W9-ABQ-253

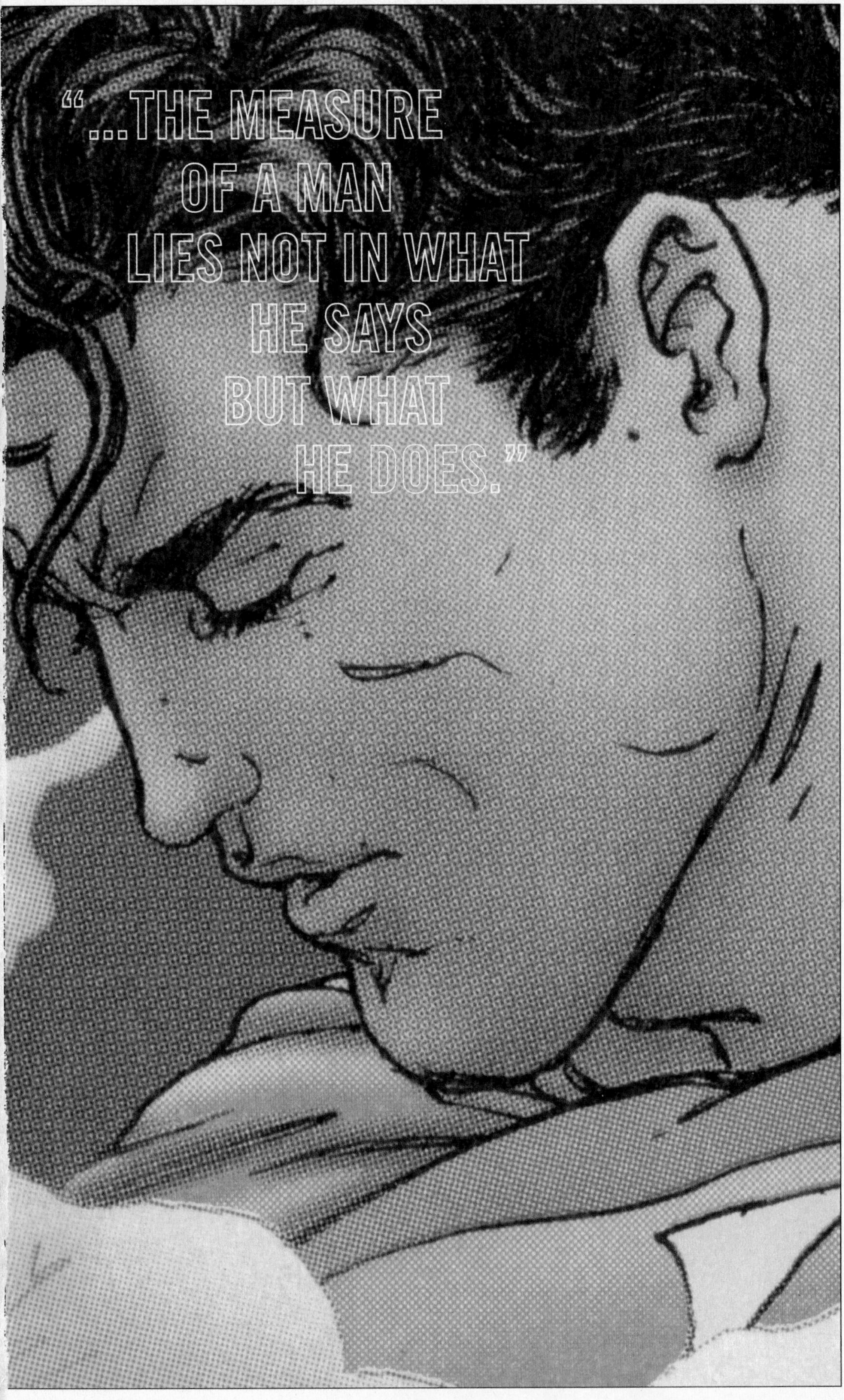
"...THE MEASURE
OF A MAN
LIES NOT IN WHAT
HE SAYS
BUT WHAT
HE DOES."

volume 1

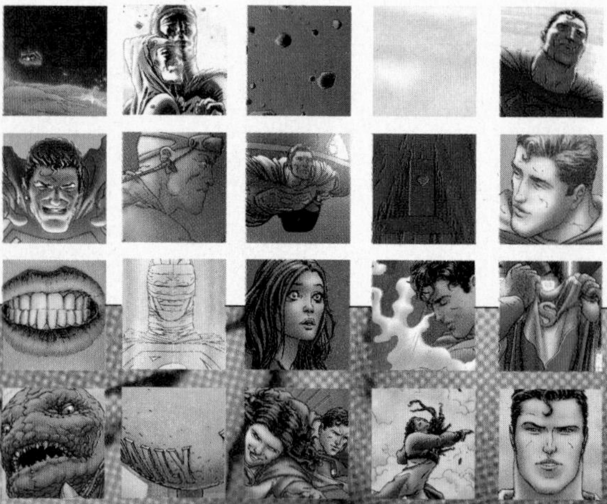

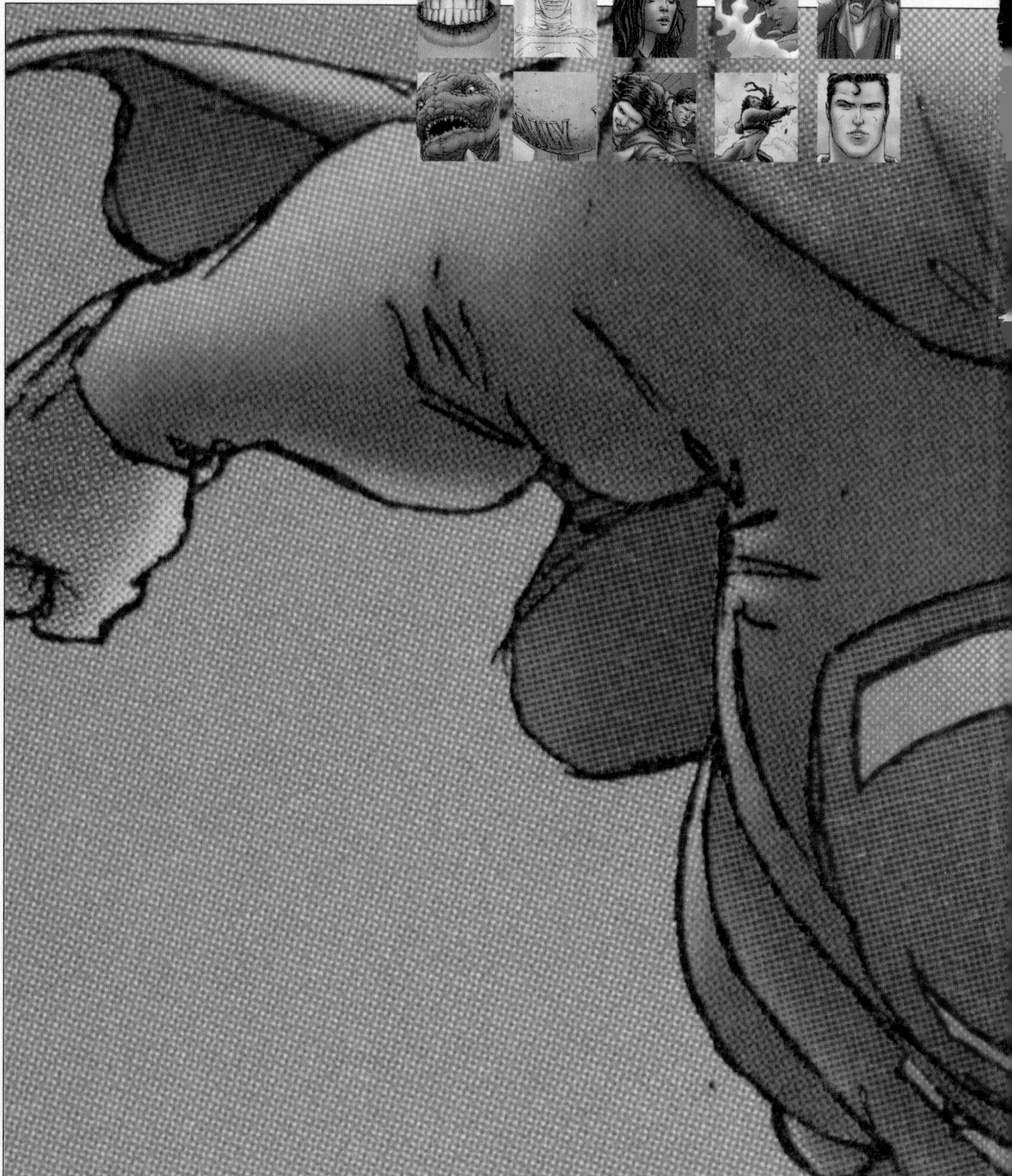

ALL-STAR SUPERMAN

Written by **Grant Morrison** Pencilled by **Frank Quitely** Digitally inked & colored by **Jamie Grant**

Lettered by **Phil Balsman** Introduction by **Bob Schreck** **Superman** created by **Jerry Siegel & Joe Shuster**

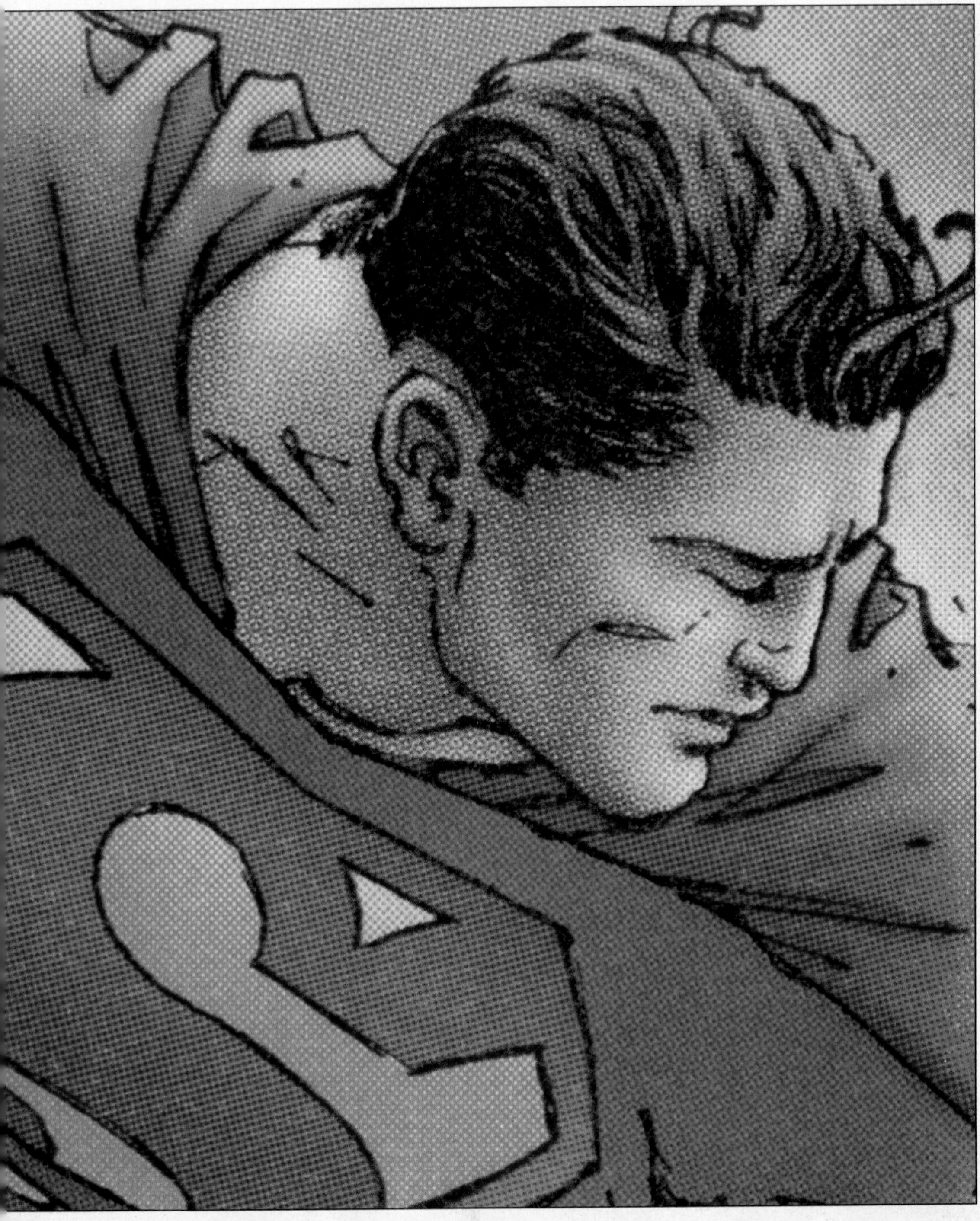

DC Comics

Dan DiDio
Senior VP-Executive Editor

Bob Schreck
Editor-original series

Brandon Montclare
Assistant Editor-original series

Bob Joy
Editor-collected edition

Robbin Brosterman
Senior Art Director

Paul Levitz
President & Publisher

Georg Brewer
VP-Design & DC Direct Creative

Richard Bruning
Senior VP-Creative Director

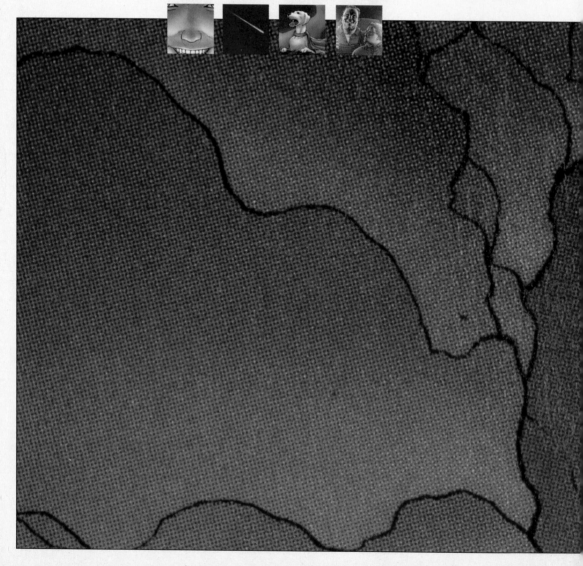

Patrick Caldon
Executive VP-Finance & Operations

Chris Caramalis
VP-Finance

John Cunningham
VP-Marketing

Terri Cunningham
VP-Managing Editor

Stephanie Fierman
Senior VP-Sales & Marketing

Alison Gill
VP-Manufacturing

Hank Kanalz
VP-General Manager, WildStorm

Jim Lee
Editorial Director-WildStorm

Paula Lowitt
Senior VP-Business & Legal Affairs

MaryEllen McLaughlin
VP-Advertising & Custom Publishing

John Nee
VP-Business Development

Gregory Noveck
Senior VP-Creative Affairs

Cheryl Rubin
Senior VP-Brand Management

Jeff Trojan
VP-Business Development, DC Direct

Bob Wayne
VP-Sales

Cover art by **Frank Quitely** and **Jamie Grant**.
Logo design by **Chip Kidd**.

ALL-STAR SUPERMAN Volume One
Published by DC Comics. Cover and compilation
copyright © 2007
DC Comics. All Rights Reserved.
Originally published in single magazine form in
ALL-STAR SUPERMAN 1-6. Copyright © 2006,2007
DC Comics. All Rights Reserved. All characters,
their distinctive likenesses and related elements
featured in this publication are trademarks
of DC Comics. The stories, characters and
incidents featured in this publication are entirely
fictional. DC Comics does not read or accept
unsolicited submissions of ideas, stories or
artwork.

DC Comics, 1700 Broadway,
New York, NY 10019
A Warner Bros. Entertainment Company
Printed in Canada. First Printing.
HC ISBN: 1-4012-0914-9
HC ISBN: 978-1-4012-0914-8
SC ISBN: 1-4012-1102-X
SC ISBN: 978-1-4012-1102-8

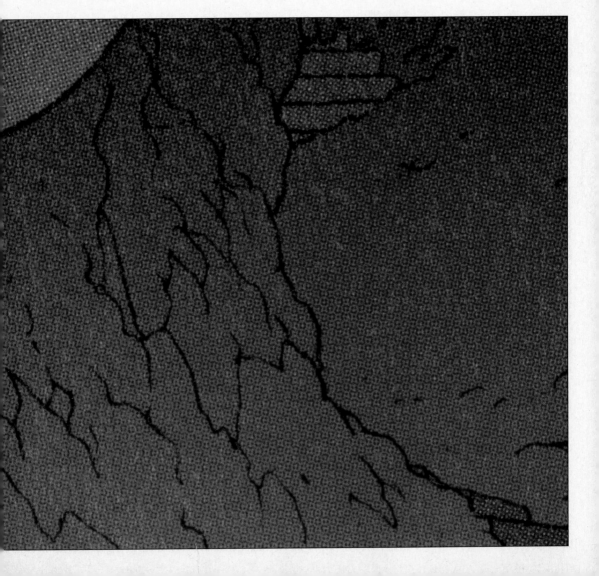

INTRODUCING ALL-STAR SUPERMAN...

Magic. They say there's none of it to be found in these modern times. I respectfully disagree.

The volume you now hold in your hands is proof positive that magic is indeed alive and well, thank you very much! It begins with the spark of Grant Morrison's seemingly limitless imagination taking this sixty-nine-year-old character, this American icon, and his supporting cast to brand new heights. Common sense tells us that every possible tale that could ever have been told with these amazing players must already have *been* told at least ten times over by now. And yet, with the craftiest sleight of hand, Grant breathes new life into each and every one of the characters while never straying from the purity of their creators' original intention. In doing so, he easily sets even the most jaded of today's readers back on their heels in awe of his disarmingly "simple" and elegant writing. While deftly moving the narrative along, he casually drops such mind-boggling concepts as genetically engineered human suicide bombers; galaxy-roving, sun-eating stars; and experimental stem-cell-accelerated — virtually unstoppable — assassins.

The magic continues as Frank Quitely then delivers his lyrical visual storytelling, encapsulating every aspect of Grant's wondrous tale onto the blank comics page — bringing them into form for the eye to see. It's an inaudible whisper of collaboration that, if I didn't know any better, would suggest these two are one and the same person. Every panel, every gesture goes straight to the core of Grant's intention while bringing it even further towards its ultimate expression. Frank's line work, like Grant's writing, appears simple, yet every line, every panel, and every page is carefully devised to achieve maximum impact on the audience. Frank gives us a totally believable, even frumpy or oafish Clark Kent, whom *no one* would ever suspect as our Superman — not even mega-genius Lex Luthor.

And for our third and final act, digital inker and colorist — the often-unsung hero of our industry — Jamie Grant painstakingly brings this world into focus. Never has the title "colorist" been less descriptive in the case of what Jamie brings to this book. The transformation — from pencils to living, breathing atmospheres and landscapes conjured for each and every scene — is flat-out astounding, not only bringing color, but shape and real dimension to every corner of the incredible universe that all three creators have built together.

Even the nuts-and-bolts, real-world physical way this book is produced, via today's state-of-the-art technology, is magical: computer files transported through time and space all the way from Glasgow, Scotland to a little, virtual town in New York named FTP. It's downright creepy! Of course, once in our clutches, a special nod goes to Phil Balsman, for his exacting attention to detail, as he letters each issue, capturing tone and emphasis for every nuance of each character's voice.

In keeping with our theme, very little of this book actually "exists" until the moment it rolls off the presses in Montreal and into your local store. Truly magical — from start to finish! Beginning with an origin summed up in four simple panels and four terse captions, and including a half-million-ton house key, a super-romantic birthday kiss on the moon, front-row seats to see "Frankenstein on Ice," Lex Luthor's prison break aided and abetted by none other than star reporter Clark Kent, and the coolest game of fetch that anyone's ever played with "man's" best friend... Well, if this is your first time reading this, you're in for a real treat.

My assistant, Brandon Montclare, and I are truly honored to be able to usher this very special book through DC's hallowed halls. We literally sit front row and center as these artisans work their craft, and even *we* still can't believe our own eyes.

Magic. Pure and simple.

Bob Schreck, Group Editor - DC Comics January 2007

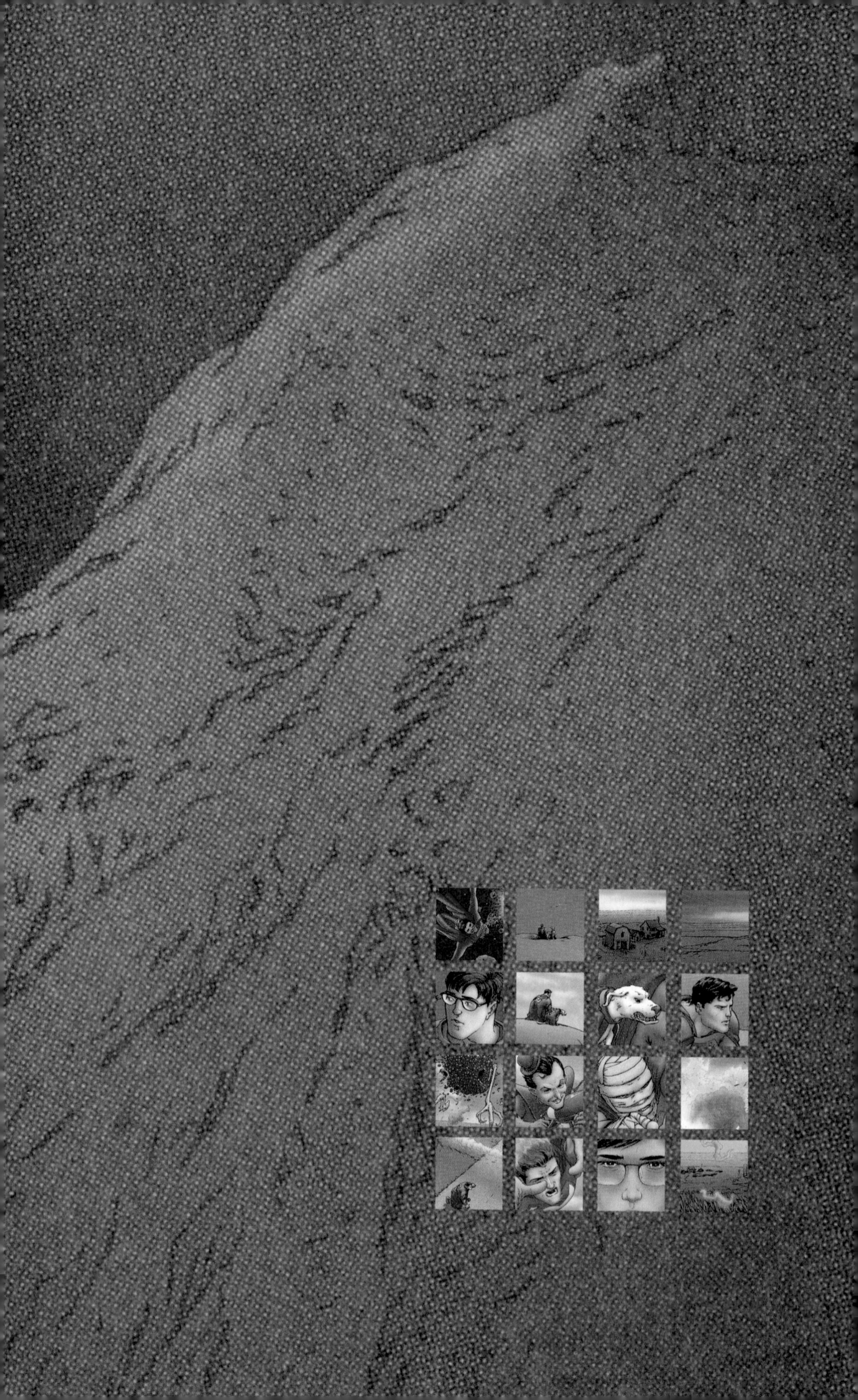

Episode 1

... FASTER...

Cover FRANK QUITELY with JAMIE GRANT

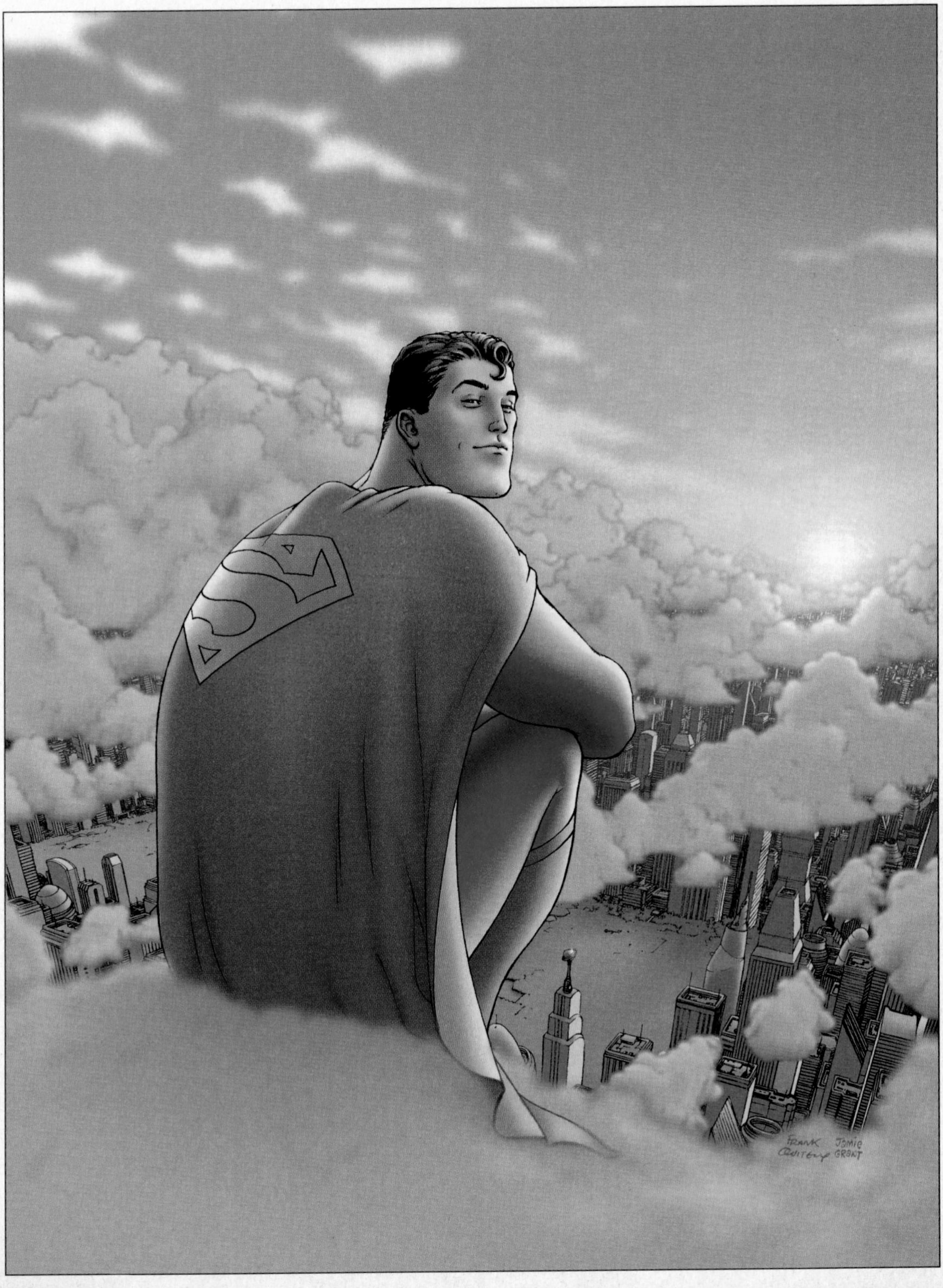

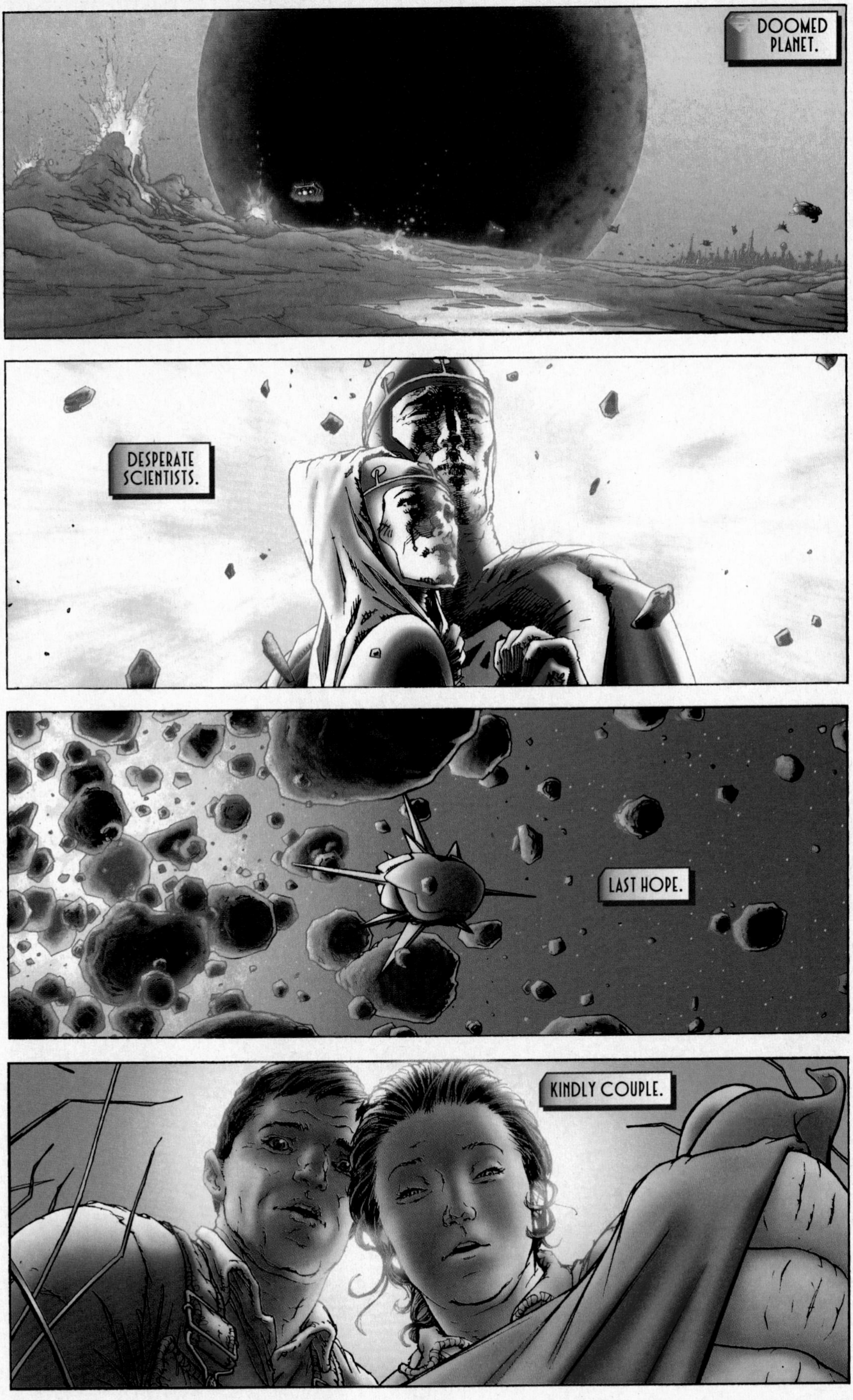
DOOMED PLANET.
DESPERATE SCIENTISTS.
LAST HOPE.
KINDLY COUPLE.

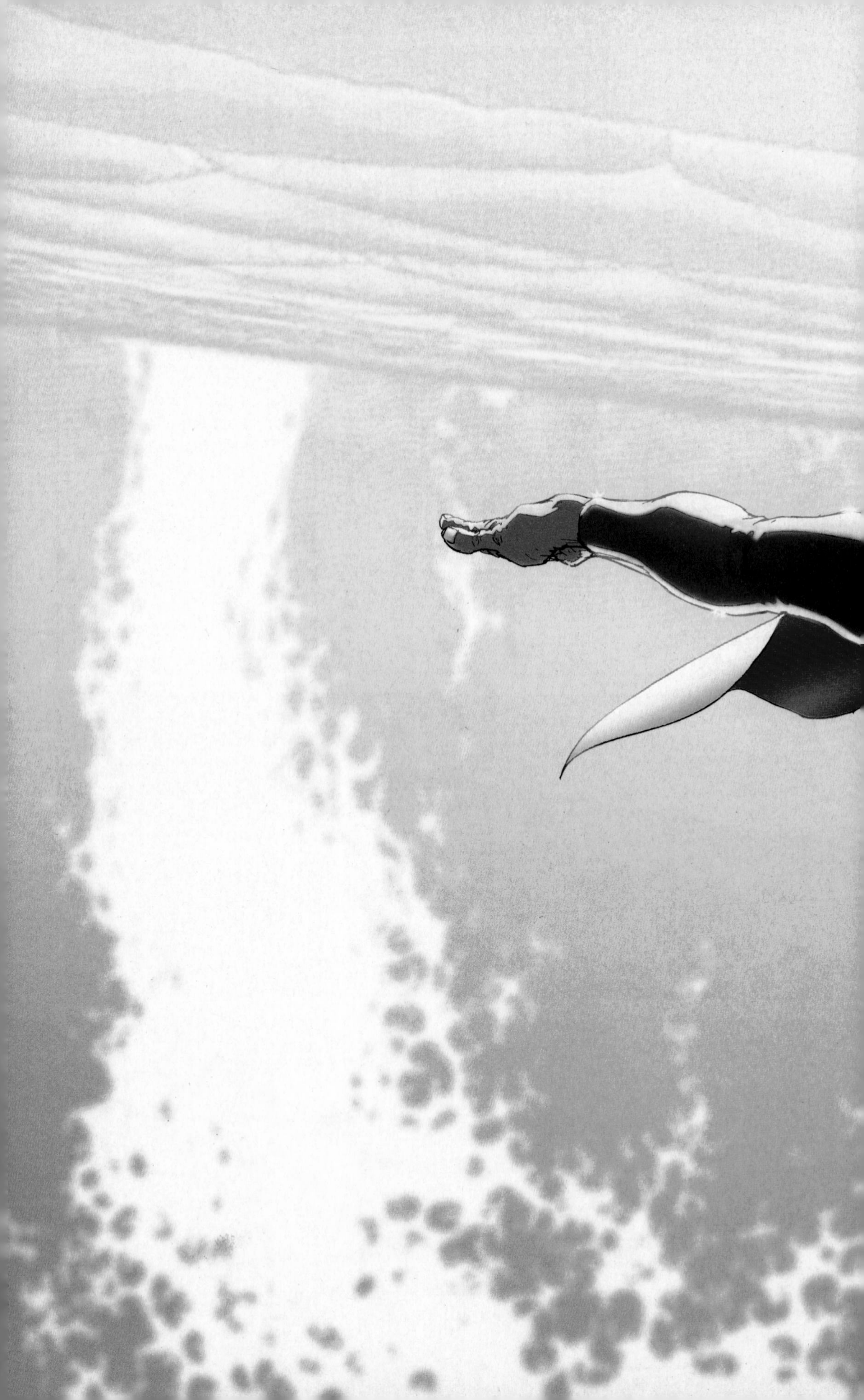

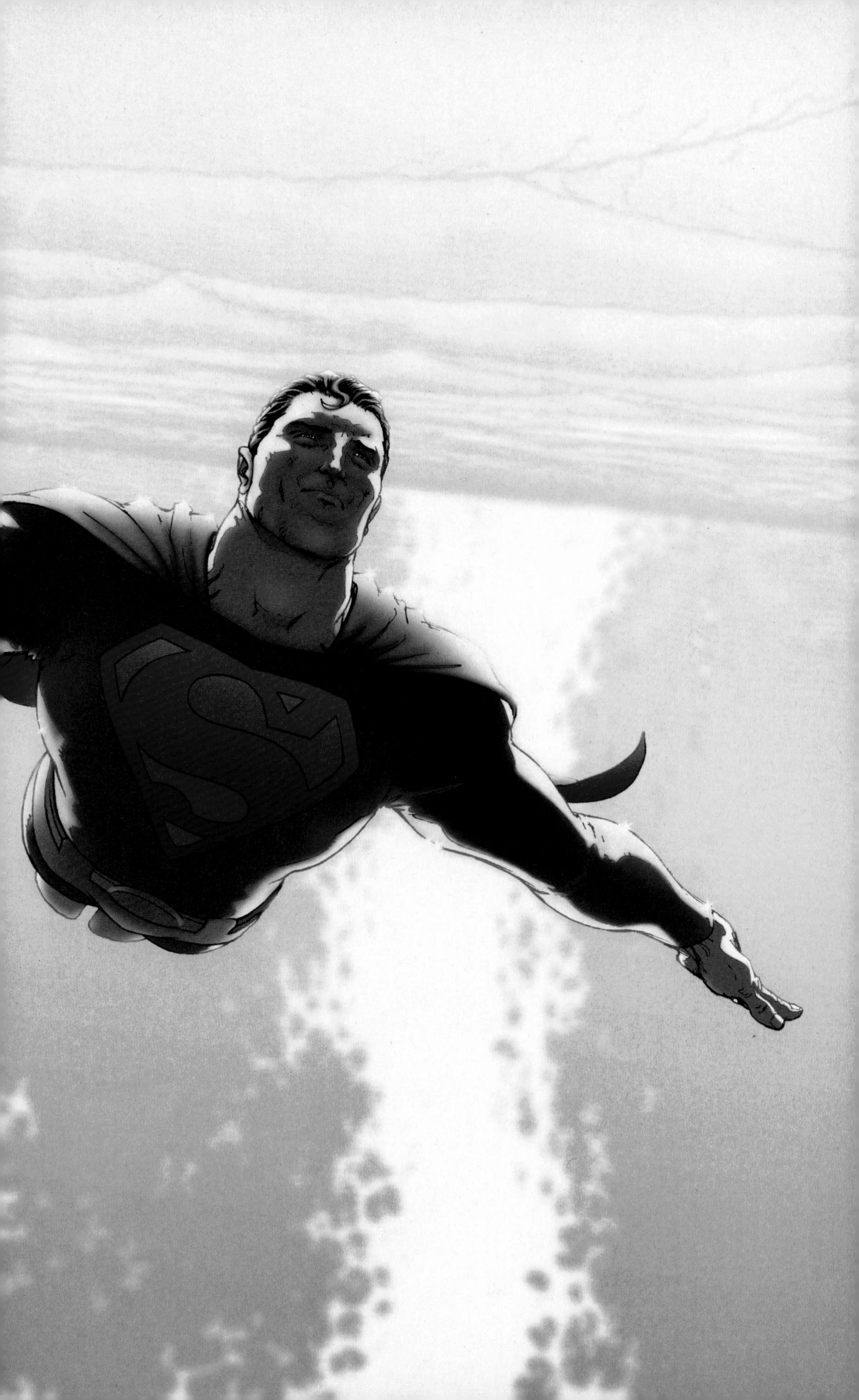

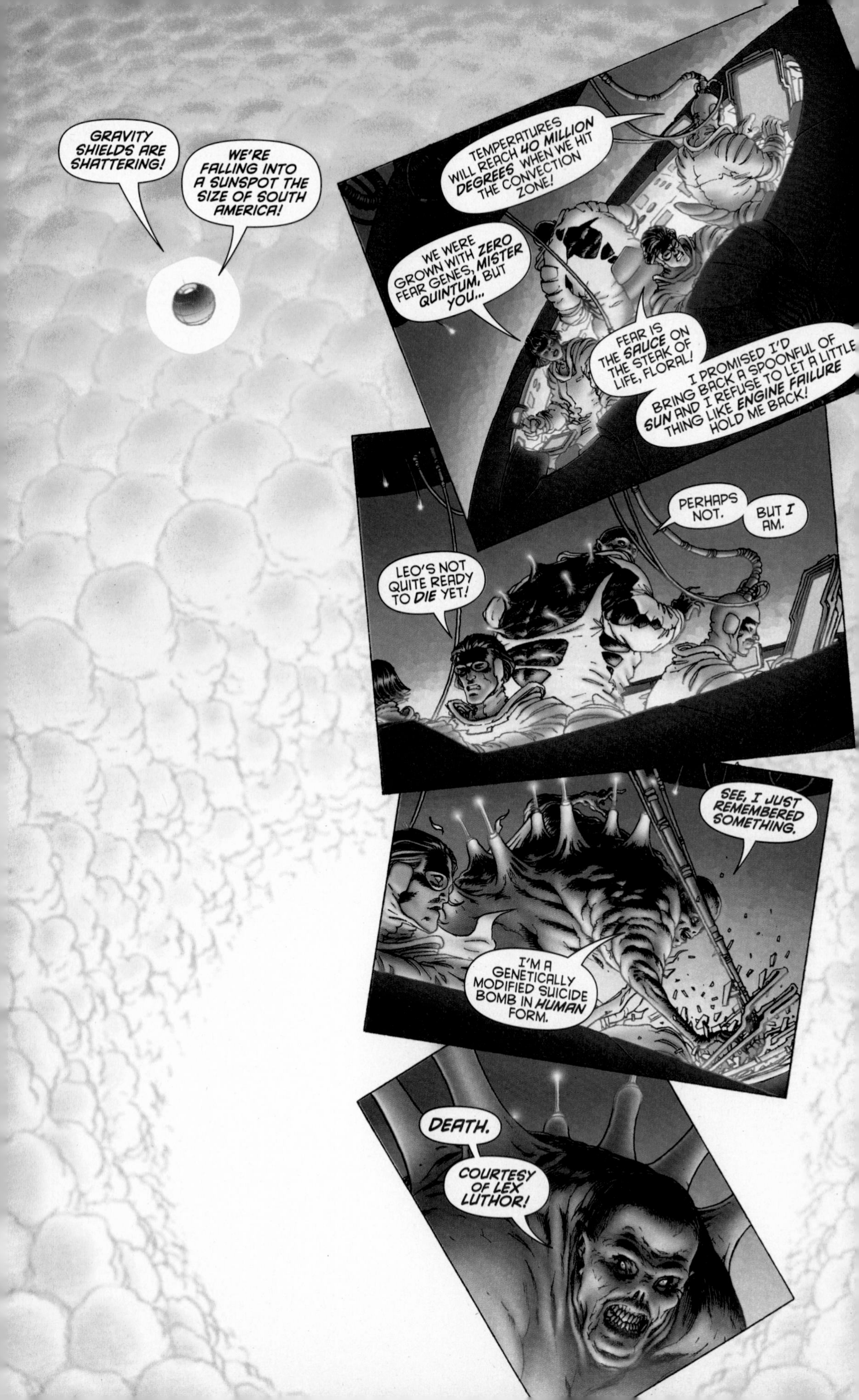

GRAVITY SHIELDS ARE SHATTERING!
WE'RE FALLING INTO A SUNSPOT THE SIZE OF SOUTH AMERICA!
TEMPERATURES WILL REACH 40 MILLION DEGREES WHEN WE HIT THE CONVECTION ZONE!
WE WERE GROWN WITH ZERO FEAR GENES, MISTER QUINTUM, BUT YOU...
FEAR IS THE SAUCE ON THE STEAK OF LIFE, FLORAL!
I PROMISED I'D BRING BACK A SPOONFUL OF SUN AND I REFUSE TO LET A LITTLE THING LIKE ENGINE FAILURE HOLD ME BACK!
LEO'S NOT QUITE READY TO DIE YET!
PERHAPS NOT.
BUT I AM.
SEE, I JUST REMEMBERED SOMETHING.
I'M A GENETICALLY MODIFIED SUICIDE BOMB IN HUMAN FORM.
DEATH.
COURTESY OF LEX LUTHOR!

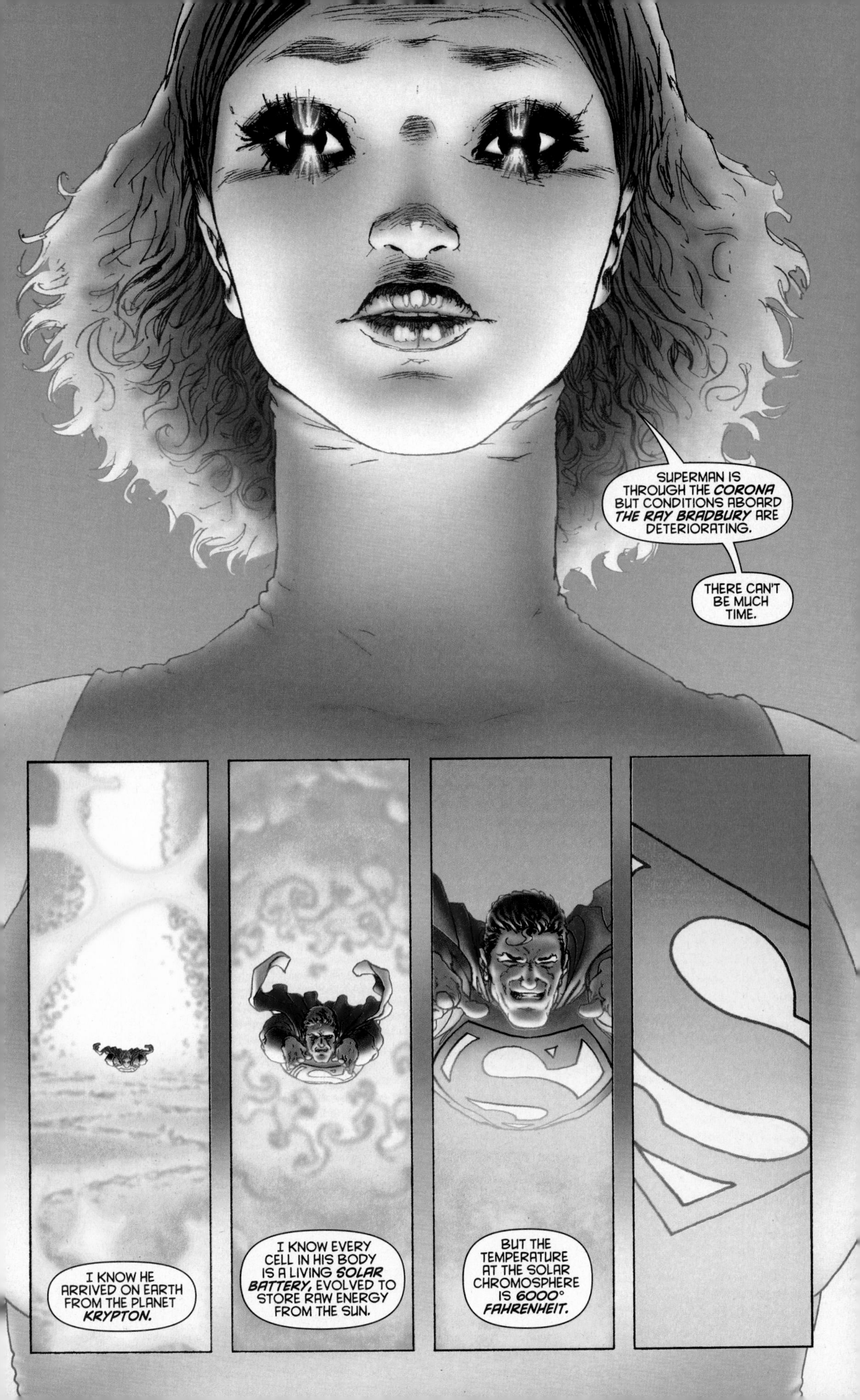
SUPERMAN IS THROUGH THE CORONA BUT CONDITIONS ABOARD THE RAY BRADBURY ARE DETERIORATING.
THERE CAN'T BE MUCH TIME.
I KNOW HE ARRIVED ON EARTH FROM THE PLANET KRYPTON.
I KNOW EVERY CELL IN HIS BODY IS A LIVING SOLAR BATTERY, EVOLVED TO STORE RAW ENERGY FROM THE SUN.
BUT THE TEMPERATURE AT THE SOLAR CHROMOSPHERE IS 6000° FAHRENHEIT.

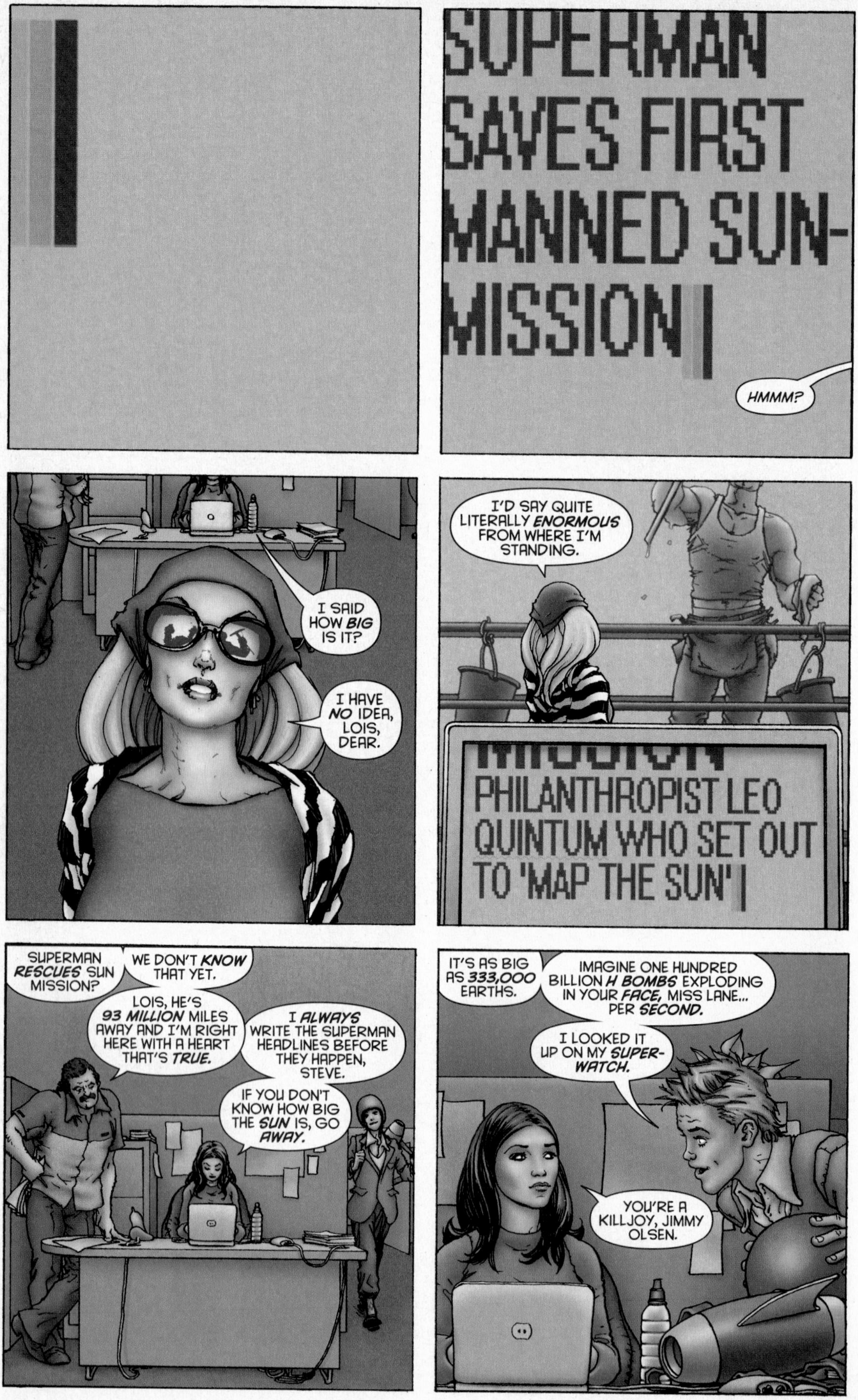

SUPERMAN SAVES FIRST MANNED SUN-MISSION
HMMM?
I SAID HOW BIG IS IT?
I HAVE NO IDEA, LOIS, DEAR.
I'D SAY QUITE LITERALLY ENORMOUS FROM WHERE I'M STANDING.
PHILANTHROPIST LEO QUINTUM WHO SET OUT TO 'MAP THE SUN'
SUPERMAN RESCUES SUN MISSION?
WE DON'T KNOW THAT YET.
LOIS, HE'S 93 MILLION MILES AWAY AND I'M RIGHT HERE WITH A HEART THAT'S TRUE.
I ALWAYS WRITE THE SUPERMAN HEADLINES BEFORE THEY HAPPEN, STEVE.
IF YOU DON'T KNOW HOW BIG THE SUN IS, GO AWAY.
IT'S AS BIG AS 333,000 EARTHS.
IMAGINE ONE HUNDRED BILLION H BOMBS EXPLODING IN YOUR FACE, MISS LANE... PER SECOND.
I LOOKED IT UP ON MY SUPER-WATCH.
YOU'RE A KILLJOY, JIMMY OLSEN.

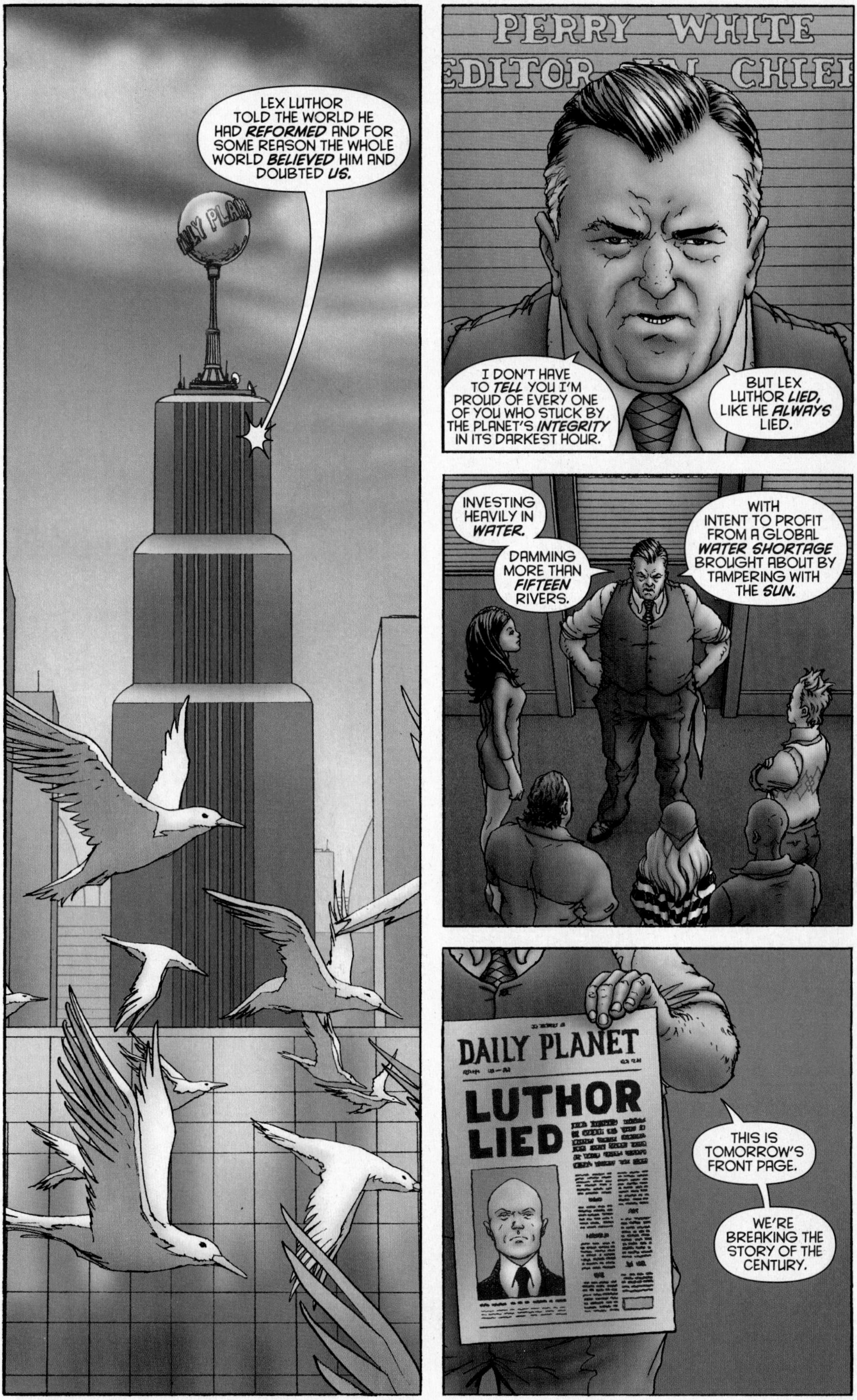
LEX LUTHOR TOLD THE WORLD HE HAD *REFORMED* AND FOR SOME REASON THE WHOLE WORLD *BELIEVED* HIM AND DOUBTED *US.*
PERRY WHITE
I DON'T HAVE TO *TELL* YOU I'M PROUD OF EVERY ONE OF YOU WHO STUCK BY THE PLANET'S *INTEGRITY* IN ITS DARKEST HOUR.
BUT LEX LUTHOR *LIED,* LIKE HE *ALWAYS* LIED.
INVESTING HEAVILY IN *WATER.*
DAMMING MORE THAN *FIFTEEN* RIVERS.
WITH INTENT TO PROFIT FROM A GLOBAL *WATER SHORTAGE* BROUGHT ABOUT BY TAMPERING WITH THE *SUN.*
DAILY PLANET
LUTHOR LIED
THIS IS TOMORROW'S FRONT PAGE.
WE'RE BREAKING THE STORY OF THE CENTURY.

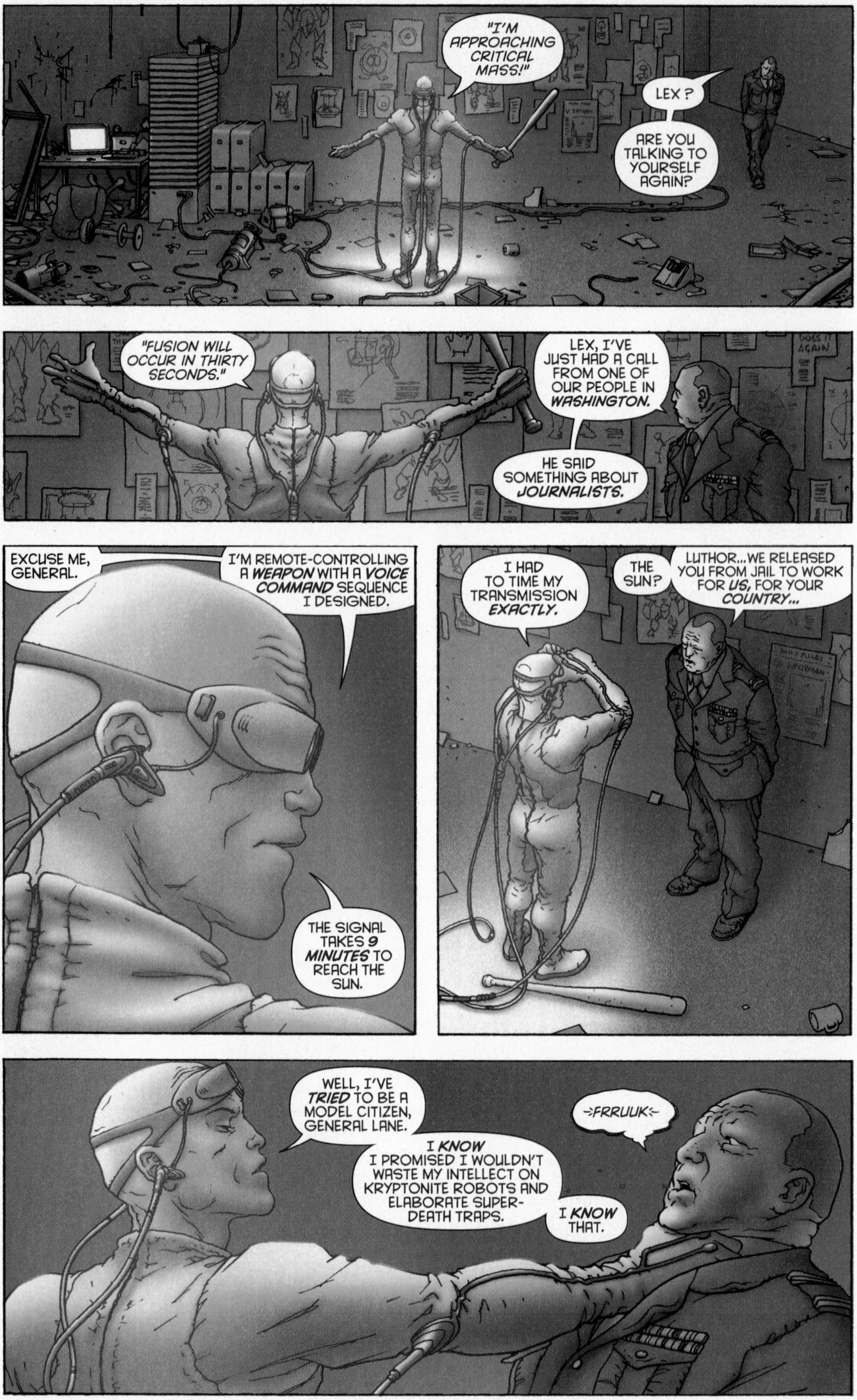
"I'M APPROACHING CRITICAL MASS!"
LEX?
ARE YOU TALKING TO YOURSELF AGAIN?
"FUSION WILL OCCUR IN THIRTY SECONDS."
LEX, I'VE JUST HAD A CALL FROM ONE OF OUR PEOPLE IN WASHINGTON.
HE SAID SOMETHING ABOUT JOURNALISTS.
EXCUSE ME, GENERAL.
I'M REMOTE-CONTROLLING A WEAPON WITH A VOICE COMMAND SEQUENCE I DESIGNED.
THE SIGNAL TAKES 9 MINUTES TO REACH THE SUN.
I HAD TO TIME MY TRANSMISSION EXACTLY.
THE SUN?
LUTHOR...WE RELEASED YOU FROM JAIL TO WORK FOR US, FOR YOUR COUNTRY...
WELL, I'VE TRIED TO BE A MODEL CITIZEN, GENERAL LANE.
I KNOW I PROMISED I WOULDN'T WASTE MY INTELLECT ON KRYPTONITE ROBOTS AND ELABORATE SUPER-DEATH TRAPS.
I KNOW THAT.
FRRUUK

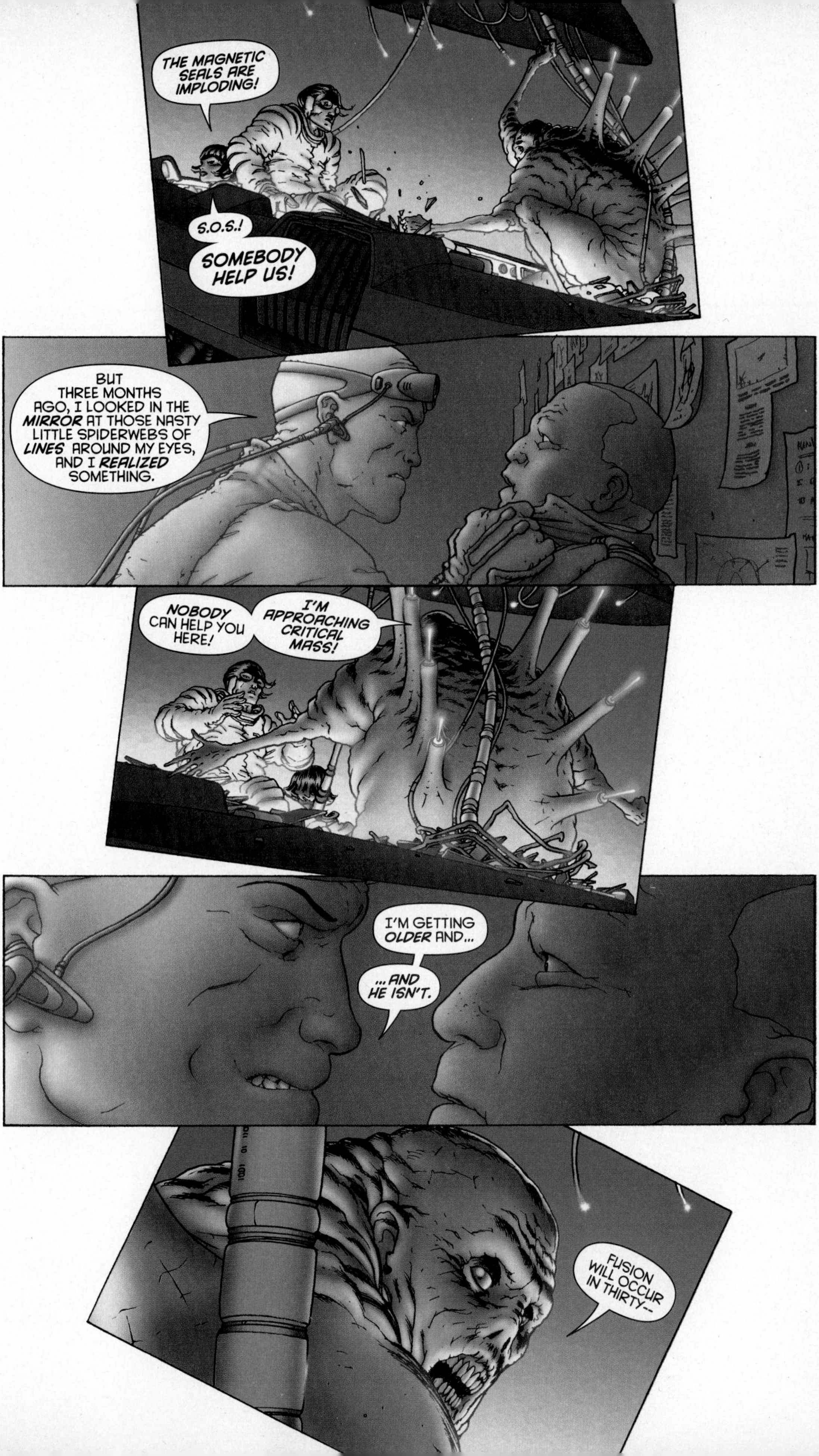
THE MAGNETIC SEALS ARE IMPLODING!
S.O.S.!
SOMEBODY HELP US!
BUT THREE MONTHS AGO, I LOOKED IN THE MIRROR AT THOSE NASTY LITTLE SPIDERWEBS OF LINES AROUND MY EYES, AND I REALIZED SOMETHING.
NOBODY CAN HELP YOU HERE!
I'M APPROACHING CRITICAL MASS!
I'M GETTING OLDER AND...
...AND HE ISN'T.
FUSION WILL OCCUR IN THIRTY--

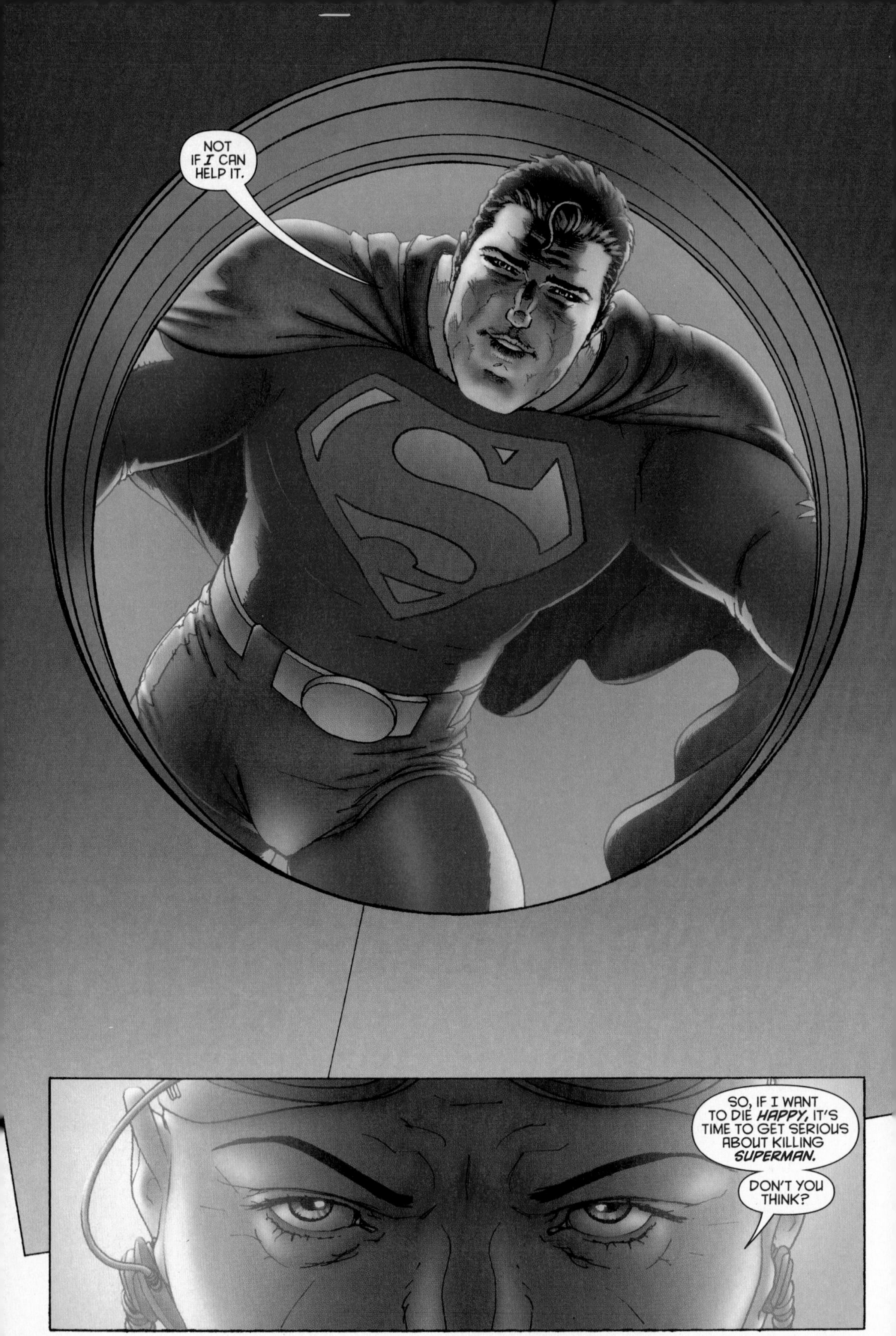
NOT IF *I* CAN HELP IT.
SO, IF I WANT TO DIE *HAPPY*, IT'S TIME TO GET SERIOUS ABOUT KILLING *SUPERMAN*.
DON'T YOU THINK?

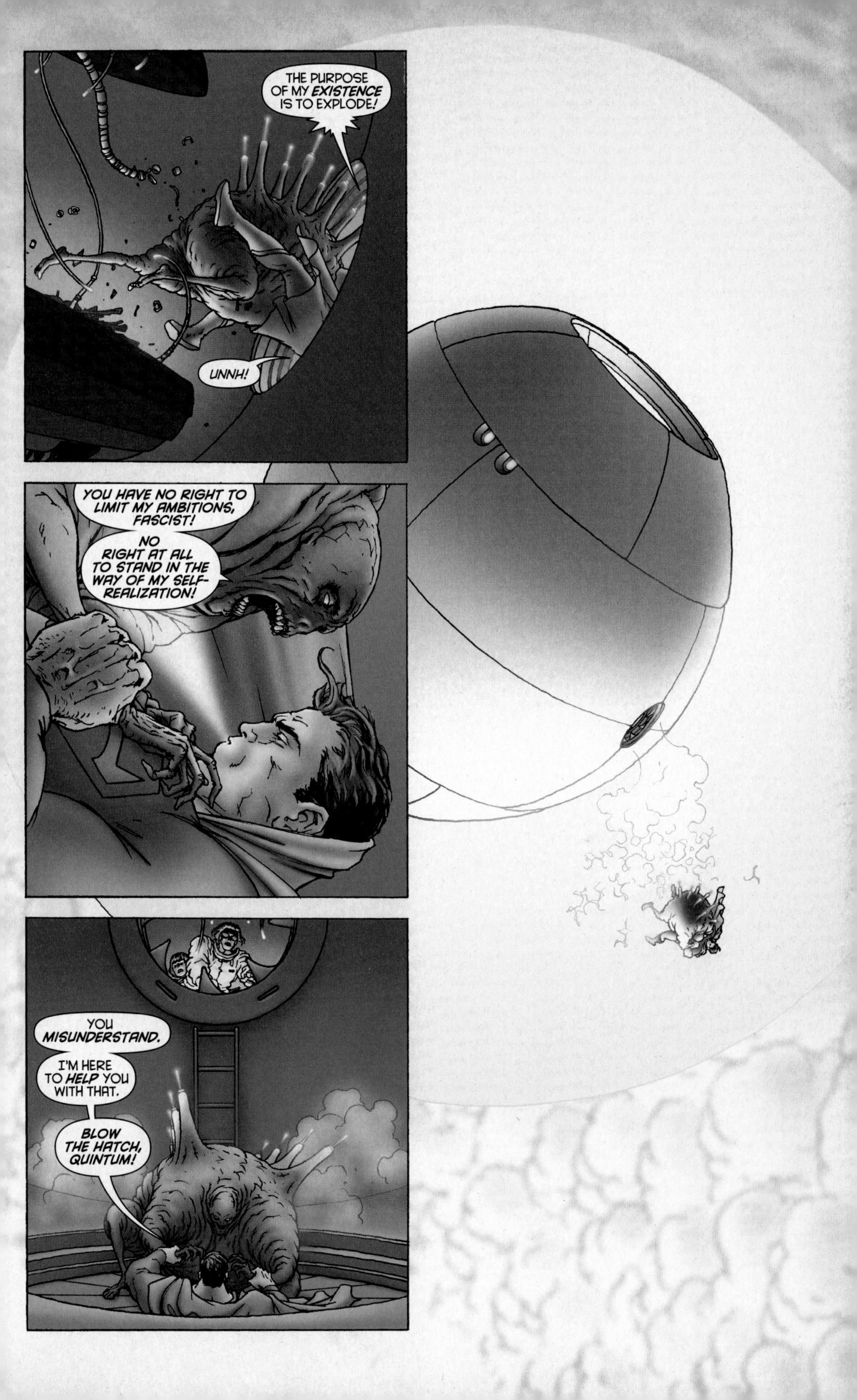
THE PURPOSE OF MY EXISTENCE IS TO EXPLODE!
UNNH!
YOU HAVE NO RIGHT TO LIMIT MY AMBITIONS, FASCIST!
NO RIGHT AT ALL TO STAND IN THE WAY OF MY SELF-REALIZATION!
YOU MISUNDERSTAND.
I'M HERE TO HELP YOU WITH THAT.
BLOW THE HATCH, QUINTUM!

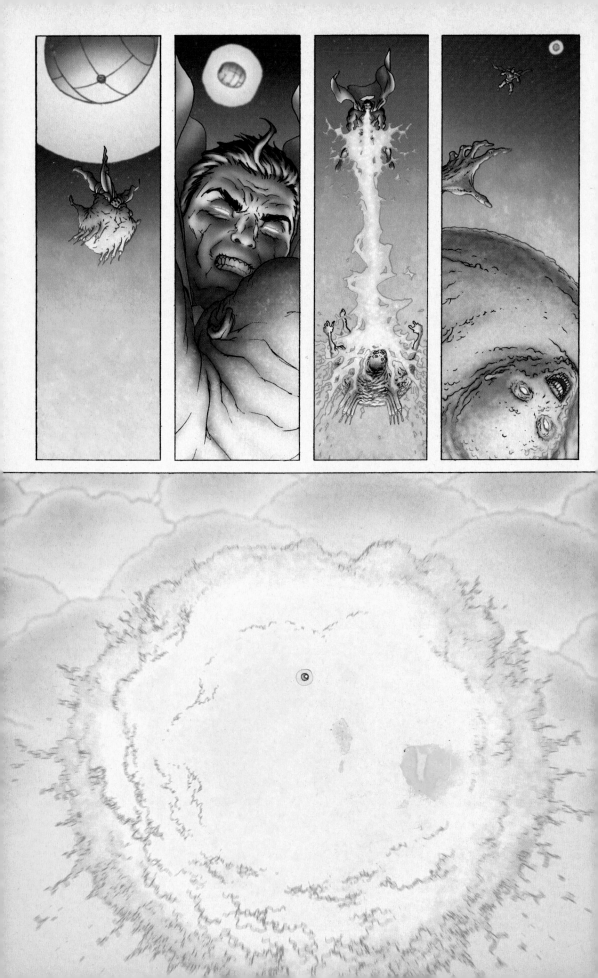

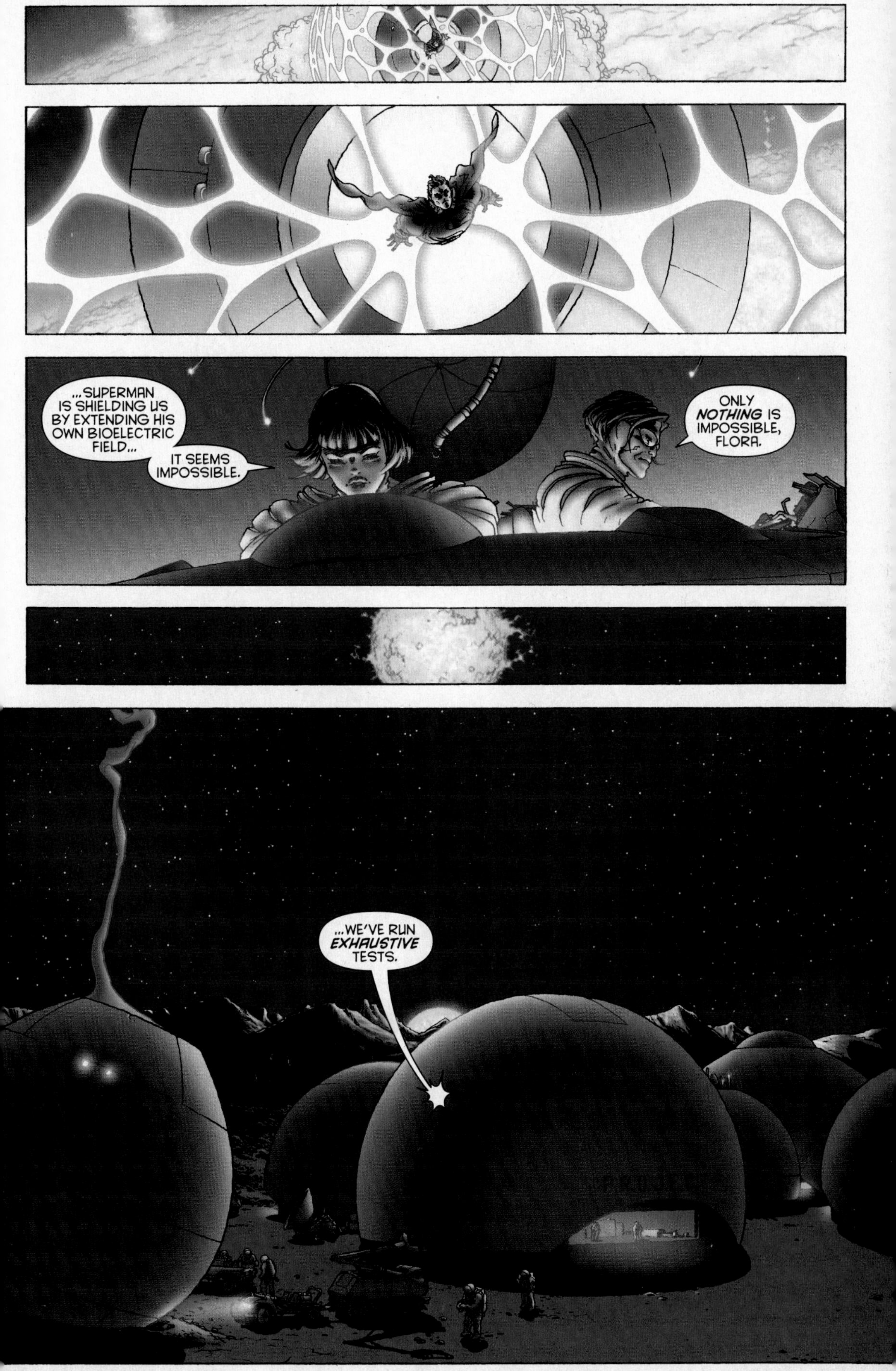
...SUPERMAN IS SHIELDING US BY EXTENDING HIS OWN BIOELECTRIC FIELD...
IT SEEMS IMPOSSIBLE.
ONLY NOTHING IS IMPOSSIBLE, FLORA.
...WE'VE RUN EXHAUSTIVE TESTS.

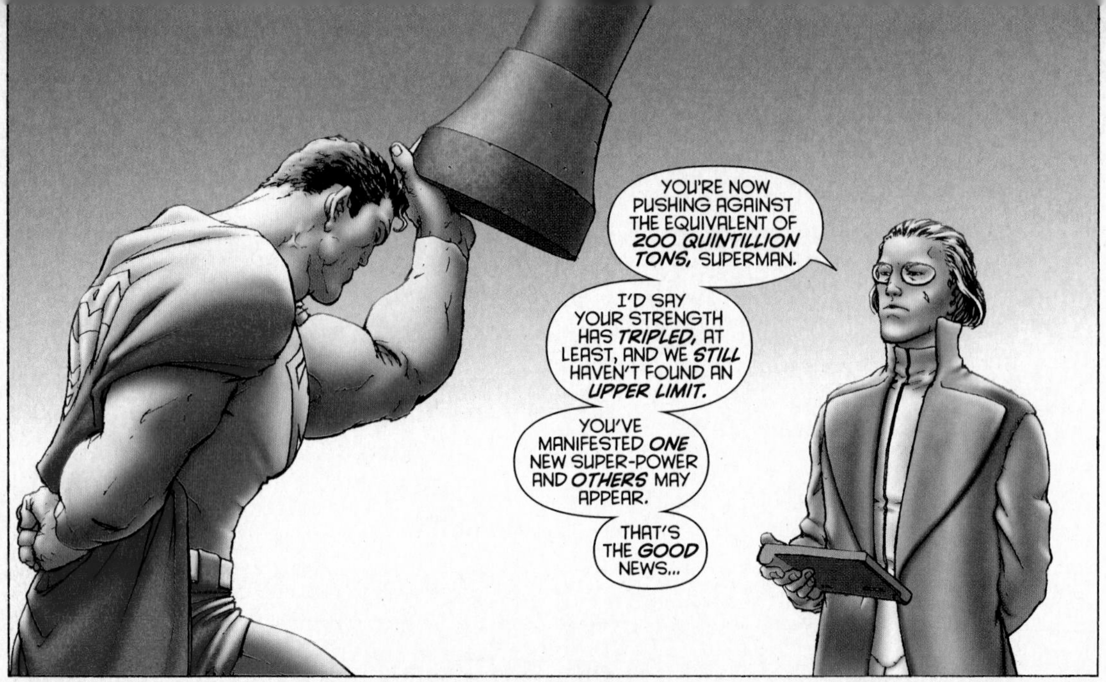
YOU'RE NOW PUSHING AGAINST THE EQUIVALENT OF ZOO QUINTILLION TONS, SUPERMAN.
I'D SAY YOUR STRENGTH HAS TRIPLED, AT LEAST, AND WE STILL HAVEN'T FOUND AN UPPER LIMIT.
YOU'VE MANIFESTED ONE NEW SUPER-POWER AND OTHERS MAY APPEAR.
THAT'S THE GOOD NEWS...

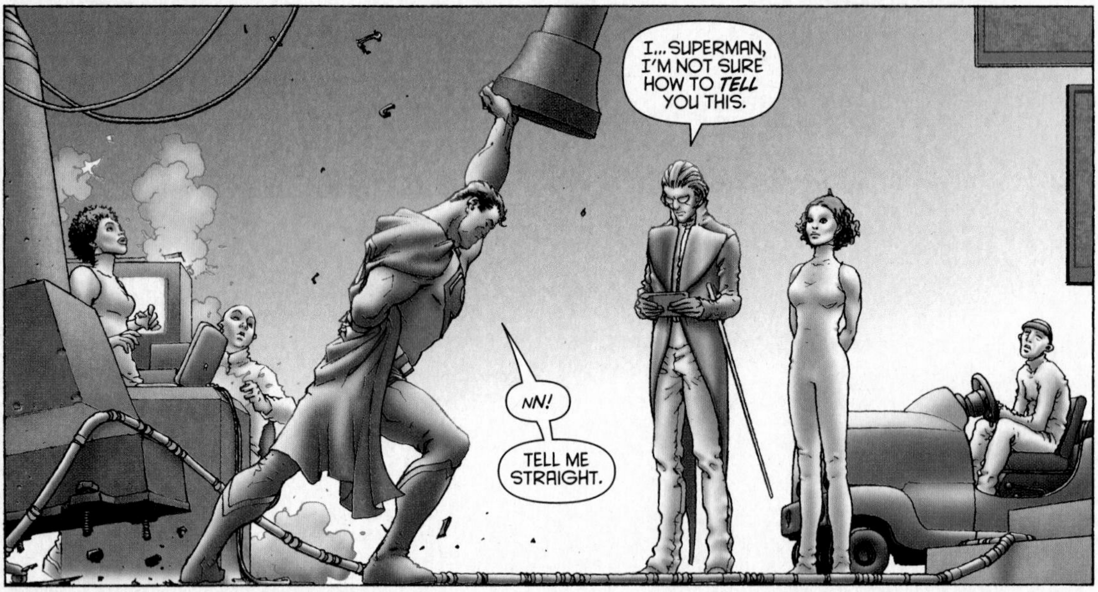
I...SUPERMAN, I'M NOT SURE HOW TO TELL YOU THIS.
NN!
TELL ME STRAIGHT.

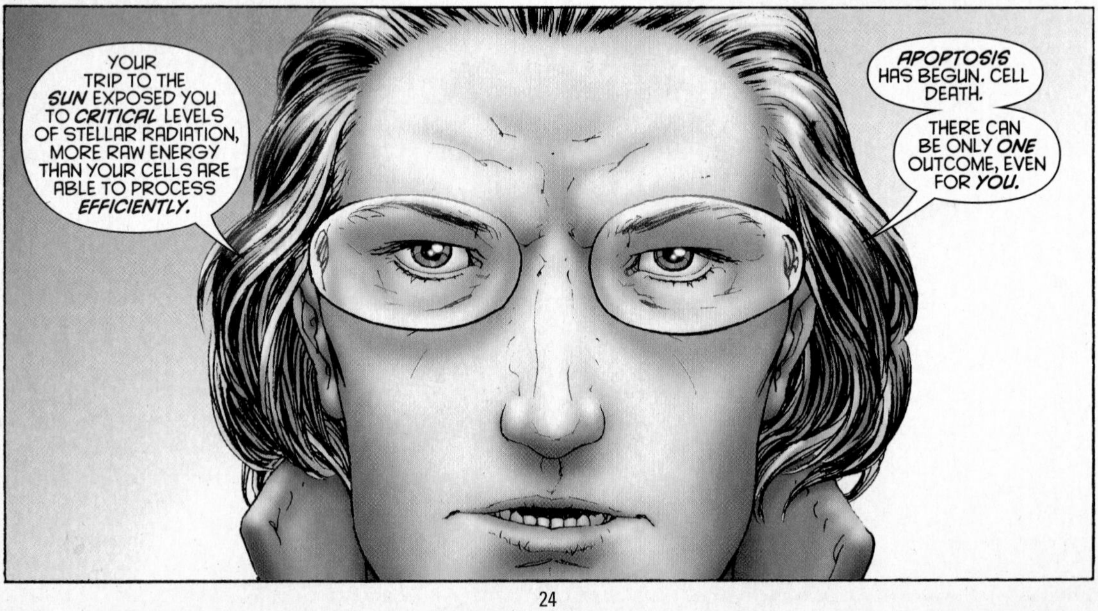
YOUR TRIP TO THE SUN EXPOSED YOU TO CRITICAL LEVELS OF STELLAR RADIATION, MORE RAW ENERGY THAN YOUR CELLS ARE ABLE TO PROCESS EFFICIENTLY.
APOPTOSIS HAS BEGUN. CELL DEATH.
THERE CAN BE ONLY ONE OUTCOME, EVEN FOR YOU.

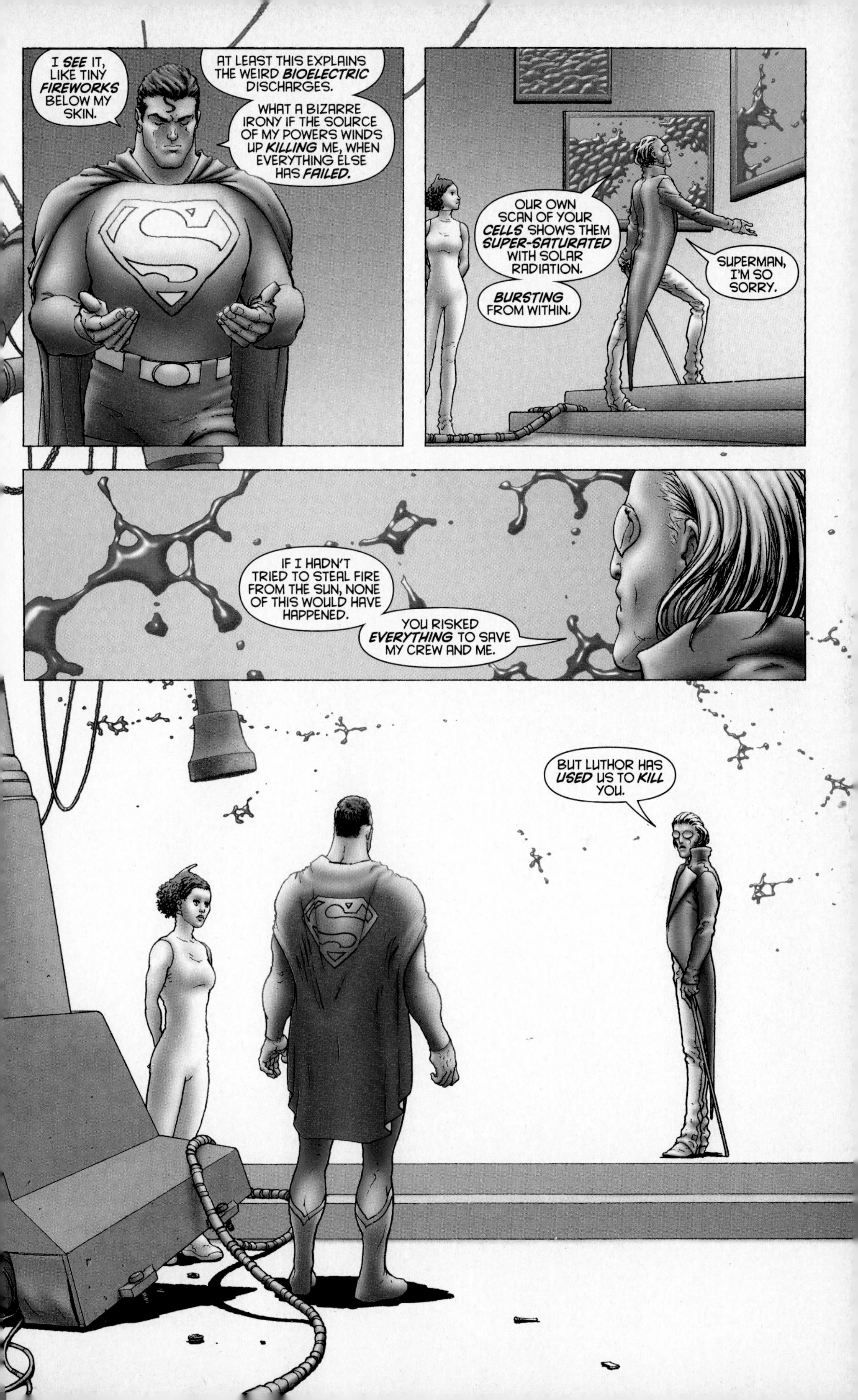
I SEE IT, LIKE TINY FIREWORKS BELOW MY SKIN.
AT LEAST THIS EXPLAINS THE WEIRD BIOELECTRIC DISCHARGES.
WHAT A BIZARRE IRONY IF THE SOURCE OF MY POWERS WINDS UP KILLING ME, WHEN EVERYTHING ELSE HAS FAILED.
OUR OWN SCAN OF YOUR CELLS SHOWS THEM SUPER-SATURATED WITH SOLAR RADIATION.
BURSTING FROM WITHIN.
SUPERMAN, I'M SO SORRY.
IF I HADN'T TRIED TO STEAL FIRE FROM THE SUN, NONE OF THIS WOULD HAVE HAPPENED.
YOU RISKED EVERYTHING TO SAVE MY CREW AND ME.
BUT LUTHOR HAS USED US TO KILL YOU.

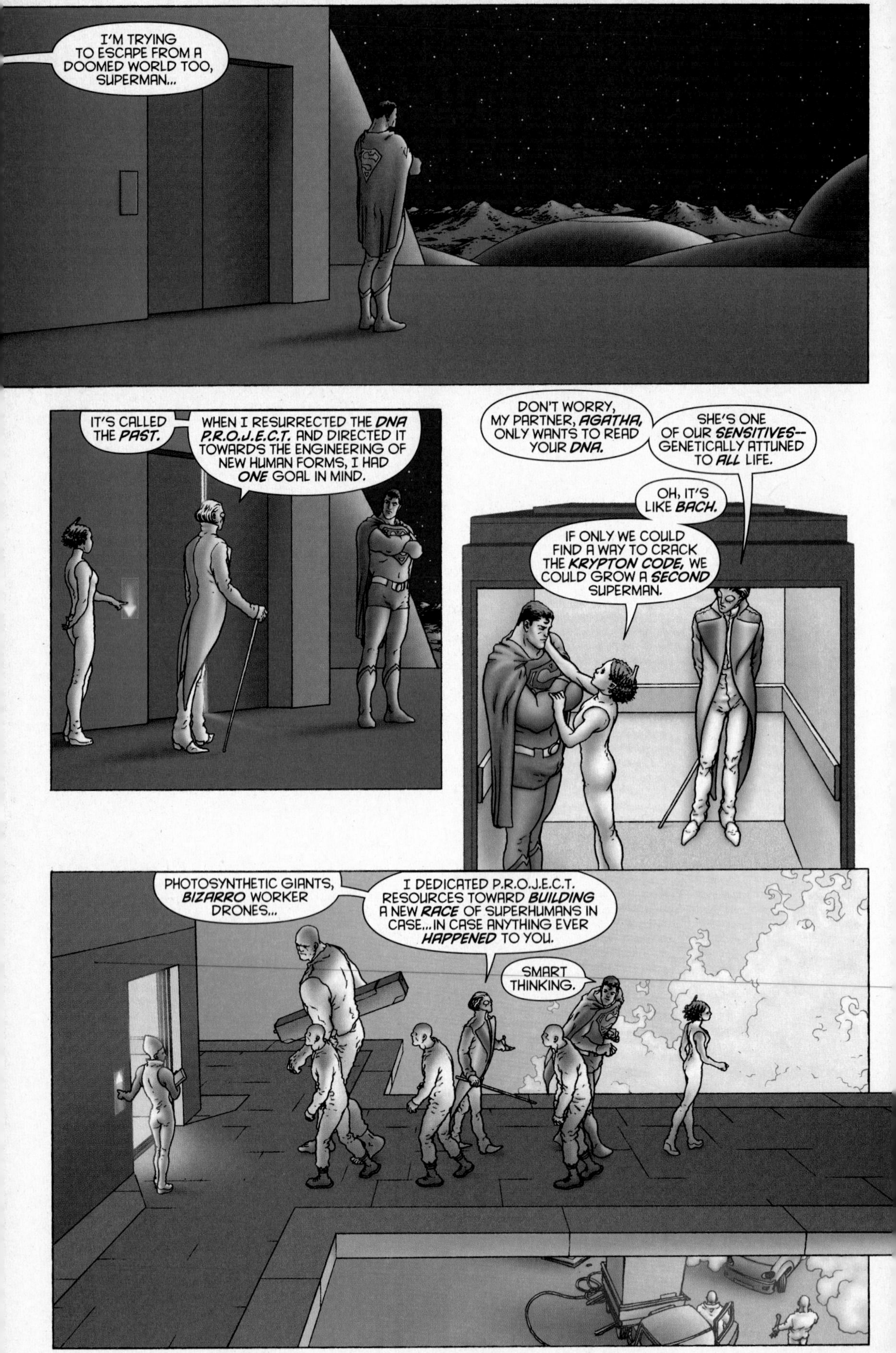
I'M TRYING TO ESCAPE FROM A DOOMED WORLD TOO, SUPERMAN...
IT'S CALLED THE PAST.
WHEN I RESURRECTED THE DNA P.R.O.J.E.C.T. AND DIRECTED IT TOWARDS THE ENGINEERING OF NEW HUMAN FORMS, I HAD ONE GOAL IN MIND.
DON'T WORRY, MY PARTNER, AGATHA, ONLY WANTS TO READ YOUR DNA.
SHE'S ONE OF OUR SENSITIVES-- GENETICALLY ATTUNED TO ALL LIFE.
OH, IT'S LIKE BACH.
IF ONLY WE COULD FIND A WAY TO CRACK THE KRYPTON CODE, WE COULD GROW A SECOND SUPERMAN.
PHOTOSYNTHETIC GIANTS, BIZARRO WORKER DRONES...
I DEDICATED P.R.O.J.E.C.T. RESOURCES TOWARD BUILDING A NEW RACE OF SUPERHUMANS IN CASE...IN CASE ANYTHING EVER HAPPENED TO YOU.
SMART THINKING.

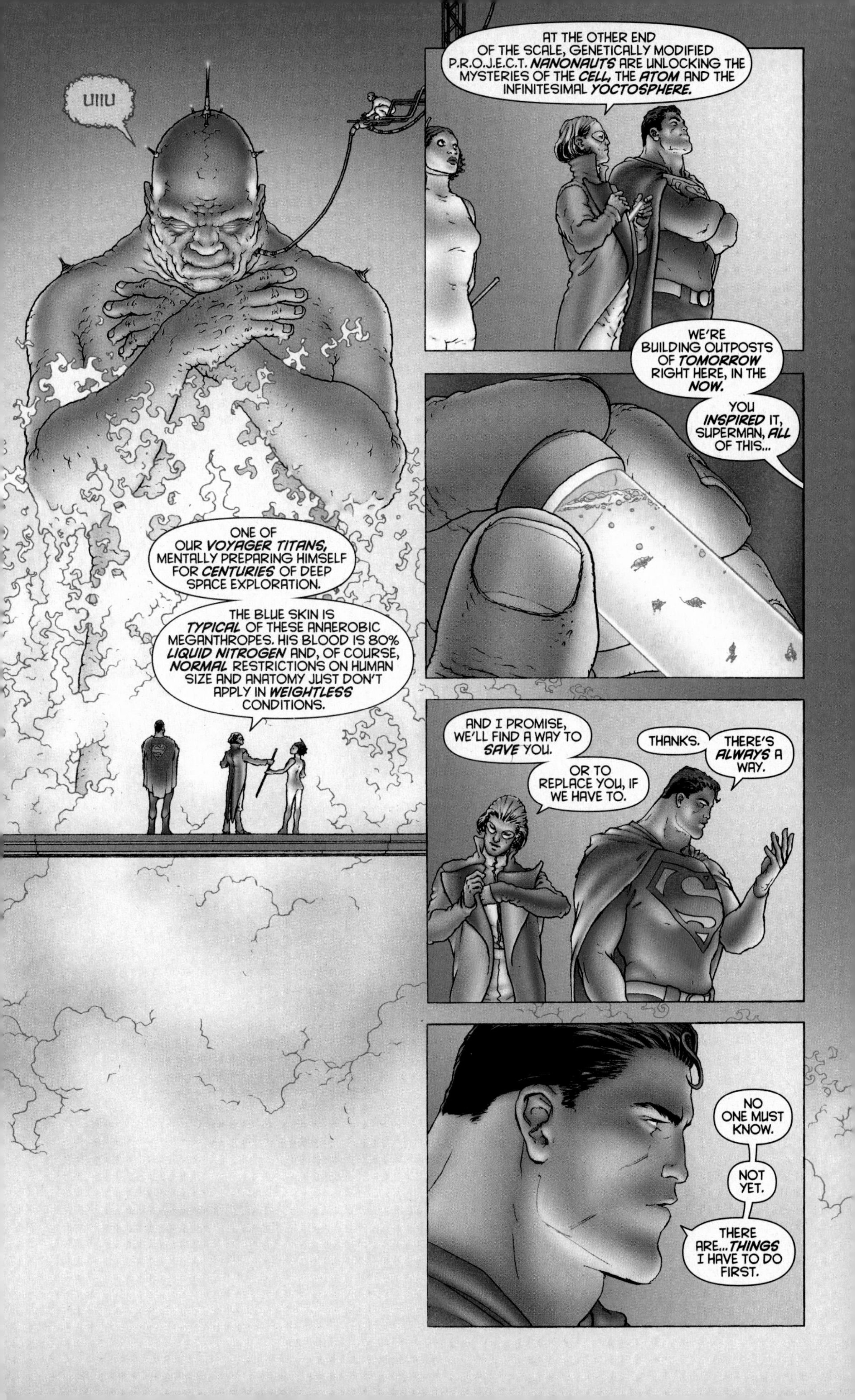
UIIU
ONE OF OUR VOYAGER TITANS, MENTALLY PREPARING HIMSELF FOR CENTURIES OF DEEP SPACE EXPLORATION.
THE BLUE SKIN IS TYPICAL OF THESE ANAEROBIC MEGANTHROPES. HIS BLOOD IS 80% LIQUID NITROGEN AND, OF COURSE, NORMAL RESTRICTIONS ON HUMAN SIZE AND ANATOMY JUST DON'T APPLY IN WEIGHTLESS CONDITIONS.
AT THE OTHER END OF THE SCALE, GENETICALLY MODIFIED P.R.O.J.E.C.T. NANONAUTS ARE UNLOCKING THE MYSTERIES OF THE CELL, THE ATOM AND THE INFINITESIMAL YOCTOSPHERE.
WE'RE BUILDING OUTPOSTS OF TOMORROW RIGHT HERE, IN THE NOW.
YOU INSPIRED IT, SUPERMAN, ALL OF THIS...
AND I PROMISE, WE'LL FIND A WAY TO SAVE YOU.
OR TO REPLACE YOU, IF WE HAVE TO.
THANKS.
THERE'S ALWAYS A WAY.
NO ONE MUST KNOW.
NOT YET.
THERE ARE...THINGS I HAVE TO DO FIRST.

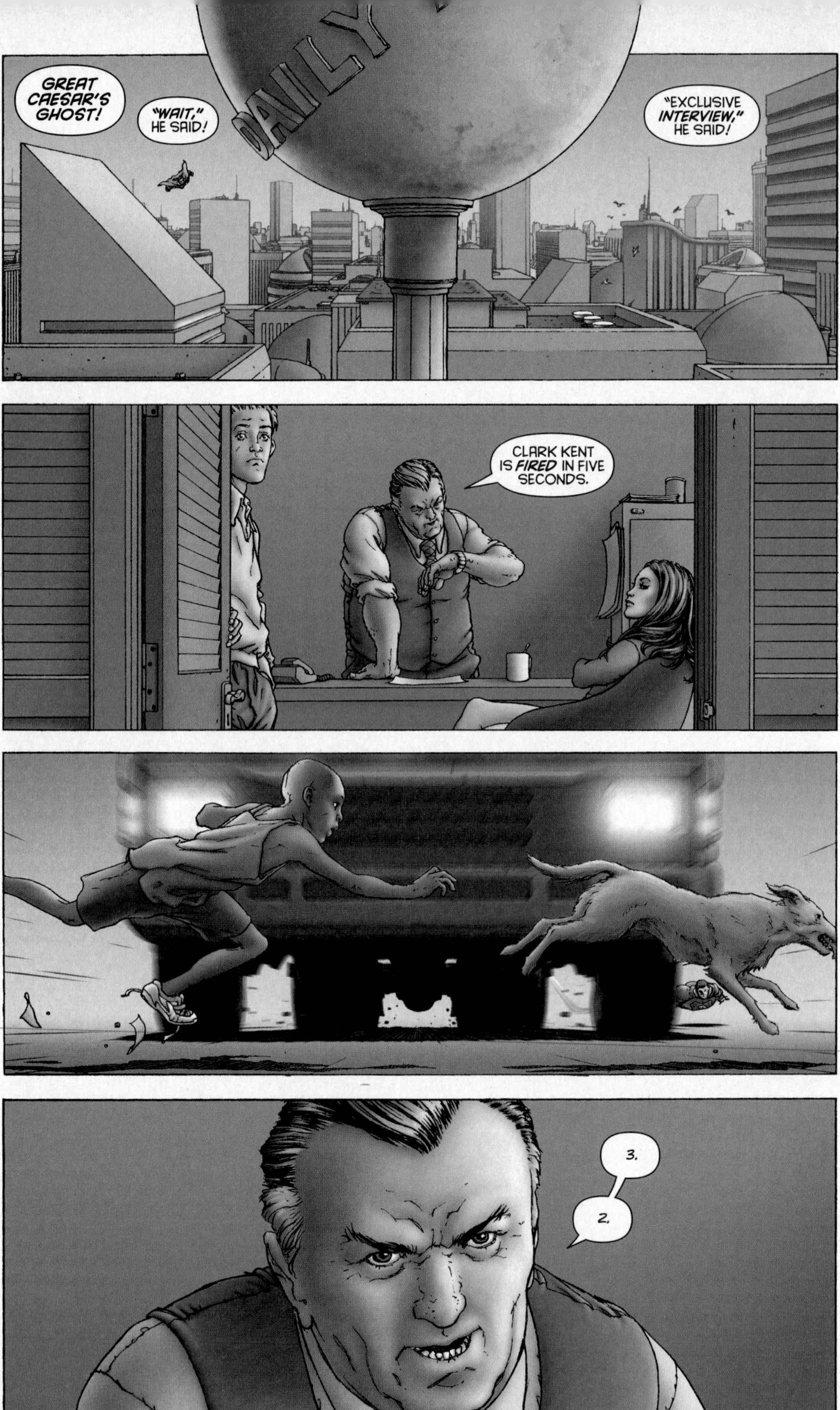
GREAT CAESAR'S GHOST!
"WAIT," HE SAID!
"EXCLUSIVE INTERVIEW," HE SAID!
CLARK KENT IS FIRED IN FIVE SECONDS.
3,
2,

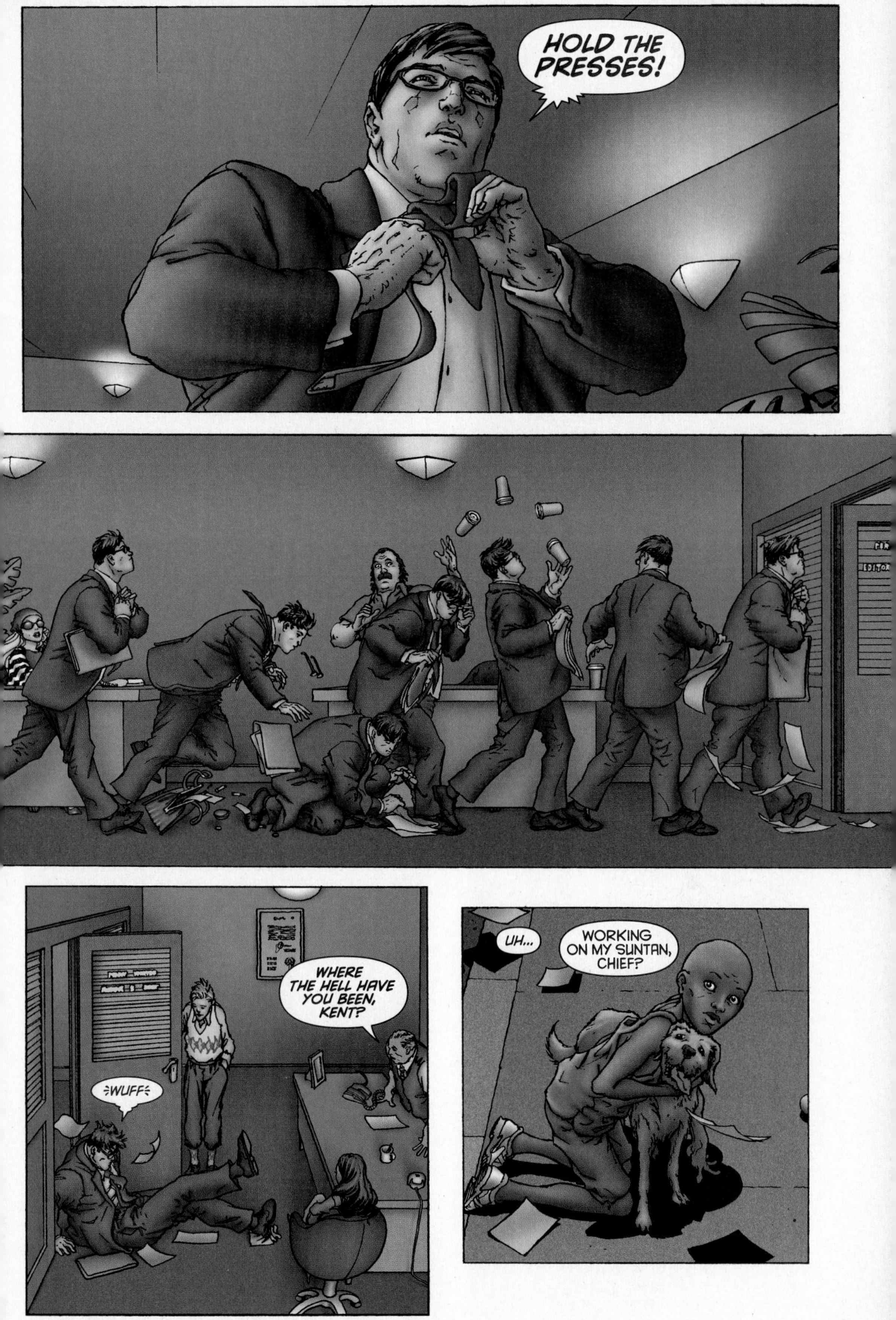
HOLD THE PRESSES!
WHERE THE HELL HAVE YOU BEEN, KENT?
WUFF
UH...
WORKING ON MY SUNTAN, CHIEF?

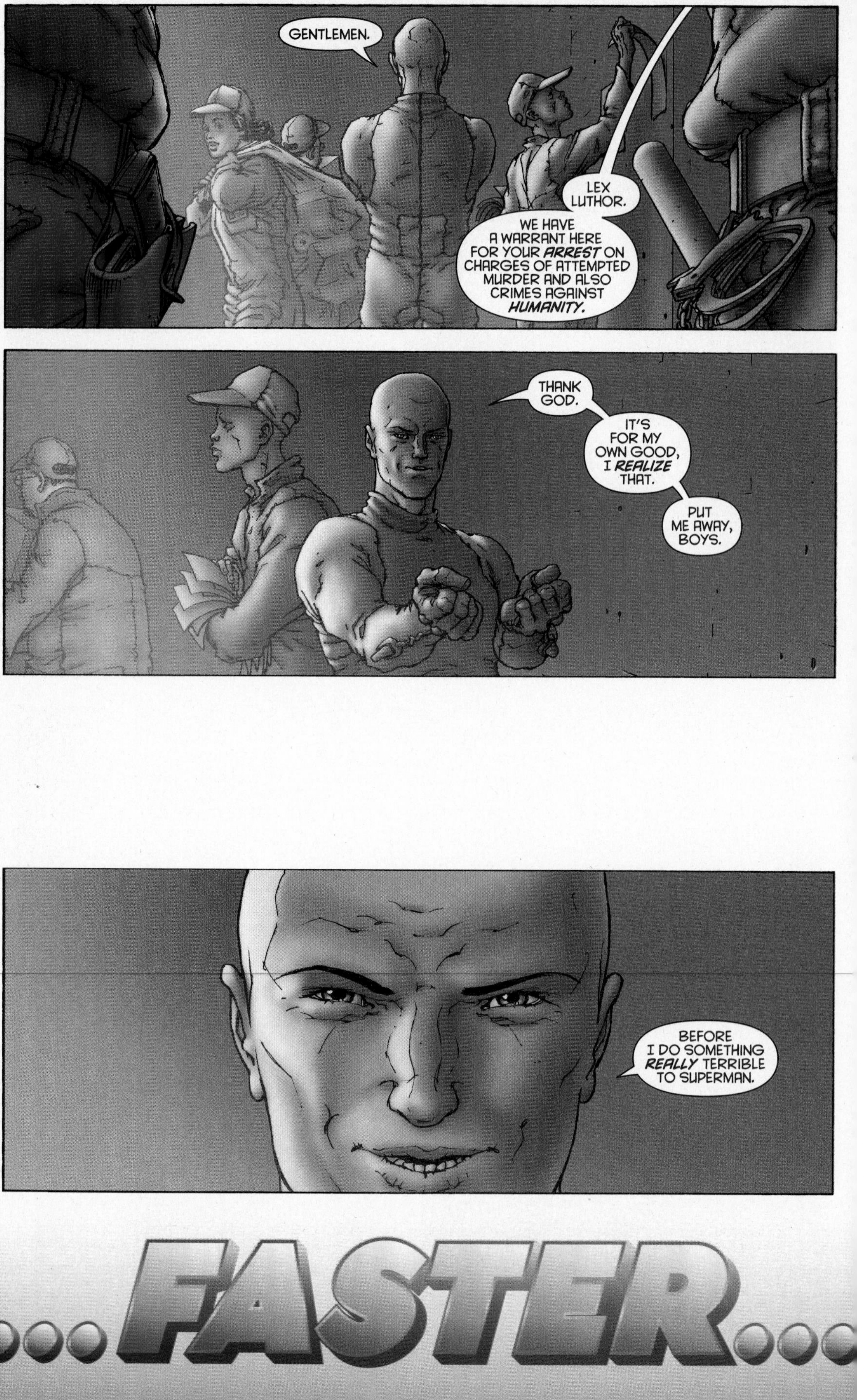
GENTLEMEN.
LEX LUTHOR.
WE HAVE A WARRANT HERE FOR YOUR ARREST ON CHARGES OF ATTEMPTED MURDER AND ALSO CRIMES AGAINST HUMANITY.
THANK GOD.
IT'S FOR MY OWN GOOD, I REALIZE THAT.
PUT ME AWAY, BOYS.
BEFORE I DO SOMETHING REALLY TERRIBLE TO SUPERMAN.
...FASTER...

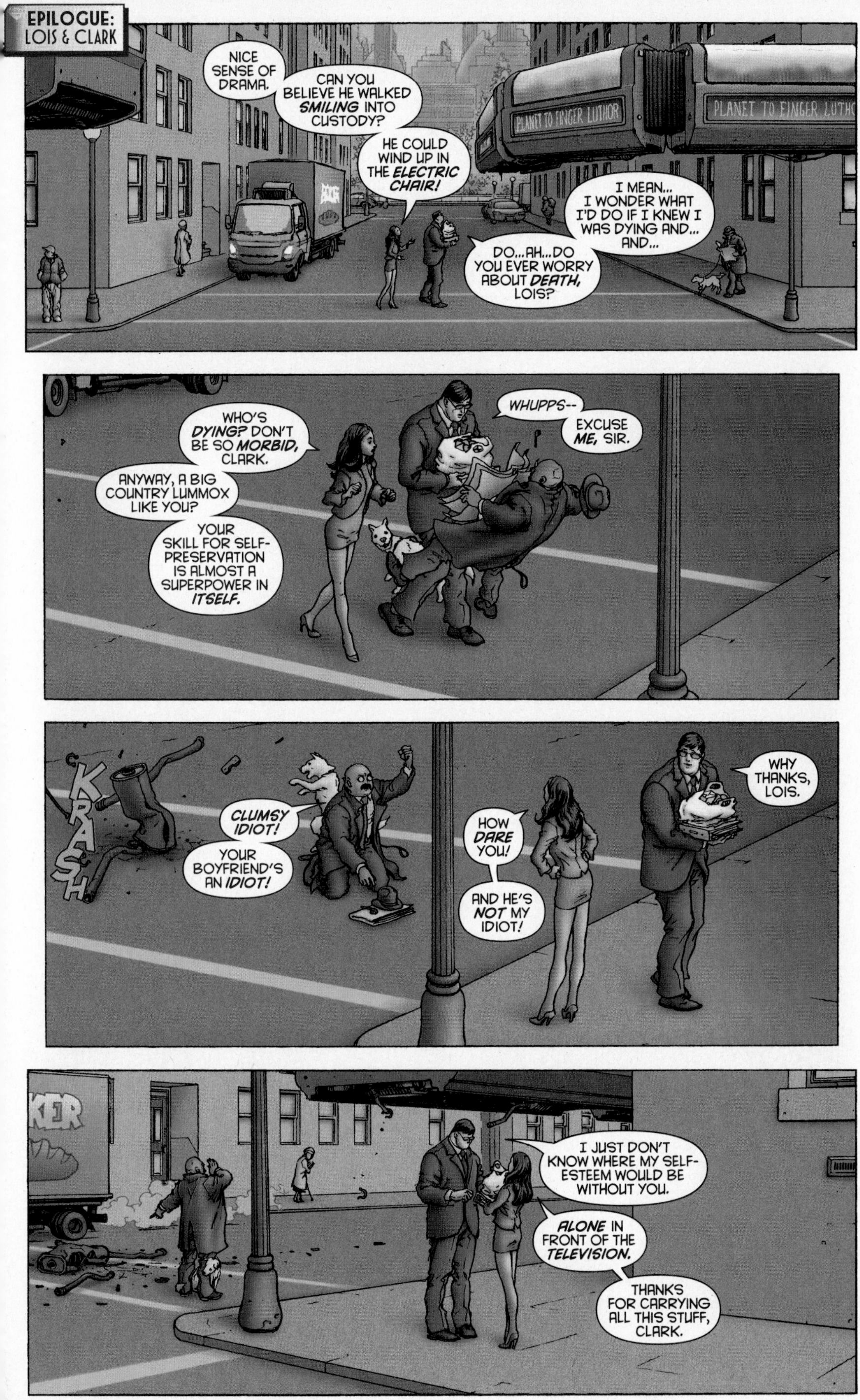
EPILOGUE: LOIS & CLARK
NICE SENSE OF DRAMA.
CAN YOU BELIEVE HE WALKED SMILING INTO CUSTODY?
HE COULD WIND UP IN THE ELECTRIC CHAIR!
PLANET TO FINGER LUTHOR
I MEAN... I WONDER WHAT I'D DO IF I KNEW I WAS DYING AND... AND...
DO...AH...DO YOU EVER WORRY ABOUT DEATH, LOIS?
WHO'S DYING? DON'T BE SO MORBID, CLARK.
WHUPPS-- EXCUSE ME, SIR.
ANYWAY, A BIG COUNTRY LUMMOX LIKE YOU?
YOUR SKILL FOR SELF-PRESERVATION IS ALMOST A SUPERPOWER IN ITSELF.
KRASH
CLUMSY IDIOT!
YOUR BOYFRIEND'S AN IDIOT!
HOW DARE YOU!
AND HE'S NOT MY IDIOT!
WHY THANKS, LOIS.
I JUST DON'T KNOW WHERE MY SELF-ESTEEM WOULD BE WITHOUT YOU.
ALONE IN FRONT OF THE TELEVISION.
THANKS FOR CARRYING ALL THIS STUFF, CLARK.

LOIS, THERE... WELL...
THERE WAS SOMETHING I WANTED TO *TELL* YOU AND...
IF THIS IS ABOUT THE *TRIAL* COVERAGE, WE CAN GO OVER ALL THAT *MAÑANA.*
I HAVE TO FLY, CLARK.
LOIS.
PLEASE STOP TALKING FOR JUST ONE SECOND.
I HAVE SOMETHING TO TELL YOU.

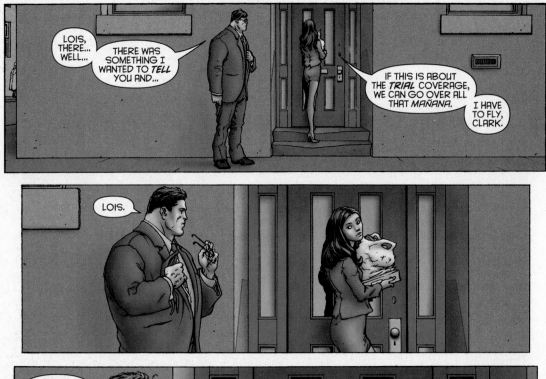

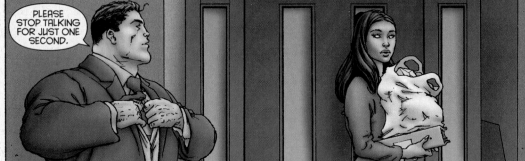

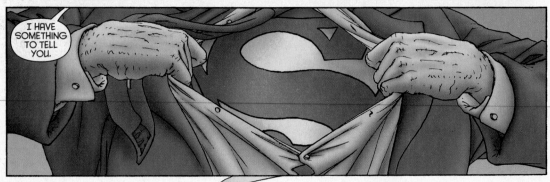

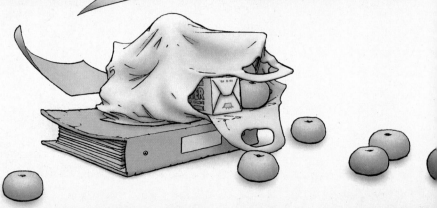

Episode 2

SUPERMAN'S FORBIDDEN ROOM

Cover FRANK QUITELY with JAMIE GRANT

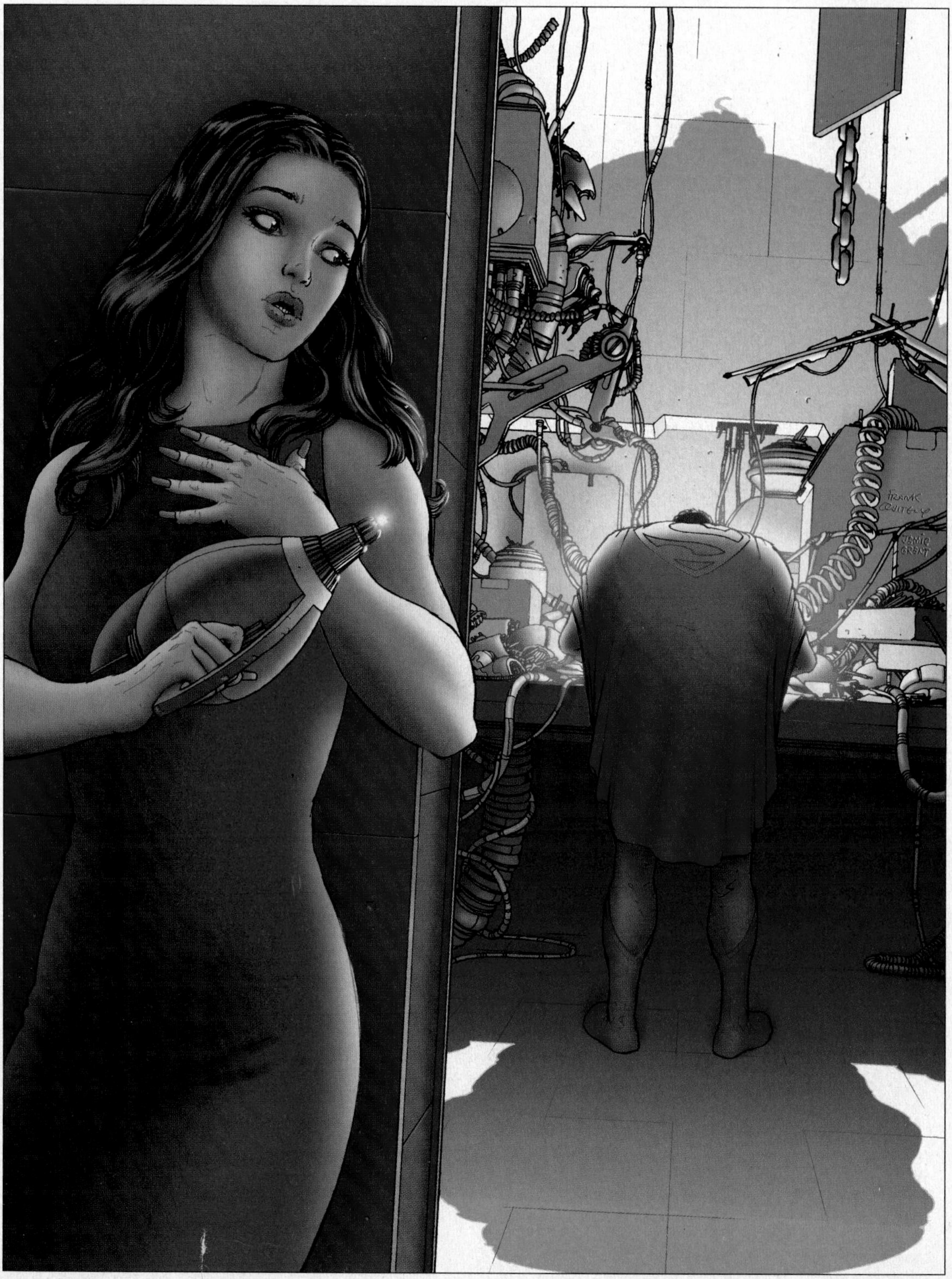
FRANK QUITELY
JAMIE GRANT

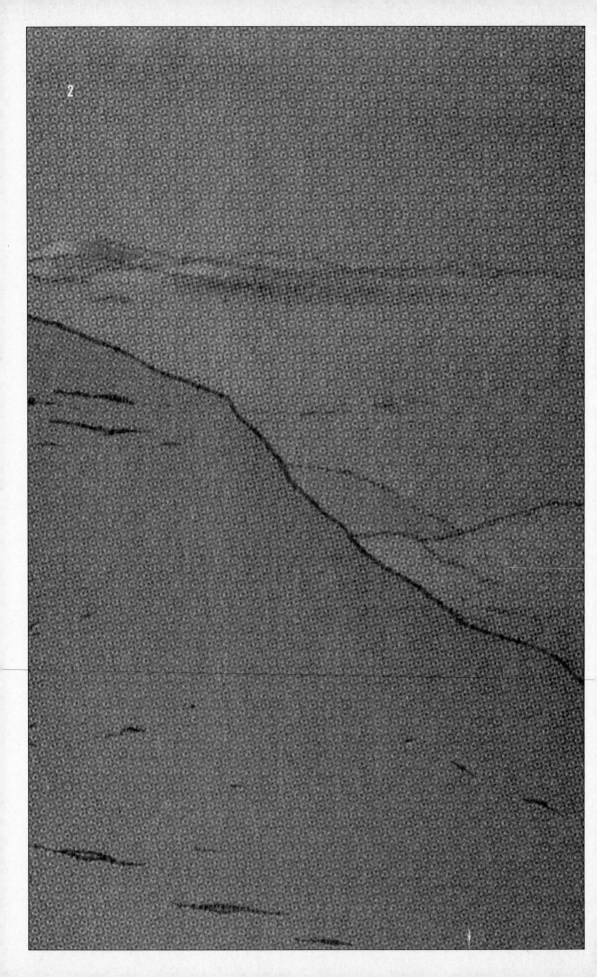

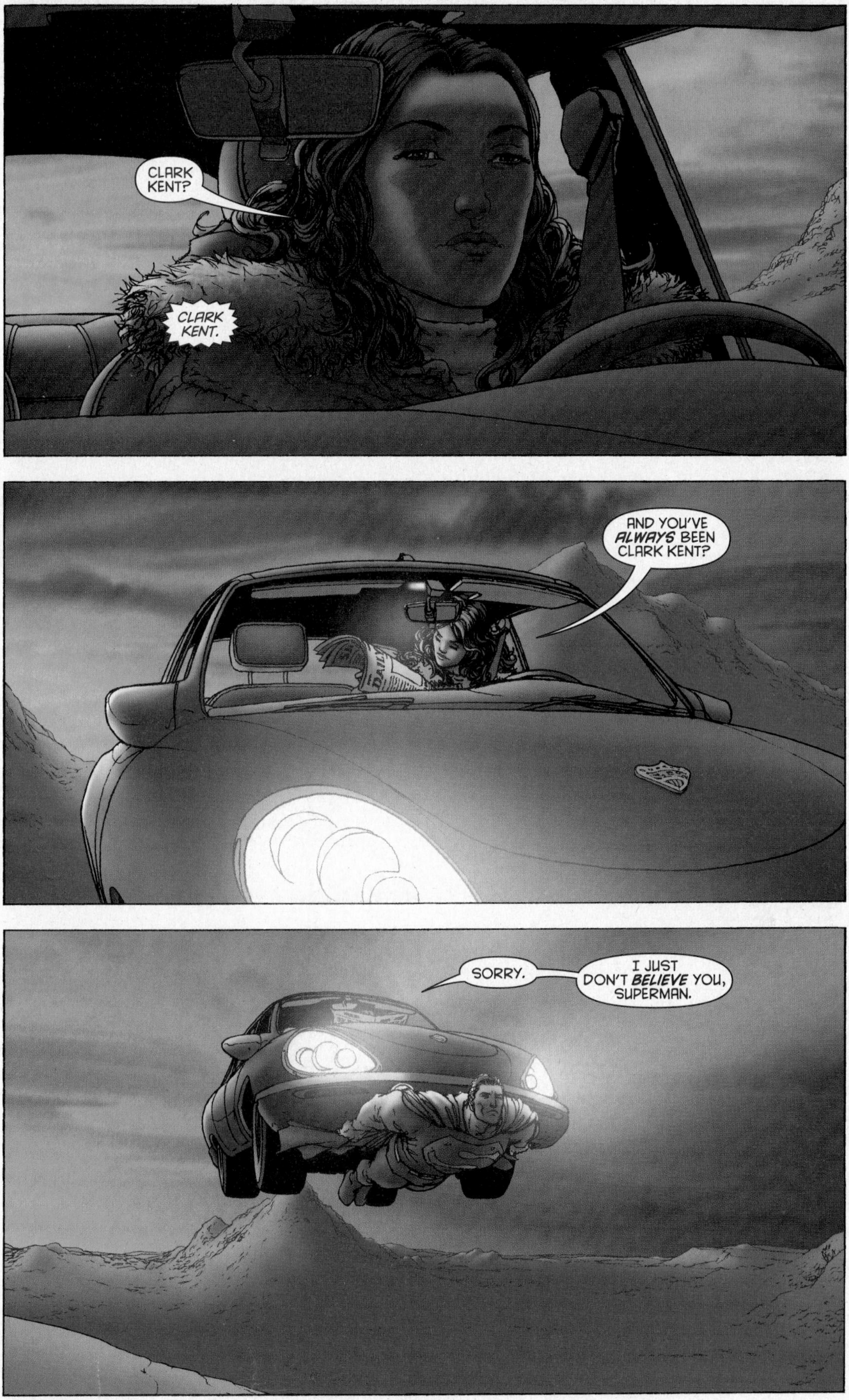
CLARK KENT?
CLARK KENT.
AND YOU'VE ALWAYS BEEN CLARK KENT?
SORRY.
I JUST DON'T BELIEVE YOU, SUPERMAN.

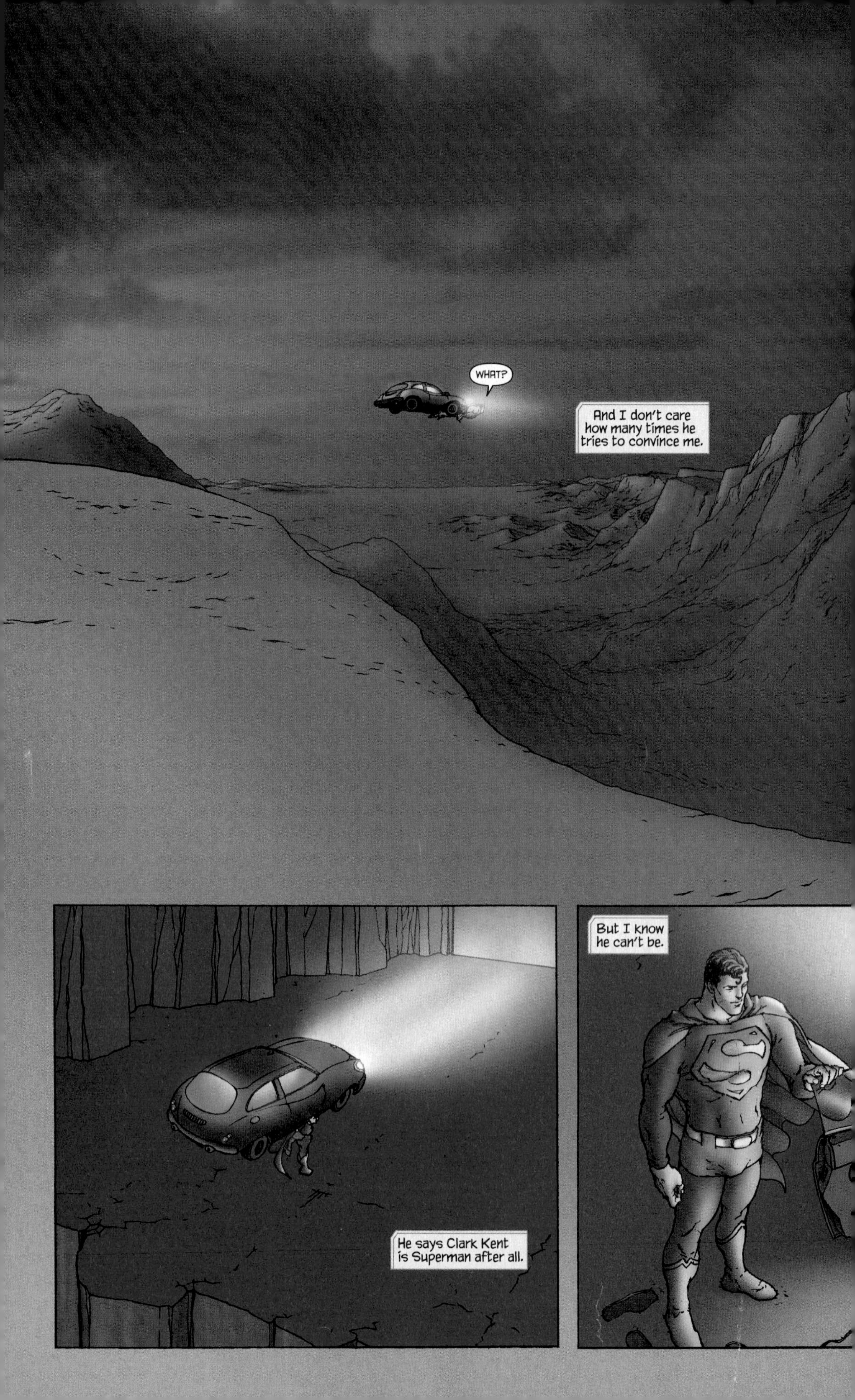
WHAT?
And I don't care how many times he tries to convince me.
He says Clark Kent is Superman after all.
But I know he can't be.

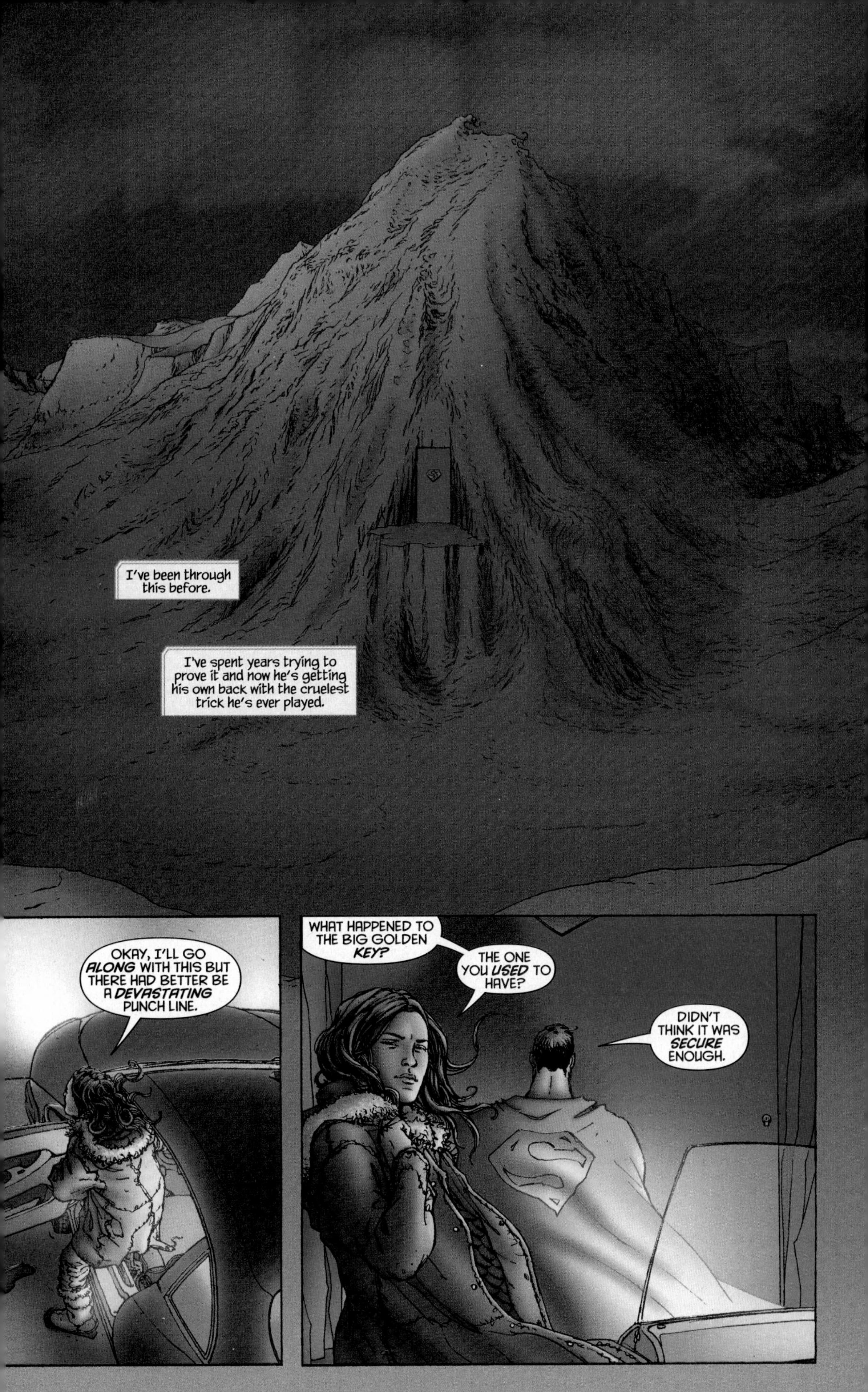
I've been through this before.
I've spent years trying to prove it and now he's getting his own back with the cruelest trick he's ever played.
OKAY, I'LL GO ALONG WITH THIS BUT THERE HAD BETTER BE A DEVASTATING PUNCH LINE.
WHAT HAPPENED TO THE BIG GOLDEN KEY?
THE ONE YOU USED TO HAVE?
DIDN'T THINK IT WAS SECURE ENOUGH.

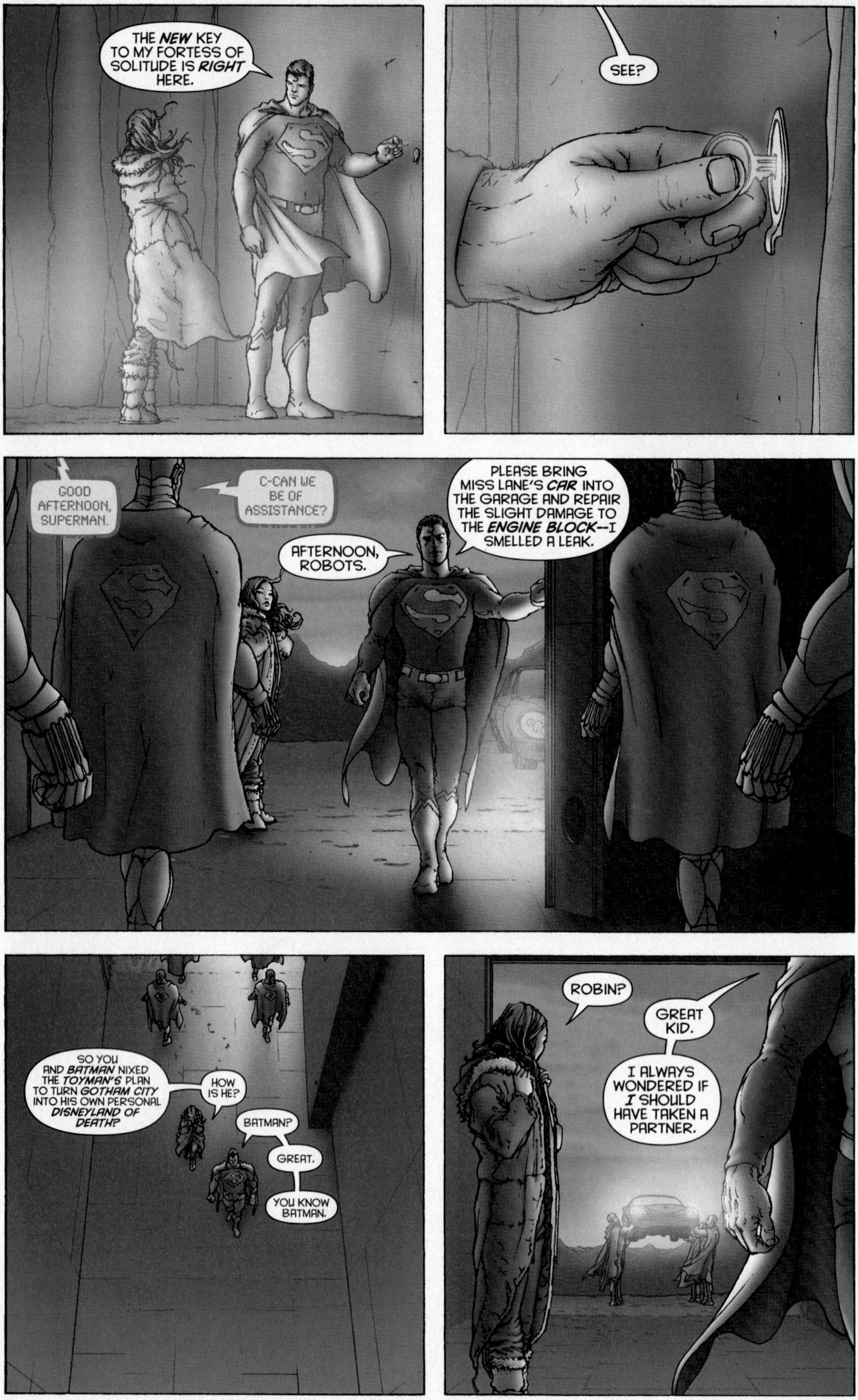
THE NEW KEY TO MY FORTESS OF SOLITUDE IS RIGHT HERE.
SEE?
GOOD AFTERNOON, SUPERMAN.
C-CAN WE BE OF ASSISTANCE?
AFTERNOON, ROBOTS.
PLEASE BRING MISS LANE'S CAR INTO THE GARAGE AND REPAIR THE SLIGHT DAMAGE TO THE ENGINE BLOCK--I SMELLED A LEAK.
SO YOU AND BATMAN NIXED THE TOYMAN'S PLAN TO TURN GOTHAM CITY INTO HIS OWN PERSONAL DISNEYLAND OF DEATH?
HOW IS HE?
BATMAN?
GREAT.
YOU KNOW BATMAN.
ROBIN?
GREAT KID.
I ALWAYS WONDERED IF I SHOULD HAVE TAKEN A PARTNER.

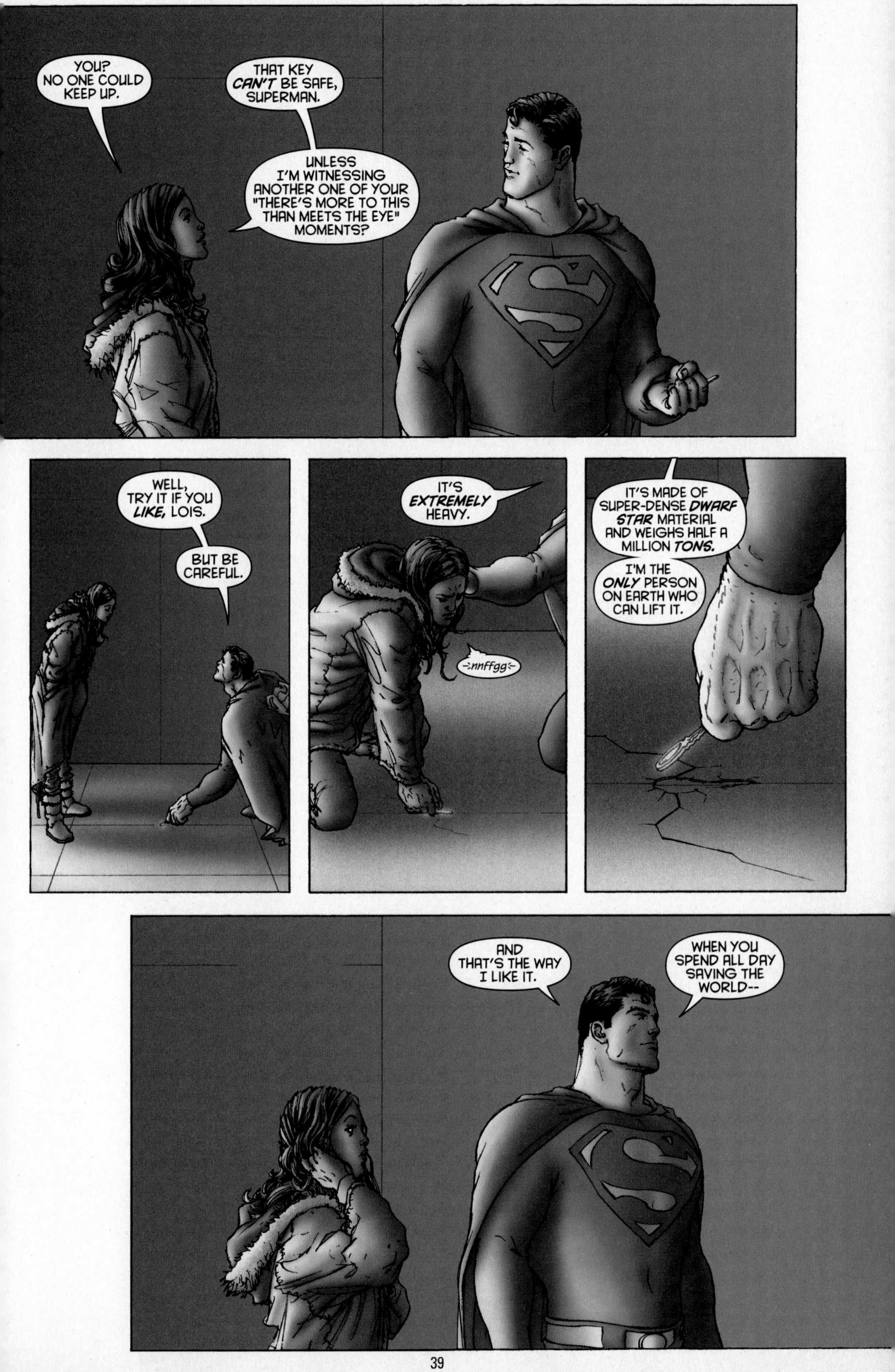

YOU? NO ONE COULD KEEP UP.
THAT KEY CAN'T BE SAFE, SUPERMAN.
UNLESS I'M WITNESSING ANOTHER ONE OF YOUR "THERE'S MORE TO THIS THAN MEETS THE EYE" MOMENTS?
WELL, TRY IT IF YOU LIKE, LOIS.
BUT BE CAREFUL.
IT'S EXTREMELY HEAVY.
nnffgg
IT'S MADE OF SUPER-DENSE DWARF STAR MATERIAL AND WEIGHS HALF A MILLION TONS.
I'M THE ONLY PERSON ON EARTH WHO CAN LIFT IT.
AND THAT'S THE WAY I LIKE IT.
WHEN YOU SPEND ALL DAY SAVING THE WORLD--

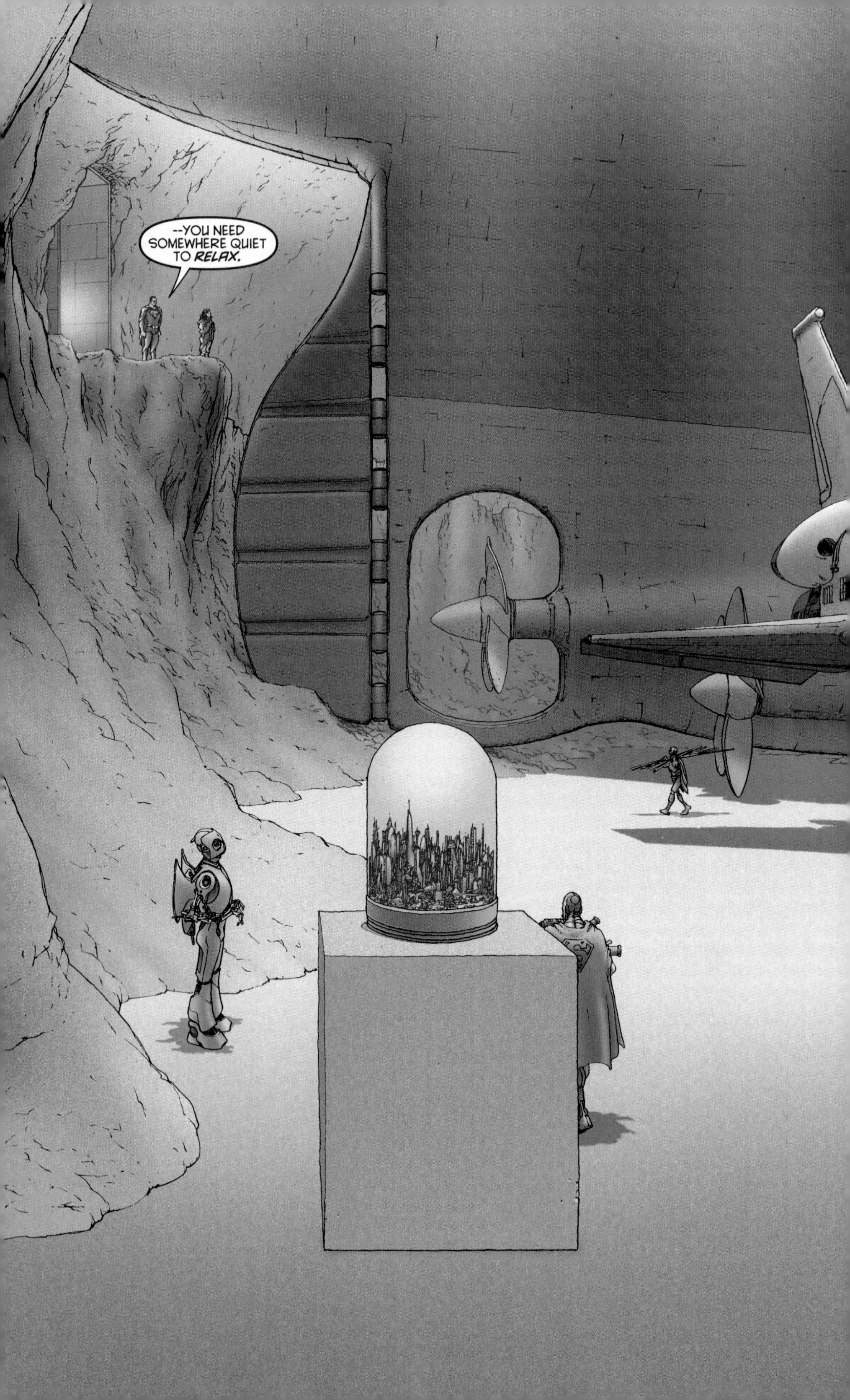
--YOU NEED SOMEWHERE QUIET TO *RELAX.*

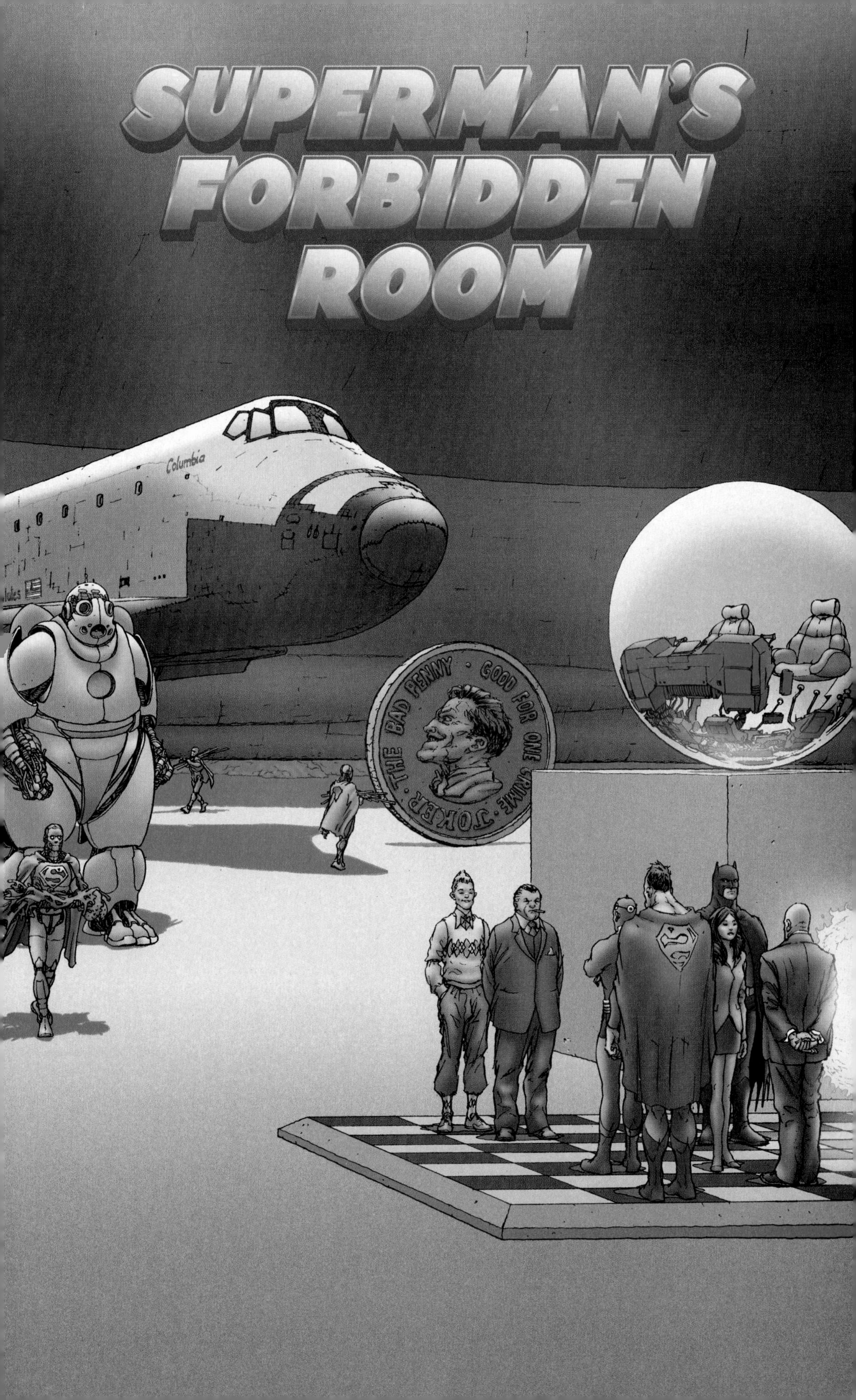
SUPERMAN'S FORBIDDEN ROOM
Columbia
THE BAD PENNY · GOOD FOR ONE CRIME · JOKER

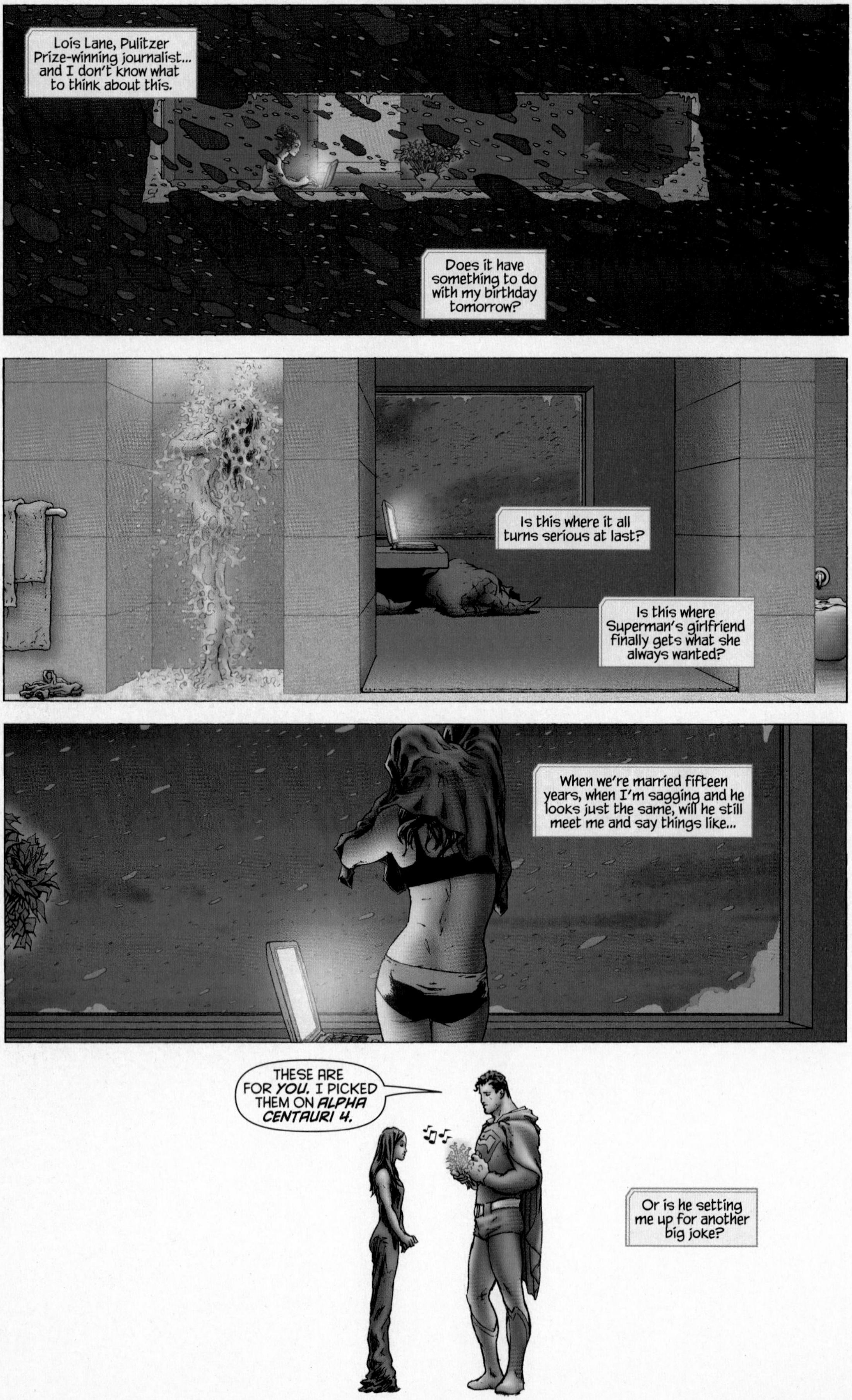

Lois Lane, Pulitzer Prize-winning journalist... and I don't know what to think about this.
Does it have something to do with my birthday tomorrow?
Is this where it all turns serious at last?
Is this where Superman's girlfriend finally gets what she always wanted?
When we're married fifteen years, when I'm sagging and he looks just the same, will he still meet me and say things like...
THESE ARE FOR YOU. I PICKED THEM ON ALPHA CENTAURI 4.
Or is he setting me up for another big joke?

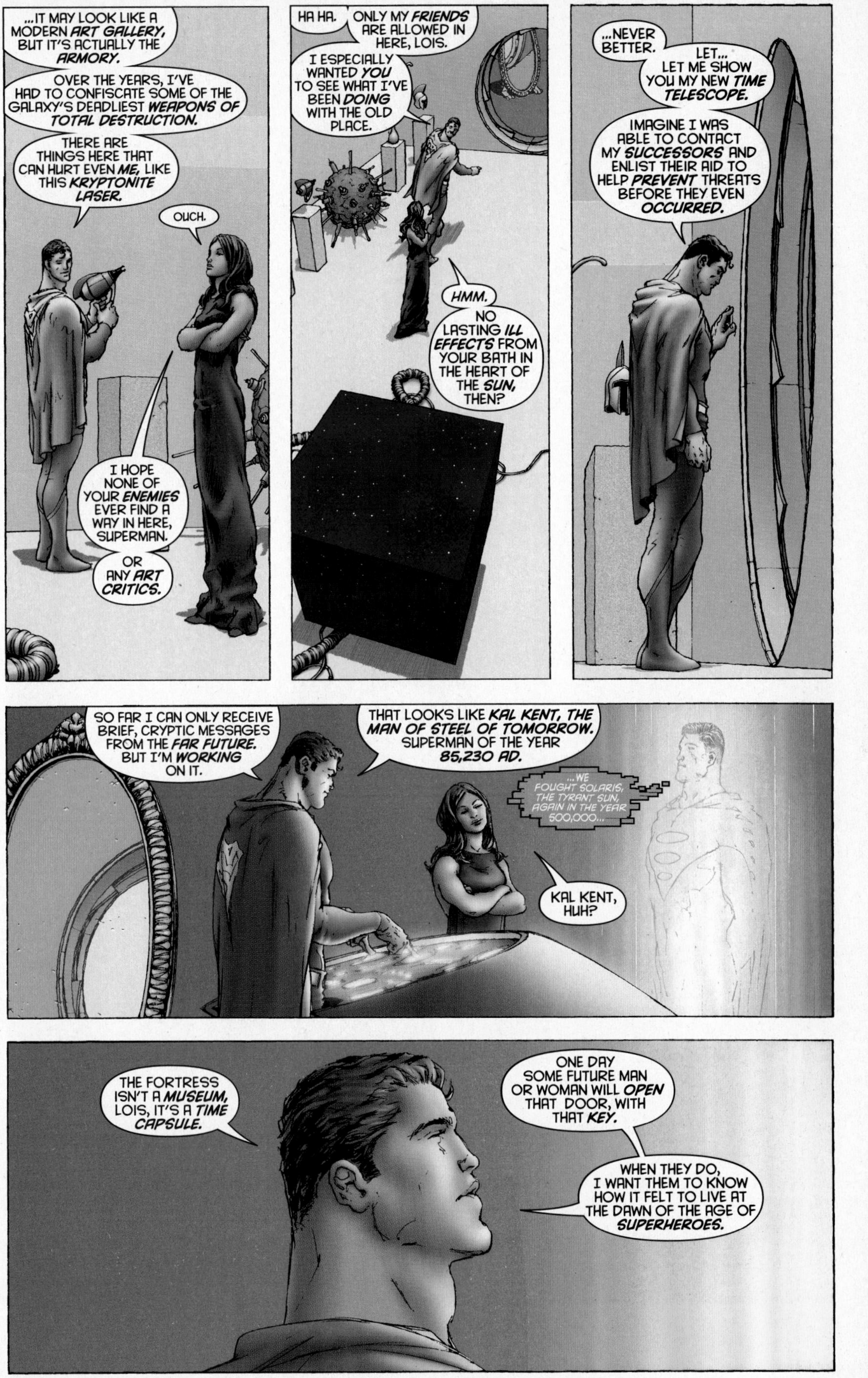
...IT MAY LOOK LIKE A MODERN ART GALLERY, BUT IT'S ACTUALLY THE ARMORY.
OVER THE YEARS, I'VE HAD TO CONFISCATE SOME OF THE GALAXY'S DEADLIEST WEAPONS OF TOTAL DESTRUCTION.
THERE ARE THINGS HERE THAT CAN HURT EVEN ME, LIKE THIS KRYPTONITE LASER.
OUCH.
I HOPE NONE OF YOUR ENEMIES EVER FIND A WAY IN HERE, SUPERMAN.
OR ANY ART CRITICS.
HA HA.
ONLY MY FRIENDS ARE ALLOWED IN HERE, LOIS.
I ESPECIALLY WANTED YOU TO SEE WHAT I'VE BEEN DOING WITH THE OLD PLACE.
HMM.
NO LASTING ILL EFFECTS FROM YOUR BATH IN THE HEART OF THE SUN, THEN?
...NEVER BETTER.
LET... LET ME SHOW YOU MY NEW TIME TELESCOPE.
IMAGINE I WAS ABLE TO CONTACT MY SUCCESSORS AND ENLIST THEIR AID TO HELP PREVENT THREATS BEFORE THEY EVEN OCCURRED.
SO FAR I CAN ONLY RECEIVE BRIEF, CRYPTIC MESSAGES FROM THE FAR FUTURE. BUT I'M WORKING ON IT.
THAT LOOKS LIKE KAL KENT, THE MAN OF STEEL OF TOMORROW. SUPERMAN OF THE YEAR 85,230 AD.
...WE FOUGHT SOLARIS, THE TYRANT SUN, AGAIN IN THE YEAR 500,000...
KAL KENT, HUH?
THE FORTRESS ISN'T A MUSEUM, LOIS, IT'S A TIME CAPSULE.
ONE DAY SOME FUTURE MAN OR WOMAN WILL OPEN THAT DOOR, WITH THAT KEY.
WHEN THEY DO, I WANT THEM TO KNOW HOW IT FELT TO LIVE AT THE DAWN OF THE AGE OF SUPERHEROES.

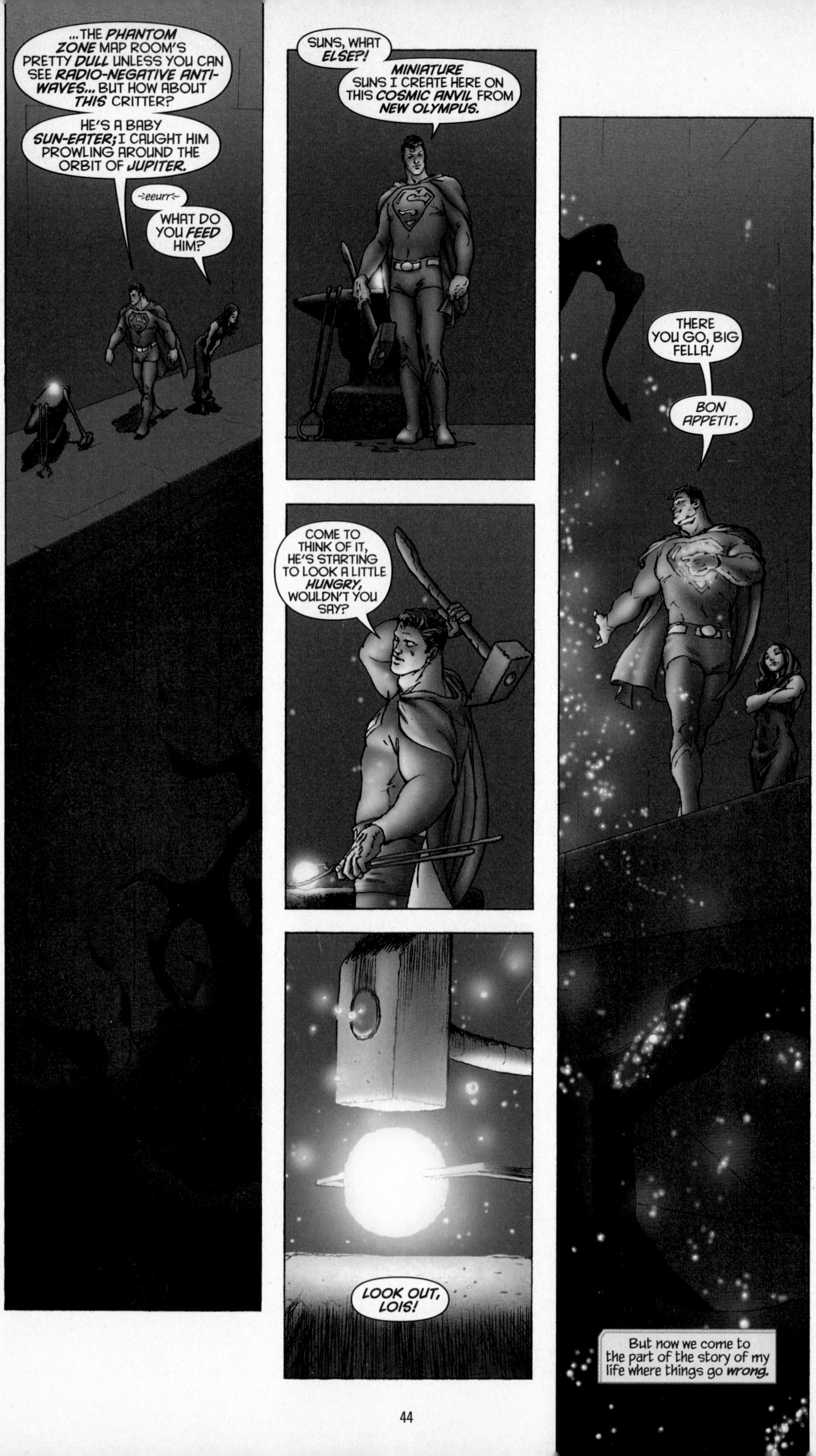
...THE PHANTOM ZONE MAP ROOM'S PRETTY DULL UNLESS YOU CAN SEE RADIO-NEGATIVE ANTI-WAVES... BUT HOW ABOUT THIS CRITTER?
HE'S A BABY SUN-EATER; I CAUGHT HIM PROWLING AROUND THE ORBIT OF JUPITER.
eeurr
WHAT DO YOU FEED HIM?
SUNS, WHAT ELSE?!
MINIATURE SUNS I CREATE HERE ON THIS COSMIC ANVIL FROM NEW OLYMPUS.
COME TO THINK OF IT, HE'S STARTING TO LOOK A LITTLE HUNGRY, WOULDN'T YOU SAY?
LOOK OUT, LOIS!
THERE YOU GO, BIG FELLA!
BON APPETIT.
But now we come to the part of the story of my life where things go wrong.

It wasn't *my fault* the door was open.

I know I wasn't supposed to see inside that weird room.

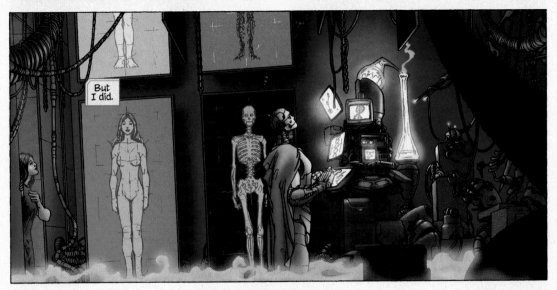

But I did.

IT'S NOT WHAT YOU *THINK.*

LOIS, *DON'T* GO IN THERE!

YOU CAN GO *ANYWHERE* IN THE FORTRESS, BUT THIS ROOM IS *OFF LIMITS.*

~wuhh~

TRUST ME.

COME THIS WAY AND LET ME SHOW YOU MY *GENETIC LIBRARY.* I USED BRAINIAC'S *SHRINKING RAY* TO STORE LIVING SAMPLES OF *EVERY* THREATENED SPECIES WITHIN A HUNDRED *LIGHT YEARS* IN A SINGLE *DRAWER...*

REPORT FOR *REPAIR,* PLEASE, ROBOT 7.

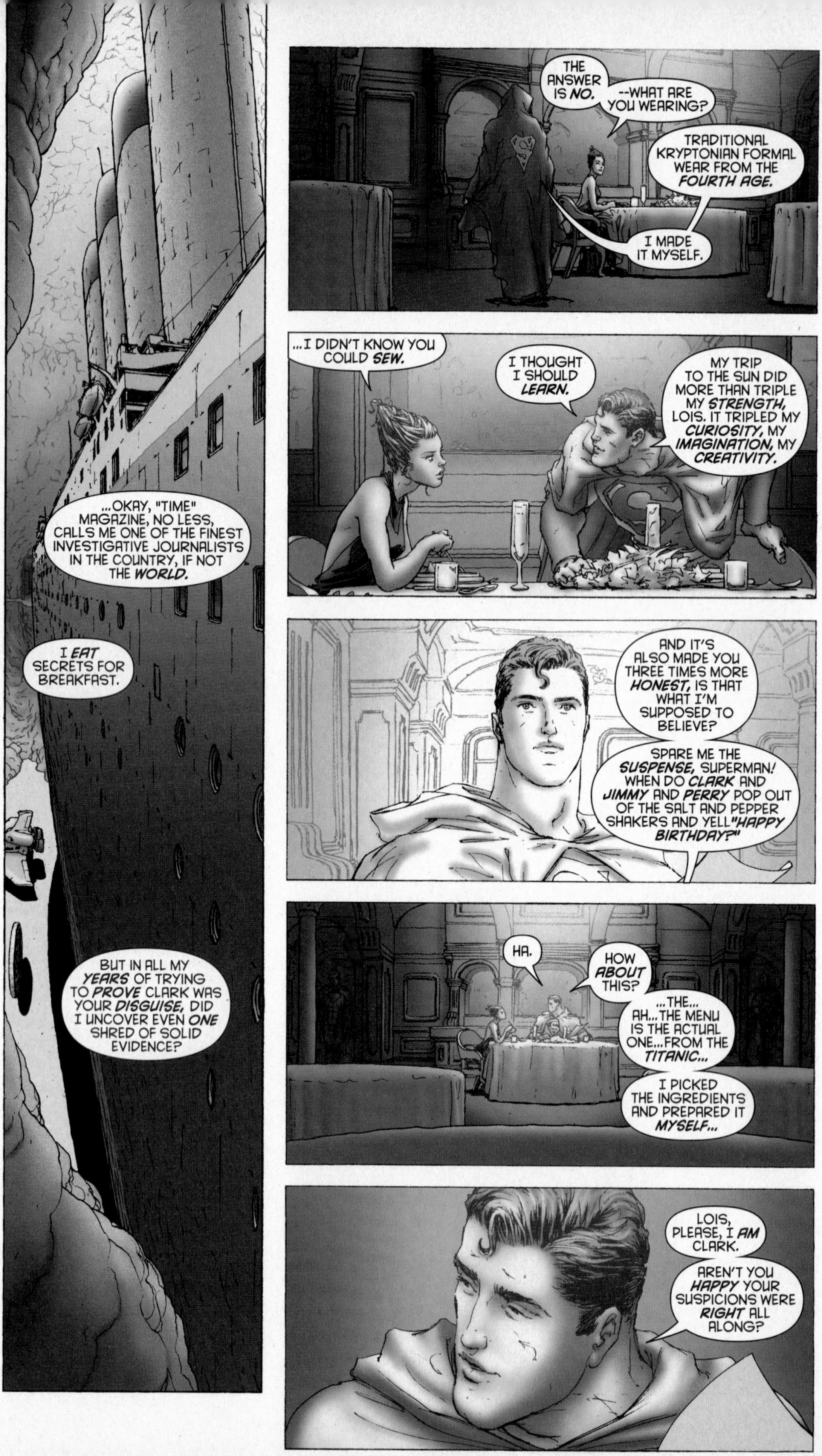

...OKAY, "TIME" MAGAZINE, NO LESS, CALLS ME ONE OF THE FINEST INVESTIGATIVE JOURNALISTS IN THE COUNTRY, IF NOT THE WORLD.
I EAT SECRETS FOR BREAKFAST.
BUT IN ALL MY YEARS OF TRYING TO PROVE CLARK WAS YOUR DISGUISE, DID I UNCOVER EVEN ONE SHRED OF SOLID EVIDENCE?
THE ANSWER IS NO.
--WHAT ARE YOU WEARING?
TRADITIONAL KRYPTONIAN FORMAL WEAR FROM THE FOURTH AGE.
I MADE IT MYSELF.
...I DIDN'T KNOW YOU COULD SEW.
I THOUGHT I SHOULD LEARN.
MY TRIP TO THE SUN DID MORE THAN TRIPLE MY STRENGTH, LOIS. IT TRIPLED MY CURIOSITY, MY IMAGINATION, MY CREATIVITY.
AND IT'S ALSO MADE YOU THREE TIMES MORE HONEST, IS THAT WHAT I'M SUPPOSED TO BELIEVE?
SPARE ME THE SUSPENSE, SUPERMAN! WHEN DO CLARK AND JIMMY AND PERRY POP OUT OF THE SALT AND PEPPER SHAKERS AND YELL "HAPPY BIRTHDAY?"
HA.
HOW ABOUT THIS?
...THE... AH...THE MENU IS THE ACTUAL ONE...FROM THE TITANIC...
I PICKED THE INGREDIENTS AND PREPARED IT MYSELF...
LOIS, PLEASE, I AM CLARK.
AREN'T YOU HAPPY YOUR SUSPICIONS WERE RIGHT ALL ALONG?

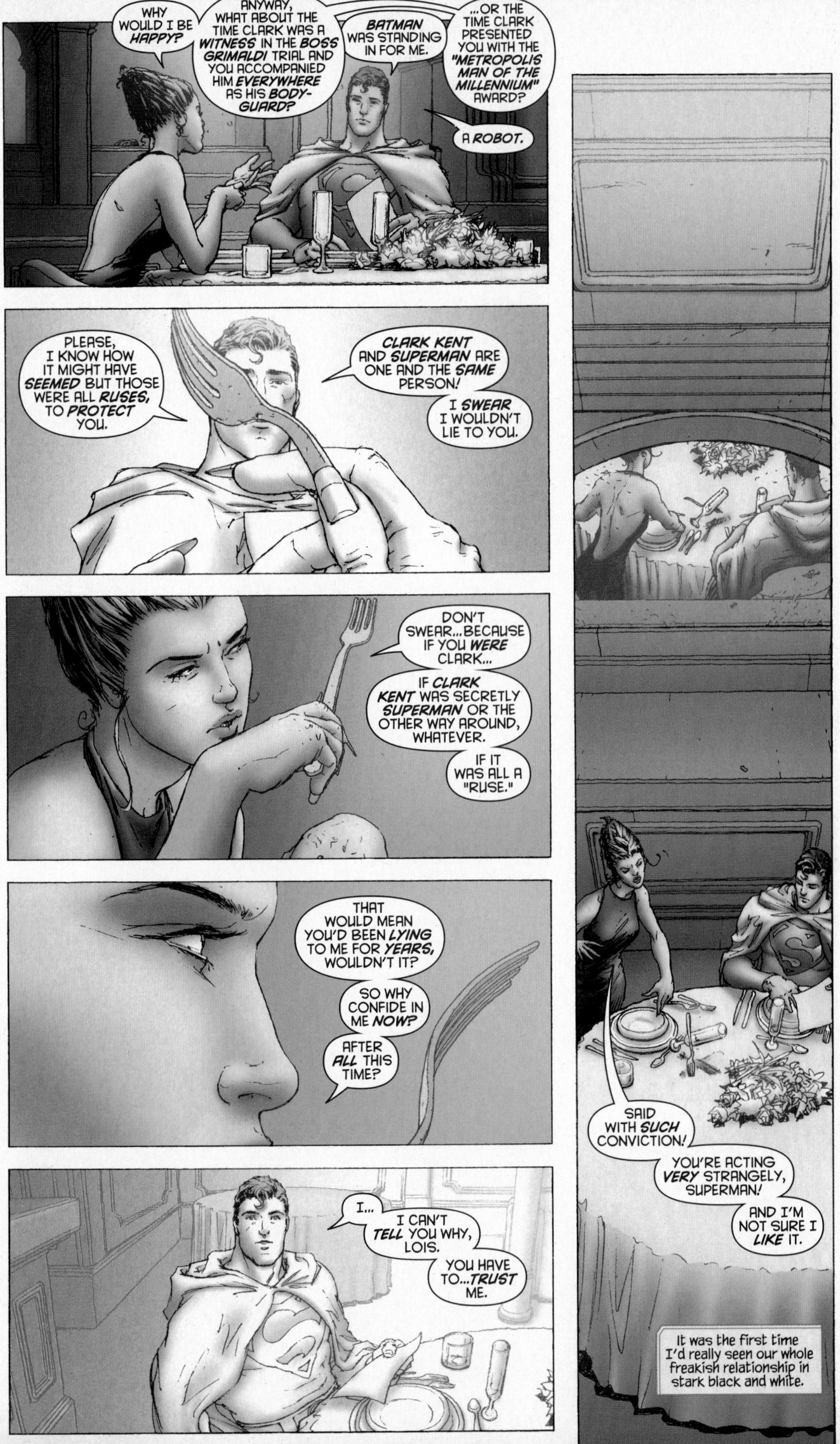
WHY WOULD I BE HAPPY?
ANYWAY, WHAT ABOUT THE TIME CLARK WAS A WITNESS IN THE BOSS GRIMALDI TRIAL AND YOU ACCOMPANIED HIM EVERYWHERE AS HIS BODY-GUARD?
BATMAN WAS STANDING IN FOR ME.
...OR THE TIME CLARK PRESENTED YOU WITH THE "METROPOLIS MAN OF THE MILLENNIUM" AWARD?
A ROBOT.
PLEASE, I KNOW HOW IT MIGHT HAVE SEEMED BUT THOSE WERE ALL RUSES, TO PROTECT YOU.
CLARK KENT AND SUPERMAN ARE ONE AND THE SAME PERSON!
I SWEAR I WOULDN'T LIE TO YOU.
DON'T SWEAR...BECAUSE IF YOU WERE CLARK...
IF CLARK KENT WAS SECRETLY SUPERMAN OR THE OTHER WAY AROUND, WHATEVER.
IF IT WAS ALL A "RUSE."
THAT WOULD MEAN YOU'D BEEN LYING TO ME FOR YEARS, WOULDN'T IT?
SO WHY CONFIDE IN ME NOW?
AFTER ALL THIS TIME?
I... I CAN'T TELL YOU WHY, LOIS.
YOU HAVE TO...TRUST ME.
SAID WITH SUCH CONVICTION!
YOU'RE ACTING VERY STRANGELY, SUPERMAN!
AND I'M NOT SURE I LIKE IT.
It was the first time I'd really seen our whole freakish relationship in stark black and white.

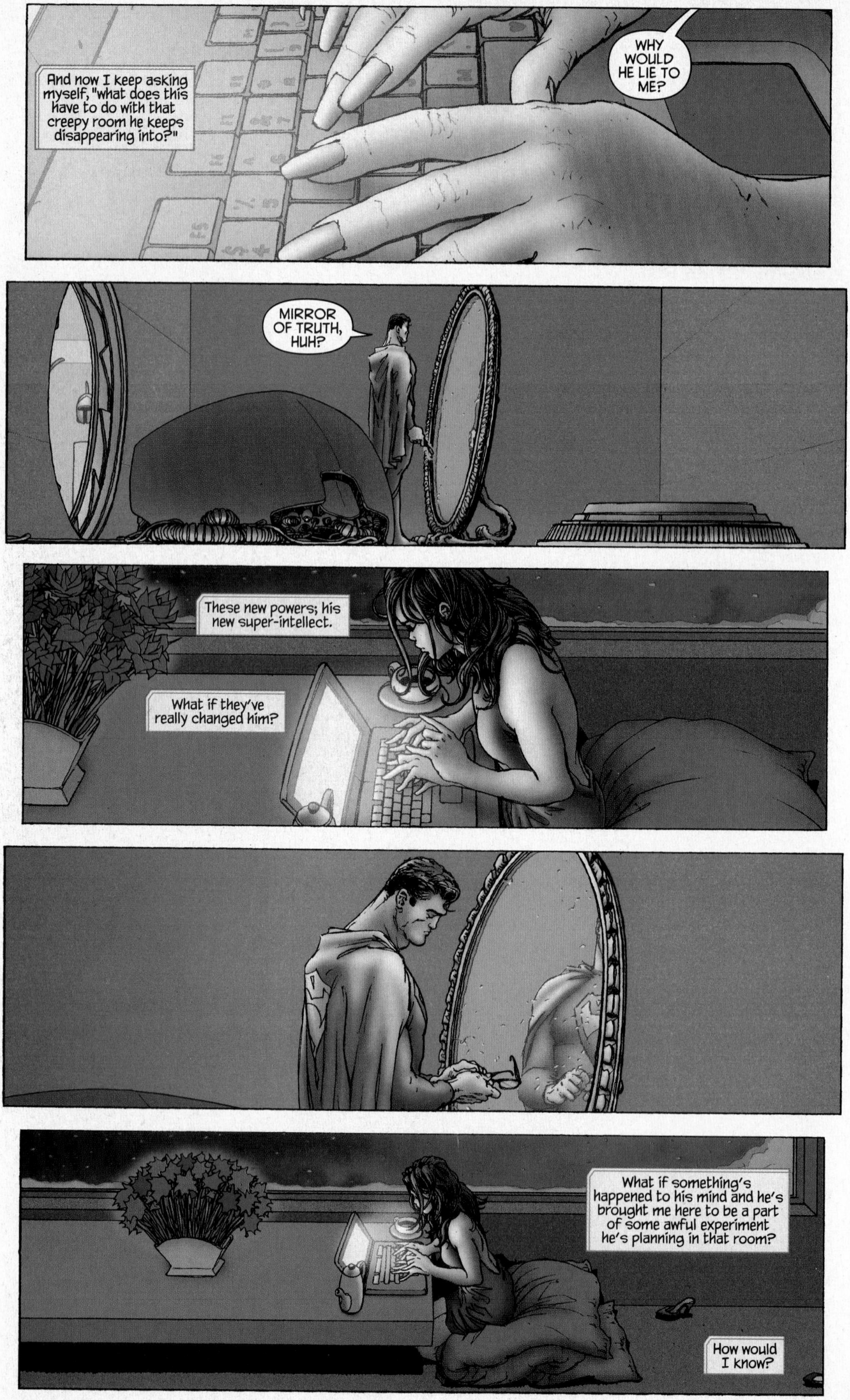
And now I keep asking myself, "what does this have to do with that creepy room he keeps disappearing into?"
WHY WOULD HE LIE TO ME?
MIRROR OF TRUTH, HUH?
These new powers; his new super-intellect.
What if they've really changed him?
What if something's happened to his mind and he's brought me here to be a part of some awful experiment he's planning in that room?
How would I know?

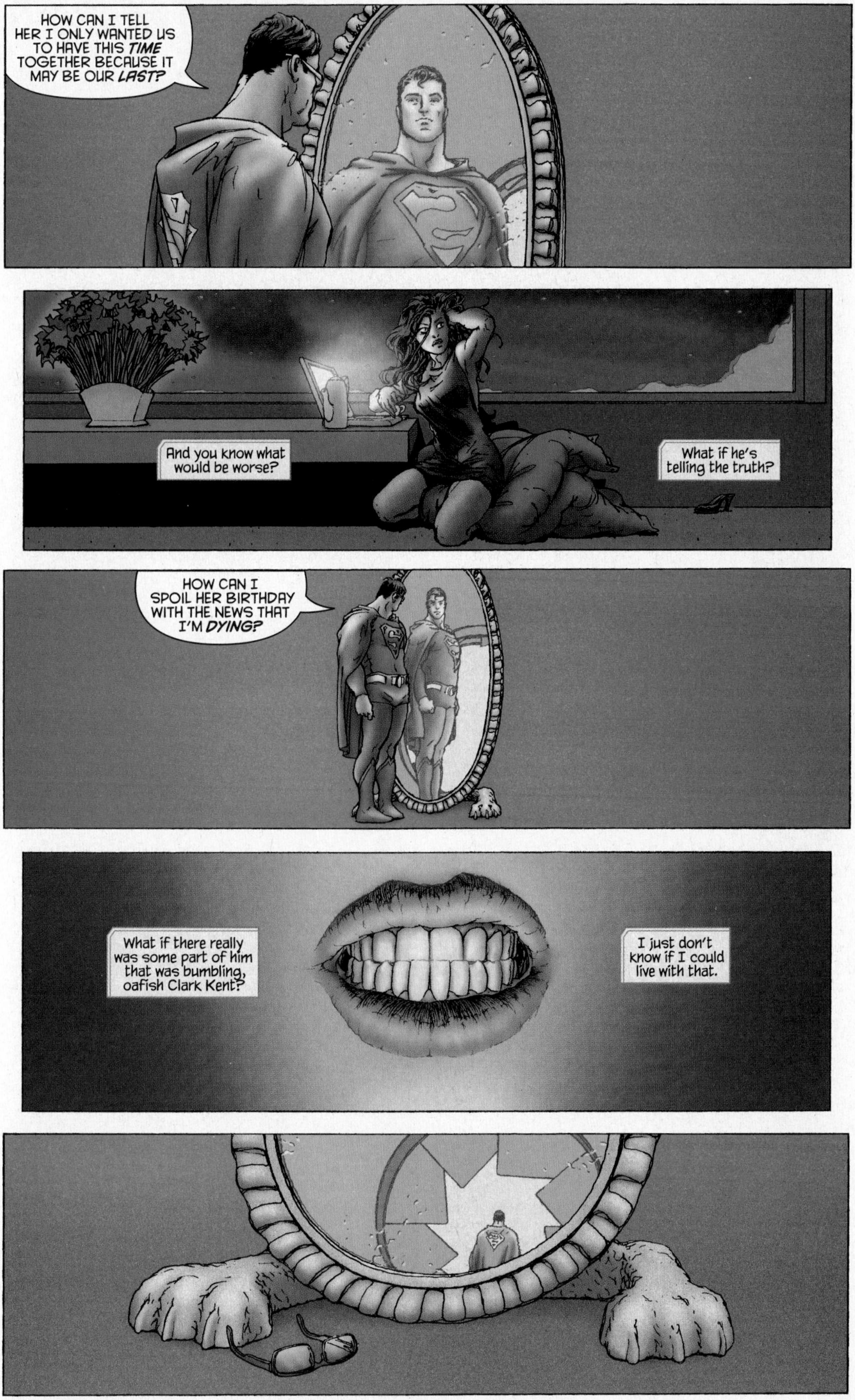
HOW CAN I TELL HER I ONLY WANTED US TO HAVE THIS *TIME* TOGETHER BECAUSE IT MAY BE OUR *LAST?*
And you know what would be worse?
What if he's telling the truth?
HOW CAN I SPOIL HER BIRTHDAY WITH THE NEWS THAT I'M *DYING?*
What if there really was some part of him that was bumbling, oafish Clark Kent?
I just don't know if I could live with that.

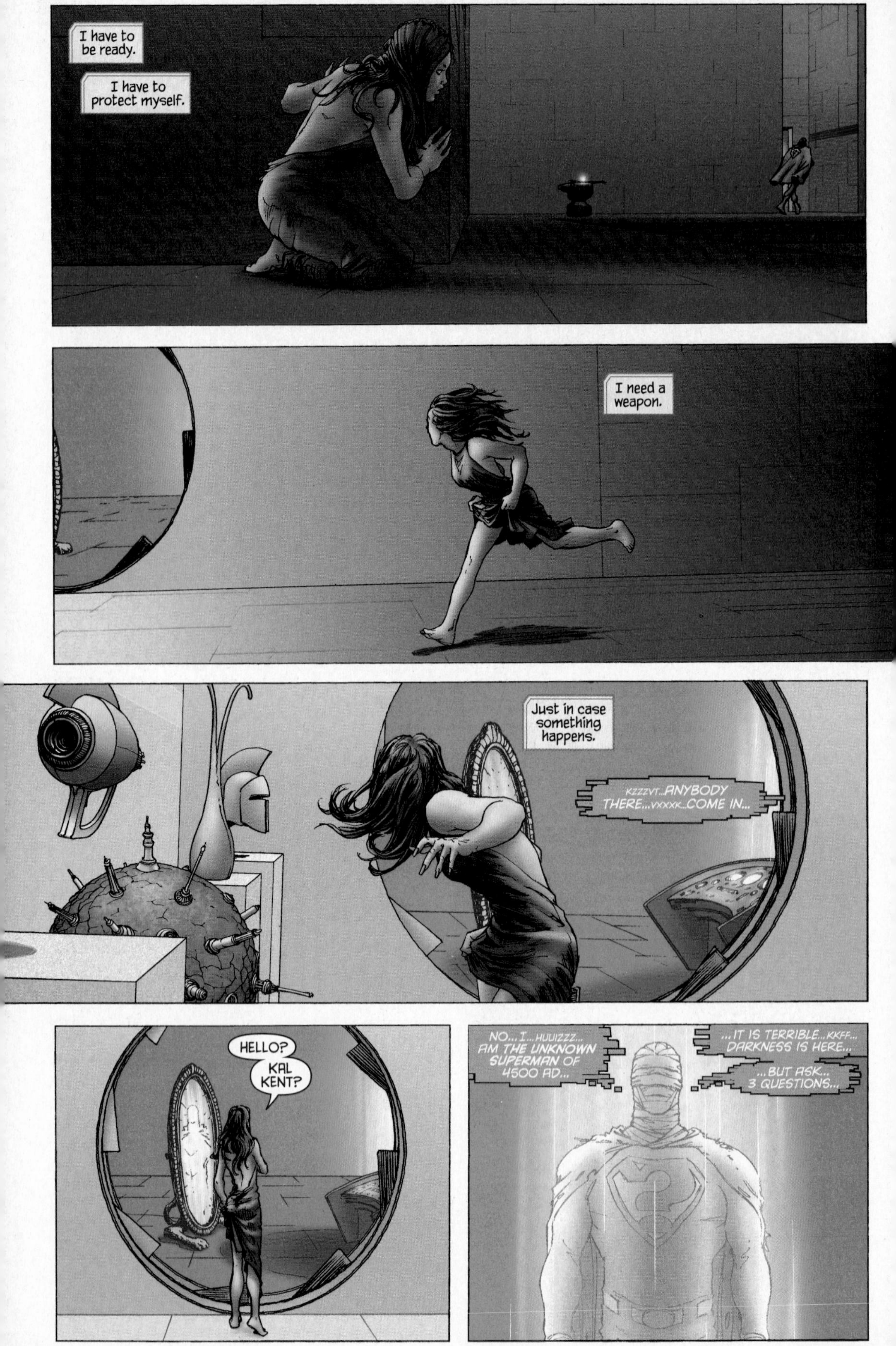
I have to be ready.
I have to protect myself.
I need a weapon.
Just in case something happens.
KZZZVT...ANYBODY THERE...VXXXK...COME IN...
HELLO? KAL KENT?
NO... I...HUUIZZZ... AM THE UNKNOWN SUPERMAN OF 4500 AD...
...IT IS TERRIBLE...KKFF... DARKNESS IS HERE...
...BUT ASK... 3 QUESTIONS...

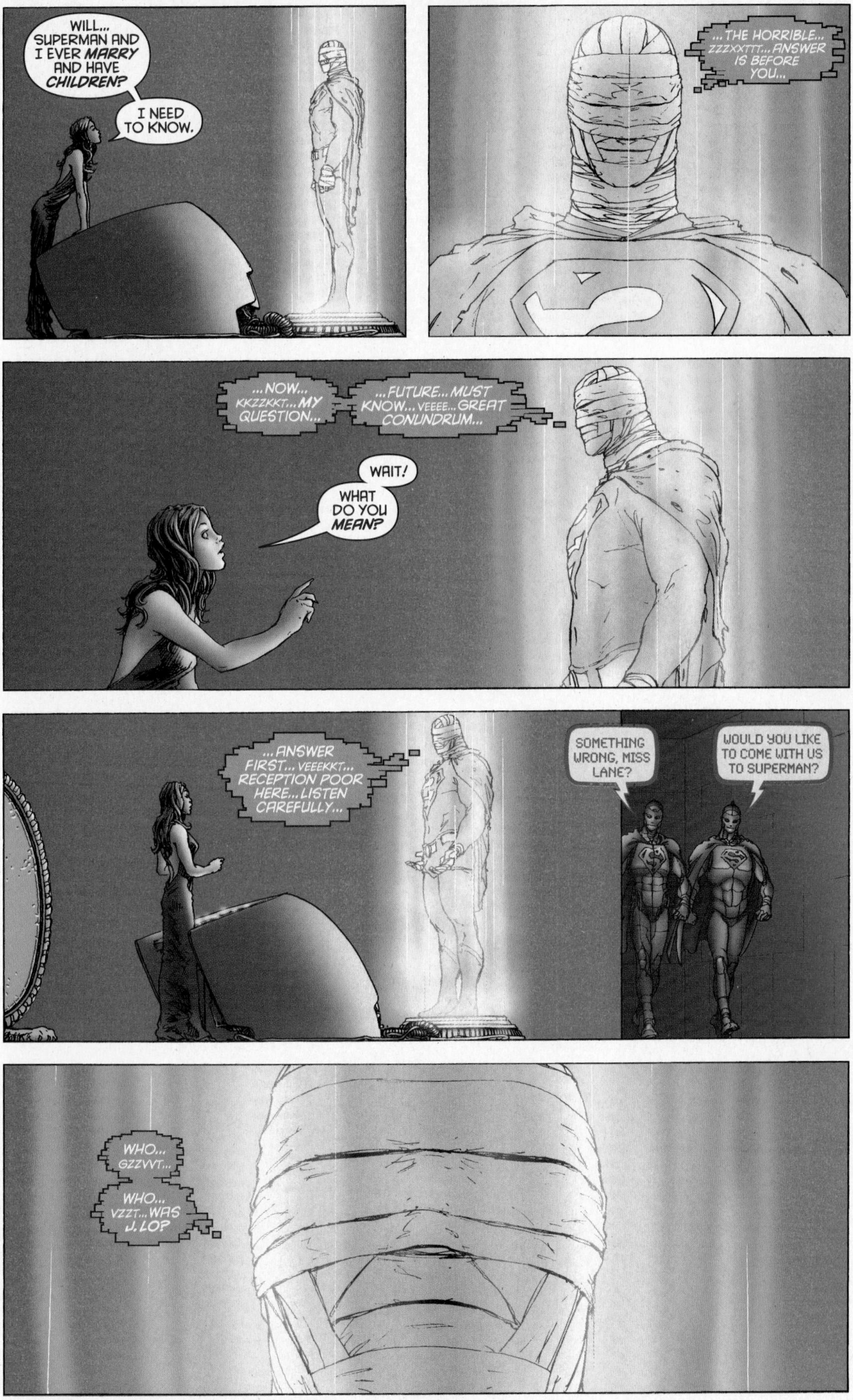
WILL... SUPERMAN AND I EVER MARRY AND HAVE CHILDREN?
I NEED TO KNOW.
...THE HORRIBLE... ZZZXXTTT... ANSWER IS BEFORE YOU...
...NOW... KKZZKKT... MY QUESTION...
...FUTURE... MUST KNOW... VEEEE... GREAT CONUNDRUM...
WAIT!
WHAT DO YOU MEAN?
...ANSWER FIRST... VEEEKKT... RECEPTION POOR HERE... LISTEN CAREFULLY...
SOMETHING WRONG, MISS LANE?
WOULD YOU LIKE TO COME WITH US TO SUPERMAN?
WHO... GZZVVT...
WHO... VZZT... WAS J. LO?

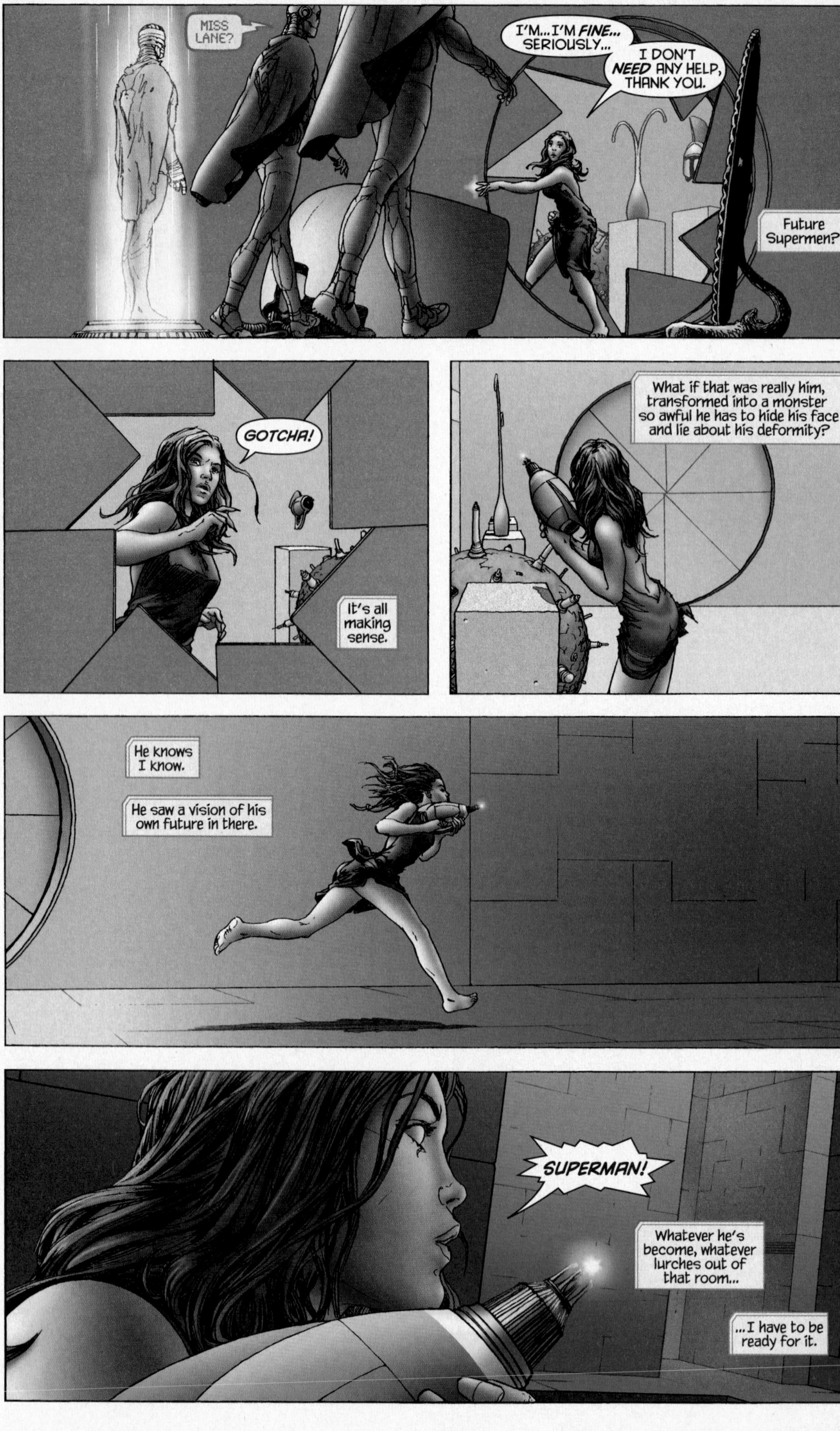
MISS LANE?
I'M...I'M FINE... SERIOUSLY...
I DON'T NEED ANY HELP, THANK YOU.
Future Supermen?
GOTCHA!
It's all making sense.
What if that was really him, transformed into a monster so awful he has to hide his face and lie about his deformity?
He knows I know.
He saw a vision of his own future in there.
SUPERMAN!
Whatever he's become, whatever lurches out of that room...
...I have to be ready for it.

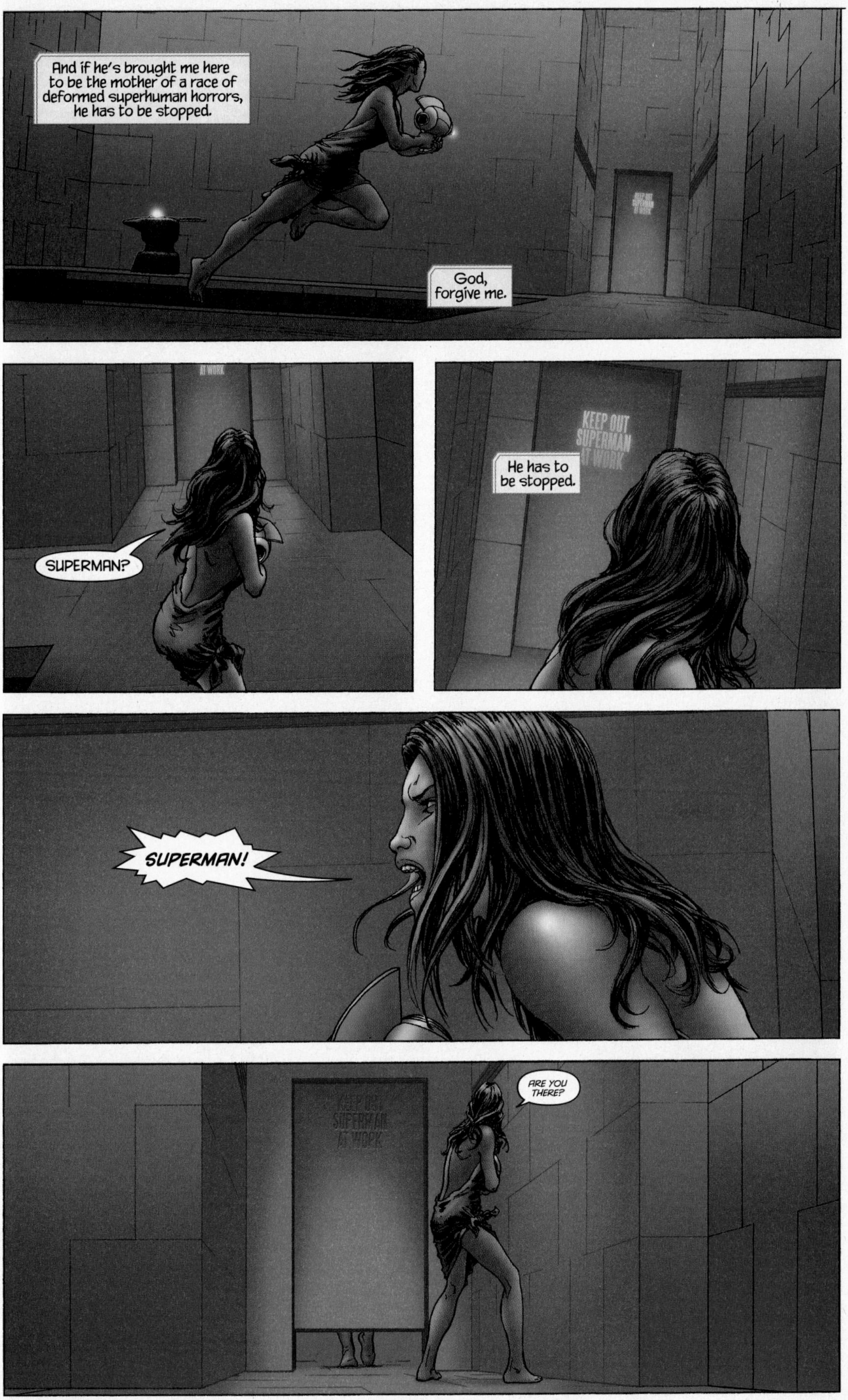
And if he's brought me here to be the mother of a race of deformed superhuman horrors, he has to be stopped.
God, forgive me.
SUPERMAN?
KEEP OUT SUPERMAN AT WORK
He has to be stopped.
SUPERMAN!
KEEP OUT SUPERMAN AT WORK
ARE YOU THERE?

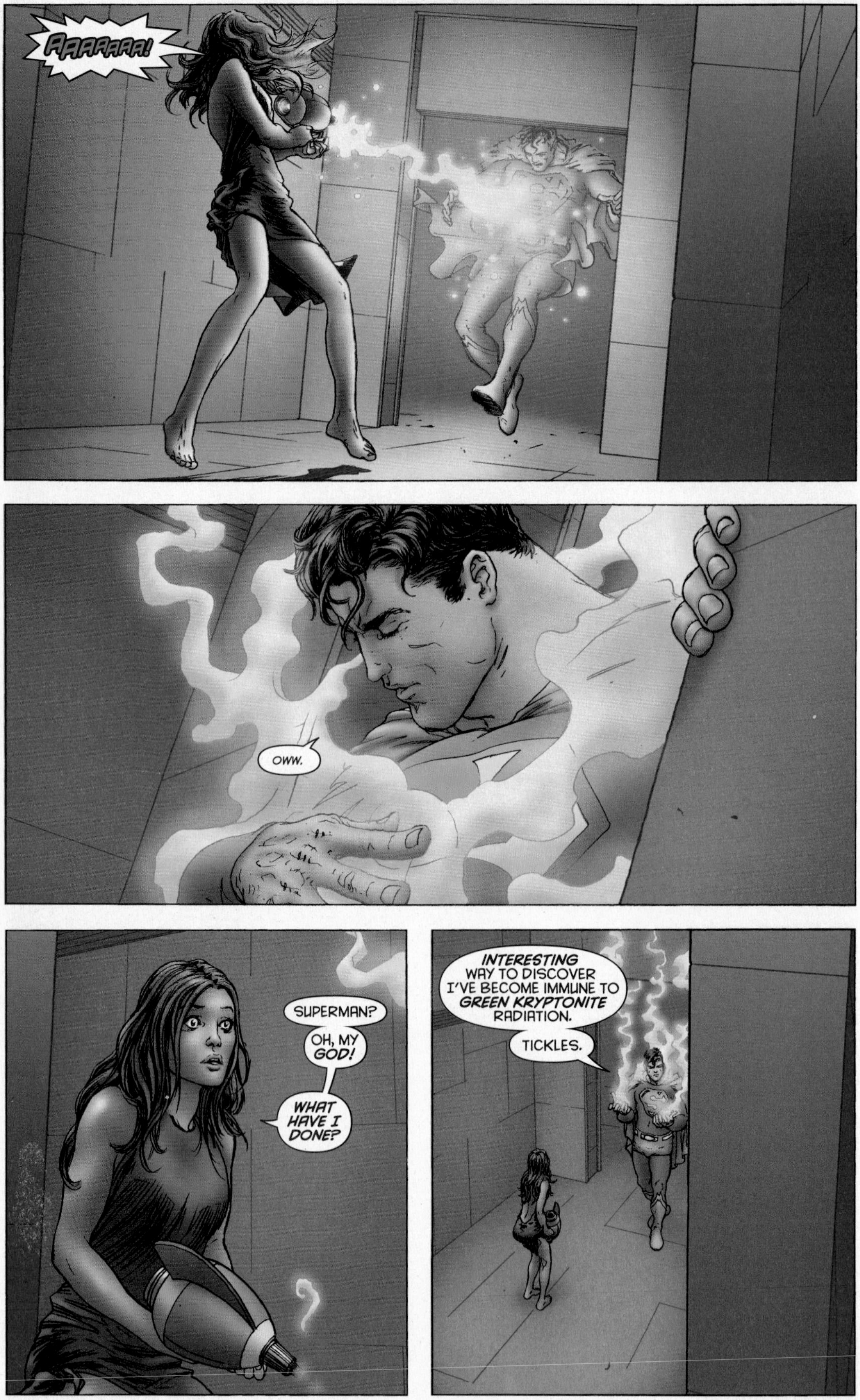
AAAAAAA!
OWW.
SUPERMAN?
OH, MY GOD!
WHAT HAVE I DONE?
INTERESTING WAY TO DISCOVER I'VE BECOME IMMUNE TO GREEN KRYPTONITE RADIATION.
TICKLES.

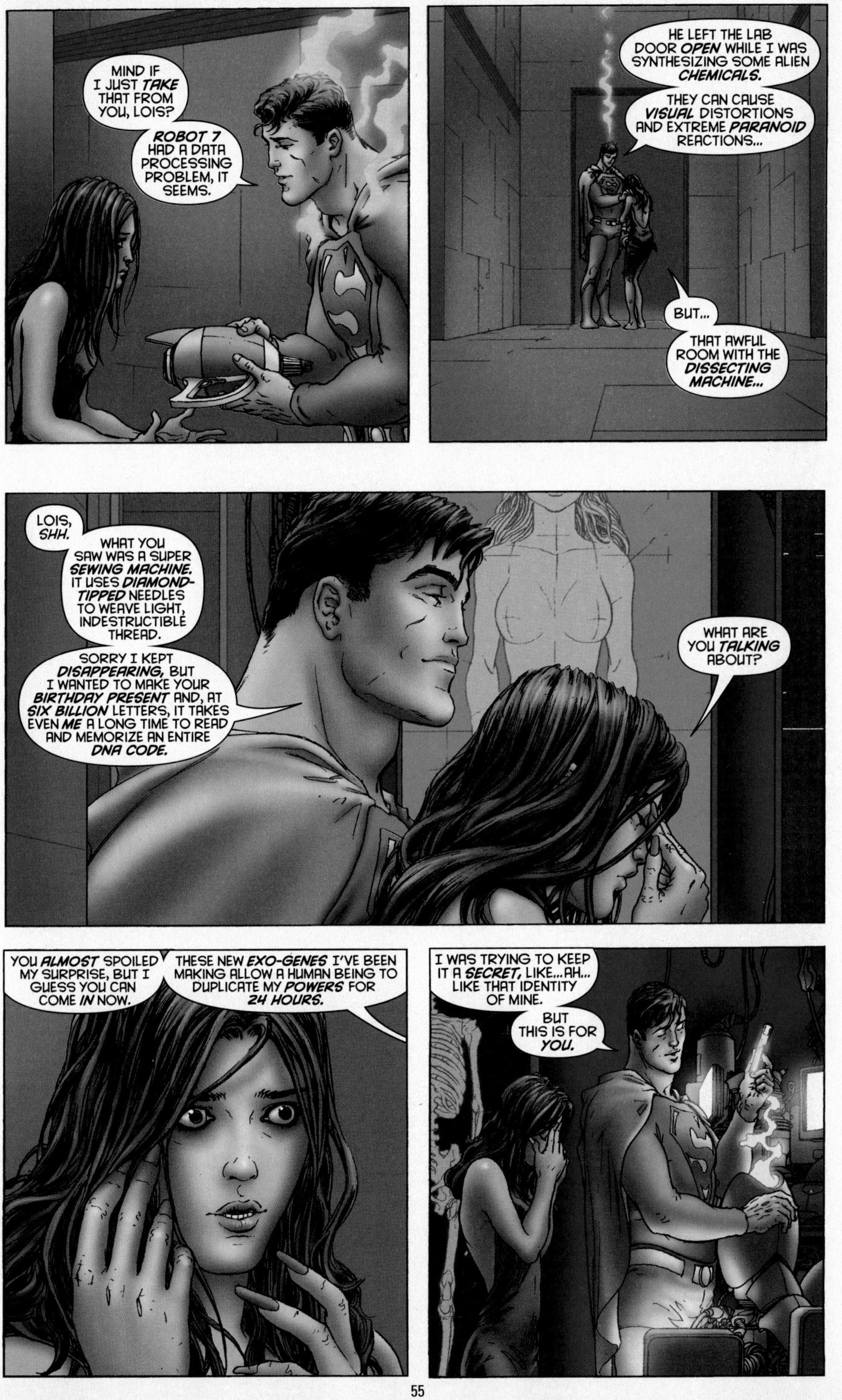
MIND IF I JUST TAKE THAT FROM YOU, LOIS?
ROBOT 7 HAD A DATA PROCESSING PROBLEM, IT SEEMS.
HE LEFT THE LAB DOOR OPEN WHILE I WAS SYNTHESIZING SOME ALIEN CHEMICALS.
THEY CAN CAUSE VISUAL DISTORTIONS AND EXTREME PARANOID REACTIONS...
BUT...
THAT AWFUL ROOM WITH THE DISSECTING MACHINE...
LOIS, SHH.
WHAT YOU SAW WAS A SUPER SEWING MACHINE. IT USES DIAMOND-TIPPED NEEDLES TO WEAVE LIGHT, INDESTRUCTIBLE THREAD.
SORRY I KEPT DISAPPEARING, BUT I WANTED TO MAKE YOUR BIRTHDAY PRESENT AND, AT SIX BILLION LETTERS, IT TAKES EVEN ME A LONG TIME TO READ AND MEMORIZE AN ENTIRE DNA CODE.
WHAT ARE YOU TALKING ABOUT?
YOU ALMOST SPOILED MY SURPRISE, BUT I GUESS YOU CAN COME IN NOW.
THESE NEW EXO-GENES I'VE BEEN MAKING ALLOW A HUMAN BEING TO DUPLICATE MY POWERS FOR 24 HOURS.
I WAS TRYING TO KEEP IT A SECRET, LIKE...AH... LIKE THAT IDENTITY OF MINE.
BUT THIS IS FOR YOU.

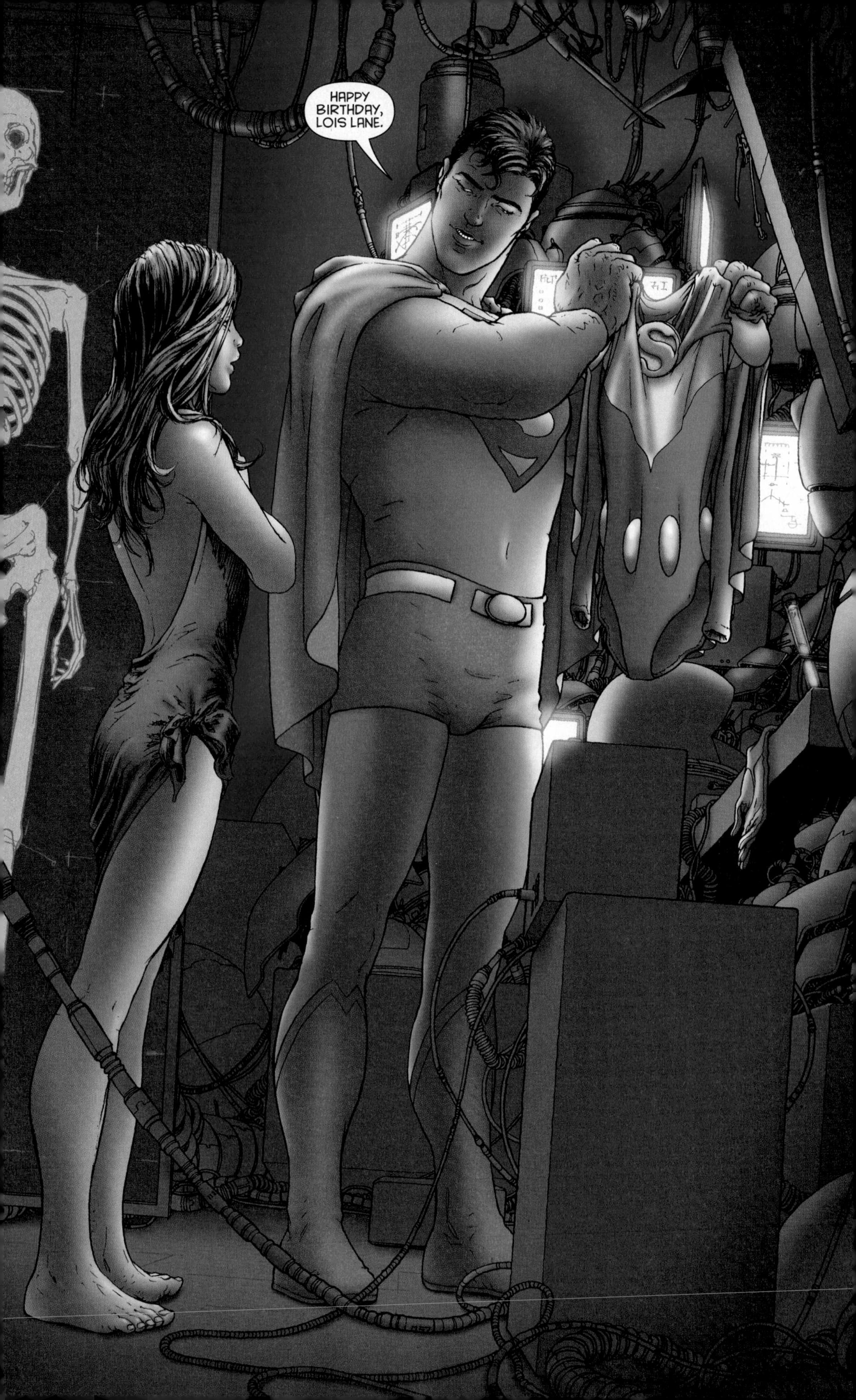
HAPPY BIRTHDAY, LOIS LANE.

Episode 3

SWEET DREAMS, SUPER WOMAN...

Cover FRANK QUITELY with JAMIE GRANT

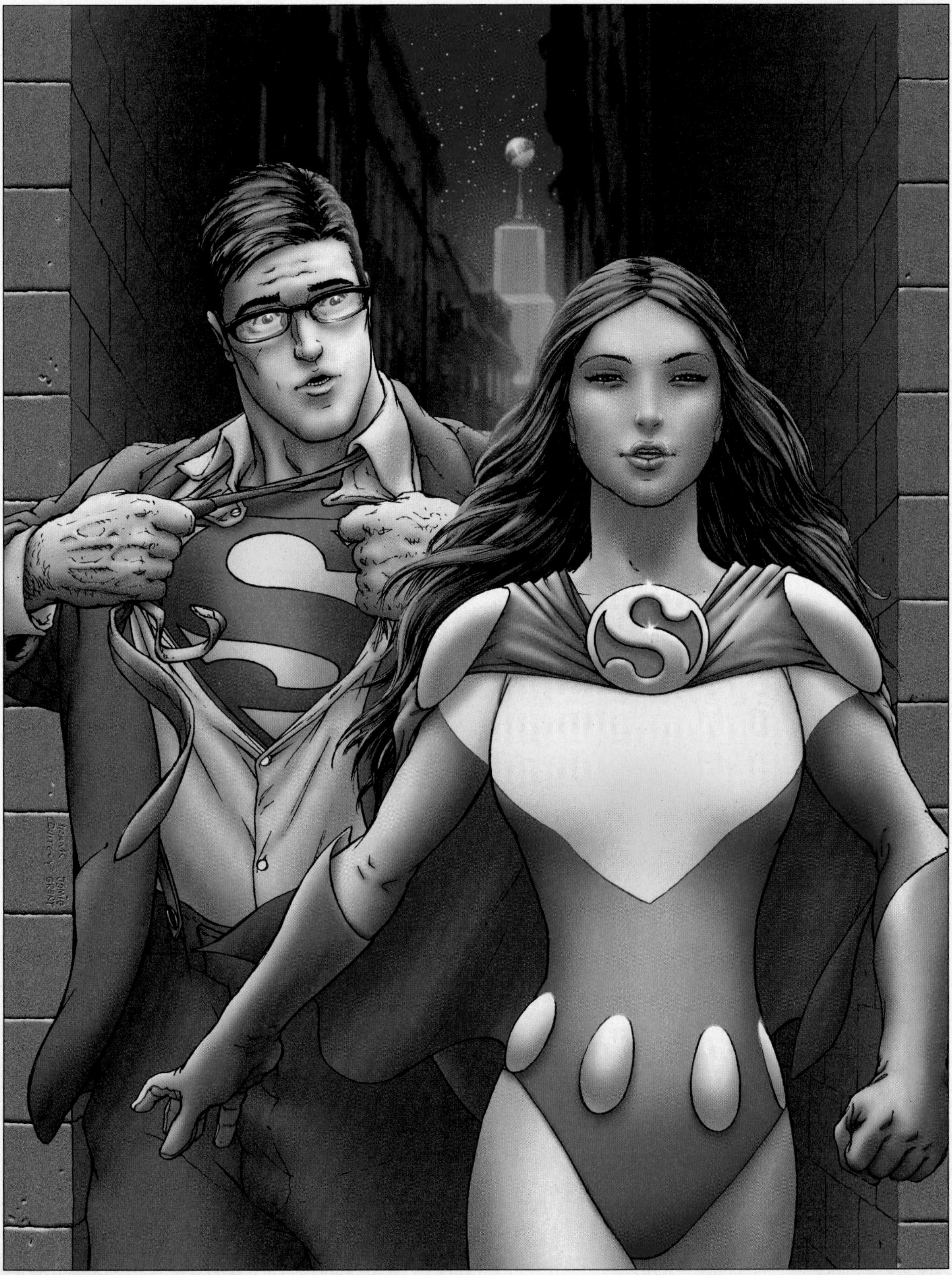

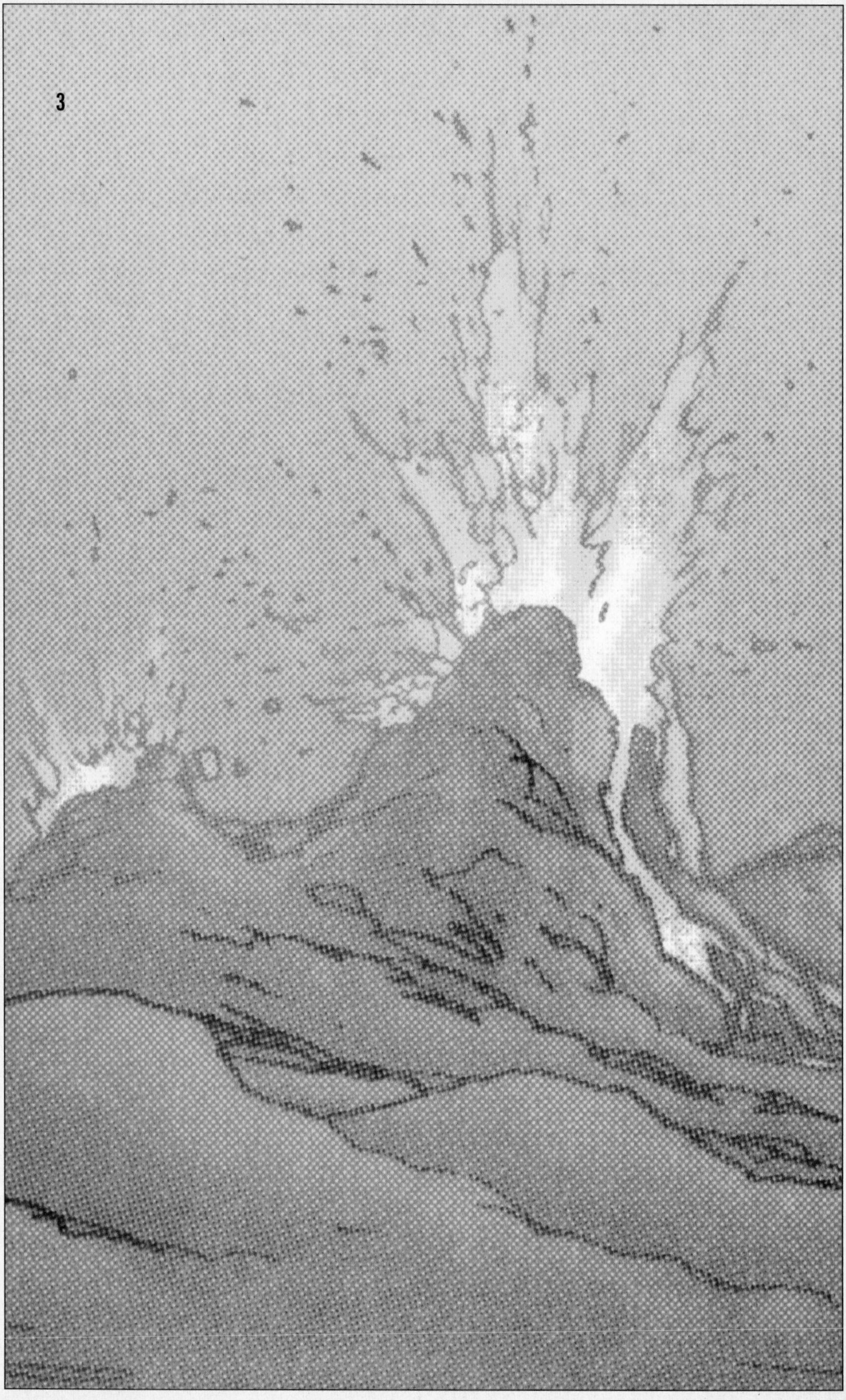
3

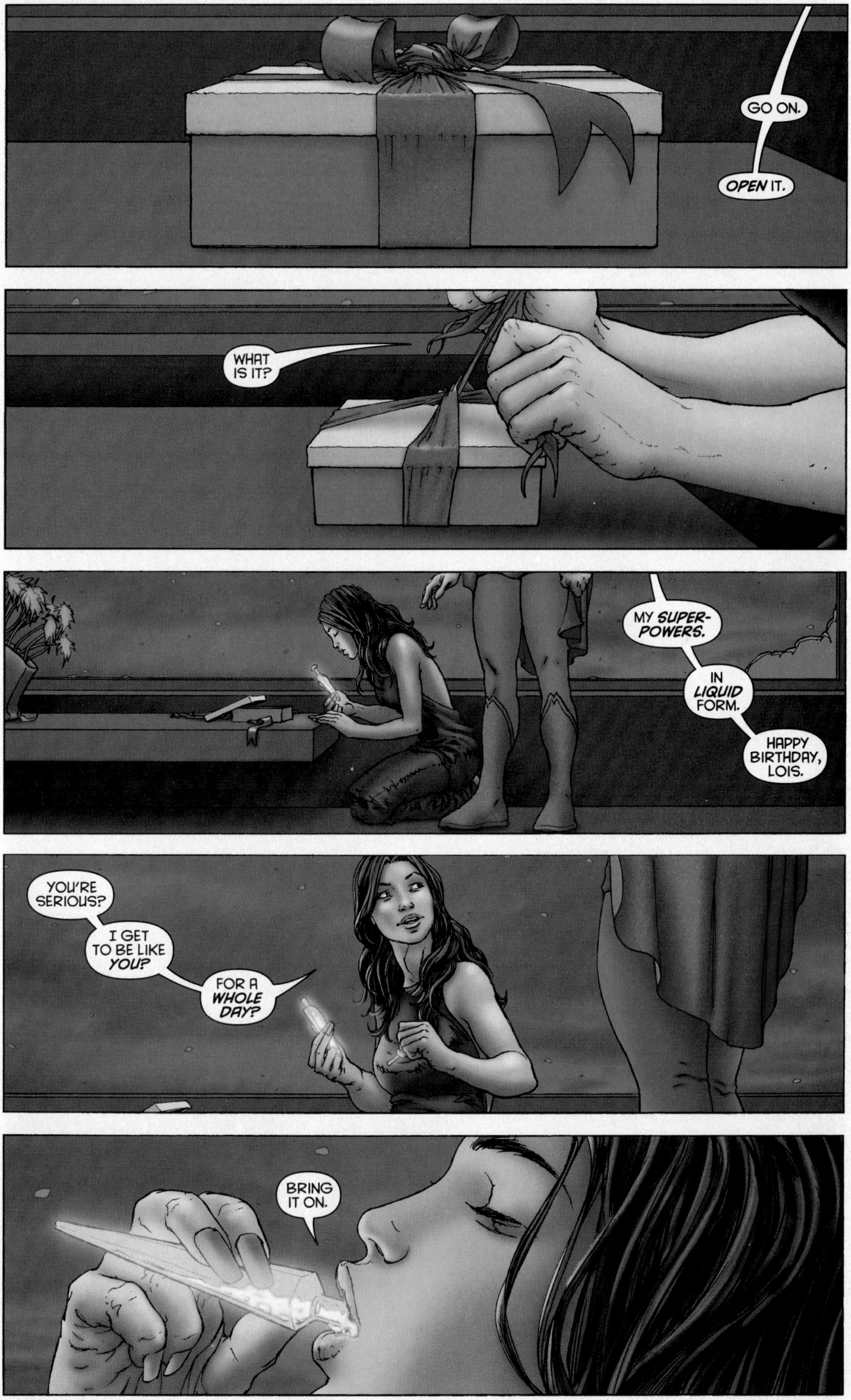
GO ON.
OPEN IT.
WHAT IS IT?
MY *SUPER-POWERS.*
IN *LIQUID* FORM.
HAPPY BIRTHDAY, LOIS.
YOU'RE SERIOUS?
I GET TO BE LIKE *YOU?*
FOR A *WHOLE DAY?*
BRING IT ON.

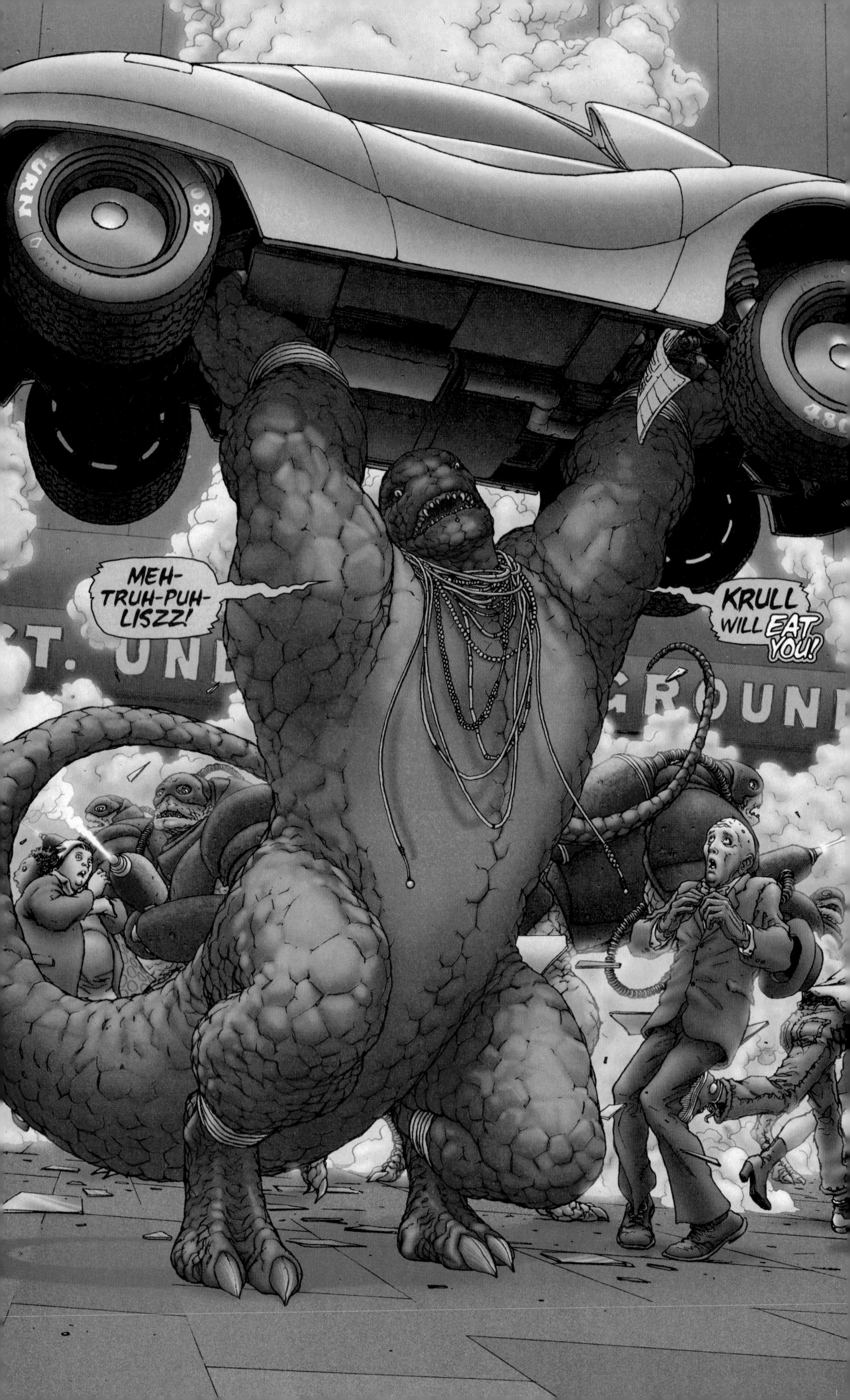
MEH-TRUH-PUH-LISZZ!
KRULL WILL EAT YOU!

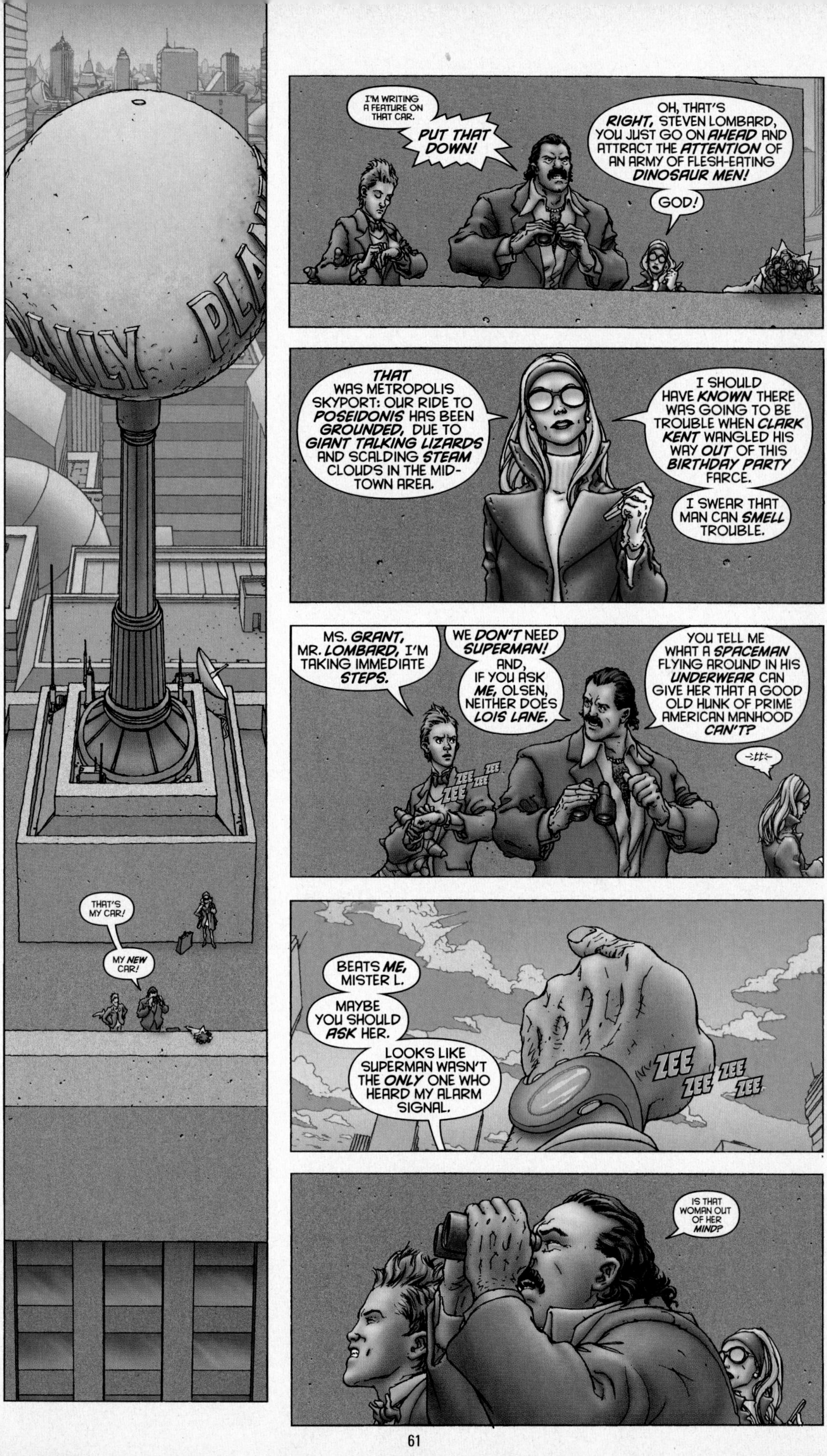

THAT'S MY CAR!
MY NEW CAR!
I'M WRITING A FEATURE ON THAT CAR.
PUT THAT DOWN!
OH, THAT'S RIGHT, STEVEN LOMBARD, YOU JUST GO ON AHEAD AND ATTRACT THE ATTENTION OF AN ARMY OF FLESH-EATING DINOSAUR MEN!
GOD!
THAT WAS METROPOLIS SKYPORT: OUR RIDE TO POSEIDONIS HAS BEEN GROUNDED, DUE TO GIANT TALKING LIZARDS AND SCALDING STEAM CLOUDS IN THE MID-TOWN AREA.
I SHOULD HAVE KNOWN THERE WAS GOING TO BE TROUBLE WHEN CLARK KENT WANGLED HIS WAY OUT OF THIS BIRTHDAY PARTY FARCE.
I SWEAR THAT MAN CAN SMELL TROUBLE.
MS. GRANT, MR. LOMBARD, I'M TAKING IMMEDIATE STEPS.
WE DON'T NEED SUPERMAN!
AND, IF YOU ASK ME, OLSEN, NEITHER DOES LOIS LANE.
YOU TELL ME WHAT A SPACEMAN FLYING AROUND IN HIS UNDERWEAR CAN GIVE HER THAT A GOOD OLD HUNK OF PRIME AMERICAN MANHOOD CAN'T?
ZEE ZEE ZEE ZEE
BEATS ME, MISTER L.
MAYBE YOU SHOULD ASK HER.
LOOKS LIKE SUPERMAN WASN'T THE ONLY ONE WHO HEARD MY ALARM SIGNAL.
ZEE ZEE ZEE ZEE
IS THAT WOMAN OUT OF HER MIND?

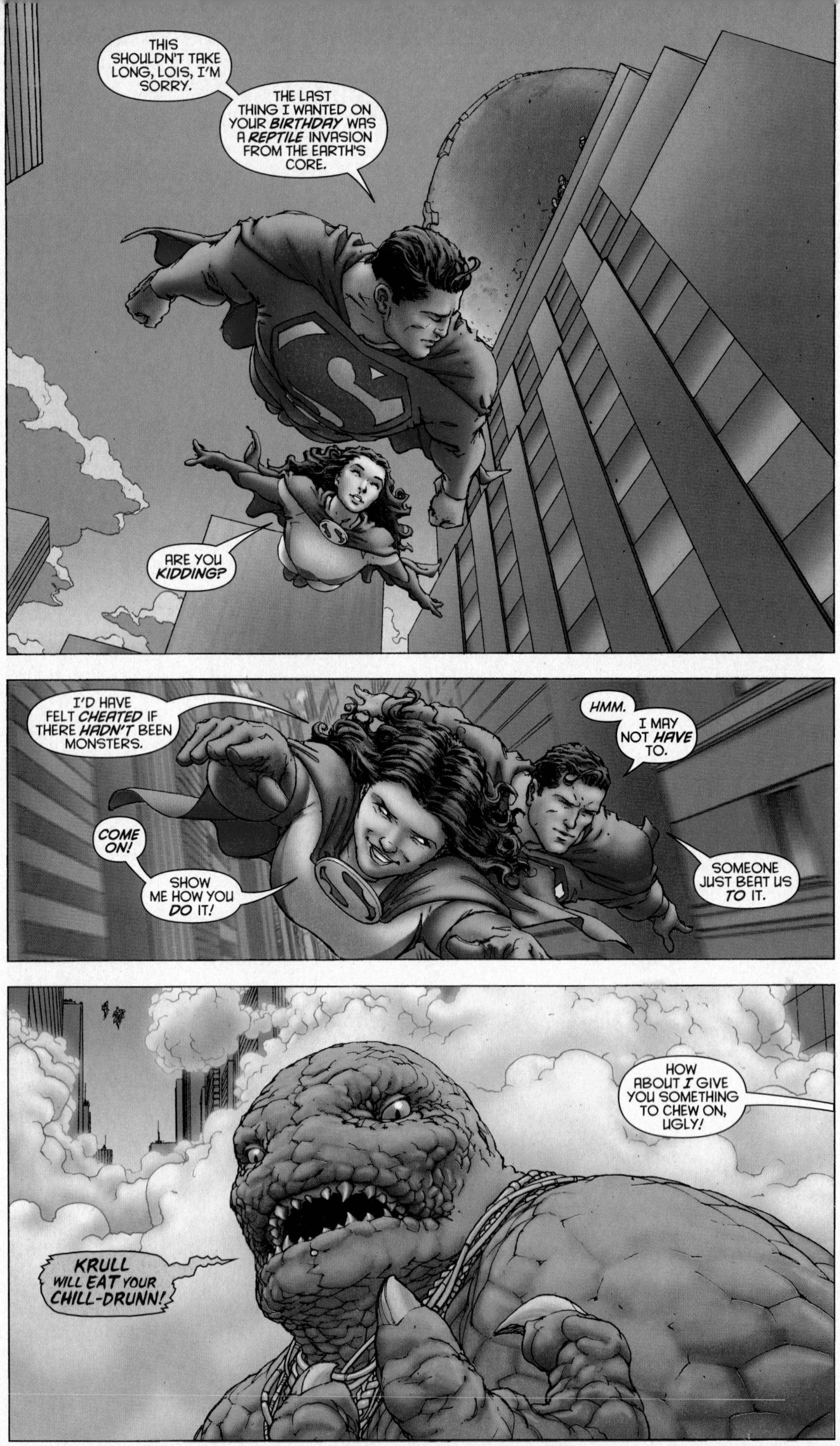
THIS SHOULDN'T TAKE LONG, LOIS, I'M SORRY.
THE LAST THING I WANTED ON YOUR BIRTHDAY WAS A REPTILE INVASION FROM THE EARTH'S CORE.
ARE YOU KIDDING?
I'D HAVE FELT CHEATED IF THERE HADN'T BEEN MONSTERS.
COME ON!
SHOW ME HOW YOU DO IT!
HMM.
I MAY NOT HAVE TO.
SOMEONE JUST BEAT US TO IT.
HOW ABOUT I GIVE YOU SOMETHING TO CHEW ON, UGLY!
KRULL WILL EAT YOUR CHILL-DRUNN!

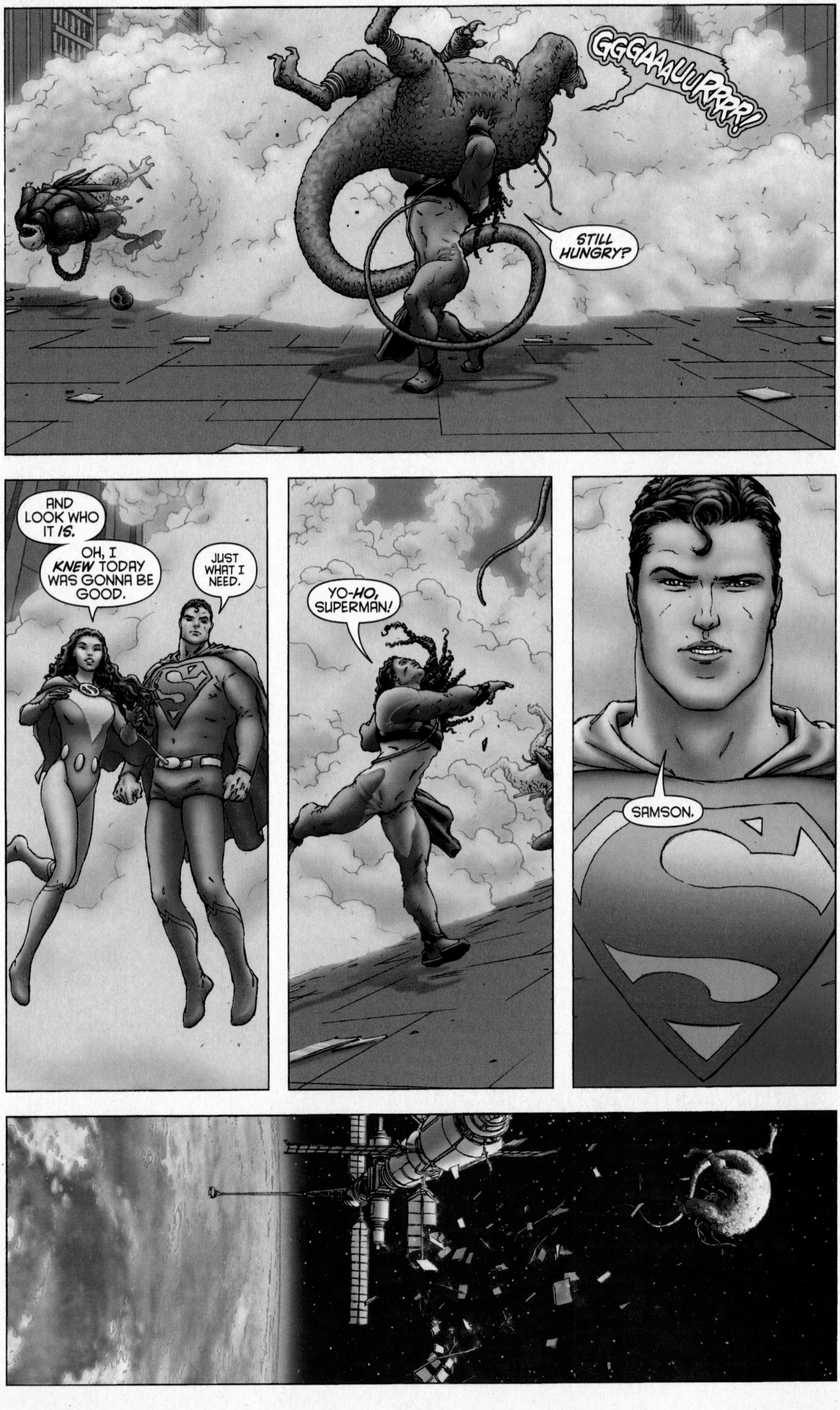
GGGAAAUURRRR!
STILL HUNGRY?
AND LOOK WHO IT IS.
OH, I KNEW TODAY WAS GONNA BE GOOD.
JUST WHAT I NEED.
YO-HO, SUPERMAN!
SAMSON.

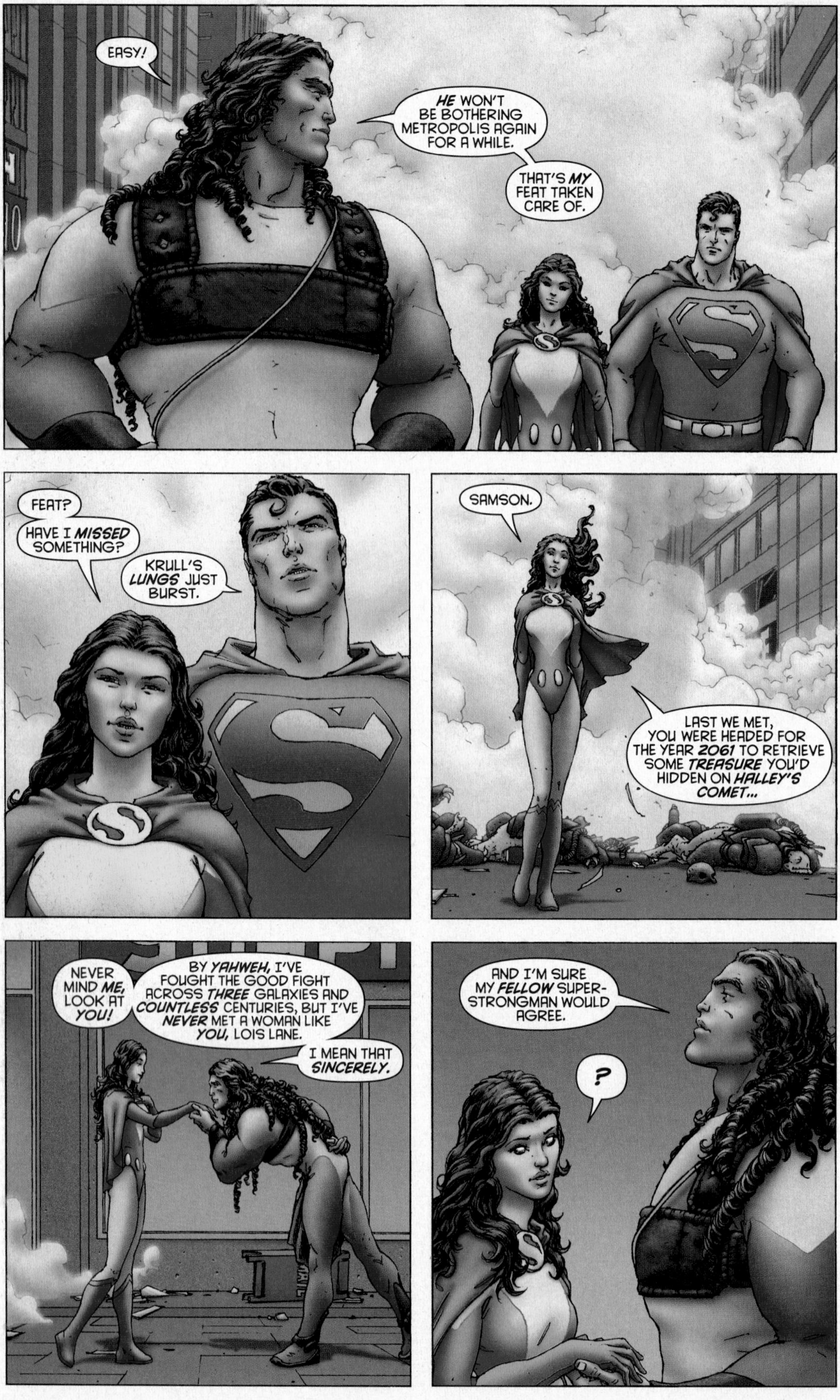
EASY!
HE WON'T BE BOTHERING METROPOLIS AGAIN FOR A WHILE.
THAT'S MY FEAT TAKEN CARE OF.
FEAT?
HAVE I MISSED SOMETHING?
KRULL'S LUNGS JUST BURST.
SAMSON.
LAST WE MET, YOU WERE HEADED FOR THE YEAR 2061 TO RETRIEVE SOME TREASURE YOU'D HIDDEN ON HALLEY'S COMET...
NEVER MIND ME, LOOK AT YOU!
BY YAHWEH, I'VE FOUGHT THE GOOD FIGHT ACROSS THREE GALAXIES AND COUNTLESS CENTURIES, BUT I'VE NEVER MET A WOMAN LIKE YOU, LOIS LANE.
I MEAN THAT SINCERELY.
AND I'M SURE MY FELLOW SUPER-STRONGMAN WOULD AGREE.
?

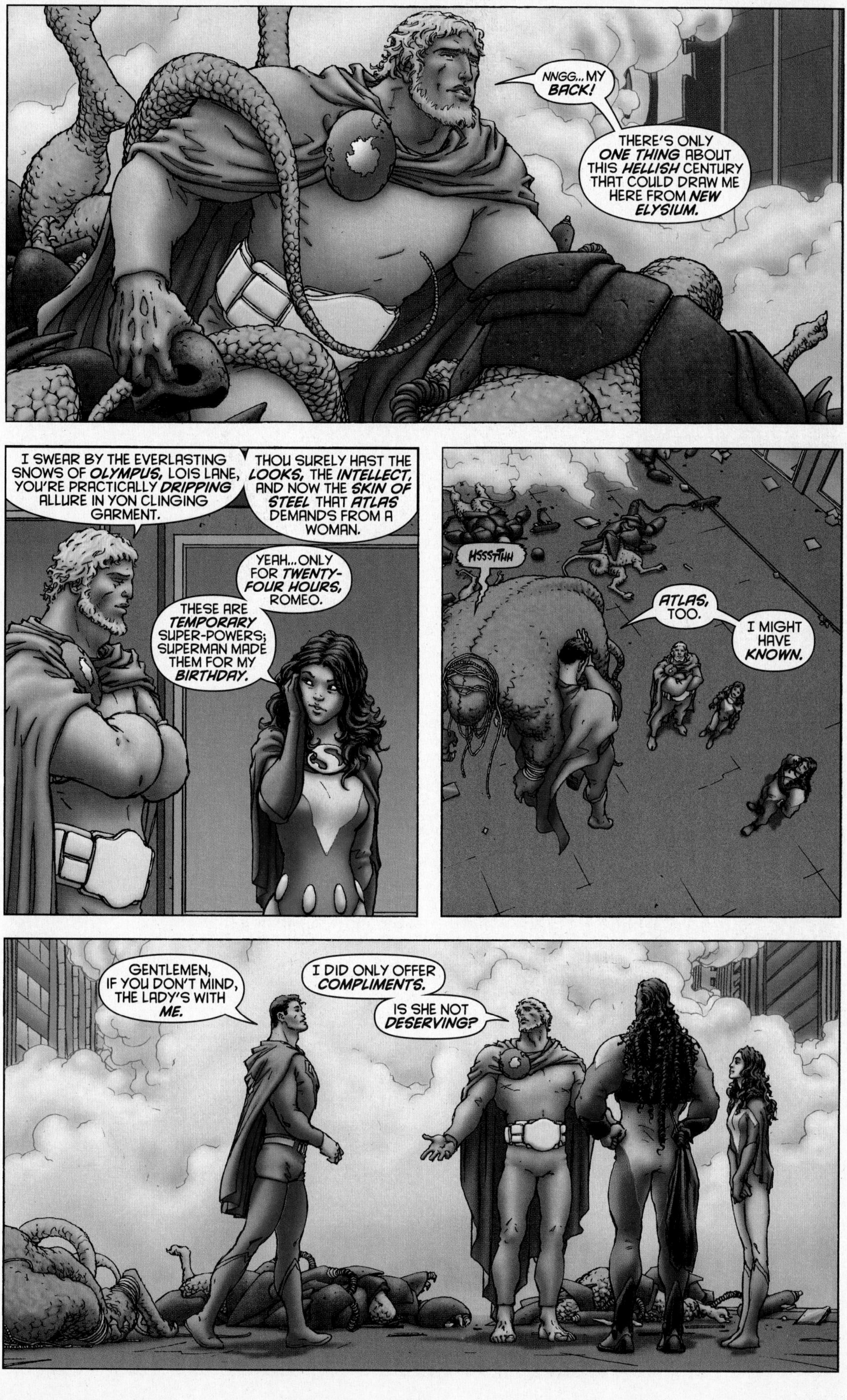
NNGG... MY BACK!
THERE'S ONLY ONE THING ABOUT THIS HELLISH CENTURY THAT COULD DRAW ME HERE FROM NEW ELYSIUM.
I SWEAR BY THE EVERLASTING SNOWS OF OLYMPUS, LOIS LANE, YOU'RE PRACTICALLY DRIPPING ALLURE IN YON CLINGING GARMENT.
THOU SURELY HAST THE LOOKS, THE INTELLECT, AND NOW THE SKIN OF STEEL THAT ATLAS DEMANDS FROM A WOMAN.
YEAH... ONLY FOR TWENTY-FOUR HOURS, ROMEO.
THESE ARE TEMPORARY SUPER-POWERS; SUPERMAN MADE THEM FOR MY BIRTHDAY.
HSSSTHH
ATLAS, TOO.
I MIGHT HAVE KNOWN.
GENTLEMEN, IF YOU DON'T MIND, THE LADY'S WITH ME.
I DID ONLY OFFER COMPLIMENTS.
IS SHE NOT DESERVING?

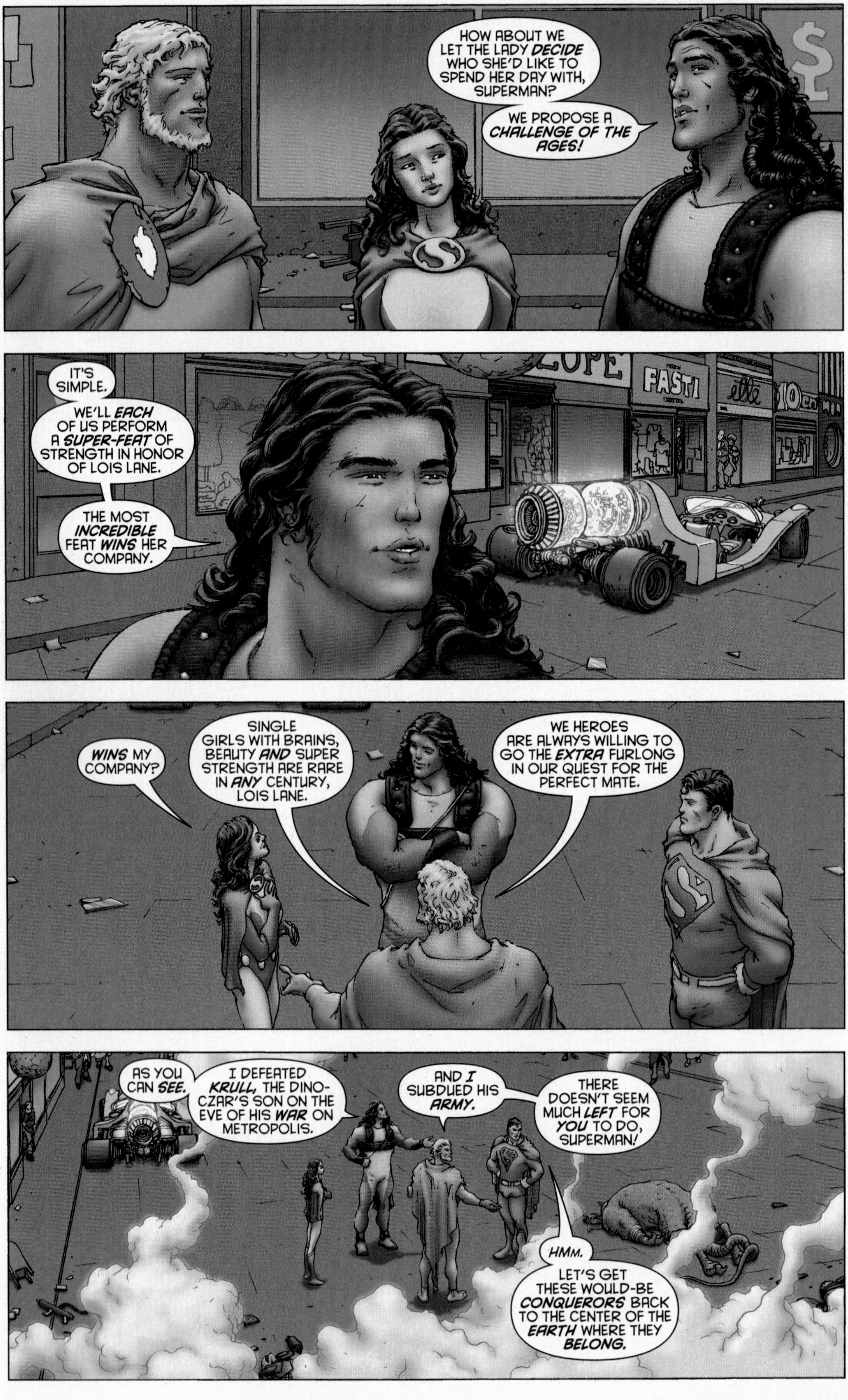
HOW ABOUT WE LET THE LADY DECIDE WHO SHE'D LIKE TO SPEND HER DAY WITH, SUPERMAN?
WE PROPOSE A CHALLENGE OF THE AGES!
IT'S SIMPLE.
WE'LL EACH OF US PERFORM A SUPER-FEAT OF STRENGTH IN HONOR OF LOIS LANE.
THE MOST INCREDIBLE FEAT WINS HER COMPANY.
WINS MY COMPANY?
SINGLE GIRLS WITH BRAINS, BEAUTY AND SUPER STRENGTH ARE RARE IN ANY CENTURY, LOIS LANE.
WE HEROES ARE ALWAYS WILLING TO GO THE EXTRA FURLONG IN OUR QUEST FOR THE PERFECT MATE.
AS YOU CAN SEE.
I DEFEATED KRULL, THE DINO-CZAR'S SON ON THE EVE OF HIS WAR ON METROPOLIS.
AND I SUBDUED HIS ARMY.
THERE DOESN'T SEEM MUCH LEFT FOR YOU TO DO, SUPERMAN!
HMM.
LET'S GET THESE WOULD-BE CONQUERORS BACK TO THE CENTER OF THE EARTH WHERE THEY BELONG.

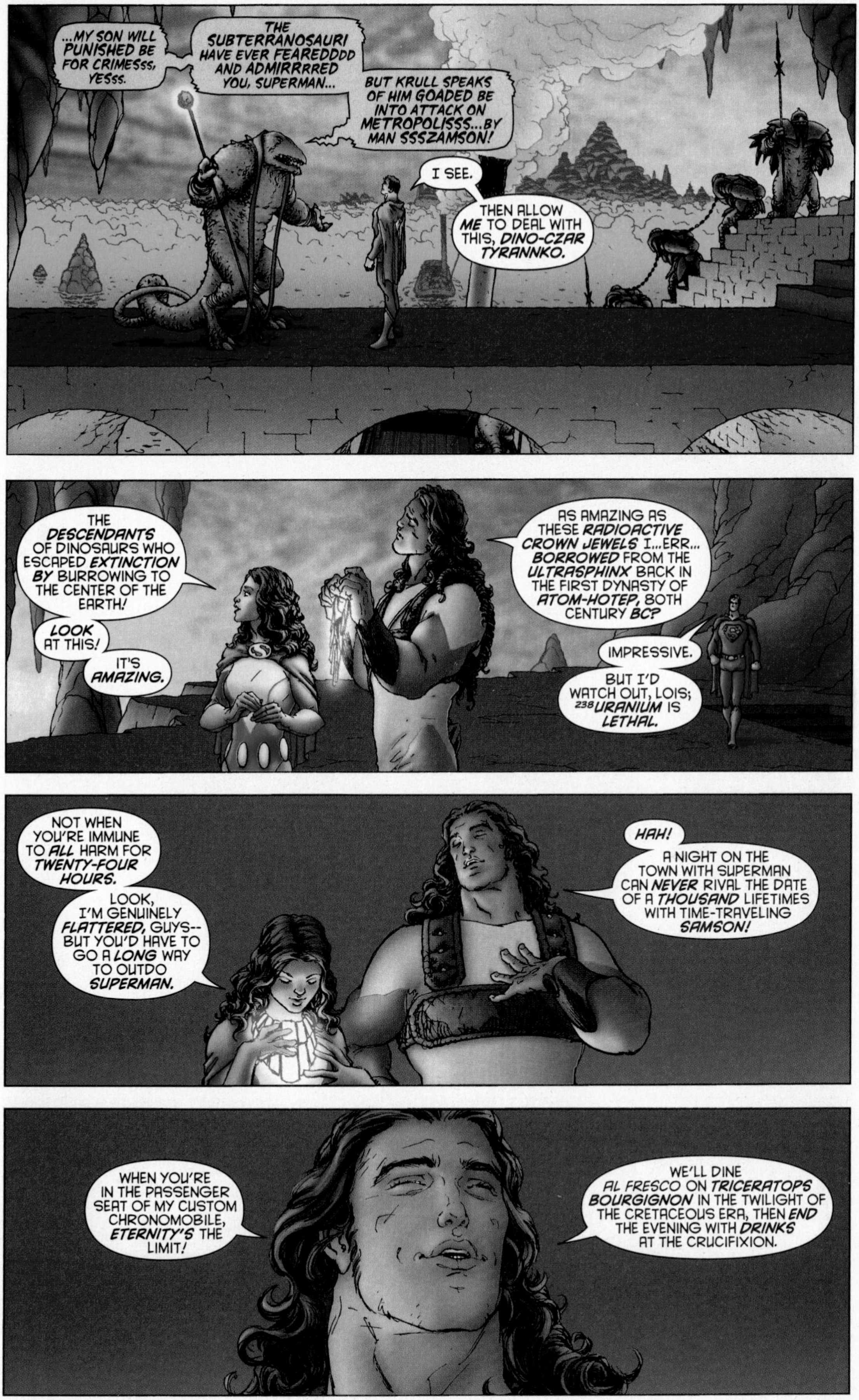
...MY SON WILL PUNISHED BE FOR CRIMESss, YESss.
THE SUBTERRANOSAURI HAVE EVER FEAREDDDD AND ADMIRRRRED YOU, SUPERMAN...
BUT KRULL SPEAKS OF HIM GOADED BE INTO ATTACK ON METROPOLISSS...BY MAN SSSZAMSON!
I SEE.
THEN ALLOW ME TO DEAL WITH THIS, DINO-CZAR TYRANNKO.
THE DESCENDANTS OF DINOSAURS WHO ESCAPED EXTINCTION BY BURROWING TO THE CENTER OF THE EARTH!
LOOK AT THIS!
IT'S AMAZING.
AS AMAZING AS THESE RADIOACTIVE CROWN JEWELS I...ERR... BORROWED FROM THE ULTRASPHINX BACK IN THE FIRST DYNASTY OF ATOM-HOTEP, 80TH CENTURY BC?
IMPRESSIVE.
BUT I'D WATCH OUT, LOIS; ^{238}URANIUM IS LETHAL.
NOT WHEN YOU'RE IMMUNE TO ALL HARM FOR TWENTY-FOUR HOURS.
LOOK, I'M GENUINELY FLATTERED, GUYS-- BUT YOU'D HAVE TO GO A LONG WAY TO OUTDO SUPERMAN.
HAH!
A NIGHT ON THE TOWN WITH SUPERMAN CAN NEVER RIVAL THE DATE OF A THOUSAND LIFETIMES WITH TIME-TRAVELING SAMSON!
WHEN YOU'RE IN THE PASSENGER SEAT OF MY CUSTOM CHRONOMOBILE, ETERNITY'S THE LIMIT!
WE'LL DINE AL FRESCO ON TRICERATOPS BOURGIGNON IN THE TWILIGHT OF THE CRETACEOUS ERA, THEN END THE EVENING WITH DRINKS AT THE CRUCIFIXION.

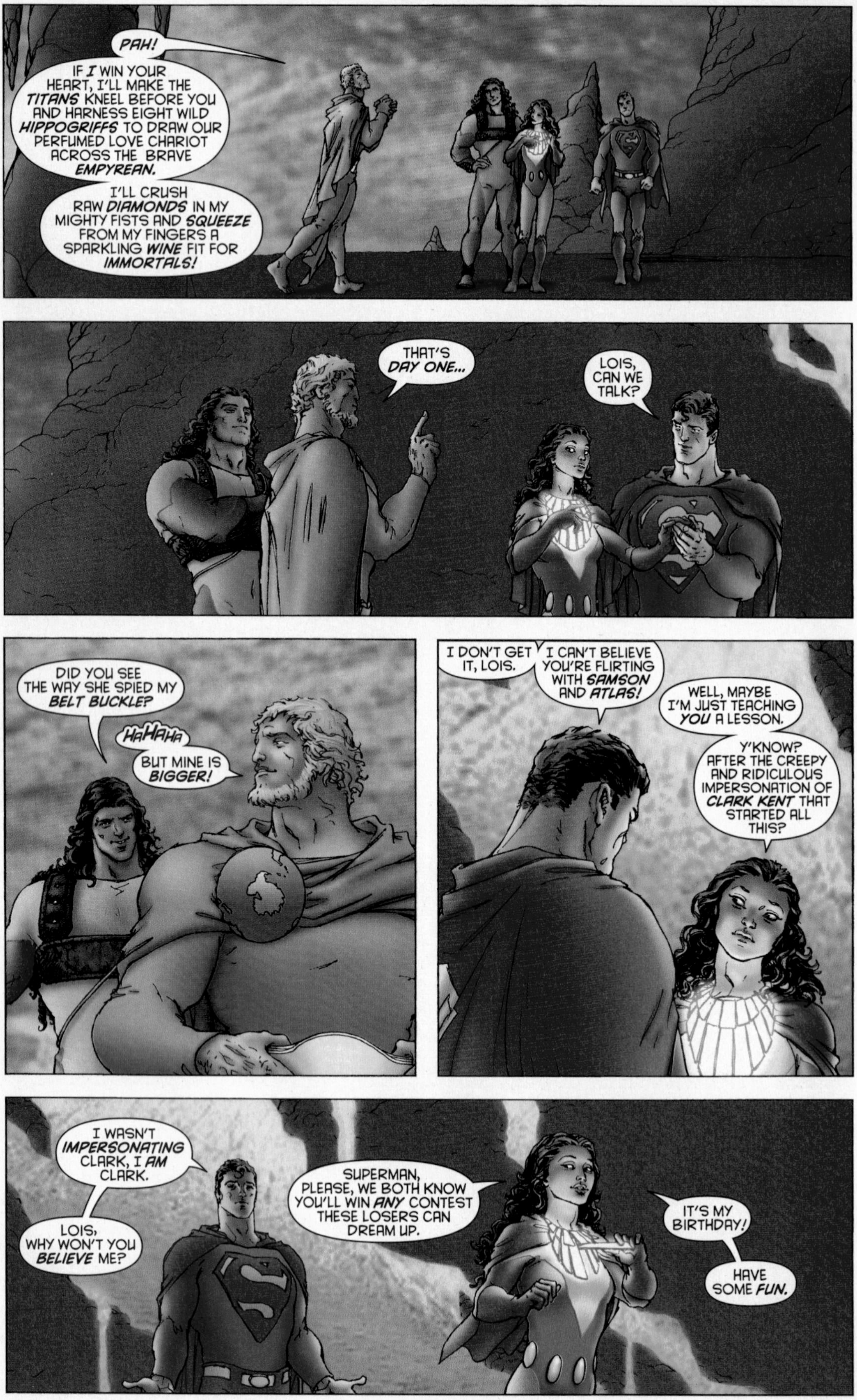
PAH!
IF I WIN YOUR HEART, I'LL MAKE THE TITANS KNEEL BEFORE YOU AND HARNESS EIGHT WILD HIPPOGRIFFS TO DRAW OUR PERFUMED LOVE CHARIOT ACROSS THE BRAVE EMPYREAN.
I'LL CRUSH RAW DIAMONDS IN MY MIGHTY FISTS AND SQUEEZE FROM MY FINGERS A SPARKLING WINE FIT FOR IMMORTALS!
THAT'S DAY ONE...
LOIS, CAN WE TALK?
DID YOU SEE THE WAY SHE SPIED MY BELT BUCKLE?
HAHAHA
BUT MINE IS BIGGER!
I DON'T GET IT, LOIS.
I CAN'T BELIEVE YOU'RE FLIRTING WITH SAMSON AND ATLAS!
WELL, MAYBE I'M JUST TEACHING YOU A LESSON.
Y'KNOW? AFTER THE CREEPY AND RIDICULOUS IMPERSONATION OF CLARK KENT THAT STARTED ALL THIS?
I WASN'T IMPERSONATING CLARK, I AM CLARK.
LOIS, WHY WON'T YOU BELIEVE ME?
SUPERMAN, PLEASE, WE BOTH KNOW YOU'LL WIN ANY CONTEST THESE LOSERS CAN DREAM UP.
IT'S MY BIRTHDAY!
HAVE SOME FUN.

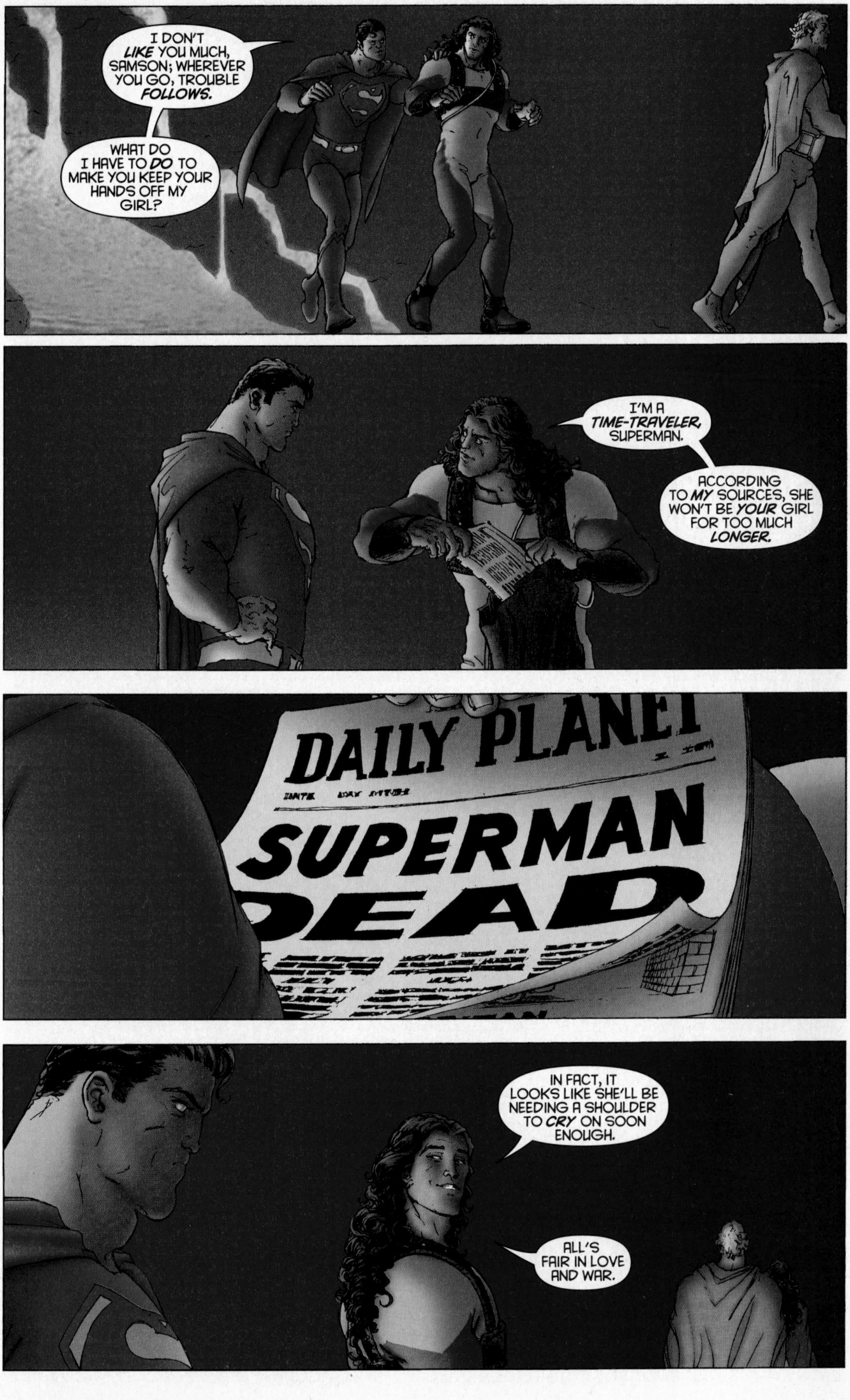
I DON'T *LIKE* YOU MUCH, SAMSON; WHEREVER YOU GO, TROUBLE *FOLLOWS.*
WHAT DO I HAVE TO *DO* TO MAKE YOU KEEP YOUR HANDS OFF MY GIRL?
I'M A *TIME-TRAVELER,* SUPERMAN.
ACCORDING TO *MY* SOURCES, SHE WON'T BE *YOUR* GIRL FOR TOO MUCH *LONGER.*
DAILY PLANET
SUPERMAN DEAD
IN FACT, IT LOOKS LIKE SHE'LL BE NEEDING A SHOULDER TO *CRY* ON SOON ENOUGH.
ALL'S FAIR IN LOVE AND WAR.

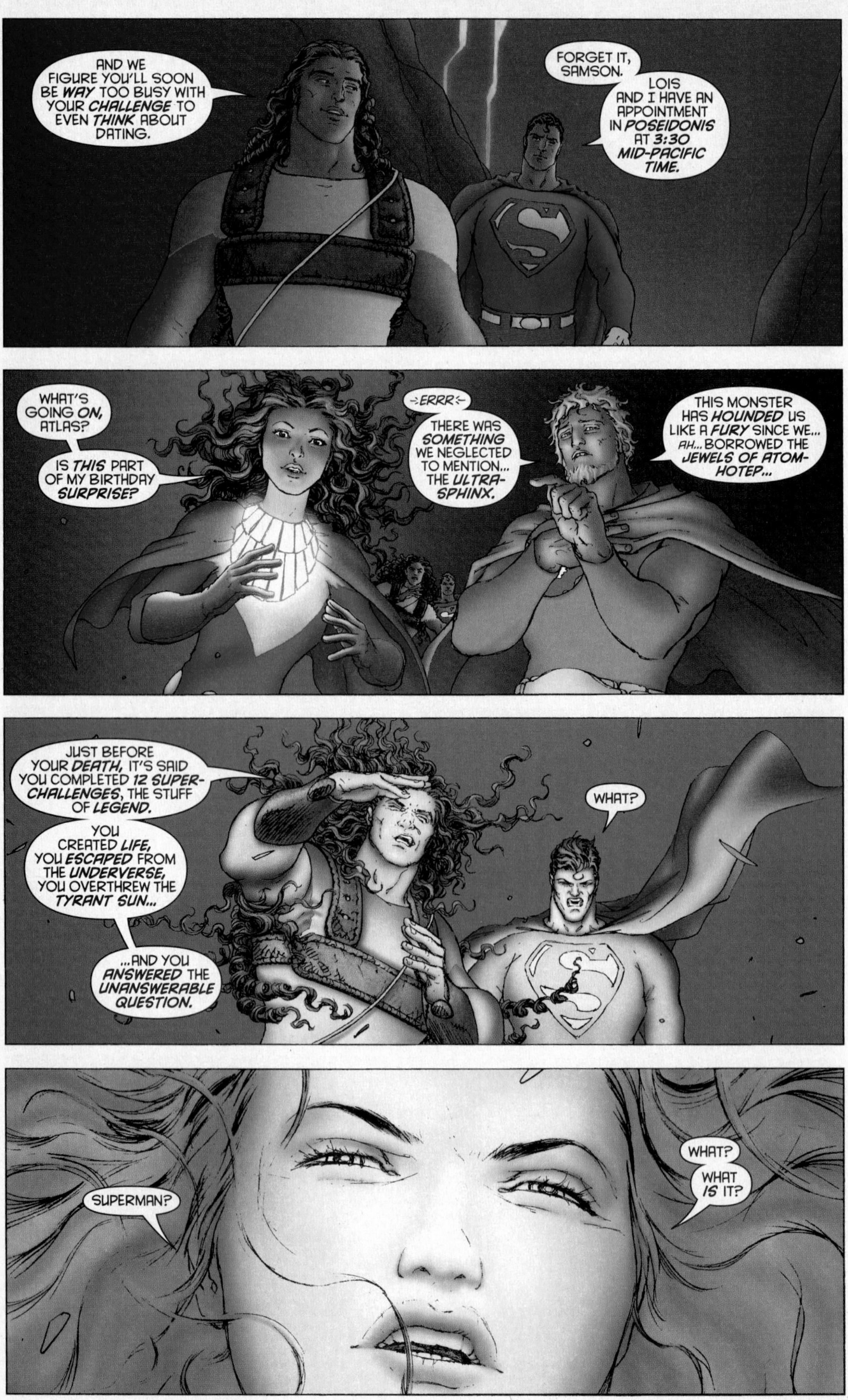
AND WE FIGURE YOU'LL SOON BE WAY TOO BUSY WITH YOUR CHALLENGE TO EVEN THINK ABOUT DATING.
FORGET IT, SAMSON.
LOIS AND I HAVE AN APPOINTMENT IN POSEIDONIS AT 3:30 MID-PACIFIC TIME.
WHAT'S GOING ON, ATLAS?
IS THIS PART OF MY BIRTHDAY SURPRISE?
ERRR
THERE WAS SOMETHING WE NEGLECTED TO MENTION... THE ULTRA-SPHINX.
THIS MONSTER HAS HOUNDED US LIKE A FURY SINCE WE... AH... BORROWED THE JEWELS OF ATOM-HOTEP...
JUST BEFORE YOUR DEATH, IT'S SAID YOU COMPLETED 12 SUPER-CHALLENGES, THE STUFF OF LEGEND.
YOU CREATED LIFE, YOU ESCAPED FROM THE UNDERVERSE, YOU OVERTHREW THE TYRANT SUN...
...AND YOU ANSWERED THE UNANSWERABLE QUESTION.
WHAT?
SUPERMAN?
WHAT? WHAT IS IT?

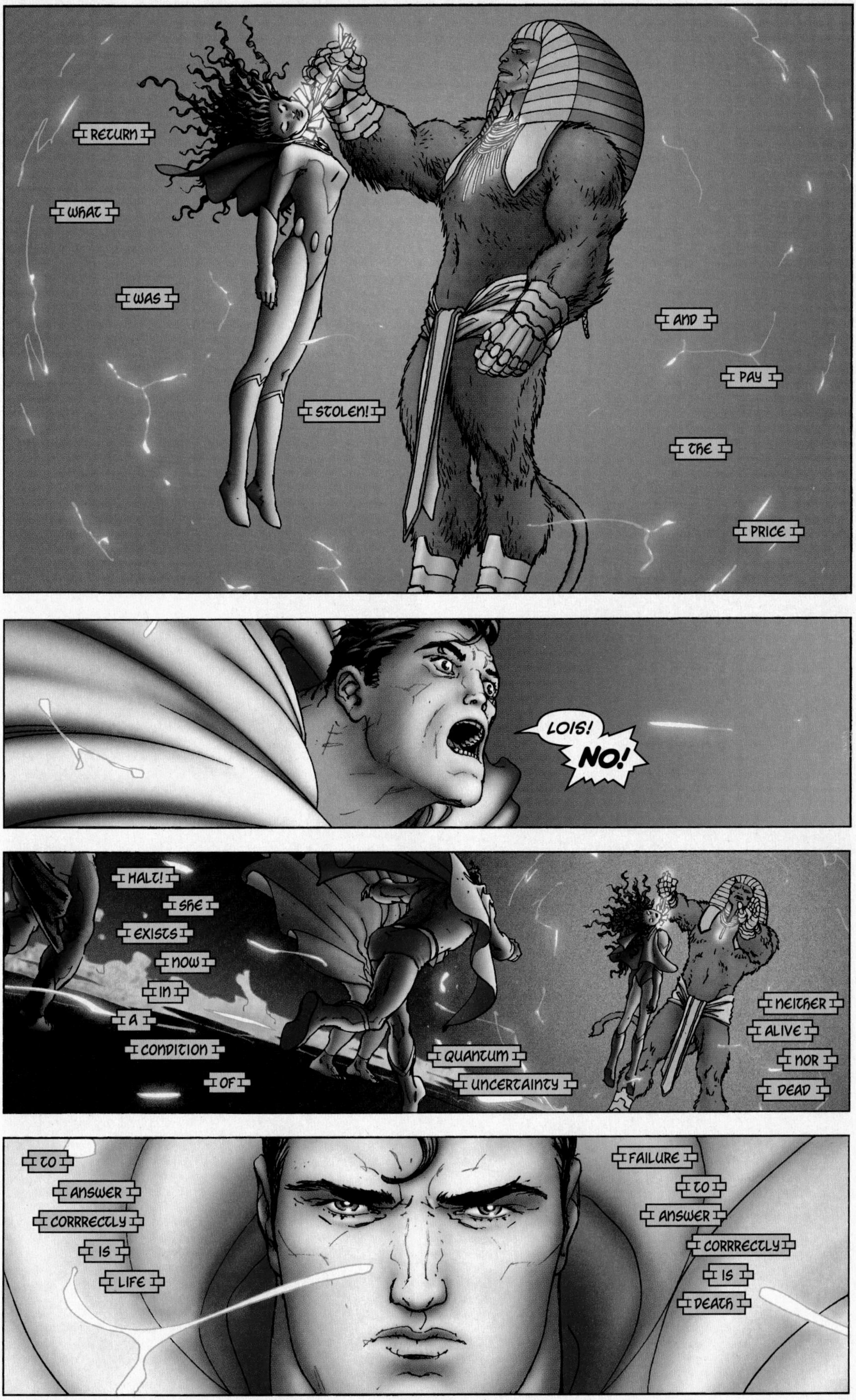
RETURN
WHAT
WAS
STOLEN!
AND
PAY
THE
PRICE
LOIS!
NO!
HALT!
SHE
EXISTS
NOW
IN
A
CONDITION
OF
QUANTUM
UNCERTAINTY
NEITHER
ALIVE
NOR
DEAD
TO
ANSWER
CORRRECTLY
IS
LIFE
FAILURE
TO
ANSWER
CORRRECTLY
IS
DEATH

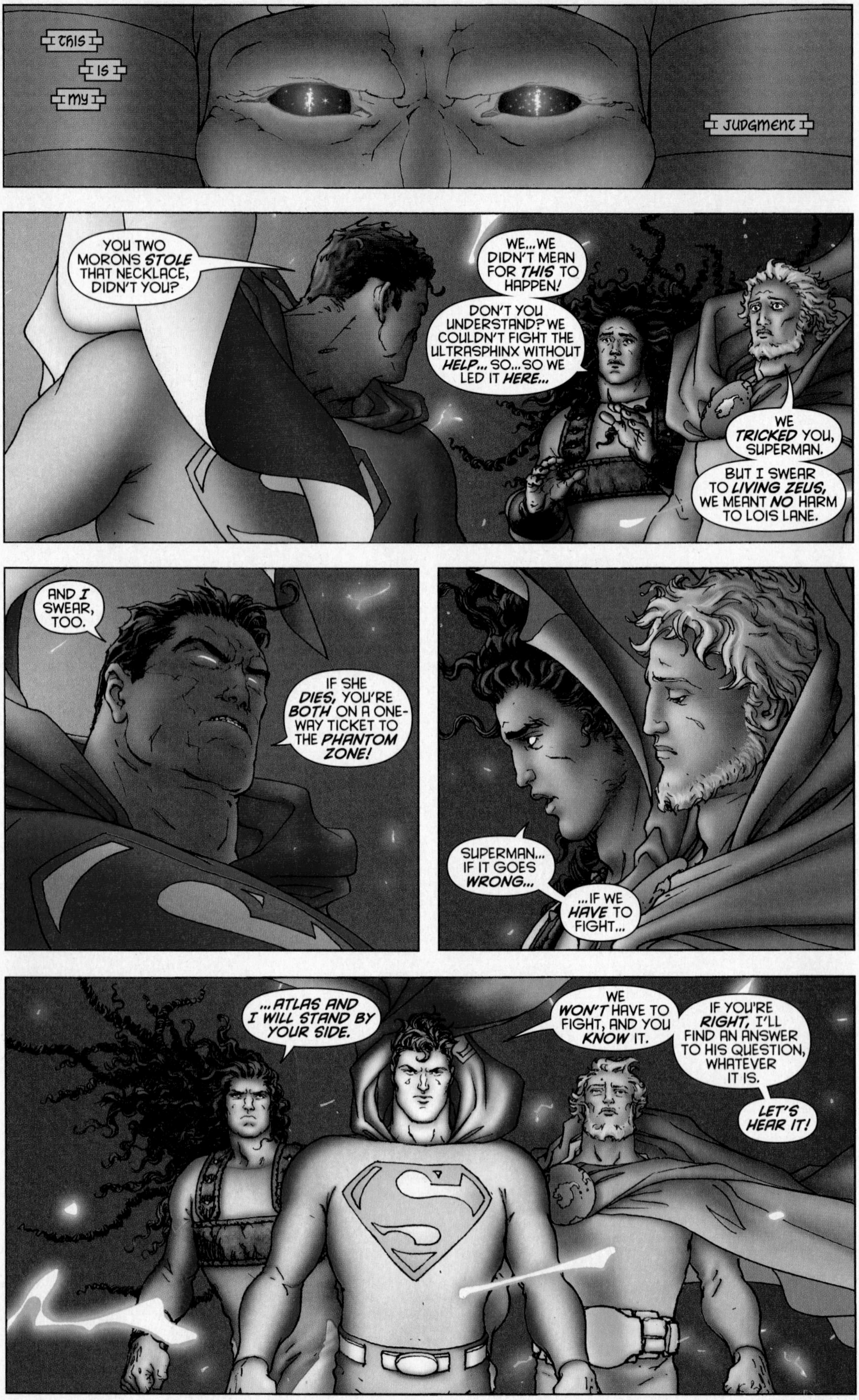
THIS
IS
MY
JUDGMENT
YOU TWO MORONS STOLE THAT NECKLACE, DIDN'T YOU?
WE... WE DIDN'T MEAN FOR THIS TO HAPPEN!
DON'T YOU UNDERSTAND? WE COULDN'T FIGHT THE ULTRASPHINX WITHOUT HELP... SO... SO WE LED IT HERE...
WE TRICKED YOU, SUPERMAN.
BUT I SWEAR TO LIVING ZEUS, WE MEANT NO HARM TO LOIS LANE.
AND I SWEAR, TOO.
IF SHE DIES, YOU'RE BOTH ON A ONE-WAY TICKET TO THE PHANTOM ZONE!
SUPERMAN... IF IT GOES WRONG...
...IF WE HAVE TO FIGHT...
...ATLAS AND I WILL STAND BY YOUR SIDE.
WE WON'T HAVE TO FIGHT, AND YOU KNOW IT.
IF YOU'RE RIGHT, I'LL FIND AN ANSWER TO HIS QUESTION, WHATEVER IT IS.
LET'S HEAR IT!

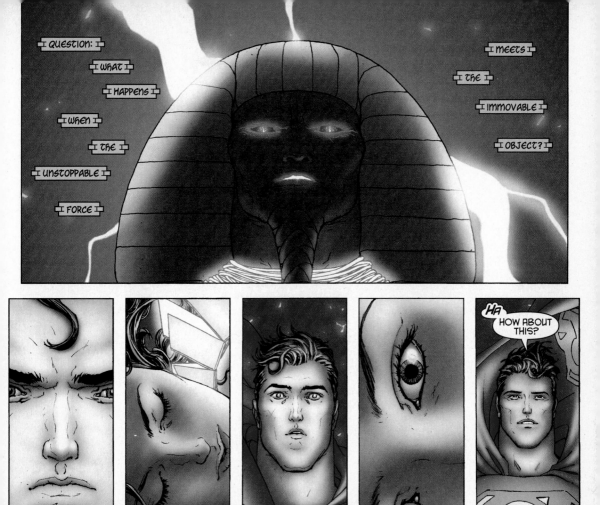

QUESTION: WHAT HAPPENS WHEN THE UNSTOPPABLE FORCE MEETS THE IMMOVABLE OBJECT?

HA HOW ABOUT THIS?

THEY SURRENDER.

RESPONSE ACCEPTABLE

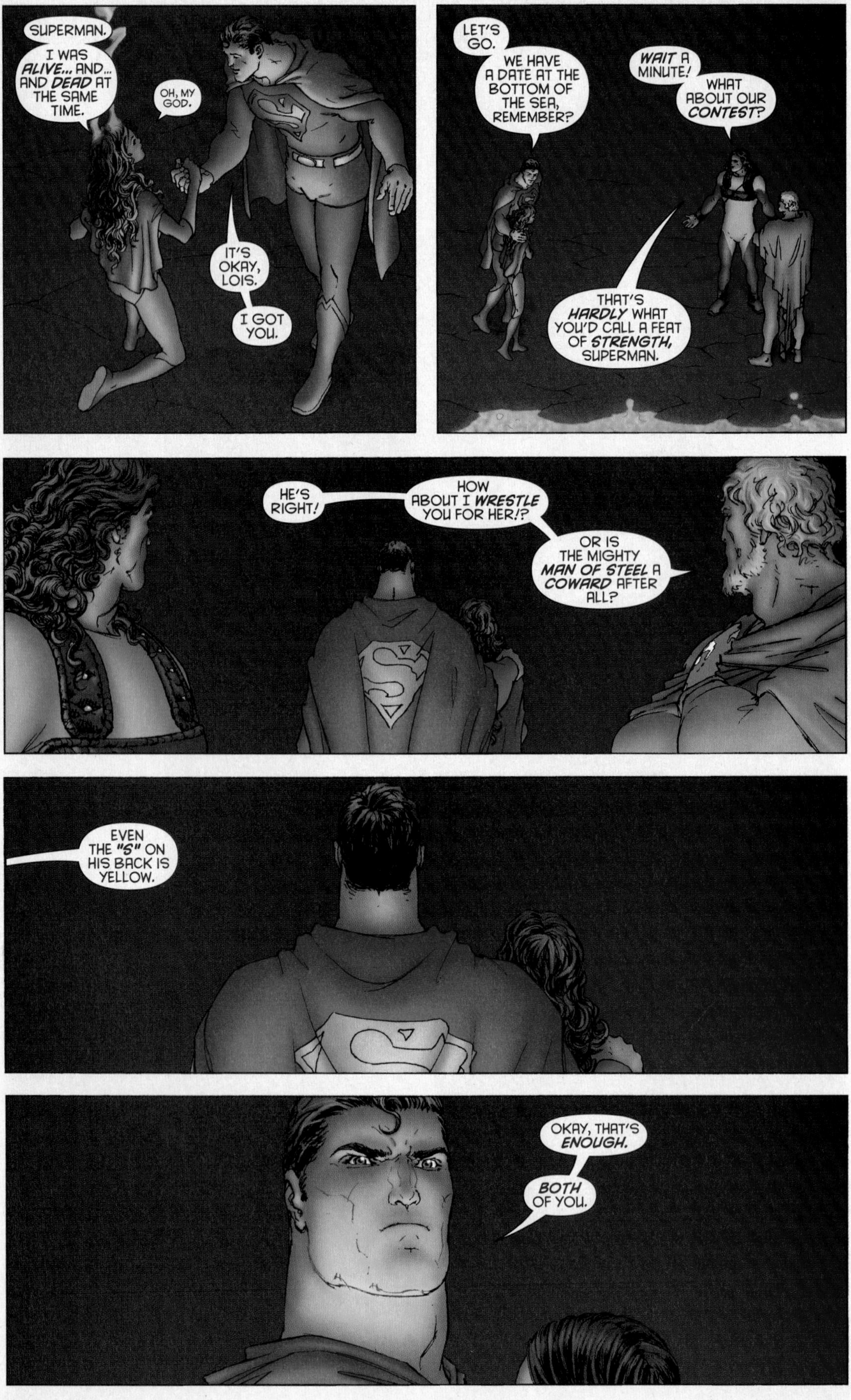

SUPERMAN.
I WAS ALIVE... AND... AND DEAD AT THE SAME TIME.
OH, MY GOD.
IT'S OKAY, LOIS.
I GOT YOU.
LET'S GO.
WE HAVE A DATE AT THE BOTTOM OF THE SEA, REMEMBER?
WAIT A MINUTE!
WHAT ABOUT OUR CONTEST?
THAT'S HARDLY WHAT YOU'D CALL A FEAT OF STRENGTH, SUPERMAN.
HE'S RIGHT!
HOW ABOUT I WRESTLE YOU FOR HER!?
OR IS THE MIGHTY MAN OF STEEL A COWARD AFTER ALL?
EVEN THE "S" ON HIS BACK IS YELLOW.
OKAY, THAT'S ENOUGH.
BOTH OF YOU.

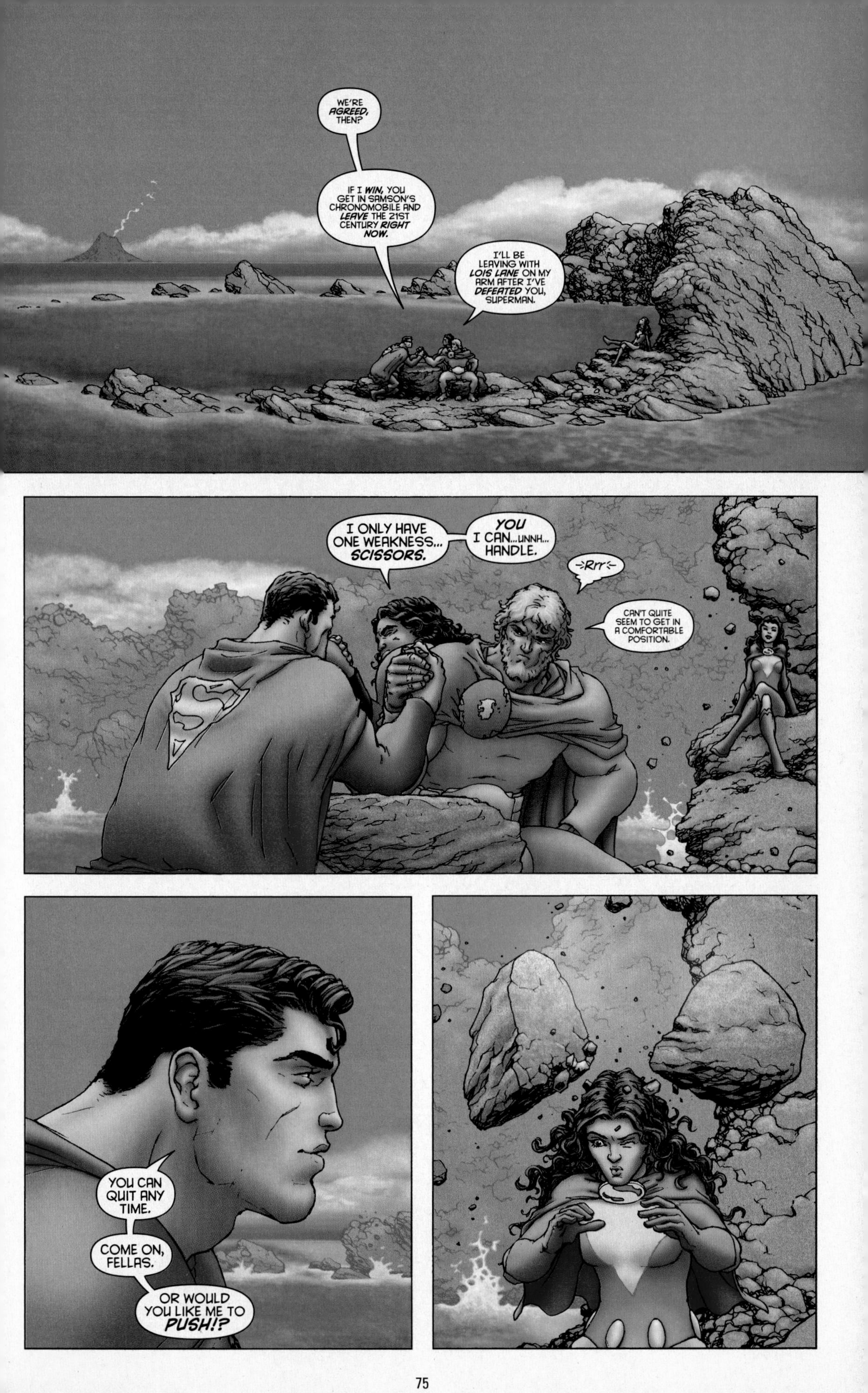
WE'RE AGREED, THEN?
IF I WIN, YOU GET IN SAMSON'S CHRONOMOBILE AND LEAVE THE 21ST CENTURY RIGHT NOW.
I'LL BE LEAVING WITH LOIS LANE ON MY ARM AFTER I'VE DEFEATED YOU, SUPERMAN.
I ONLY HAVE ONE WEAKNESS... SCISSORS.
YOU I CAN...UNNH... HANDLE.
-Rrr-
CAN'T QUITE SEEM TO GET IN A COMFORTABLE POSITION.
YOU CAN QUIT ANY TIME.
COME ON, FELLAS.
OR WOULD YOU LIKE ME TO PUSH!?

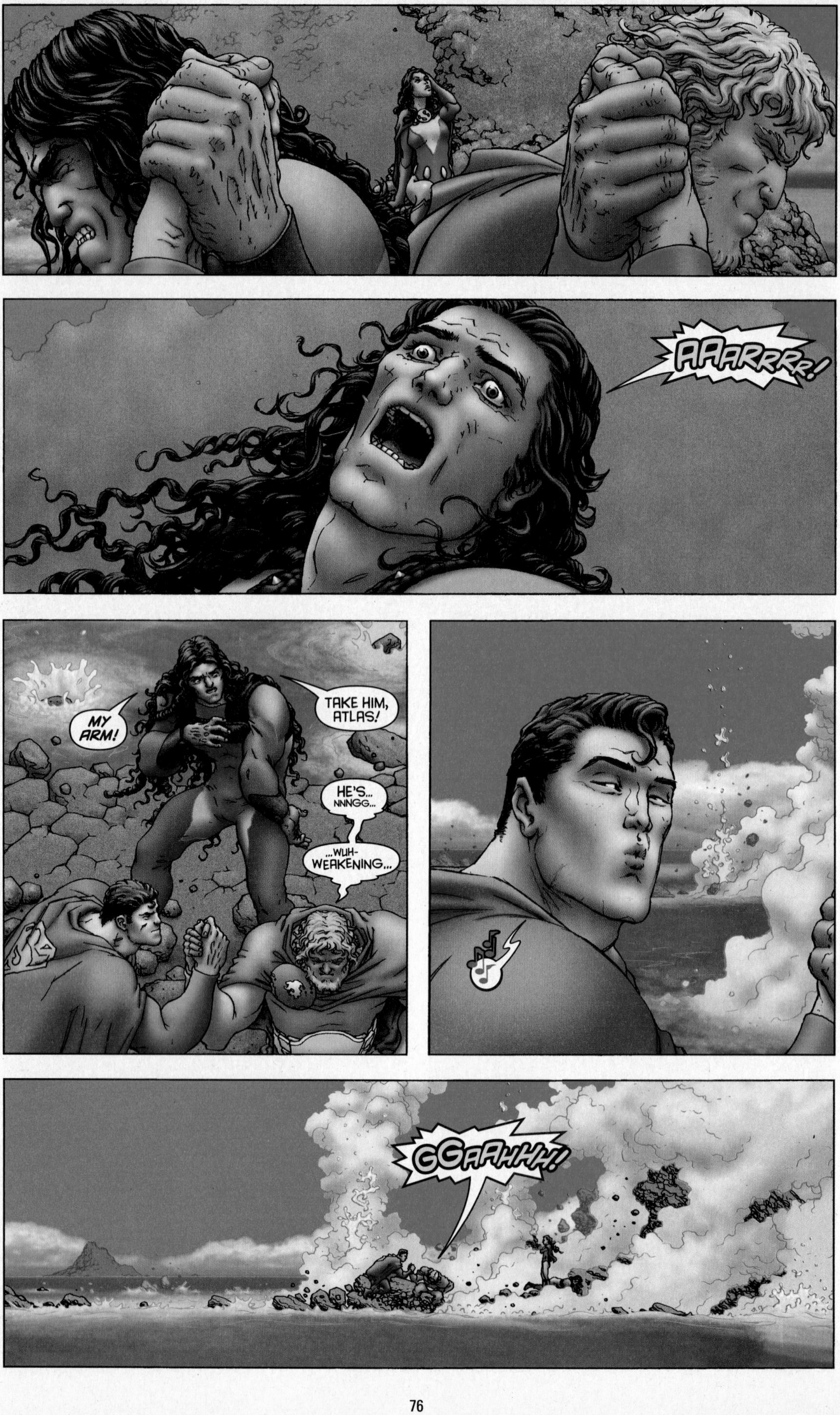
AAARRRR!
MY ARM!
TAKE HIM, ATLAS!
HE'S... NNNGG...
...WUH-WEAKENING...
GGAAHHH!

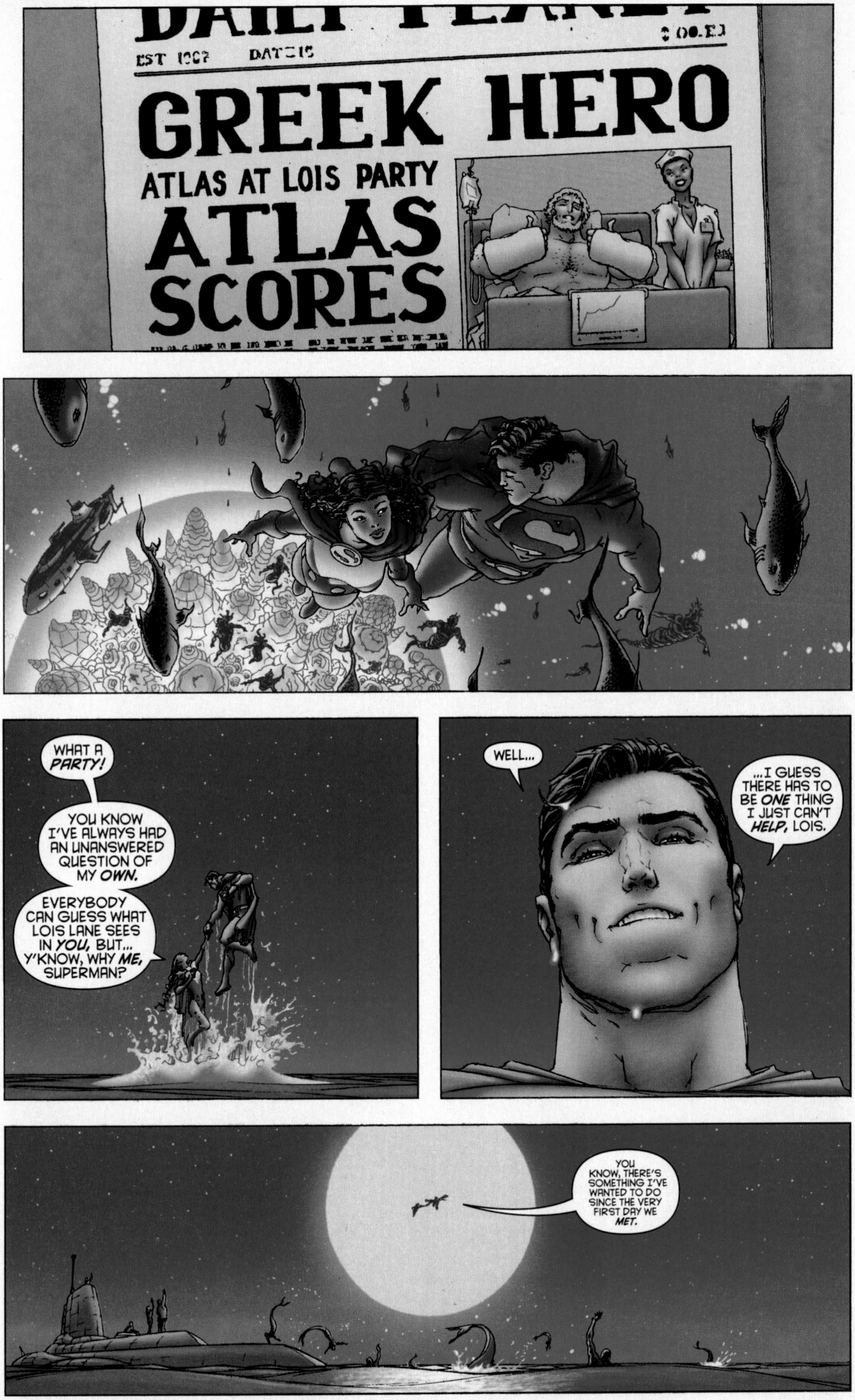
GREEK HERO
ATLAS AT LOIS PARTY
ATLAS SCORES
WHAT A PARTY!
YOU KNOW I'VE ALWAYS HAD AN UNANSWERED QUESTION OF MY OWN.
EVERYBODY CAN GUESS WHAT LOIS LANE SEES IN YOU, BUT... Y'KNOW, WHY ME, SUPERMAN?
WELL...
...I GUESS THERE HAS TO BE ONE THING I JUST CAN'T HELP, LOIS.
YOU KNOW, THERE'S SOMETHING I'VE WANTED TO DO SINCE THE VERY FIRST DAY WE MET.

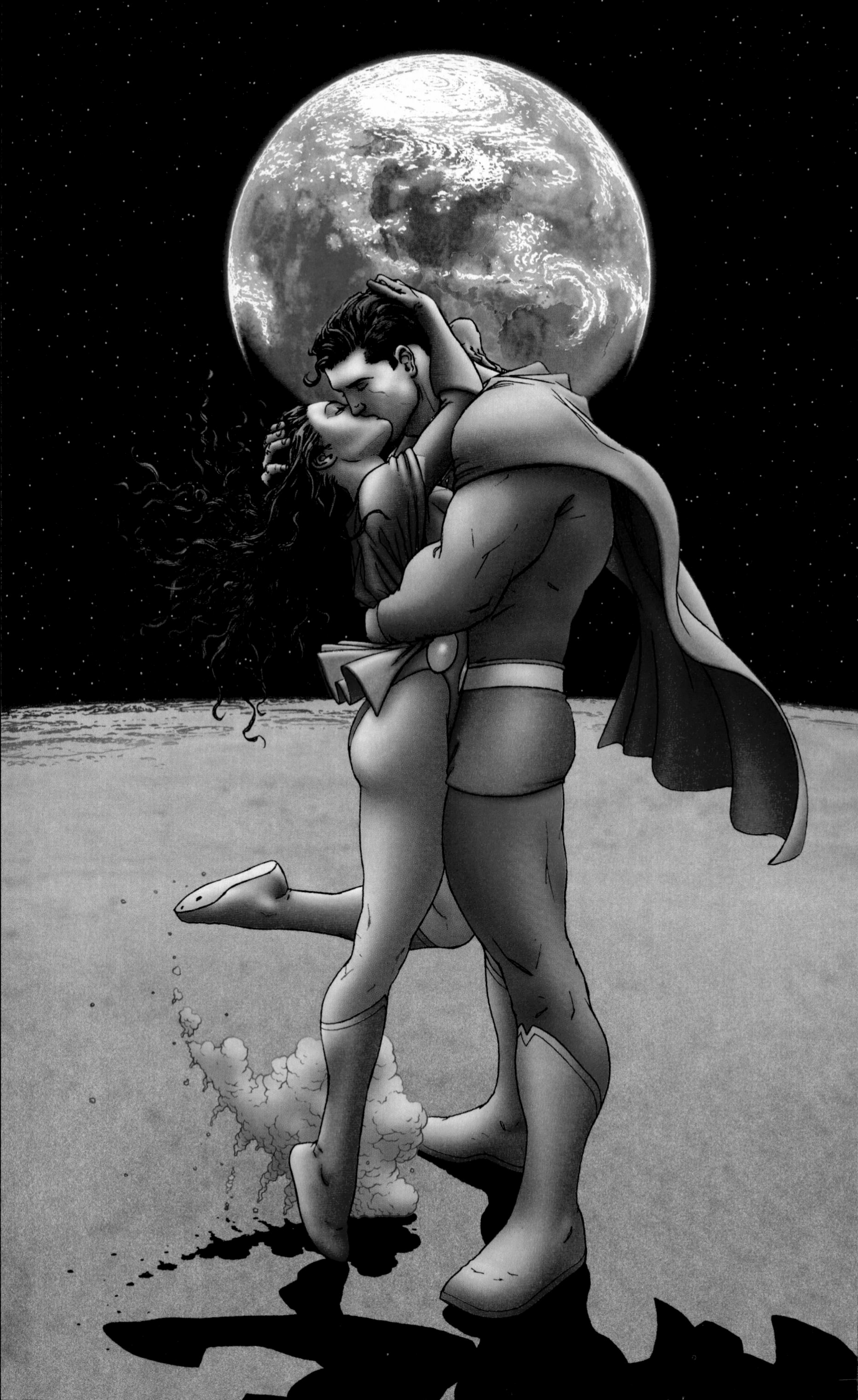

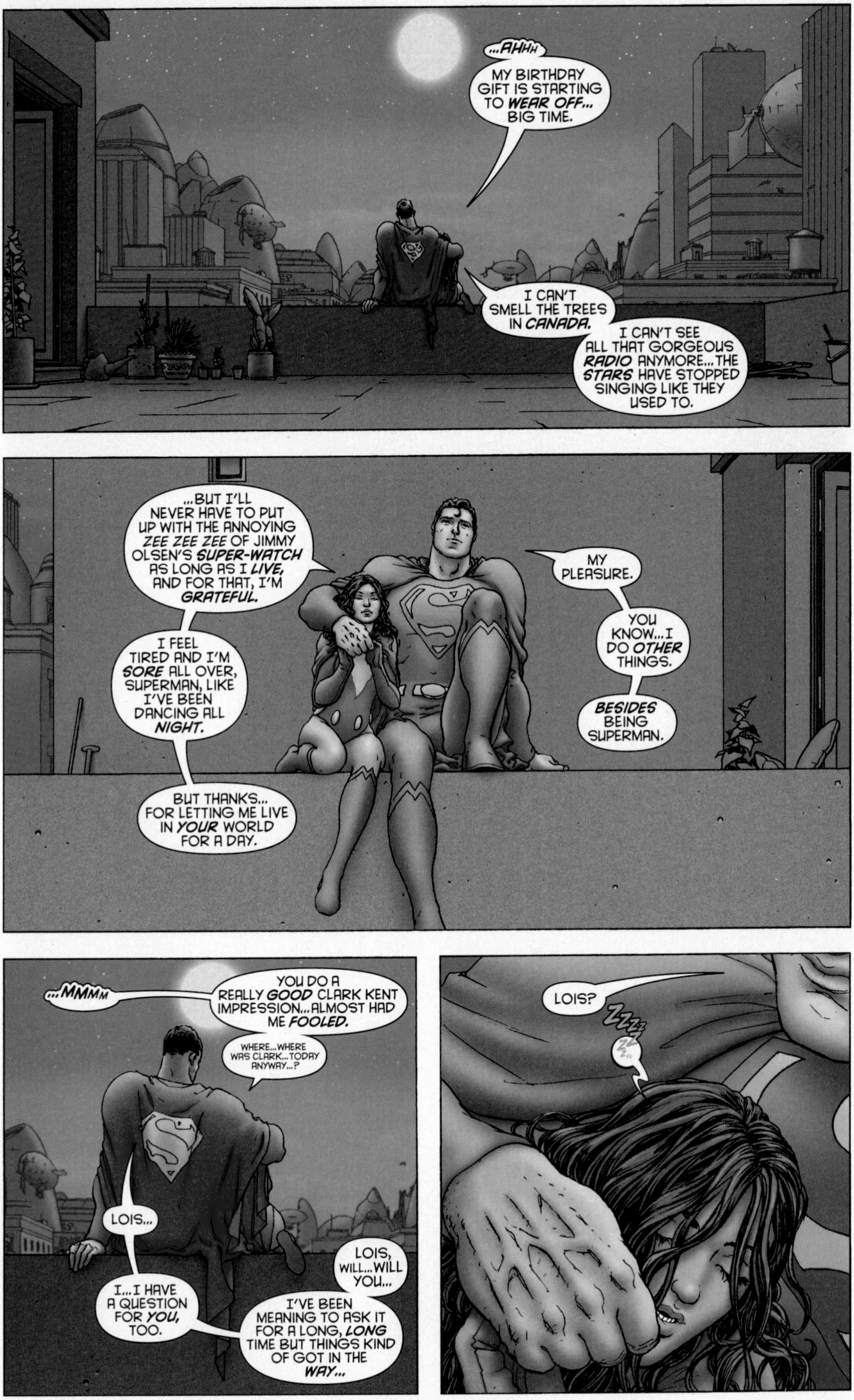

...AHHH
MY BIRTHDAY GIFT IS STARTING TO WEAR OFF... BIG TIME.
I CAN'T SMELL THE TREES IN CANADA.
I CAN'T SEE ALL THAT GORGEOUS RADIO ANYMORE...THE STARS HAVE STOPPED SINGING LIKE THEY USED TO.
...BUT I'LL NEVER HAVE TO PUT UP WITH THE ANNOYING ZEE ZEE ZEE OF JIMMY OLSEN'S SUPER-WATCH AS LONG AS I LIVE, AND FOR THAT, I'M GRATEFUL.
I FEEL TIRED AND I'M SORE ALL OVER, SUPERMAN, LIKE I'VE BEEN DANCING ALL NIGHT.
BUT THANKS... FOR LETTING ME LIVE IN YOUR WORLD FOR A DAY.
MY PLEASURE.
YOU KNOW...I DO OTHER THINGS.
BESIDES BEING SUPERMAN.
...MMMM
YOU DO A REALLY GOOD CLARK KENT IMPRESSION...ALMOST HAD ME FOOLED.
WHERE...WHERE WAS CLARK...TODAY ANYWAY...?
LOIS...
I...I HAVE A QUESTION FOR YOU, TOO.
LOIS, WILL...WILL YOU...
I'VE BEEN MEANING TO ASK IT FOR A LONG, LONG TIME BUT THINGS KIND OF GOT IN THE WAY...
LOIS?
ZZZZ

SWEET DREAMS, SUPERWOMAN...
DAILY PLANET
SUPERMAN DEAD
BY CLARK KENT
WHAT HAPPENS WHEN THE UNSTOPPABLE FORCE MEETS THE IMMOVABLE OBJECT?
SURRENDER TO THE NEW LUXUS SAMARITAN
LUXUS
SAMARITAN

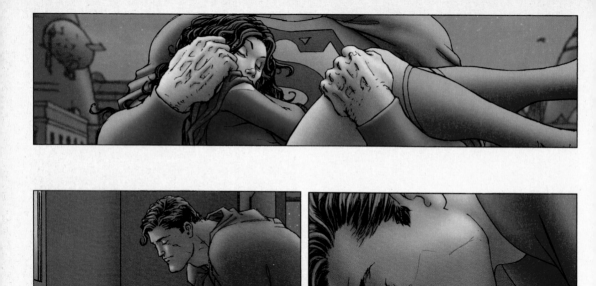

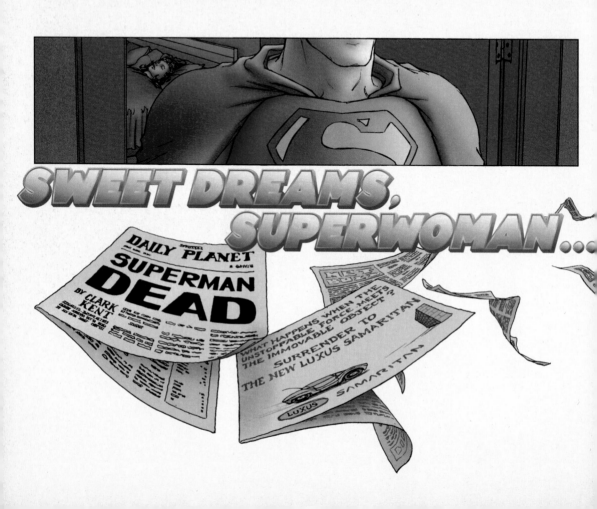

Episode 4

THE SUPERMAN/JIMMY OLSEN WAR!

Cover FRANK QUITELY with JAMIE GRANT

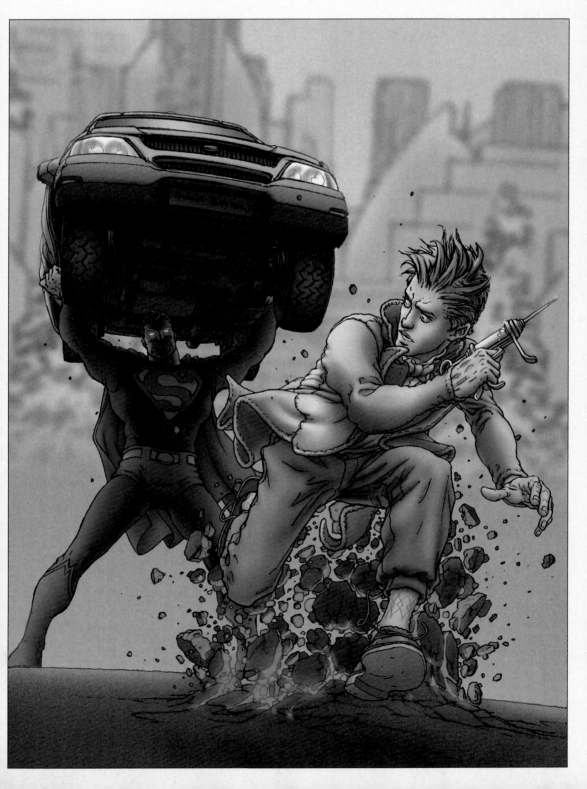

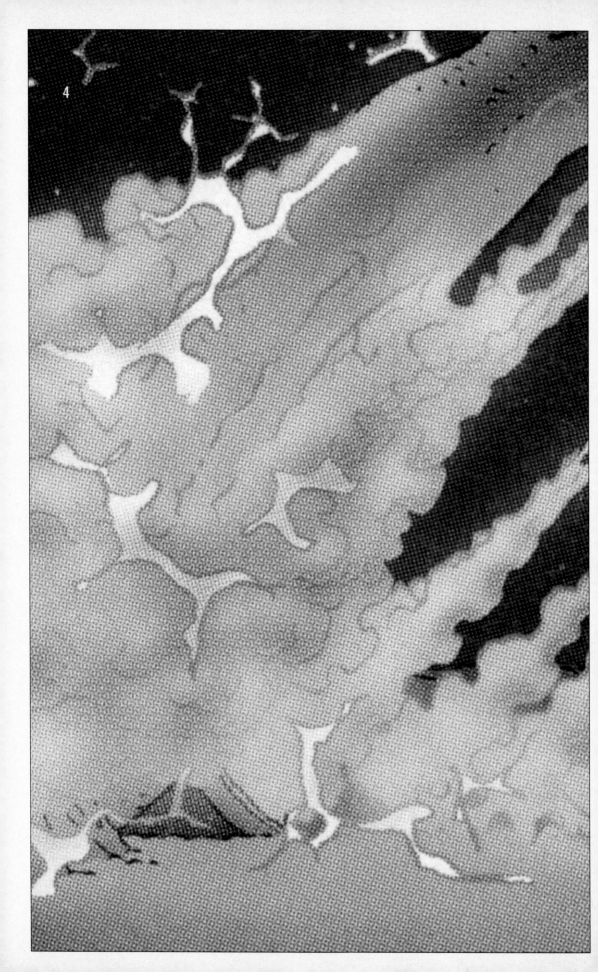

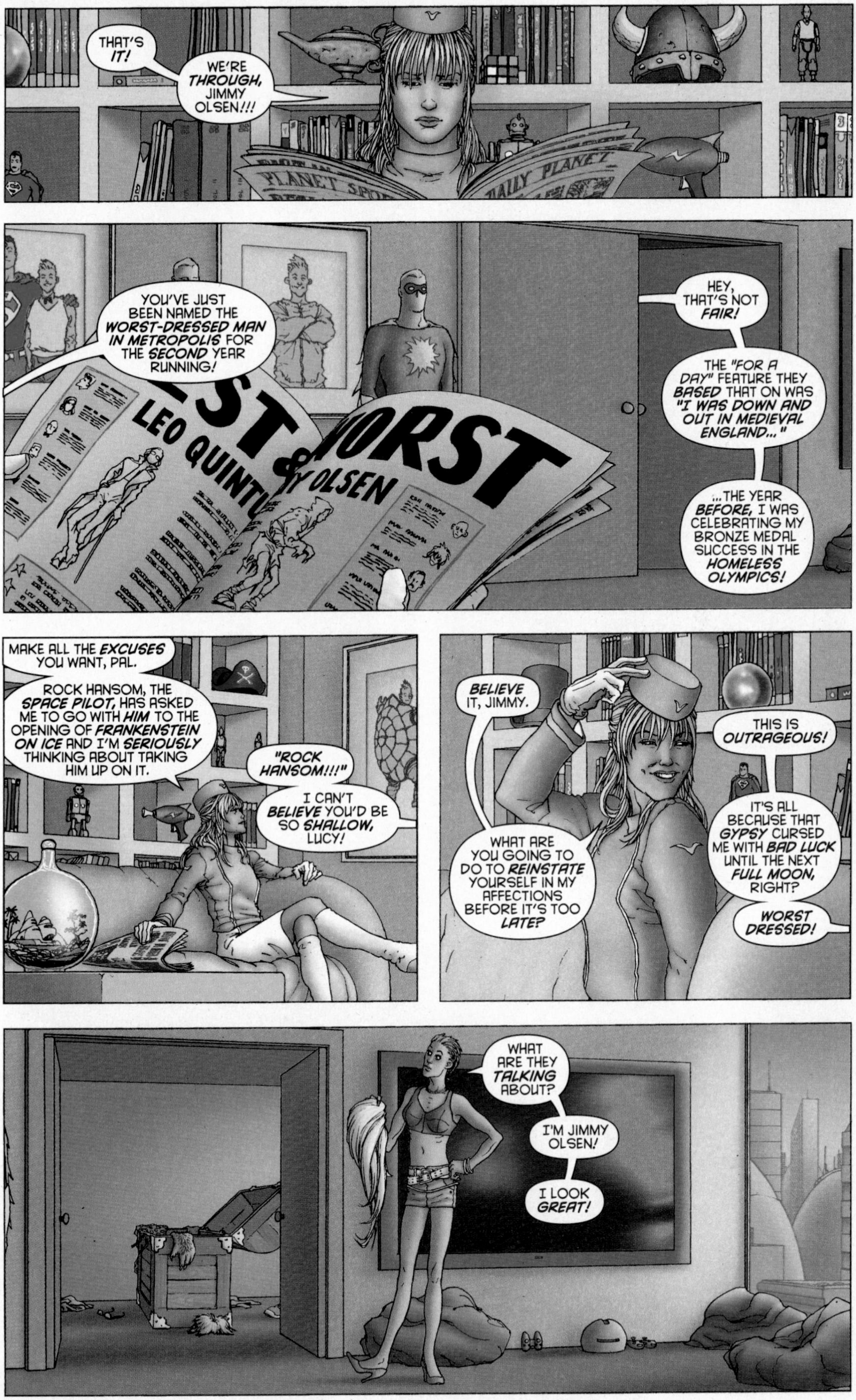
THAT'S *IT!*
WE'RE *THROUGH,* JIMMY OLSEN*!!!*
DAILY PLANET
YOU'VE JUST BEEN NAMED THE *WORST-DRESSED MAN IN METROPOLIS* FOR THE *SECOND* YEAR RUNNING!
WORST
HEY, THAT'S NOT *FAIR!*
THE *"FOR A DAY"* FEATURE THEY *BASED* THAT ON WAS *"I WAS DOWN AND OUT IN MEDIEVAL ENGLAND..."*
...THE YEAR *BEFORE,* I WAS CELEBRATING MY BRONZE MEDAL SUCCESS IN THE *HOMELESS OLYMPICS!*
MAKE ALL THE *EXCUSES* YOU WANT, PAL.
ROCK HANSOM, THE *SPACE PILOT,* HAS ASKED ME TO GO WITH *HIM* TO THE OPENING OF *FRANKENSTEIN ON ICE* AND I'M *SERIOUSLY* THINKING ABOUT TAKING HIM UP ON IT.
"ROCK HANSOM!!!"
I CAN'T *BELIEVE* YOU'D BE SO *SHALLOW,* LUCY!
BELIEVE IT, JIMMY.
WHAT ARE YOU GOING TO DO TO *REINSTATE* YOURSELF IN MY AFFECTIONS BEFORE IT'S TOO *LATE?*
THIS IS *OUTRAGEOUS!*
IT'S ALL BECAUSE THAT *GYPSY* CURSED ME WITH *BAD LUCK* UNTIL THE NEXT *FULL MOON,* RIGHT?
WORST DRESSED!
WHAT ARE THEY *TALKING* ABOUT?
I'M JIMMY OLSEN!
I LOOK *GREAT!*

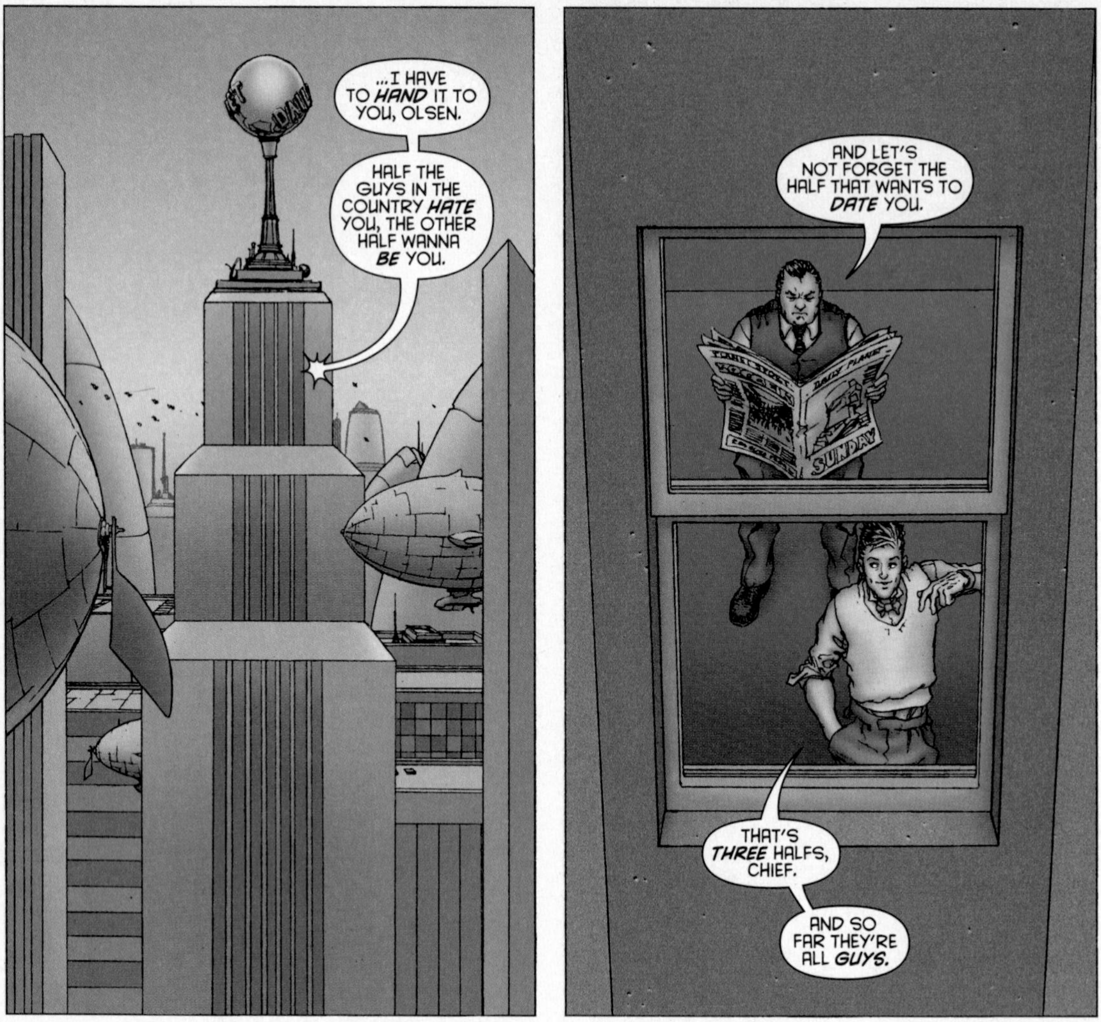
...I HAVE TO HAND IT TO YOU, OLSEN.
HALF THE GUYS IN THE COUNTRY HATE YOU, THE OTHER HALF WANNA BE YOU.
AND LET'S NOT FORGET THE HALF THAT WANTS TO DATE YOU.
SUNDAY
THAT'S THREE HALFS, CHIEF.
AND SO FAR THEY'RE ALL GUYS.

THE SUPERMAN

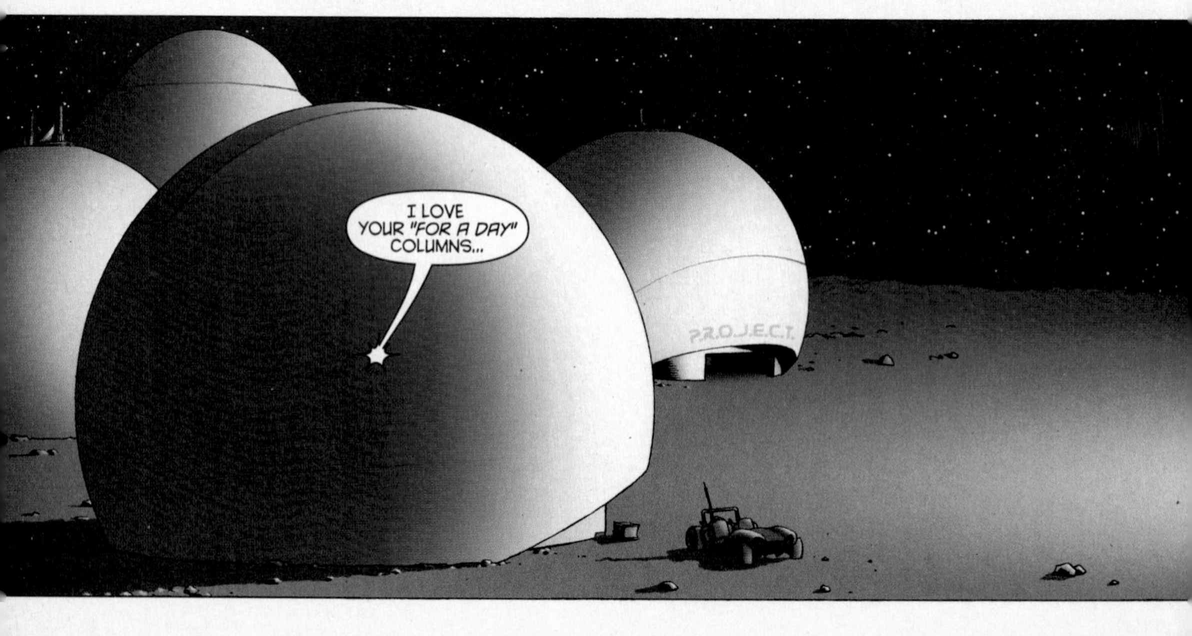
I LOVE YOUR "FOR A DAY" COLUMNS...
P.R.O.J.E.C.T.

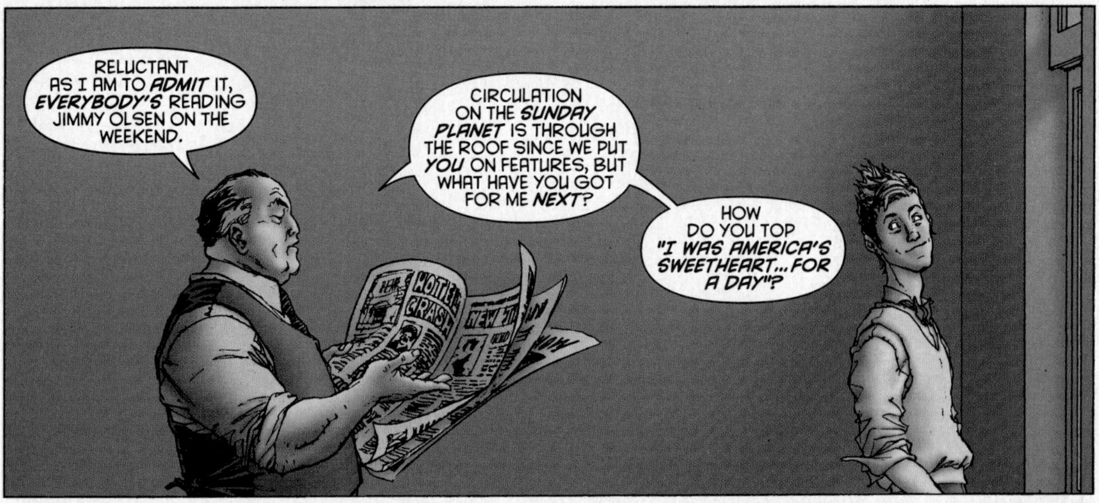
RELUCTANT AS I AM TO ADMIT IT, EVERYBODY'S READING JIMMY OLSEN ON THE WEEKEND.
CIRCULATION ON THE SUNDAY PLANET IS THROUGH THE ROOF SINCE WE PUT YOU ON FEATURES, BUT WHAT HAVE YOU GOT FOR ME NEXT?
HOW DO YOU TOP "I WAS AMERICA'S SWEETHEART... FOR A DAY"?

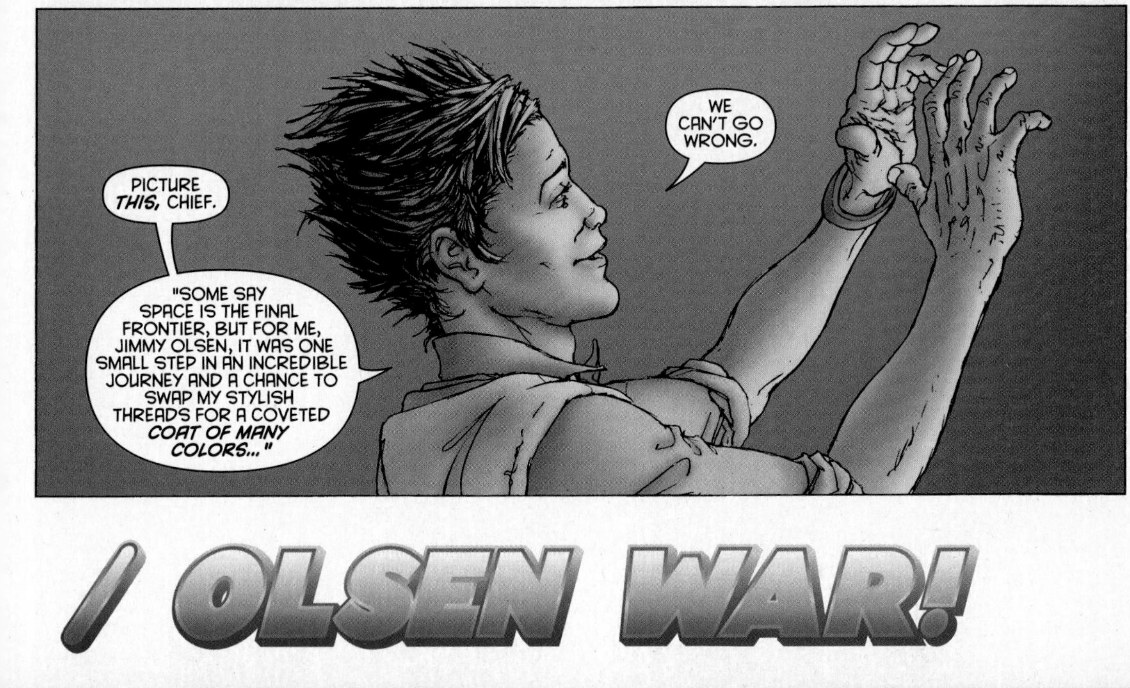
WE CAN'T GO WRONG.
PICTURE THIS, CHIEF.
"SOME SAY SPACE IS THE FINAL FRONTIER, BUT FOR ME, JIMMY OLSEN, IT WAS ONE SMALL STEP IN AN INCREDIBLE JOURNEY AND A CHANCE TO SWAP MY STYLISH THREADS FOR A COVETED COAT OF MANY COLORS..."

/ OLSEN WAR!

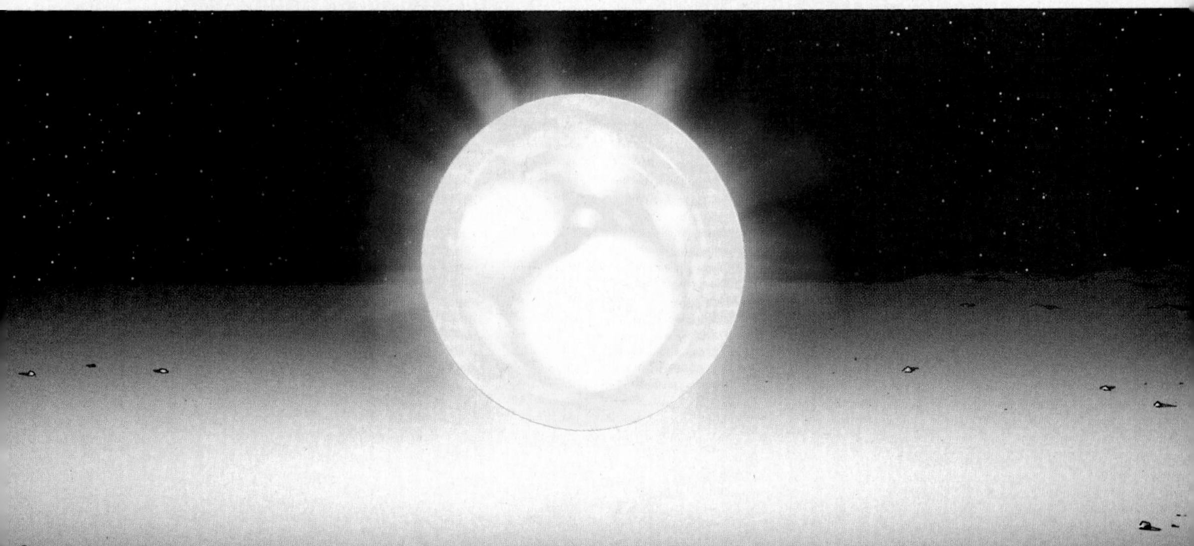

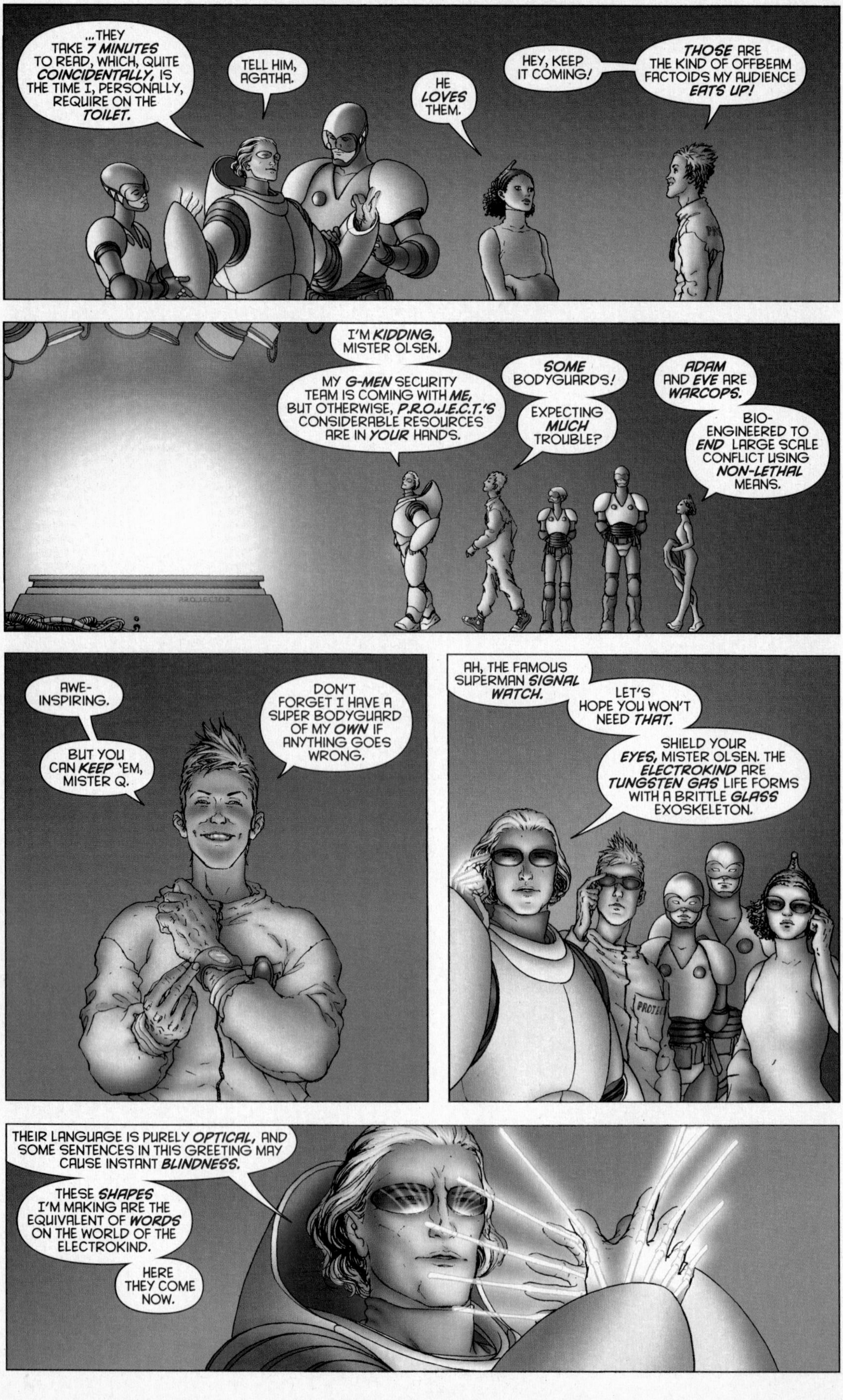
...THEY TAKE 7 MINUTES TO READ, WHICH, QUITE COINCIDENTALLY, IS THE TIME I, PERSONALLY, REQUIRE ON THE TOILET.
TELL HIM, AGATHA.
HE LOVES THEM.
HEY, KEEP IT COMING!
THOSE ARE THE KIND OF OFFBEAM FACTOIDS MY AUDIENCE EATS UP!
I'M KIDDING, MISTER OLSEN.
MY G-MEN SECURITY TEAM IS COMING WITH ME, BUT OTHERWISE, P.R.O.J.E.C.T.'S CONSIDERABLE RESOURCES ARE IN YOUR HANDS.
SOME BODYGUARDS!
EXPECTING MUCH TROUBLE?
ADAM AND EVE ARE WARCOPS.
BIO-ENGINEERED TO END LARGE SCALE CONFLICT USING NON-LETHAL MEANS.
PROJECTOR
AWE-INSPIRING.
BUT YOU CAN KEEP 'EM, MISTER Q.
DON'T FORGET I HAVE A SUPER BODYGUARD OF MY OWN IF ANYTHING GOES WRONG.
AH, THE FAMOUS SUPERMAN SIGNAL WATCH.
LET'S HOPE YOU WON'T NEED THAT.
SHIELD YOUR EYES, MISTER OLSEN. THE ELECTROKIND ARE TUNGSTEN GAS LIFE FORMS WITH A BRITTLE GLASS EXOSKELETON.
THEIR LANGUAGE IS PURELY OPTICAL, AND SOME SENTENCES IN THIS GREETING MAY CAUSE INSTANT BLINDNESS.
THESE SHAPES I'M MAKING ARE THE EQUIVALENT OF WORDS ON THE WORLD OF THE ELECTROKIND.
HERE THEY COME NOW.

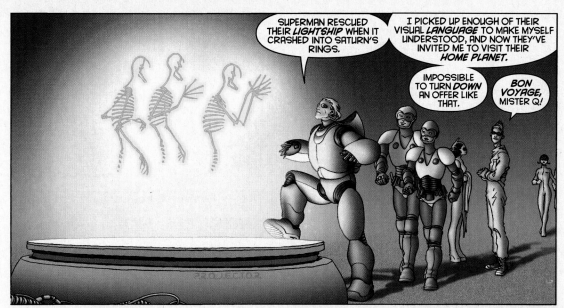

SUPERMAN RESCUED THEIR *LIGHTSHIP* WHEN IT CRASHED INTO SATURN'S RINGS.

I PICKED UP ENOUGH OF THEIR VISUAL *LANGUAGE* TO MAKE MYSELF UNDERSTOOD, AND NOW THEY'VE INVITED ME TO VISIT THEIR *HOME PLANET.*

IMPOSSIBLE TO TURN *DOWN* AN OFFER LIKE THAT.

BON VOYAGE, MISTER Q!

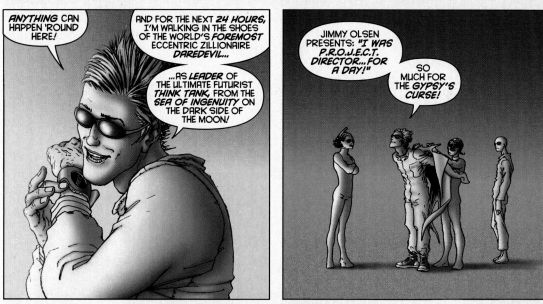

ANYTHING CAN HAPPEN 'ROUND HERE!

AND FOR THE NEXT *24 HOURS,* I'M WALKING IN THE SHOES OF THE WORLD'S *FOREMOST* ECCENTRIC ZILLIONAIRE *DAREDEVIL...*

...AS *LEADER* OF THE ULTIMATE FUTURIST *THINK TANK,* FROM THE *SEA OF INGENUITY* ON THE DARK SIDE OF THE MOON!

JIMMY OLSEN PRESENTS: *"I WAS P.R.O.J.E.C.T. DIRECTOR...FOR A DAY!"*

SO MUCH FOR THE *GYPSY'S CURSE!*

OKAY, P.R.O.J.E.C.T.'S OBVIOUSLY AN *ACRONYM:* CAN ANYONE TELL ME WHAT IT *STANDS* FOR?

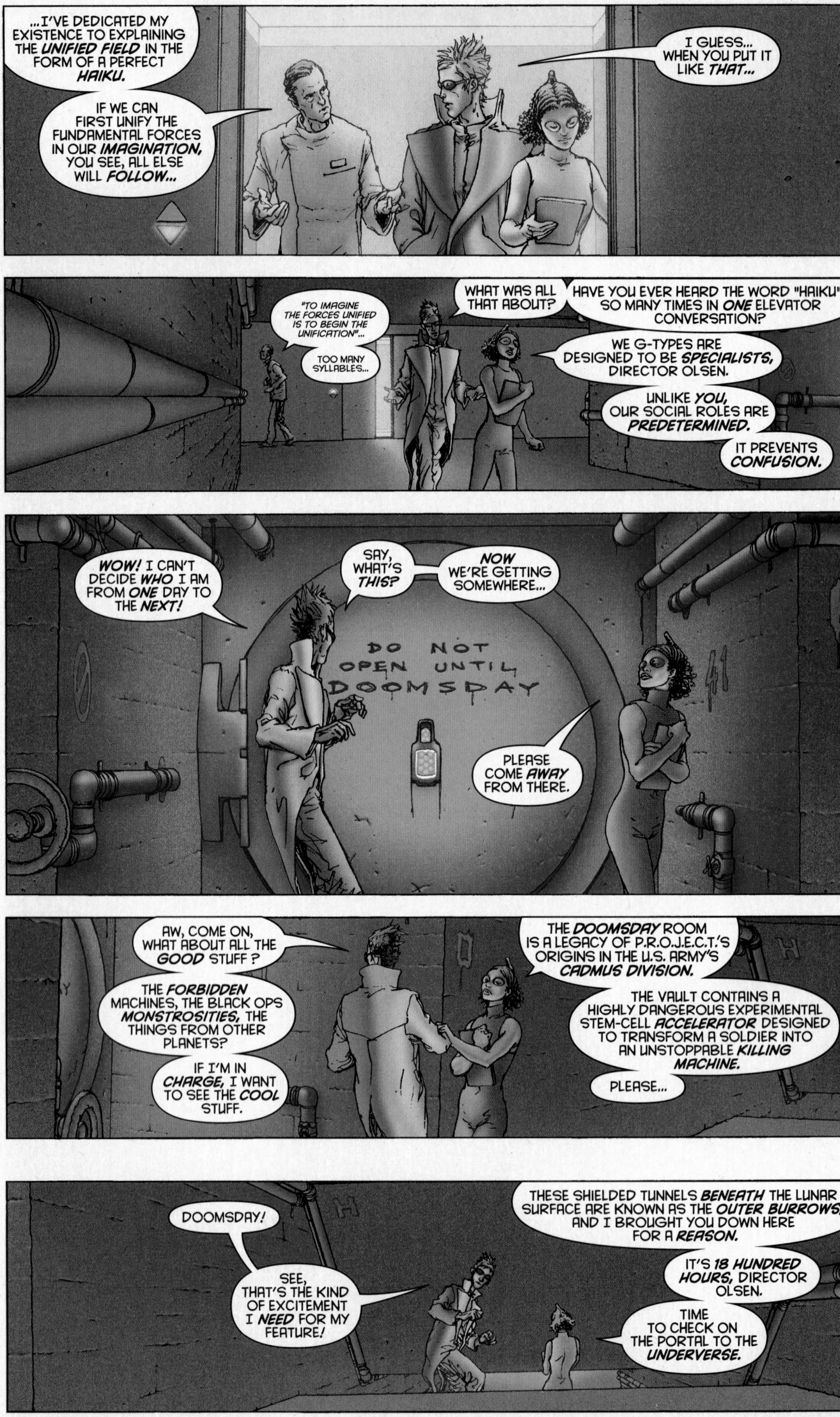

...I'VE DEDICATED MY EXISTENCE TO EXPLAINING THE UNIFIED FIELD IN THE FORM OF A PERFECT HAIKU.
IF WE CAN FIRST UNIFY THE FUNDAMENTAL FORCES IN OUR IMAGINATION, YOU SEE, ALL ELSE WILL FOLLOW...
I GUESS... WHEN YOU PUT IT LIKE THAT...
"TO IMAGINE THE FORCES UNIFIED IS TO BEGIN THE UNIFICATION"...
TOO MANY SYLLABLES...
WHAT WAS ALL THAT ABOUT?
HAVE YOU EVER HEARD THE WORD "HAIKU" SO MANY TIMES IN ONE ELEVATOR CONVERSATION?
WE G-TYPES ARE DESIGNED TO BE SPECIALISTS, DIRECTOR OLSEN.
UNLIKE YOU, OUR SOCIAL ROLES ARE PREDETERMINED.
IT PREVENTS CONFUSION.
WOW! I CAN'T DECIDE WHO I AM FROM ONE DAY TO THE NEXT!
SAY, WHAT'S THIS?
NOW WE'RE GETTING SOMEWHERE...
DO NOT OPEN UNTIL DOOMSDAY
PLEASE COME AWAY FROM THERE.
AW, COME ON, WHAT ABOUT ALL THE GOOD STUFF?
THE FORBIDDEN MACHINES, THE BLACK OPS MONSTROSITIES, THE THINGS FROM OTHER PLANETS?
IF I'M IN CHARGE, I WANT TO SEE THE COOL STUFF.
THE DOOMSDAY ROOM IS A LEGACY OF P.R.O.J.E.C.T.'S ORIGINS IN THE U.S. ARMY'S CADMUS DIVISION.
THE VAULT CONTAINS A HIGHLY DANGEROUS EXPERIMENTAL STEM-CELL ACCELERATOR DESIGNED TO TRANSFORM A SOLDIER INTO AN UNSTOPPABLE KILLING MACHINE.
PLEASE...
DOOMSDAY!
SEE, THAT'S THE KIND OF EXCITEMENT I NEED FOR MY FEATURE!
THESE SHIELDED TUNNELS BENEATH THE LUNAR SURFACE ARE KNOWN AS THE OUTER BURROWS, AND I BROUGHT YOU DOWN HERE FOR A REASON.
IT'S 18 HUNDRED HOURS, DIRECTOR OLSEN.
TIME TO CHECK ON THE PORTAL TO THE UNDERVERSE.

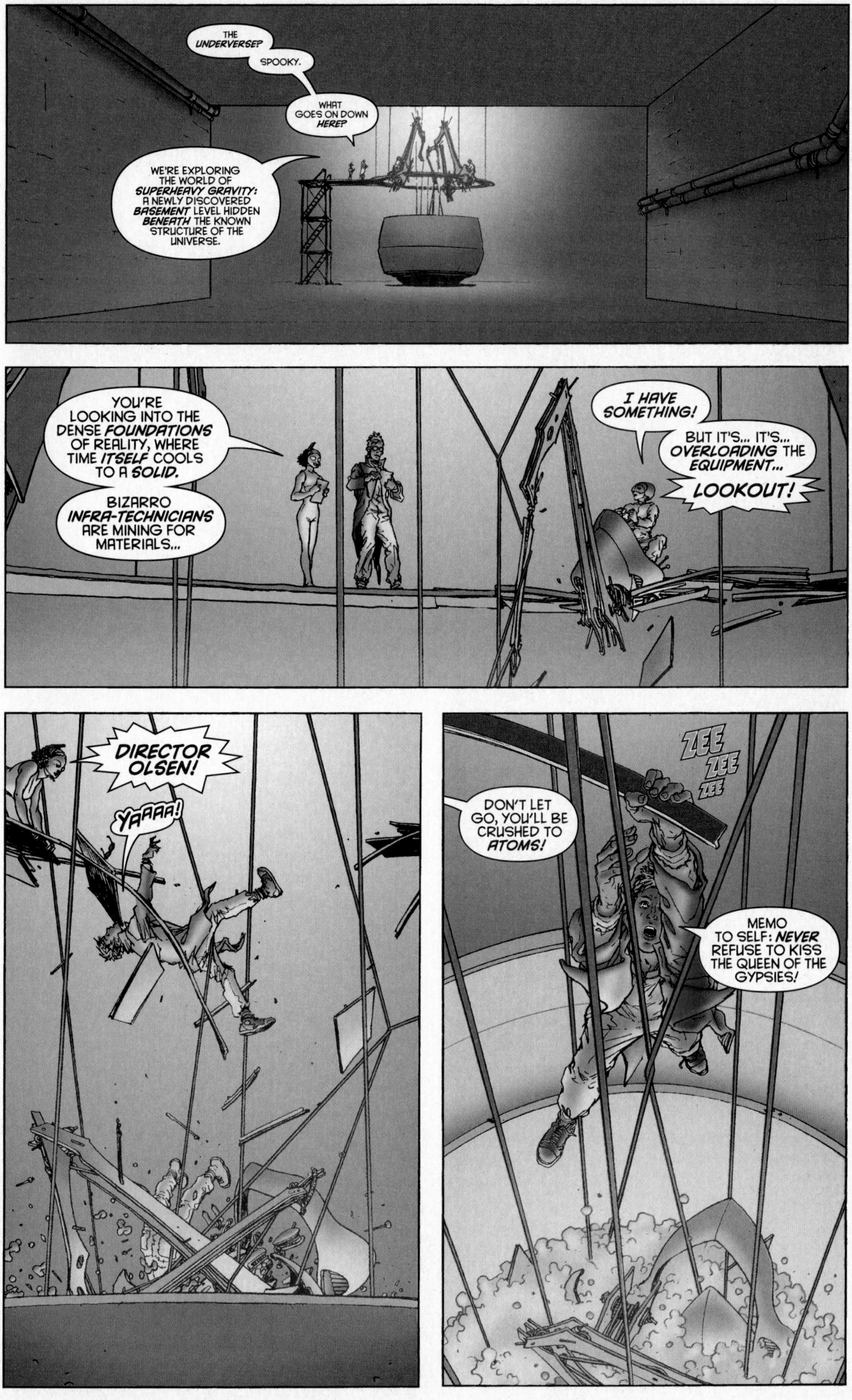
THE UNDERVERSE?
SPOOKY.
WHAT GOES ON DOWN HERE?
WE'RE EXPLORING THE WORLD OF SUPERHEAVY GRAVITY: A NEWLY DISCOVERED BASEMENT LEVEL HIDDEN BENEATH THE KNOWN STRUCTURE OF THE UNIVERSE.
YOU'RE LOOKING INTO THE DENSE FOUNDATIONS OF REALITY, WHERE TIME ITSELF COOLS TO A SOLID.
BIZARRO INFRA-TECHNICIANS ARE MINING FOR MATERIALS...
I HAVE SOMETHING!
BUT IT'S... IT'S... OVERLOADING THE EQUIPMENT...
LOOKOUT!
DIRECTOR OLSEN!
YAAAA!
ZEE ZEE ZEE
DON'T LET GO, YOU'LL BE CRUSHED TO ATOMS!
MEMO TO SELF: NEVER REFUSE TO KISS THE QUEEN OF THE GYPSIES!

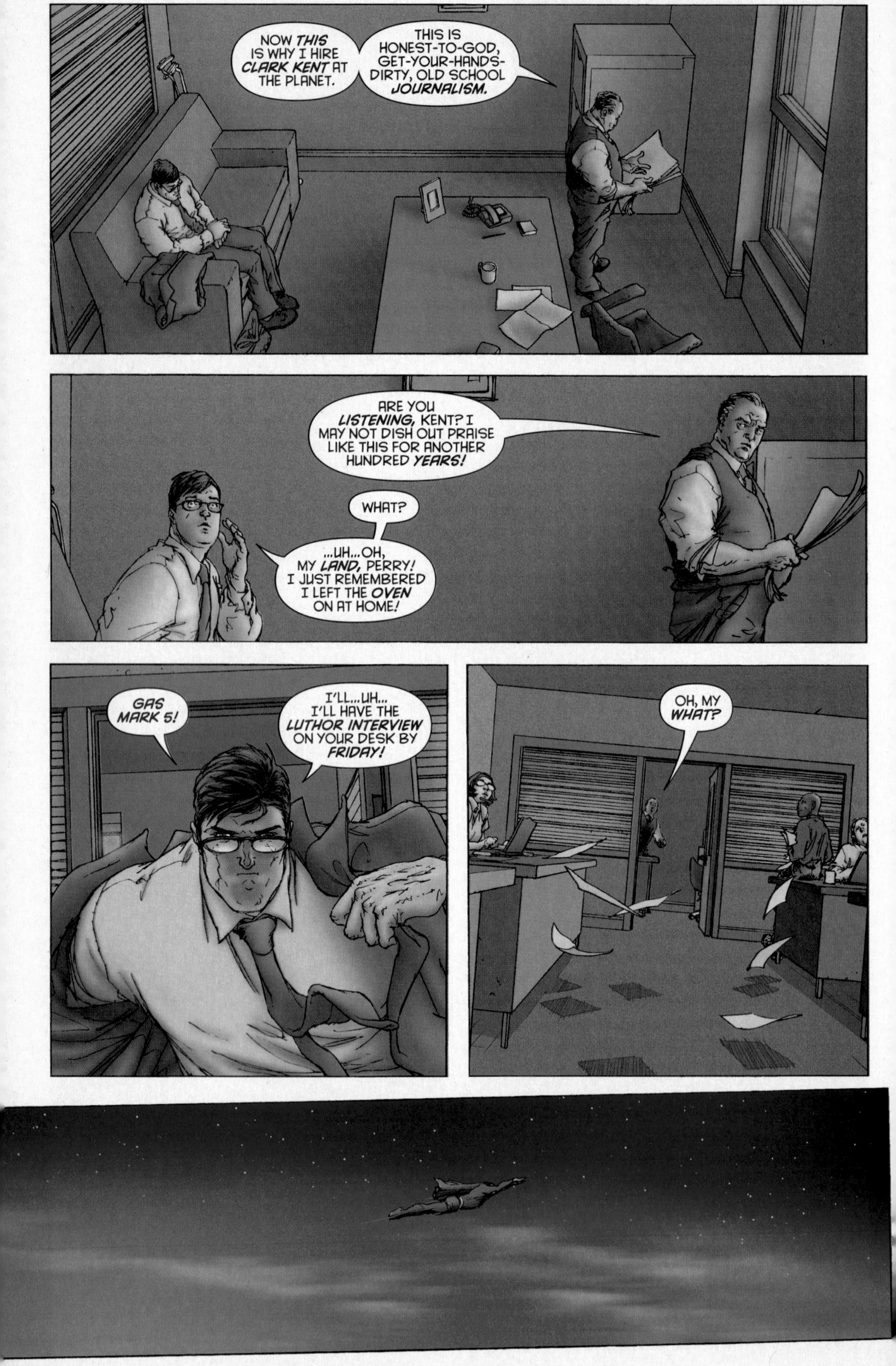
NOW THIS IS WHY I HIRE CLARK KENT AT THE PLANET.
THIS IS HONEST-TO-GOD, GET-YOUR-HANDS-DIRTY, OLD SCHOOL JOURNALISM.
ARE YOU LISTENING, KENT? I MAY NOT DISH OUT PRAISE LIKE THIS FOR ANOTHER HUNDRED YEARS!
WHAT?
...UH...OH, MY LAND, PERRY! I JUST REMEMBERED I LEFT THE OVEN ON AT HOME!
GAS MARK 5!
I'LL...UH... I'LL HAVE THE LUTHOR INTERVIEW ON YOUR DESK BY FRIDAY!
OH, MY WHAT?

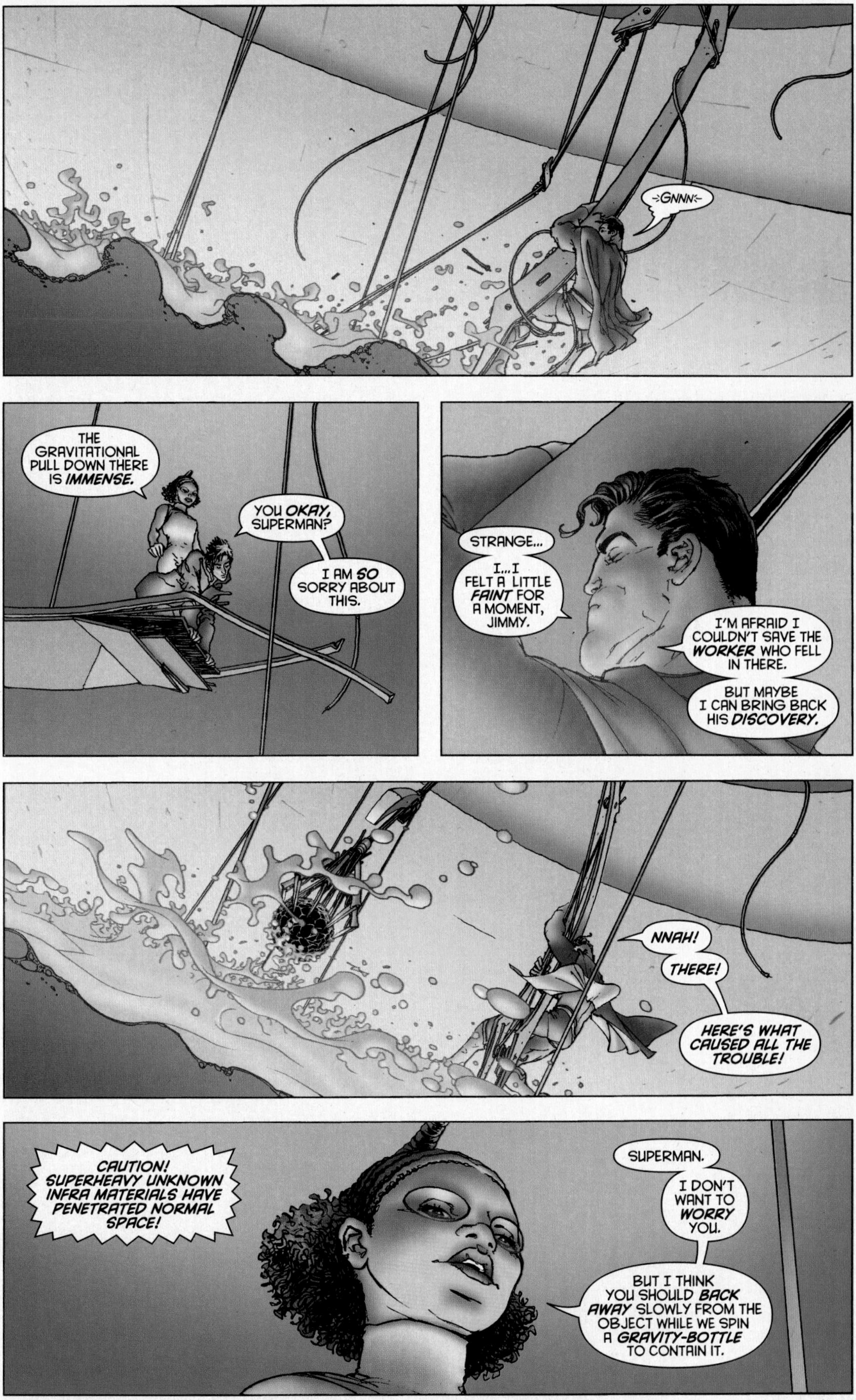

-GNNN-
THE GRAVITATIONAL PULL DOWN THERE IS IMMENSE.
YOU OKAY, SUPERMAN?
I AM SO SORRY ABOUT THIS.
STRANGE...
I...I FELT A LITTLE FAINT FOR A MOMENT, JIMMY.
I'M AFRAID I COULDN'T SAVE THE WORKER WHO FELL IN THERE.
BUT MAYBE I CAN BRING BACK HIS DISCOVERY.
NNAH!
THERE!
HERE'S WHAT CAUSED ALL THE TROUBLE!
CAUTION! SUPERHEAVY UNKNOWN INFRA MATERIALS HAVE PENETRATED NORMAL SPACE!
SUPERMAN.
I DON'T WANT TO WORRY YOU.
BUT I THINK YOU SHOULD BACK AWAY SLOWLY FROM THE OBJECT WHILE WE SPIN A GRAVITY-BOTTLE TO CONTAIN IT.

BLACK KRYPTONITE.

A NEW *ISOTOPE* AT THE LOW-FREQUENCY END OF THE *K-MINERAL* SPECTRUM.

IT SEEMS WE'VE DUG UP A RADIOACTIVE FRAGMENT OF YOUR *HOMEWORLD* THAT'S BEEN BURIED FOR YEARS IN THE *UNDERVERSE.*

A *NEW* TYPE OF KRYPTONITE!

I DON'T LIKE THE *LOOK* OF THIS, SUPERMAN.

K-RADIATION CAN *KILL* YOU.

NOT ANYMORE SINCE I BECAME *IMMUNE* TO *GREEN K,* JIMMY.

CAN'T SAY I *FEEL* ANY PHYSICAL EFFECTS FROM *THIS* SAMPLE.

I GUESS I'M *FINE.*

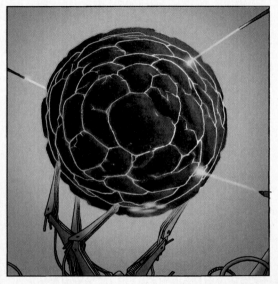

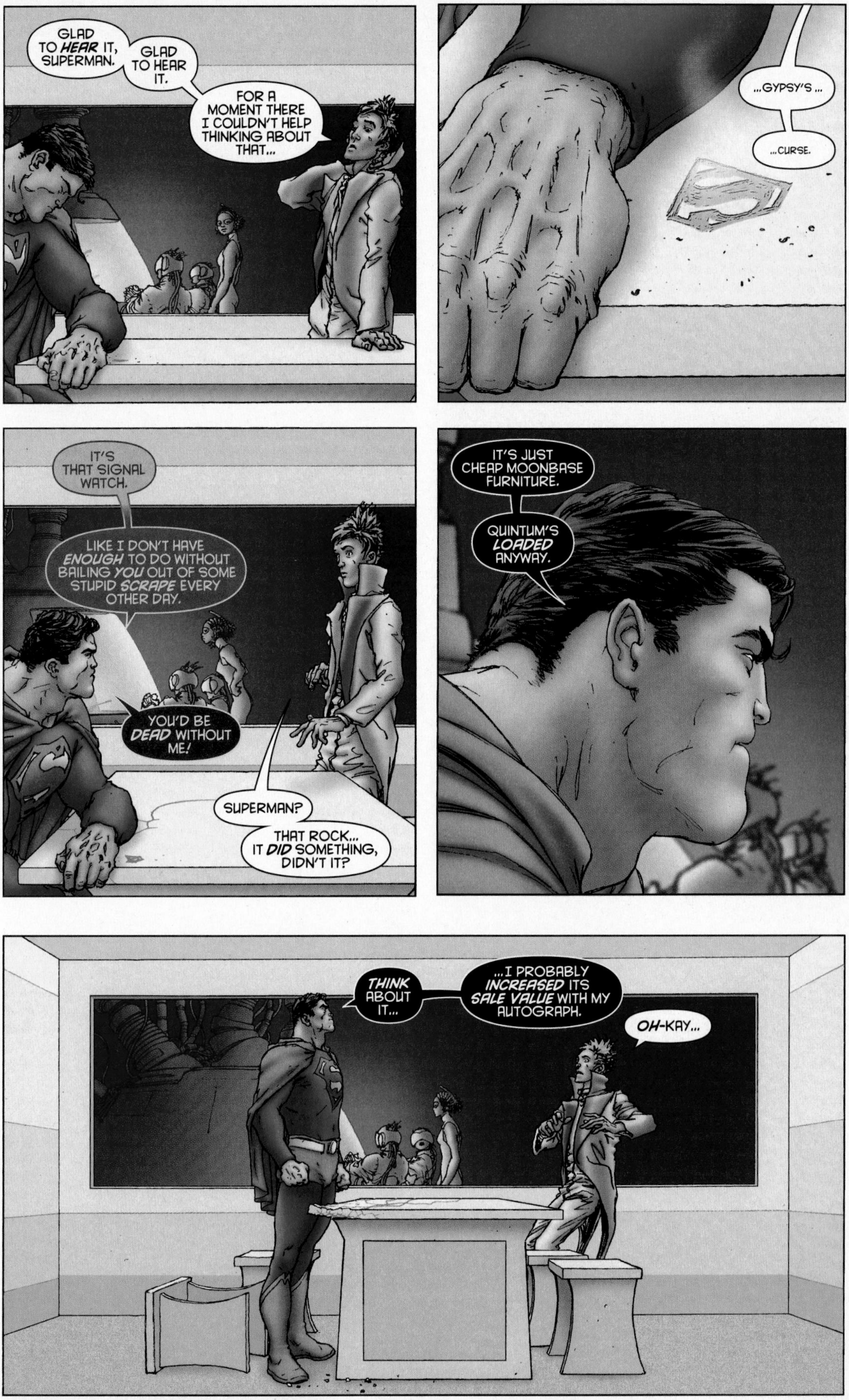
GLAD TO HEAR IT, SUPERMAN.
GLAD TO HEAR IT.
FOR A MOMENT THERE I COULDN'T HELP THINKING ABOUT THAT...
...GYPSY'S ...
...CURSE.
IT'S THAT SIGNAL WATCH.
LIKE I DON'T HAVE ENOUGH TO DO WITHOUT BAILING YOU OUT OF SOME STUPID SCRAPE EVERY OTHER DAY.
YOU'D BE DEAD WITHOUT ME!
SUPERMAN?
THAT ROCK... IT DID SOMETHING, DIDN'T IT?
IT'S JUST CHEAP MOONBASE FURNITURE.
QUINTUM'S LOADED ANYWAY.
THINK ABOUT IT...
...I PROBABLY INCREASED ITS SALE VALUE WITH MY AUTOGRAPH.
OH-KAY...

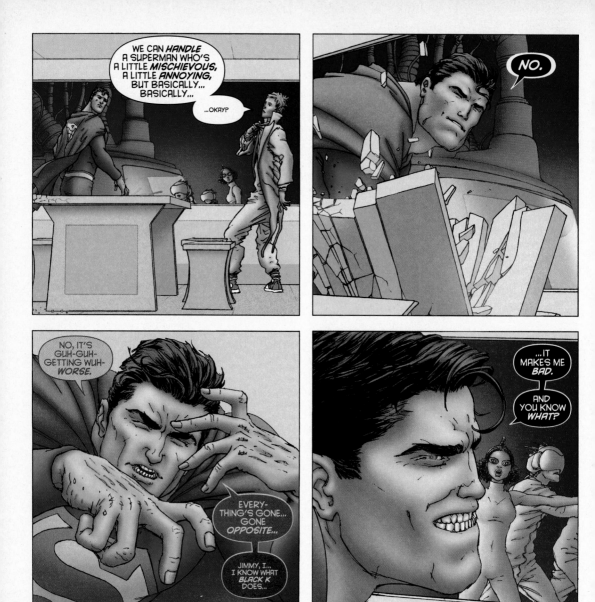

WE CAN *HANDLE* A SUPERMAN WHO'S A LITTLE *MISCHIEVOUS*, A LITTLE *ANNOYING*, BUT BASICALLY... BASICALLY...

...OKAY?

NO.

NO, IT'S GUH-GUH-GETTING WUH-*WORSE.*

EVERY-THING'S GONE... GONE *OPPOSITE...*

JIMMY, I... I KNOW WHAT *BLACK K* DOES...

...IT MAKES ME *BAD.*

AND YOU KNOW *WHAT?*

PART OF ME IS STARTING TO LIKE THAT IDEA!

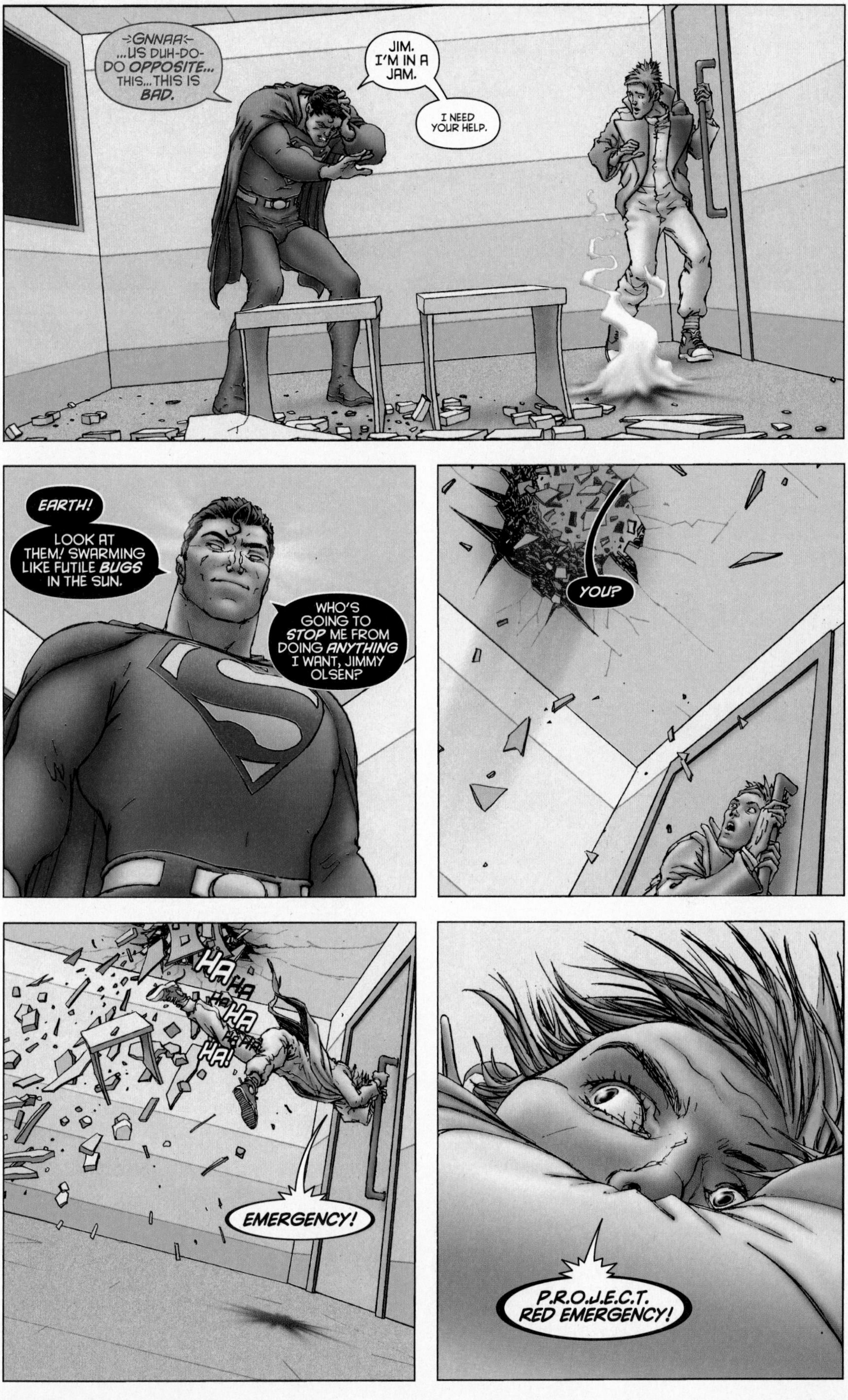
-GNNAA- ...US DUH-DO-DO OPPOSITE... THIS... THIS IS BAD.
JIM. I'M IN A JAM.
I NEED YOUR HELP.
EARTH!
LOOK AT THEM! SWARMING LIKE FUTILE BUGS IN THE SUN.
WHO'S GOING TO STOP ME FROM DOING ANYTHING I WANT, JIMMY OLSEN?
YOU?
HA HA HA HA HA HA HA!
EMERGENCY!
P.R.O.J.E.C.T. RED EMERGENCY!

SUPERMAN HIMSELF HELPED CREATE THREE *ANTI-SUPERMAN* WEAPONS.

ONE WAS *KRYPTONITE-POWERED* AND IS CURRENTLY *INEFFECTIVE.*

THE *SECOND* WEAPON, THIS *PHANTOM ZONE CANNON* WILL SHORTLY BE RELEASED FROM LEAD SHIELDING AND *FIRED* FROM AN ORBITAL LOCATION.

THE *PHANTOM ZONE!*

BUT THAT'S A *NO EXIT* RIDE TO *OBLIVION!*

WHAT *CHOICE* WOULD WE HAVE, FACED WITH AN *EVIL* SUPERMAN?

HE COULD CRACK THE *EARTH* IN HALF.

HE COULD *ENSLAVE* HUMANITY.

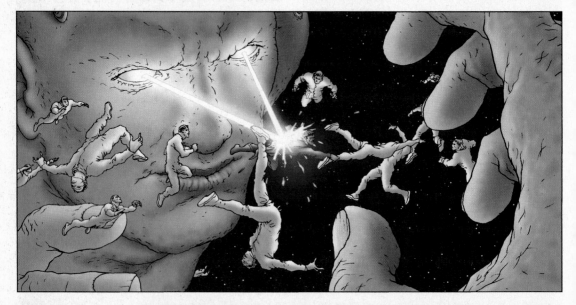

HE'S SAVED MY LIFE A ZILLION TIMES.

WHAT ABOUT THE *THIRD* WEAPON?

IT'S *DOOMSDAY,* RIGHT?

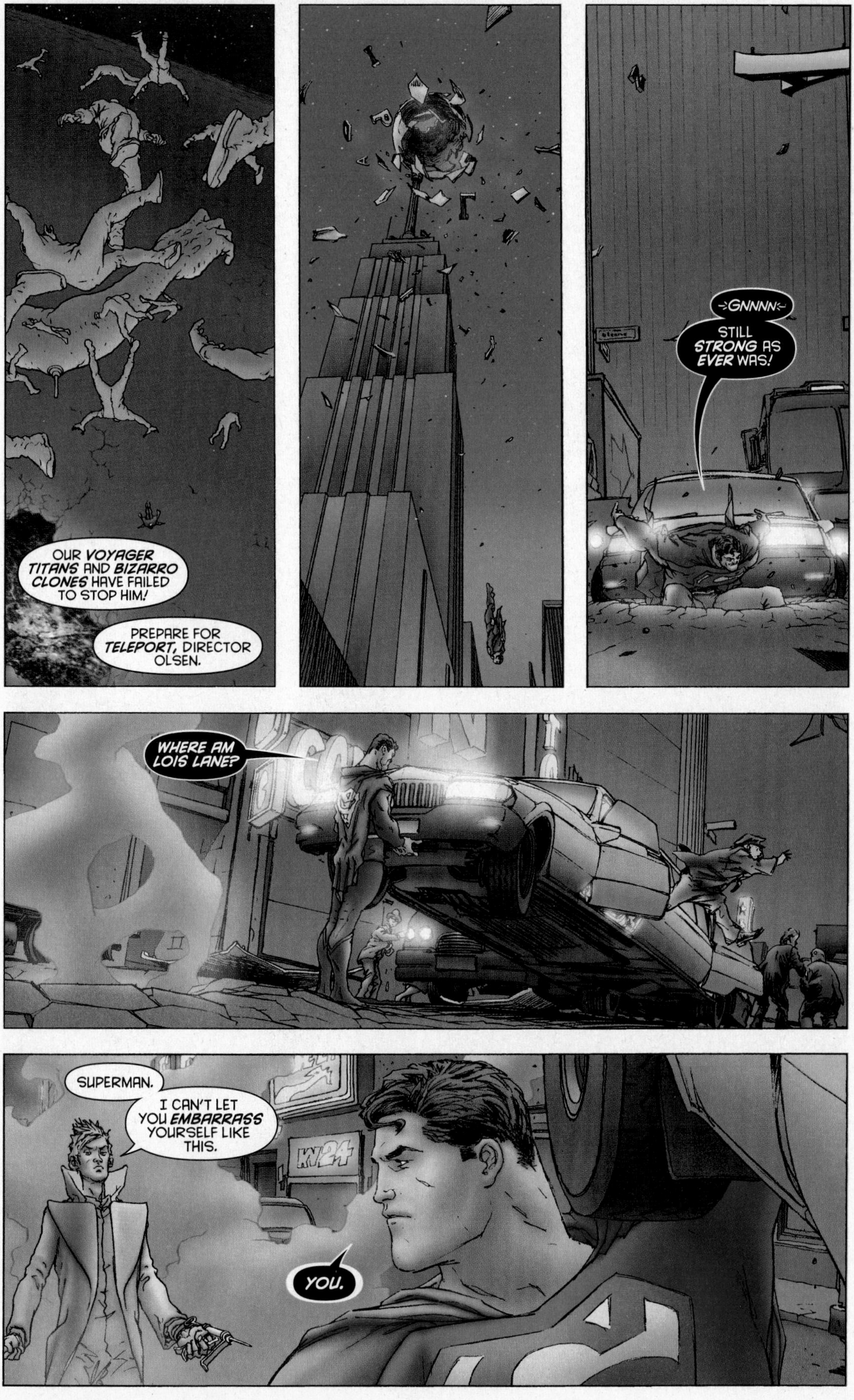
OUR VOYAGER TITANS AND BIZARRO CLONES HAVE FAILED TO STOP HIM!
PREPARE FOR TELEPORT, DIRECTOR OLSEN.
GNNNN
STILL STRONG AS EVER WAS!
WHERE AM LOIS LANE?
SUPERMAN.
I CAN'T LET YOU EMBARRASS YOURSELF LIKE THIS.
YOU.

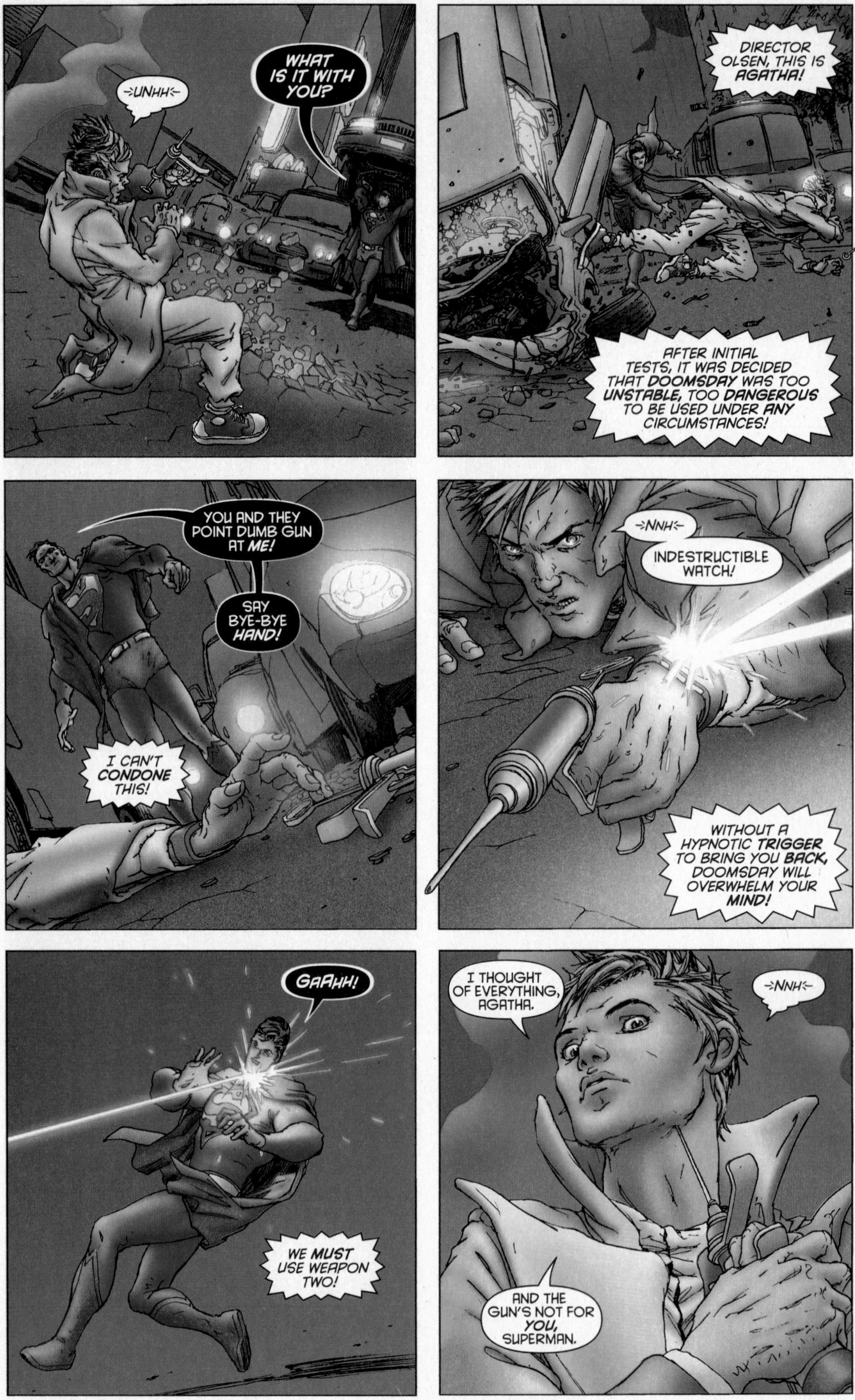

WHAT IS IT WITH YOU?
=UNHH=
DIRECTOR OLSEN, THIS IS AGATHA!
AFTER INITIAL TESTS, IT WAS DECIDED THAT DOOMSDAY WAS TOO UNSTABLE, TOO DANGEROUS TO BE USED UNDER ANY CIRCUMSTANCES!
YOU AND THEY POINT DUMB GUN AT ME!
SAY BYE-BYE HAND!
I CAN'T CONDONE THIS!
=NNH=
INDESTRUCTIBLE WATCH!
WITHOUT A HYPNOTIC TRIGGER TO BRING YOU BACK, DOOMSDAY WILL OVERWHELM YOUR MIND!
GAAHH!
WE MUST USE WEAPON TWO!
I THOUGHT OF EVERYTHING, AGATHA.
=NNH=
AND THE GUN'S NOT FOR YOU, SUPERMAN.

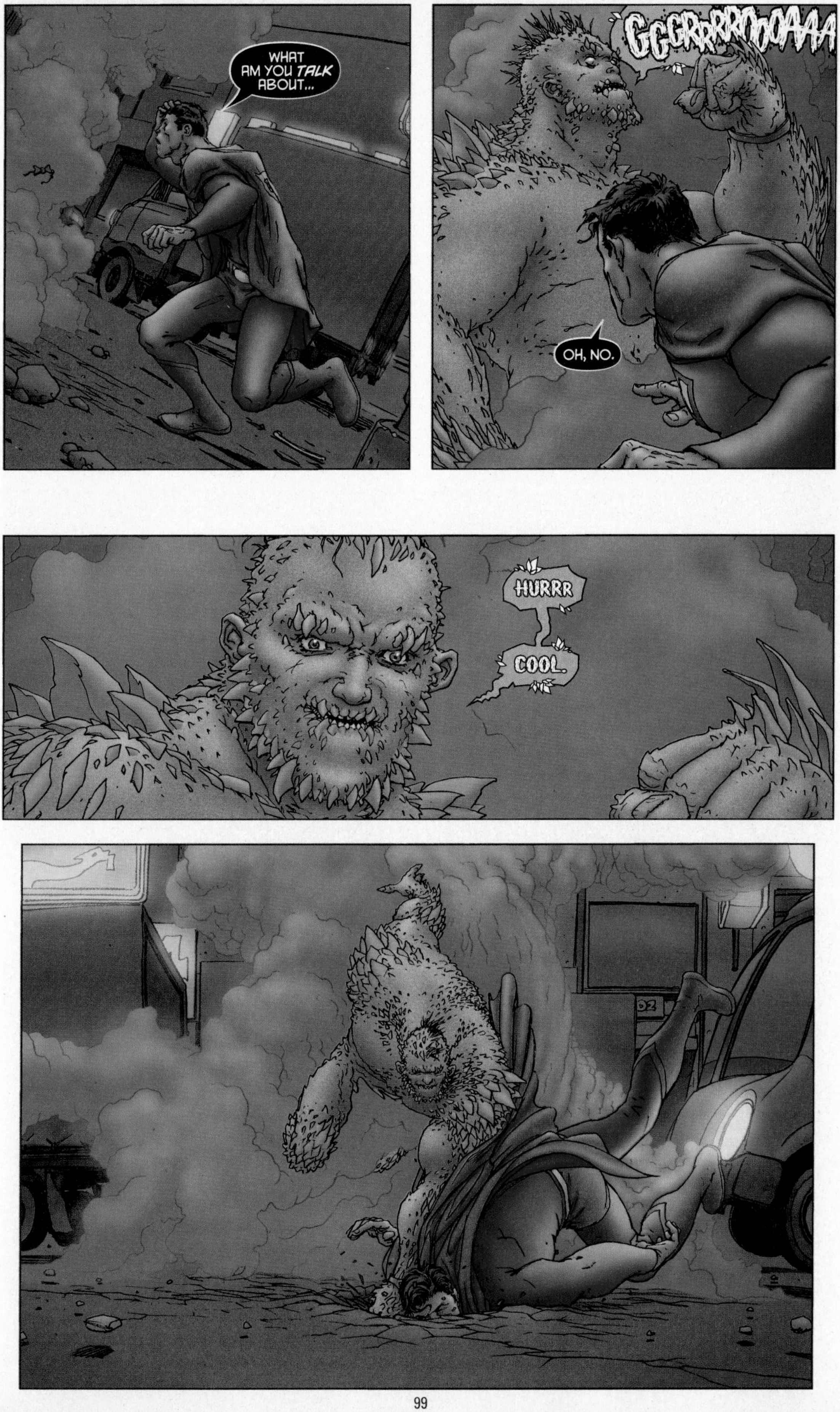
WHAT AM YOU *TALK* ABOUT...
GGGRRRRRROOAAAA
OH, NO.
HURRR
COOL.

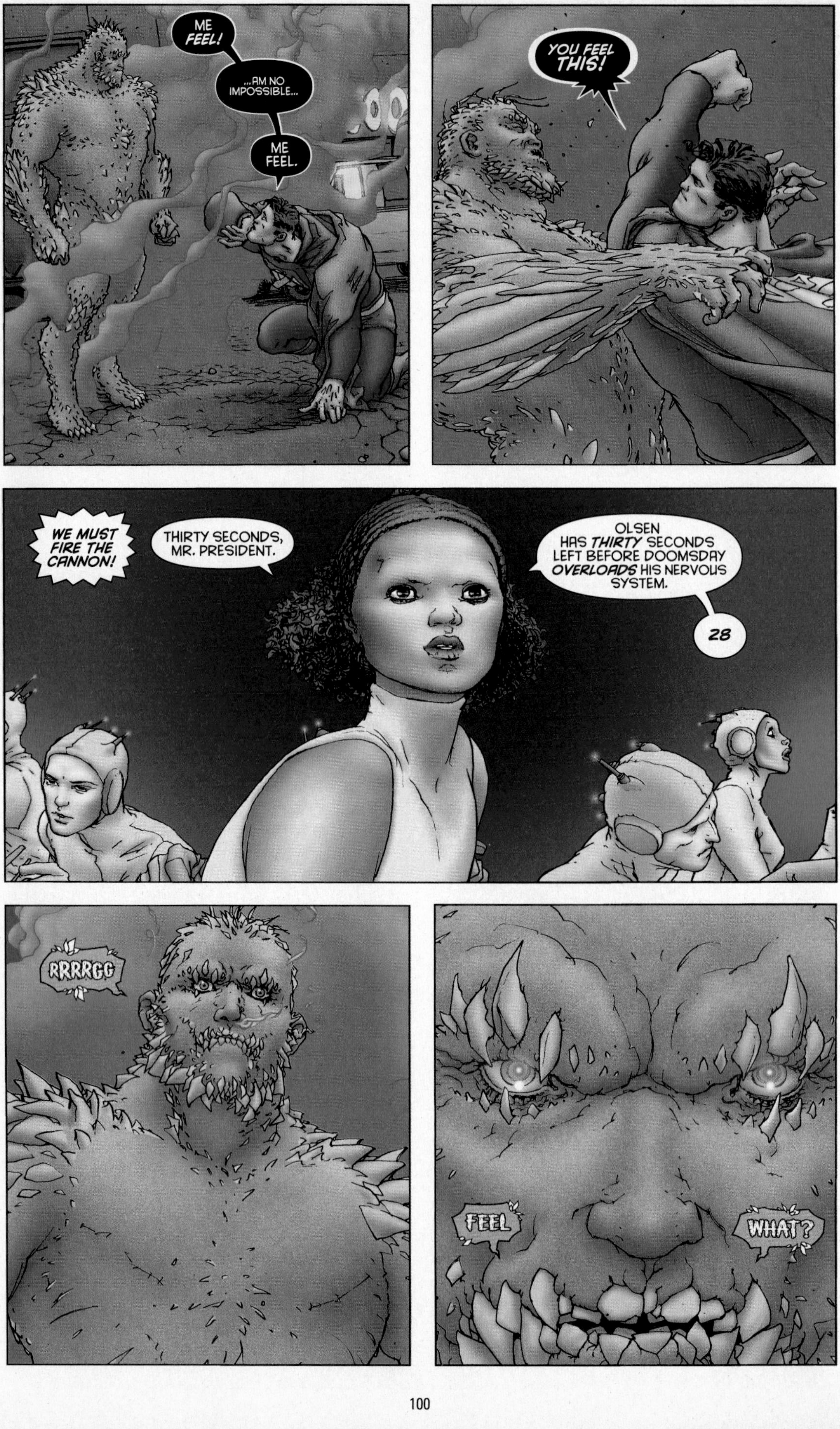
ME FEEL!
...AM NO IMPOSSIBLE...
ME FEEL.
YOU FEEL THIS!
WE MUST FIRE THE CANNON!
THIRTY SECONDS, MR. PRESIDENT.
OLSEN HAS THIRTY SECONDS LEFT BEFORE DOOMSDAY OVERLOADS HIS NERVOUS SYSTEM.
28
RRRRGG
FEEL
WHAT?

WHAT AM HAPPEN TO ME?
NO FAIR!
ME GET WEAKER...
ZEE ZEEE
ME AM DIE NOW?
NO DIE!
ME SCARED...
ZEEE ZEEEE ZEEE
ZEEE ZEEEE ZEEE ZEEEE
NO DIE.
NO CAN DIE.
AM SUPERMAN...
...NO CAN DIE.
ZEEE ZEEEE ZEEE ZEEEE

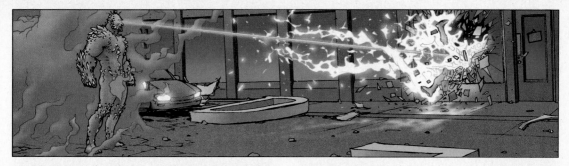

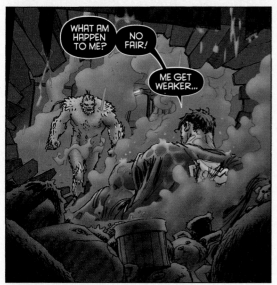

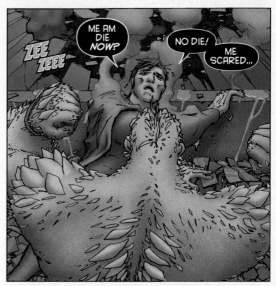

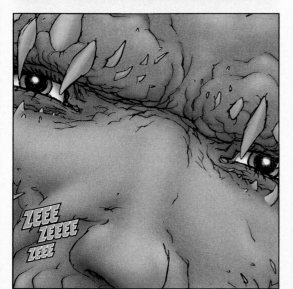

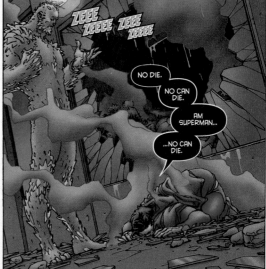

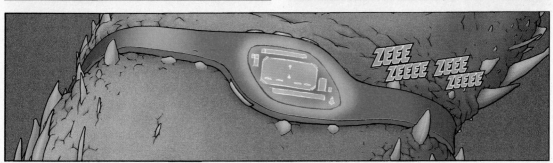

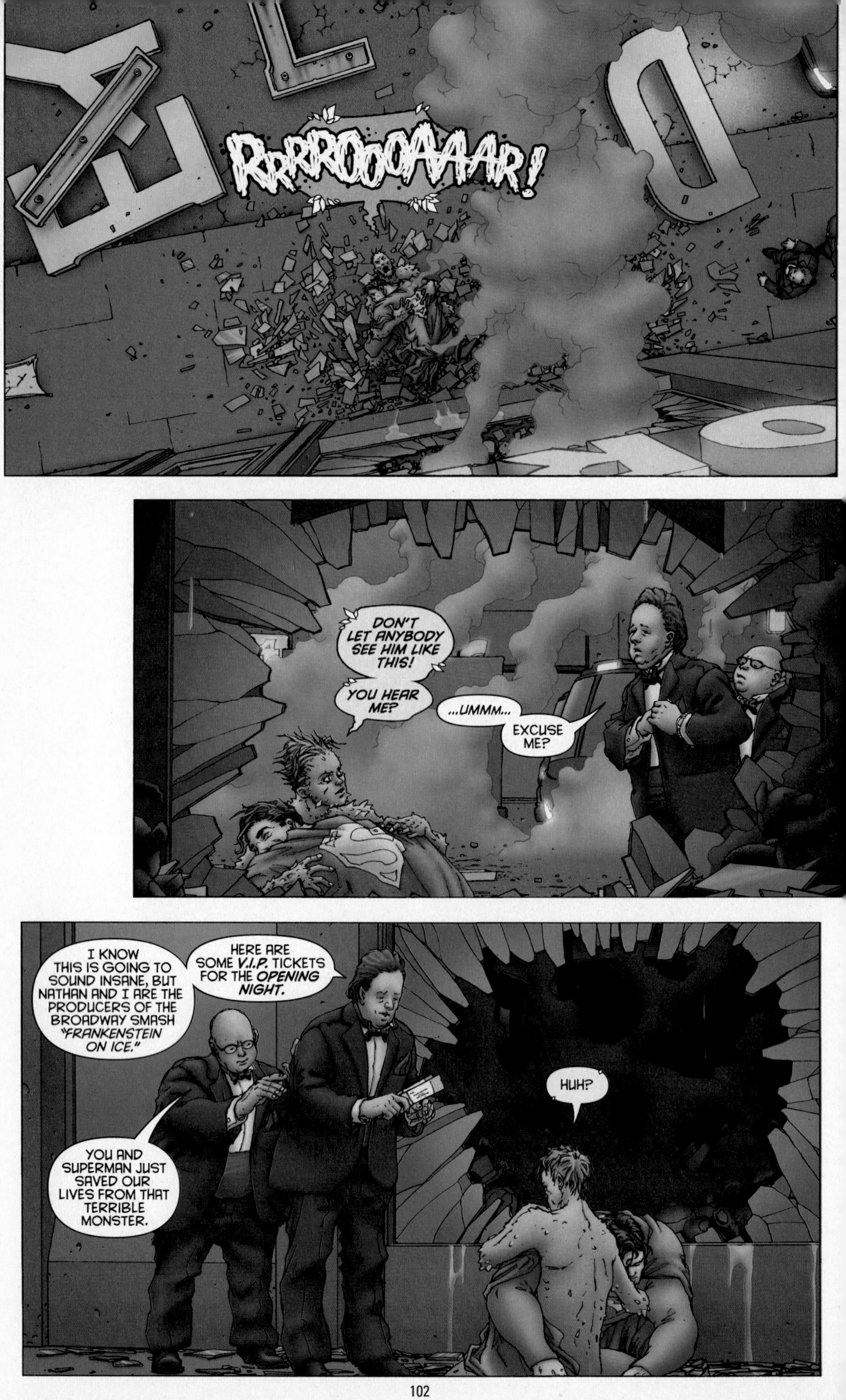
RRRROOOAAAR!
DON'T LET ANYBODY SEE HIM LIKE THIS!
YOU HEAR ME?
...UMMM... EXCUSE ME?
I KNOW THIS IS GOING TO SOUND INSANE, BUT NATHAN AND I ARE THE PRODUCERS OF THE BROADWAY SMASH "FRANKENSTEIN ON ICE."
HERE ARE SOME V.I.P. TICKETS FOR THE OPENING NIGHT.
YOU AND SUPERMAN JUST SAVED OUR LIVES FROM THAT TERRIBLE MONSTER.
HUH?

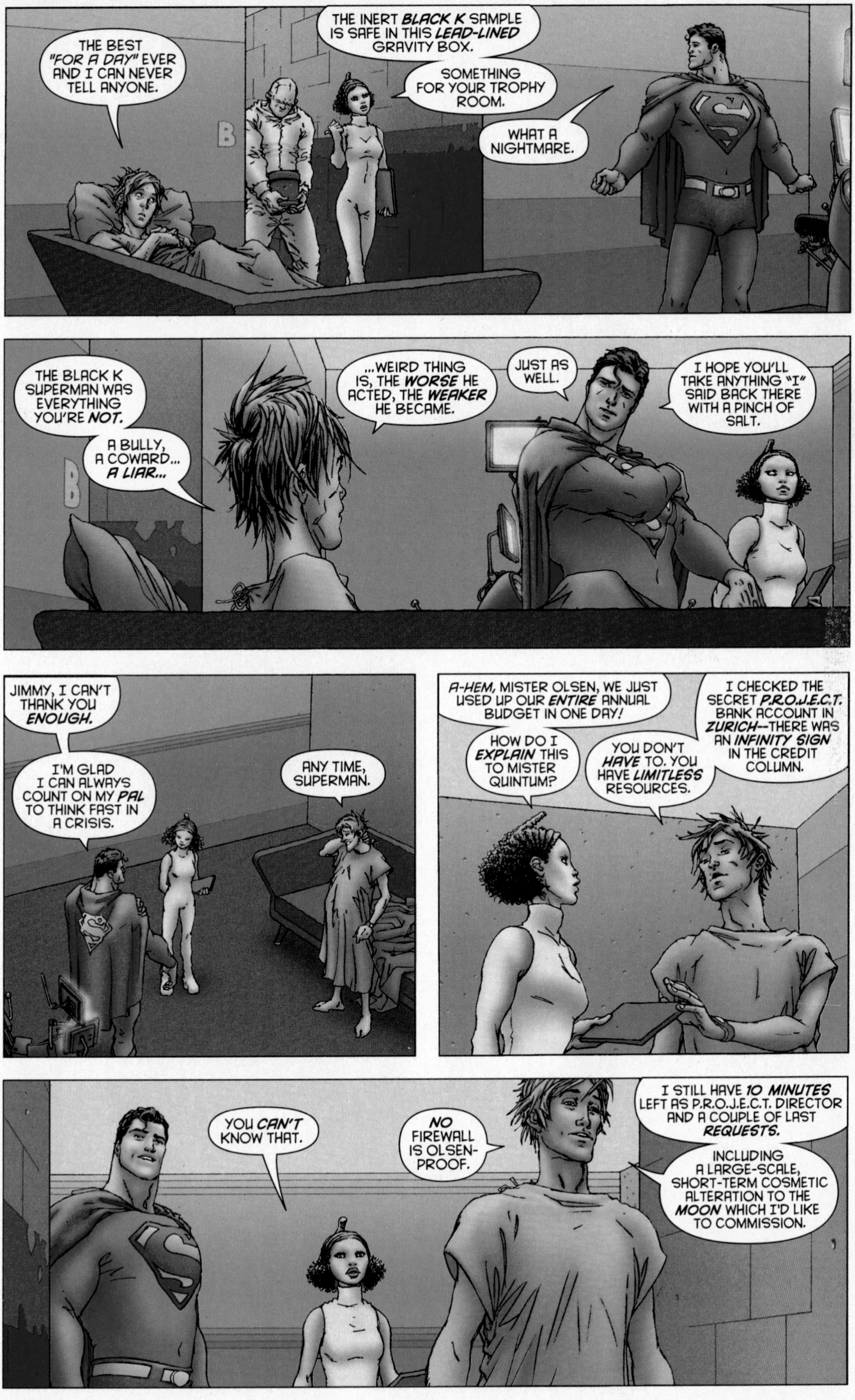
THE BEST "FOR A DAY" EVER AND I CAN NEVER TELL ANYONE.
THE INERT BLACK K SAMPLE IS SAFE IN THIS LEAD-LINED GRAVITY BOX.
SOMETHING FOR YOUR TROPHY ROOM.
WHAT A NIGHTMARE.
THE BLACK K SUPERMAN WAS EVERYTHING YOU'RE NOT.
A BULLY, A COWARD... A LIAR...
...WEIRD THING IS, THE WORSE HE ACTED, THE WEAKER HE BECAME.
JUST AS WELL.
I HOPE YOU'LL TAKE ANYTHING "I" SAID BACK THERE WITH A PINCH OF SALT.
JIMMY, I CAN'T THANK YOU ENOUGH.
I'M GLAD I CAN ALWAYS COUNT ON MY PAL TO THINK FAST IN A CRISIS.
ANY TIME, SUPERMAN.
A-HEM, MISTER OLSEN, WE JUST USED UP OUR ENTIRE ANNUAL BUDGET IN ONE DAY!
HOW DO I EXPLAIN THIS TO MISTER QUINTUM?
YOU DON'T HAVE TO. YOU HAVE LIMITLESS RESOURCES.
I CHECKED THE SECRET P.R.O.J.E.C.T. BANK ACCOUNT IN ZURICH--THERE WAS AN INFINITY SIGN IN THE CREDIT COLUMN.
YOU CAN'T KNOW THAT.
NO FIREWALL IS OLSEN-PROOF.
I STILL HAVE 10 MINUTES LEFT AS P.R.O.J.E.C.T. DIRECTOR AND A COUPLE OF LAST REQUESTS.
INCLUDING A LARGE-SCALE, SHORT-TERM COSMETIC ALTERATION TO THE MOON WHICH I'D LIKE TO COMMISSION.

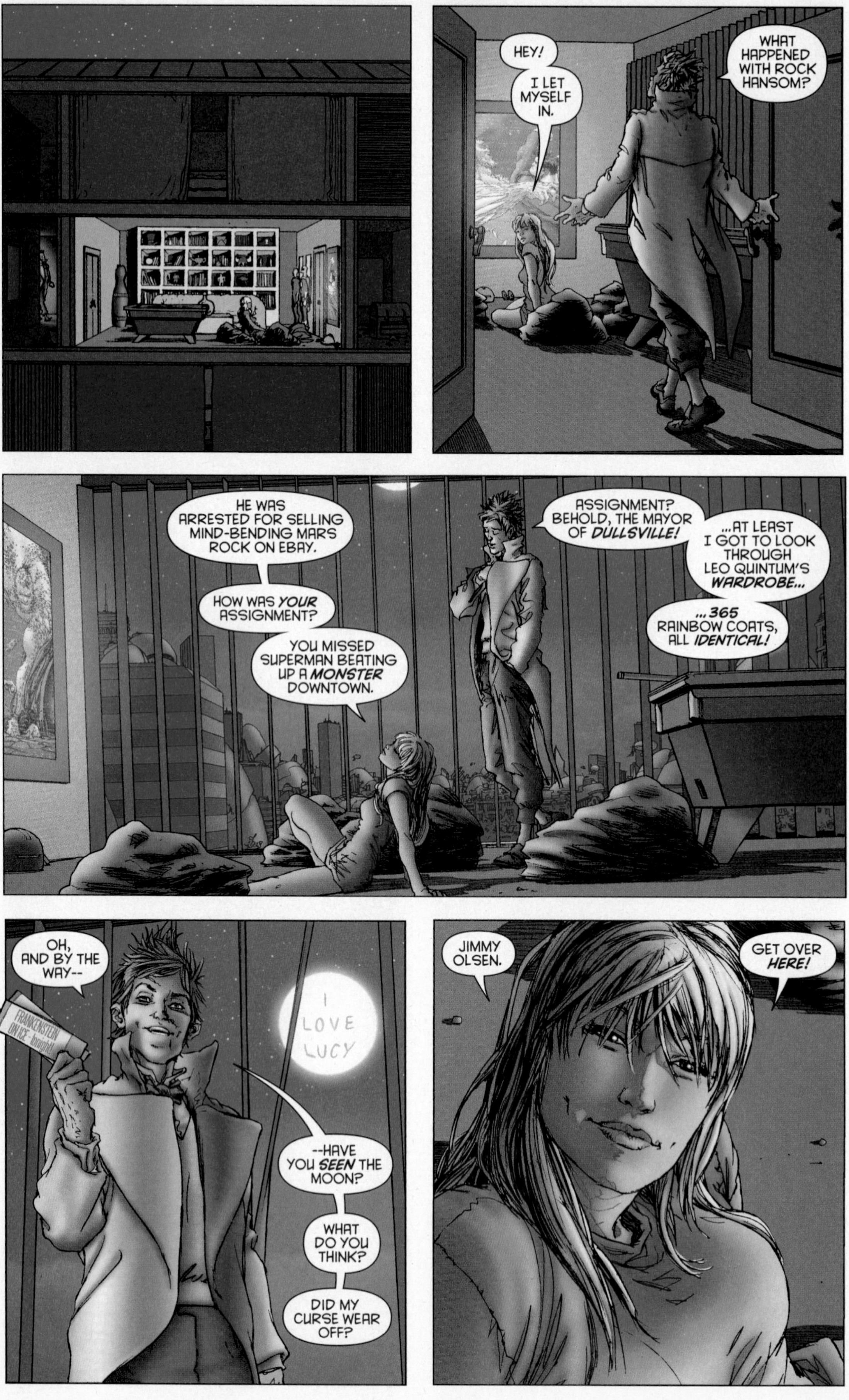
HEY!
I LET MYSELF IN.
WHAT HAPPENED WITH ROCK HANSOM?
HE WAS ARRESTED FOR SELLING MIND-BENDING MARS ROCK ON EBAY.
HOW WAS *YOUR* ASSIGNMENT?
YOU MISSED SUPERMAN BEATING UP A *MONSTER* DOWNTOWN.
ASSIGNMENT? BEHOLD, THE MAYOR OF *DULLSVILLE!*
...AT LEAST I GOT TO LOOK THROUGH LEO QUINTUM'S *WARDROBE...*
...365 RAINBOW COATS, ALL *IDENTICAL!*
OH, AND BY THE WAY--
FRANKENSTEIN ON ICE–tonight!
I LOVE LUCY
--HAVE YOU *SEEN* THE MOON?
WHAT DO YOU THINK?
DID MY CURSE WEAR OFF?
JIMMY OLSEN.
GET OVER *HERE!*

Episode 5

THE GOSPEL ACCORDING TO LEX LUTHOR

Cover FRANK QUITELY

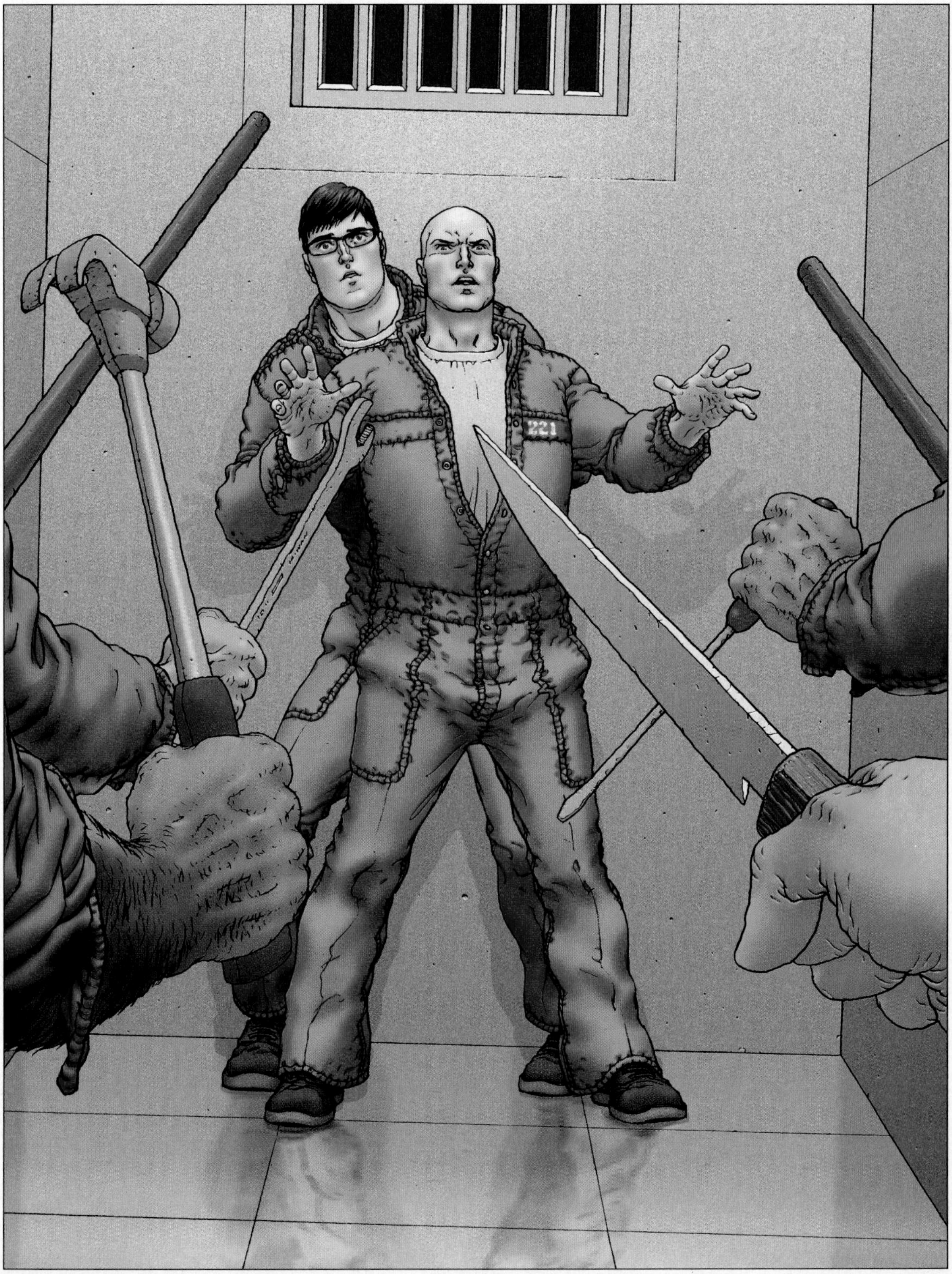
221

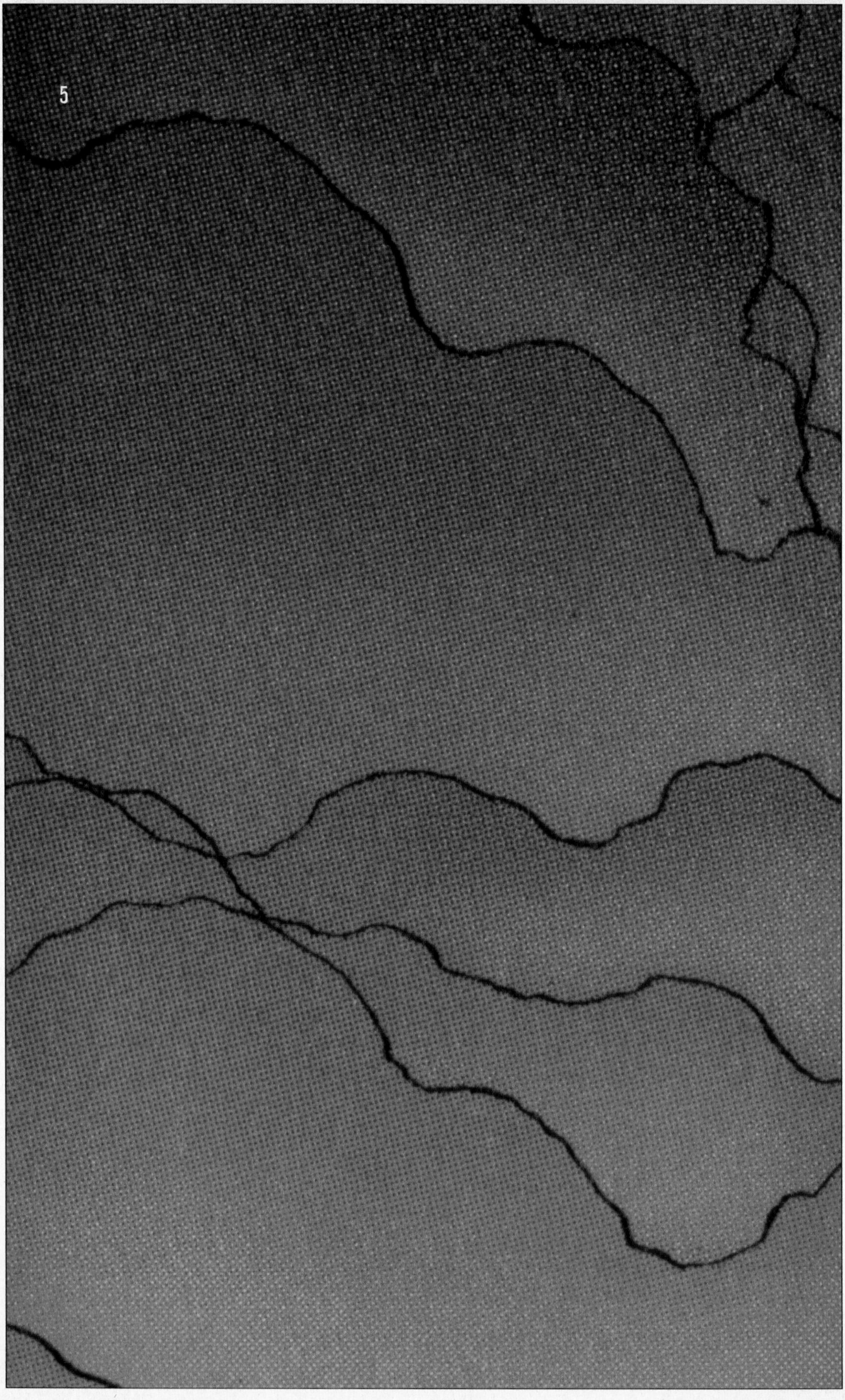
5

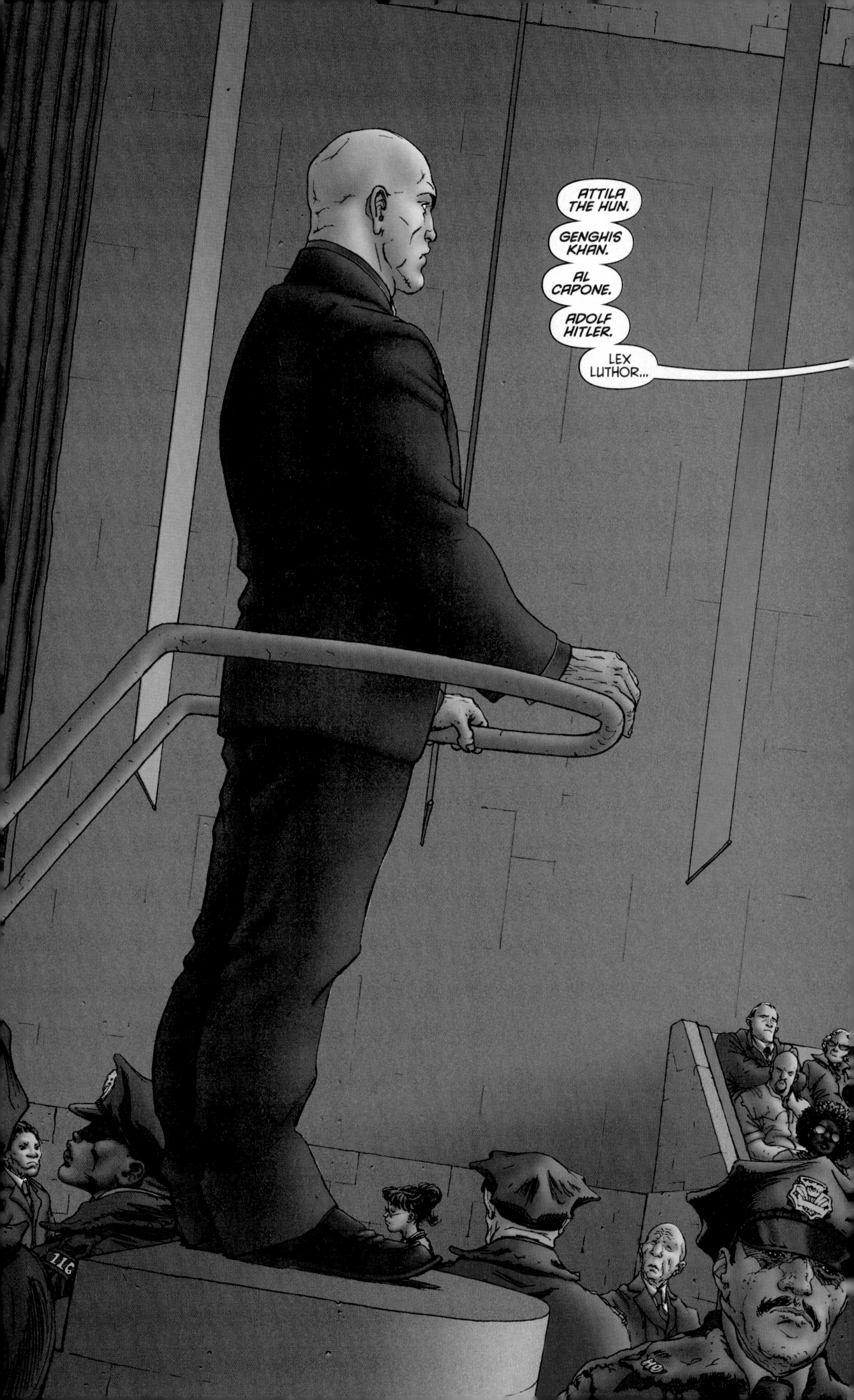
ATTILA THE HUN.
GENGHIS KHAN.
AL CAPONE.
ADOLF HITLER.
LEX LUTHOR...

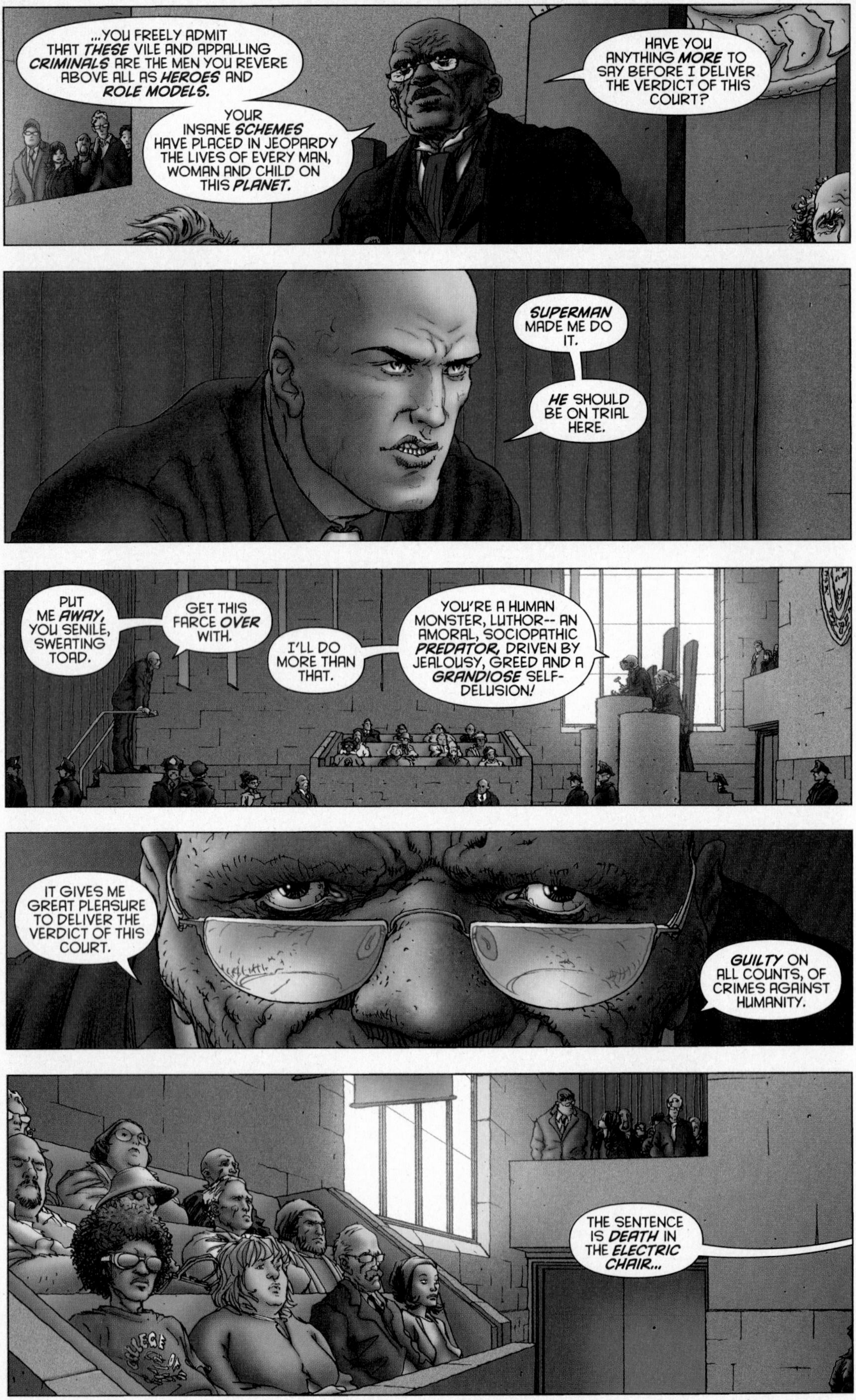
...YOU FREELY ADMIT THAT THESE VILE AND APPALLING CRIMINALS ARE THE MEN YOU REVERE ABOVE ALL AS HEROES AND ROLE MODELS.
YOUR INSANE SCHEMES HAVE PLACED IN JEOPARDY THE LIVES OF EVERY MAN, WOMAN AND CHILD ON THIS PLANET.
HAVE YOU ANYTHING MORE TO SAY BEFORE I DELIVER THE VERDICT OF THIS COURT?
SUPERMAN MADE ME DO IT.
HE SHOULD BE ON TRIAL HERE.
PUT ME AWAY, YOU SENILE, SWEATING TOAD.
GET THIS FARCE OVER WITH.
I'LL DO MORE THAN THAT.
YOU'RE A HUMAN MONSTER, LUTHOR-- AN AMORAL, SOCIOPATHIC PREDATOR, DRIVEN BY JEALOUSY, GREED AND A GRANDIOSE SELF-DELUSION!
IT GIVES ME GREAT PLEASURE TO DELIVER THE VERDICT OF THIS COURT.
GUILTY ON ALL COUNTS, OF CRIMES AGAINST HUMANITY.
THE SENTENCE IS DEATH IN THE ELECTRIC CHAIR...

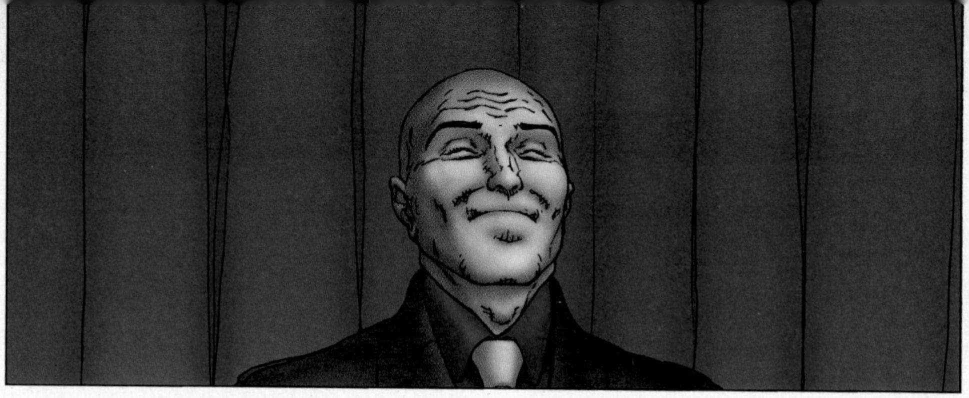

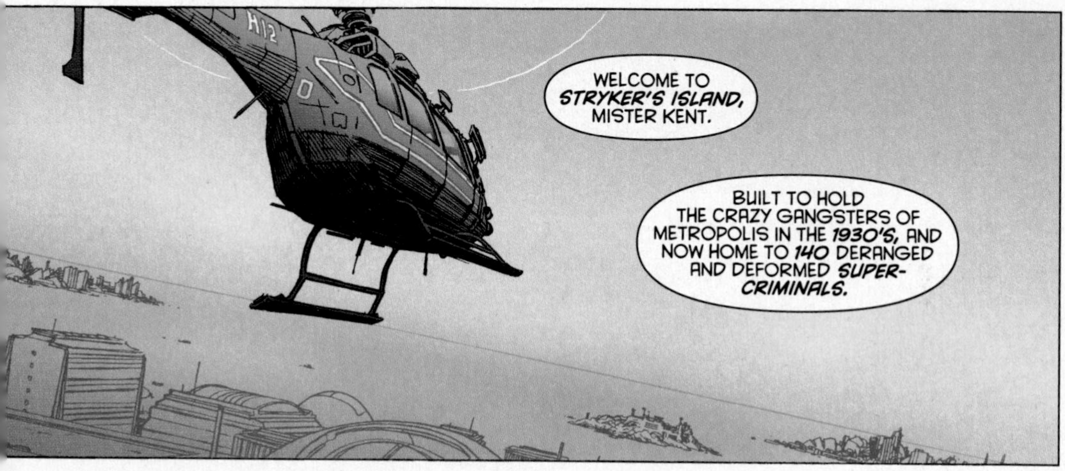
WELCOME TO *STRYKER'S ISLAND,* MISTER KENT.
BUILT TO HOLD THE CRAZY GANGSTERS OF METROPOLIS IN THE *1930'S,* AND NOW HOME TO *140* DERANGED AND DEFORMED *SUPER-CRIMINALS.*

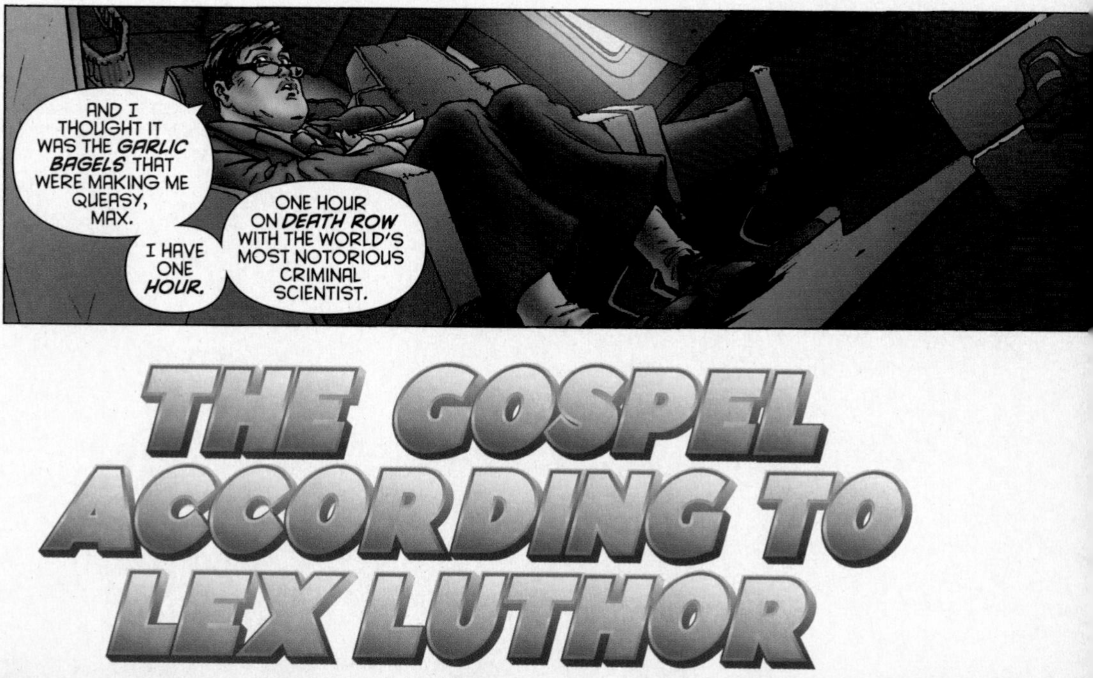
AND I THOUGHT IT WAS THE *GARLIC BAGELS* THAT WERE MAKING ME QUEASY, MAX.
I HAVE ONE *HOUR.*
ONE HOUR ON *DEATH ROW* WITH THE WORLD'S MOST NOTORIOUS CRIMINAL SCIENTIST.

THE GOSPEL ACCORDING TO LEX LUTHOR

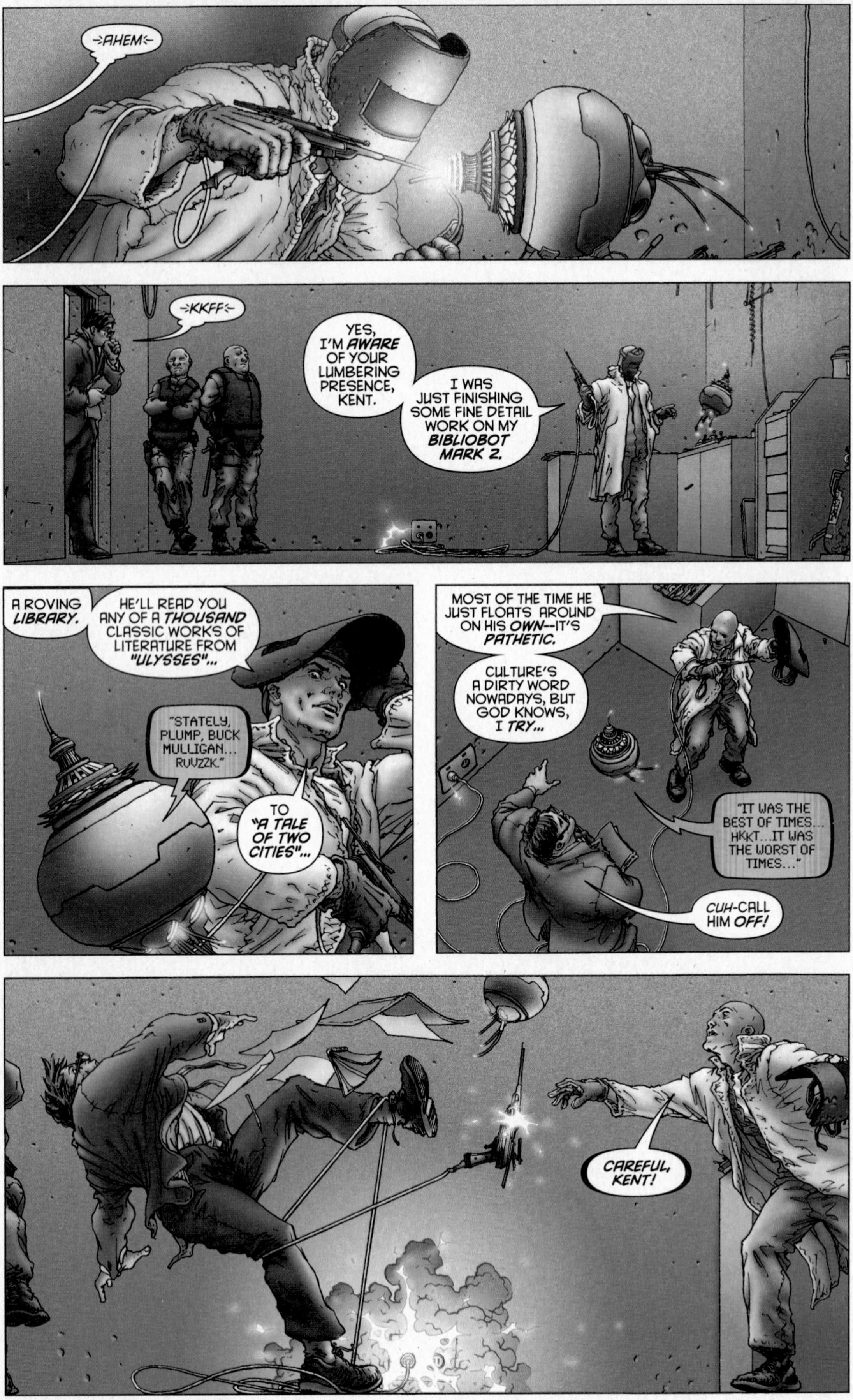

AHEM
KKFF
YES, I'M AWARE OF YOUR LUMBERING PRESENCE, KENT.
I WAS JUST FINISHING SOME FINE DETAIL WORK ON MY BIBLIOBOT MARK 2.
A ROVING LIBRARY.
HE'LL READ YOU ANY OF A THOUSAND CLASSIC WORKS OF LITERATURE FROM "ULYSSES"...
"STATELY, PLUMP, BUCK MULLIGAN... RUUZZK."
TO "A TALE OF TWO CITIES"...
MOST OF THE TIME HE JUST FLOATS AROUND ON HIS OWN--IT'S PATHETIC.
CULTURE'S A DIRTY WORD NOWADAYS, BUT GOD KNOWS, I TRY...
"IT WAS THE BEST OF TIMES... HKKT...IT WAS THE WORST OF TIMES..."
CUH-CALL HIM OFF!
CAREFUL, KENT!

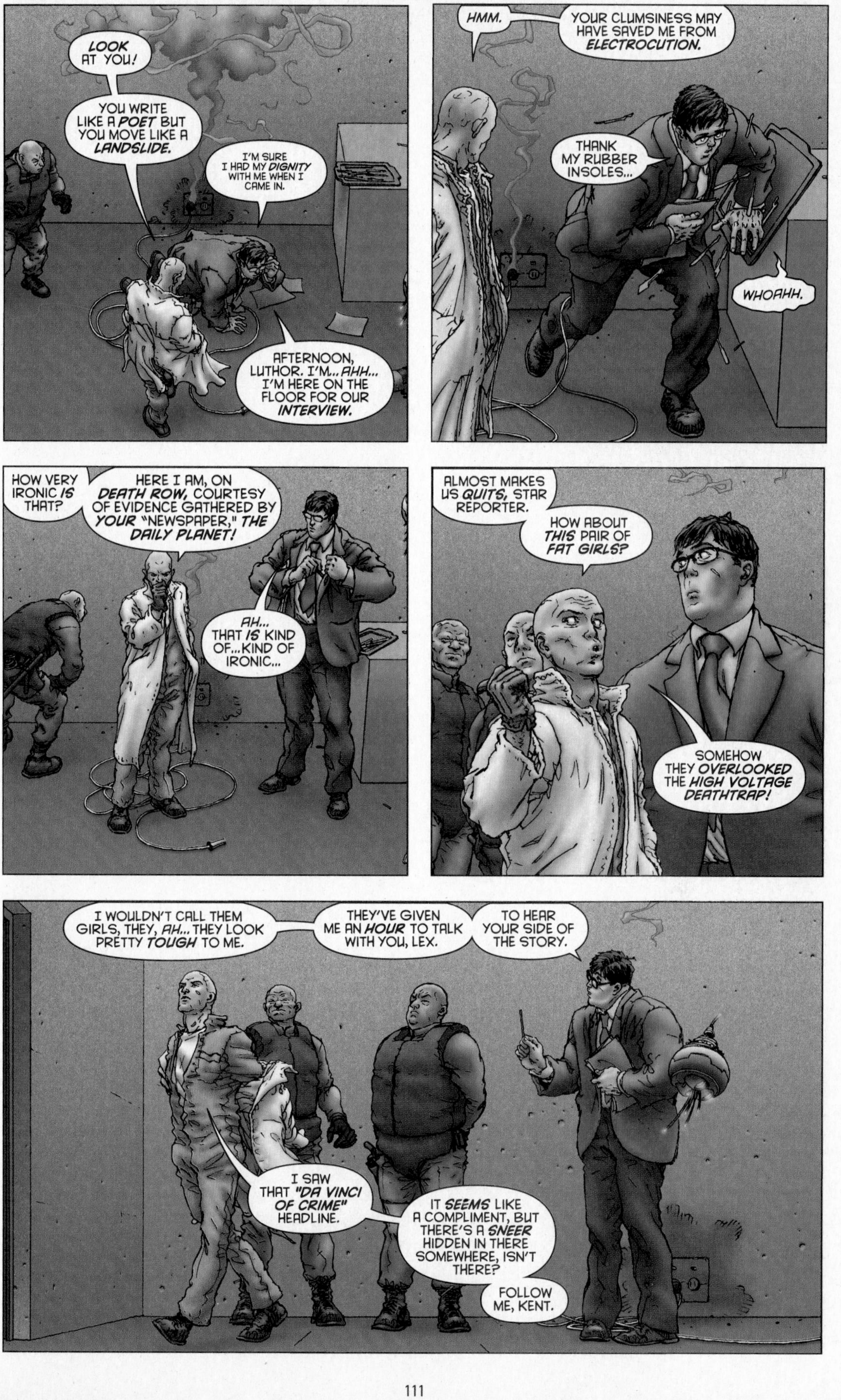
LOOK AT YOU!
YOU WRITE LIKE A POET BUT YOU MOVE LIKE A LANDSLIDE.
I'M SURE I HAD MY DIGNITY WITH ME WHEN I CAME IN.
AFTERNOON, LUTHOR. I'M... AHH... I'M HERE ON THE FLOOR FOR OUR INTERVIEW.
HMM.
YOUR CLUMSINESS MAY HAVE SAVED ME FROM ELECTROCUTION.
THANK MY RUBBER INSOLES...
WHOAHH.
HOW VERY IRONIC IS THAT?
HERE I AM, ON DEATH ROW, COURTESY OF EVIDENCE GATHERED BY YOUR "NEWSPAPER," THE DAILY PLANET!
AH... THAT IS KIND OF...KIND OF IRONIC...
ALMOST MAKES US QUITS, STAR REPORTER.
HOW ABOUT THIS PAIR OF FAT GIRLS?
SOMEHOW THEY OVERLOOKED THE HIGH VOLTAGE DEATHTRAP!
I WOULDN'T CALL THEM GIRLS, THEY, AH... THEY LOOK PRETTY TOUGH TO ME.
THEY'VE GIVEN ME AN HOUR TO TALK WITH YOU, LEX.
TO HEAR YOUR SIDE OF THE STORY.
I SAW THAT "DA VINCI OF CRIME" HEADLINE.
IT SEEMS LIKE A COMPLIMENT, BUT THERE'S A SNEER HIDDEN IN THERE SOMEWHERE, ISN'T THERE?
FOLLOW ME, KENT.

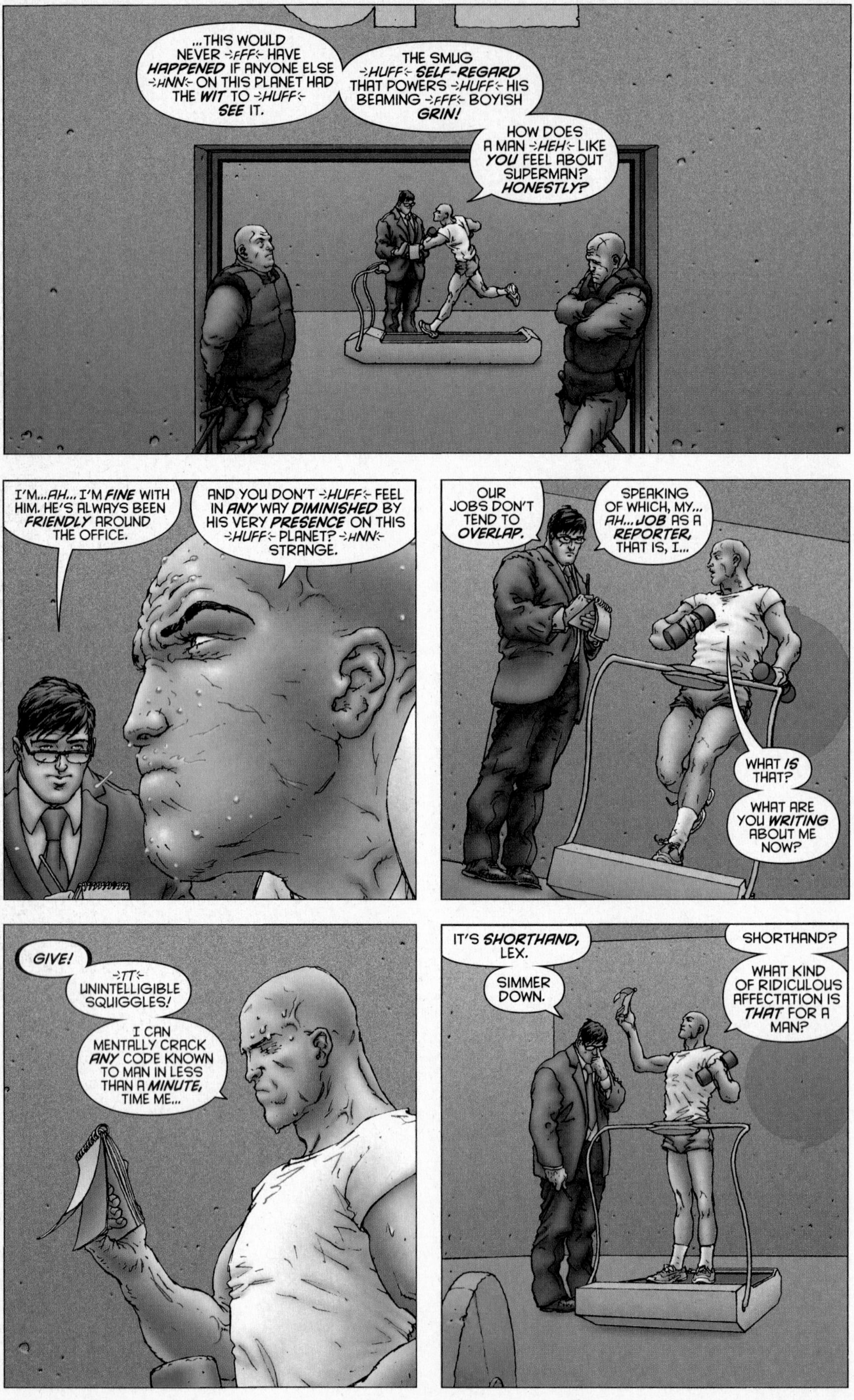
...THIS WOULD NEVER -FFF- HAVE HAPPENED IF ANYONE ELSE -HNN- ON THIS PLANET HAD THE WIT TO -HUFF- SEE IT.
THE SMUG -HUFF- SELF-REGARD THAT POWERS -HUFF- HIS BEAMING -FFF- BOYISH GRIN!
HOW DOES A MAN -HEH- LIKE YOU FEEL ABOUT SUPERMAN? HONESTLY?
I'M...AH... I'M FINE WITH HIM. HE'S ALWAYS BEEN FRIENDLY AROUND THE OFFICE.
AND YOU DON'T -HUFF- FEEL IN ANY WAY DIMINISHED BY HIS VERY PRESENCE ON THIS -HUFF- PLANET? -HNN- STRANGE.
OUR JOBS DON'T TEND TO OVERLAP.
SPEAKING OF WHICH, MY... AH... JOB AS A REPORTER, THAT IS, I...
WHAT IS THAT?
WHAT ARE YOU WRITING ABOUT ME NOW?
GIVE!
-TT- UNINTELLIGIBLE SQUIGGLES!
I CAN MENTALLY CRACK ANY CODE KNOWN TO MAN IN LESS THAN A MINUTE, TIME ME...
IT'S SHORTHAND, LEX.
SIMMER DOWN.
SHORTHAND?
WHAT KIND OF RIDICULOUS AFFECTATION IS THAT FOR A MAN?

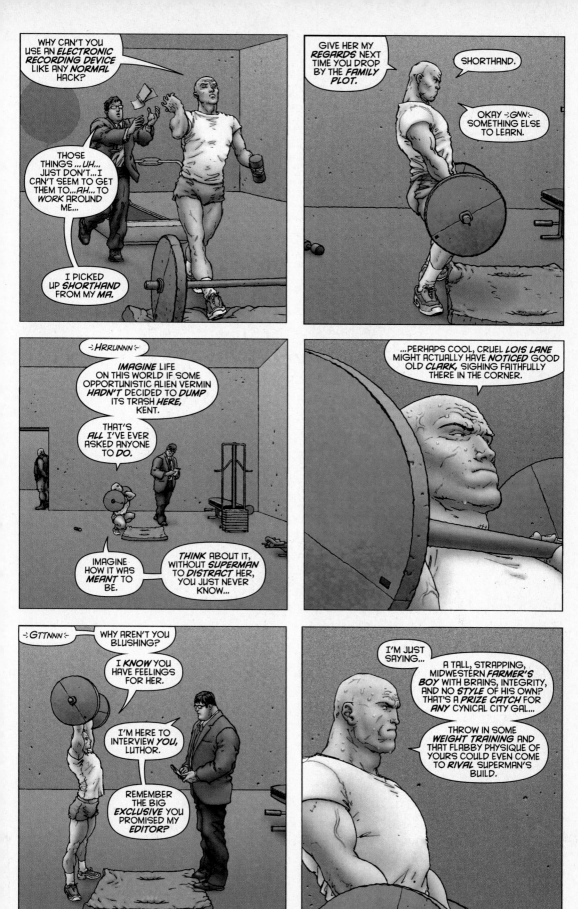

WHY CAN'T YOU USE AN *ELECTRONIC RECORDING DEVICE* LIKE ANY *NORMAL* HACK?

THOSE THINGS *...UH...* JUST DON'T...I CAN'T SEEM TO GET THEM TO...*AH...* TO *WORK* AROUND ME...

I PICKED UP *SHORTHAND* FROM MY *MA*.

GIVE HER MY *REGARDS* NEXT TIME YOU DROP BY THE *FAMILY PLOT*.

SHORTHAND.

OKAY ~*GNN*~ SOMETHING ELSE TO LEARN.

~*HRRUNNN*~

IMAGINE LIFE ON THIS WORLD IF SOME *OPPORTUNISTIC ALIEN VERMIN HADN'T* DECIDED TO *DUMP* ITS TRASH *HERE*, KENT.

THAT'S *ALL* I'VE EVER ASKED ANYONE TO *DO*.

IMAGINE HOW IT WAS *MEANT* TO BE.

THINK ABOUT IT, WITHOUT *SUPERMAN* TO *DISTRACT* HER, YOU JUST NEVER *KNOW*...

...PERHAPS COOL, CRUEL *LOIS LANE* MIGHT ACTUALLY HAVE *NOTICED* GOOD OLD *CLARK,* SIGHING FAITHFULLY THERE IN THE CORNER.

~*GTTNNN*~

WHY AREN'T YOU BLUSHING?

I *KNOW* YOU HAVE FEELINGS FOR HER.

I'M HERE TO INTERVIEW *YOU,* LUTHOR.

REMEMBER THE BIG *EXCLUSIVE* YOU PROMISED MY *EDITOR?*

I'M JUST SAYING...

A TALL, STRAPPING, MIDWESTERN *FARMER'S BOY* WITH BRAINS, INTEGRITY, AND NO *STYLE* OF HIS OWN? THAT'S A *PRIZE CATCH* FOR *ANY* CYNICAL CITY GAL...

THROW IN SOME *WEIGHT TRAINING* AND THAT FLABBY PHYSIQUE OF YOURS COULD EVEN COME TO *RIVAL* SUPERMAN'S BUILD.

113

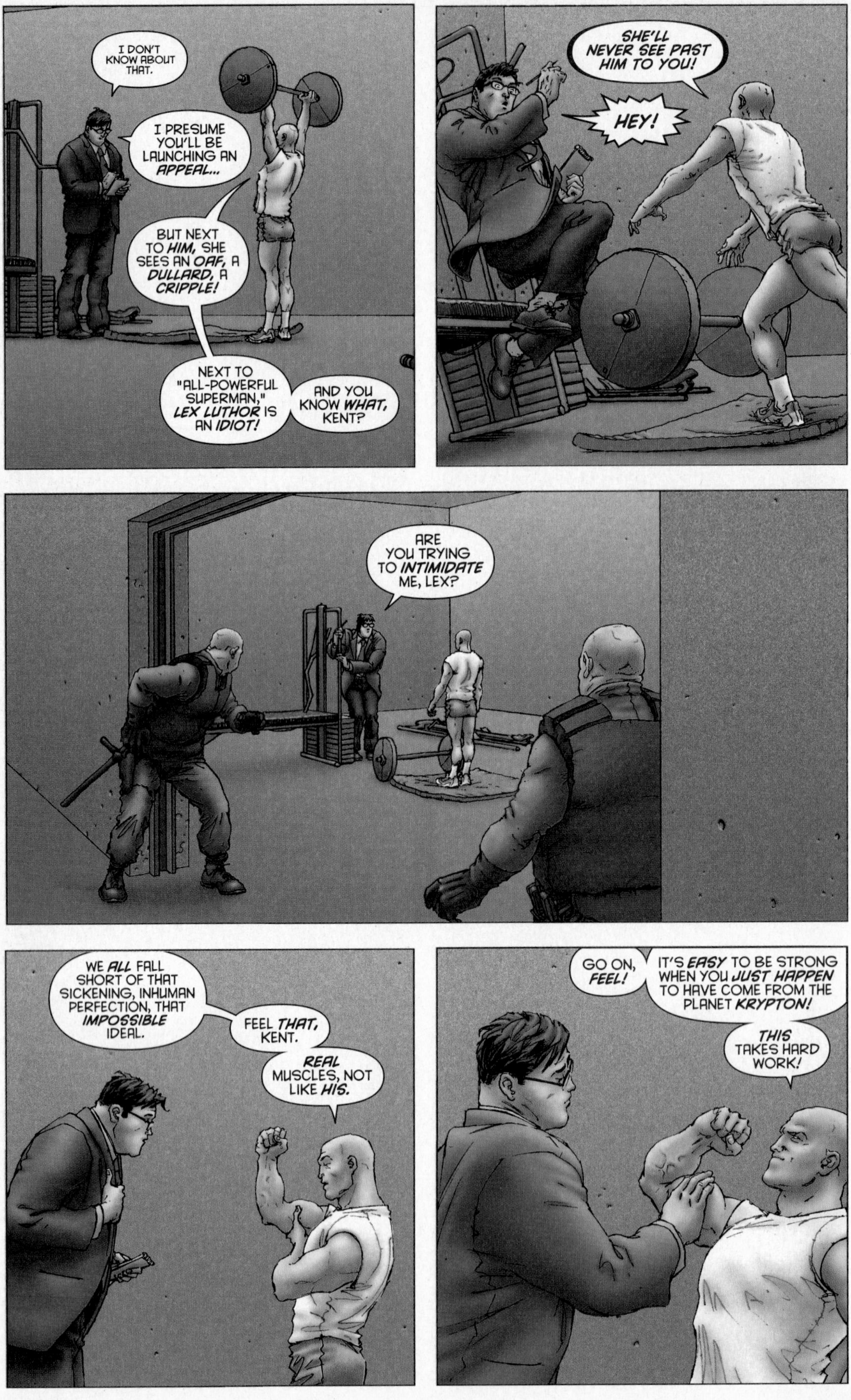

I DON'T KNOW ABOUT THAT.
I PRESUME YOU'LL BE LAUNCHING AN APPEAL...
BUT NEXT TO HIM, SHE SEES AN OAF, A DULLARD, A CRIPPLE!
NEXT TO "ALL-POWERFUL SUPERMAN," LEX LUTHOR IS AN IDIOT!
AND YOU KNOW WHAT, KENT?
SHE'LL NEVER SEE PAST HIM TO YOU!
HEY!
ARE YOU TRYING TO INTIMIDATE ME, LEX?
WE ALL FALL SHORT OF THAT SICKENING, INHUMAN PERFECTION, THAT IMPOSSIBLE IDEAL.
FEEL THAT, KENT.
REAL MUSCLES, NOT LIKE HIS.
GO ON, FEEL!
IT'S EASY TO BE STRONG WHEN YOU JUST HAPPEN TO HAVE COME FROM THE PLANET KRYPTON!
THIS TAKES HARD WORK!

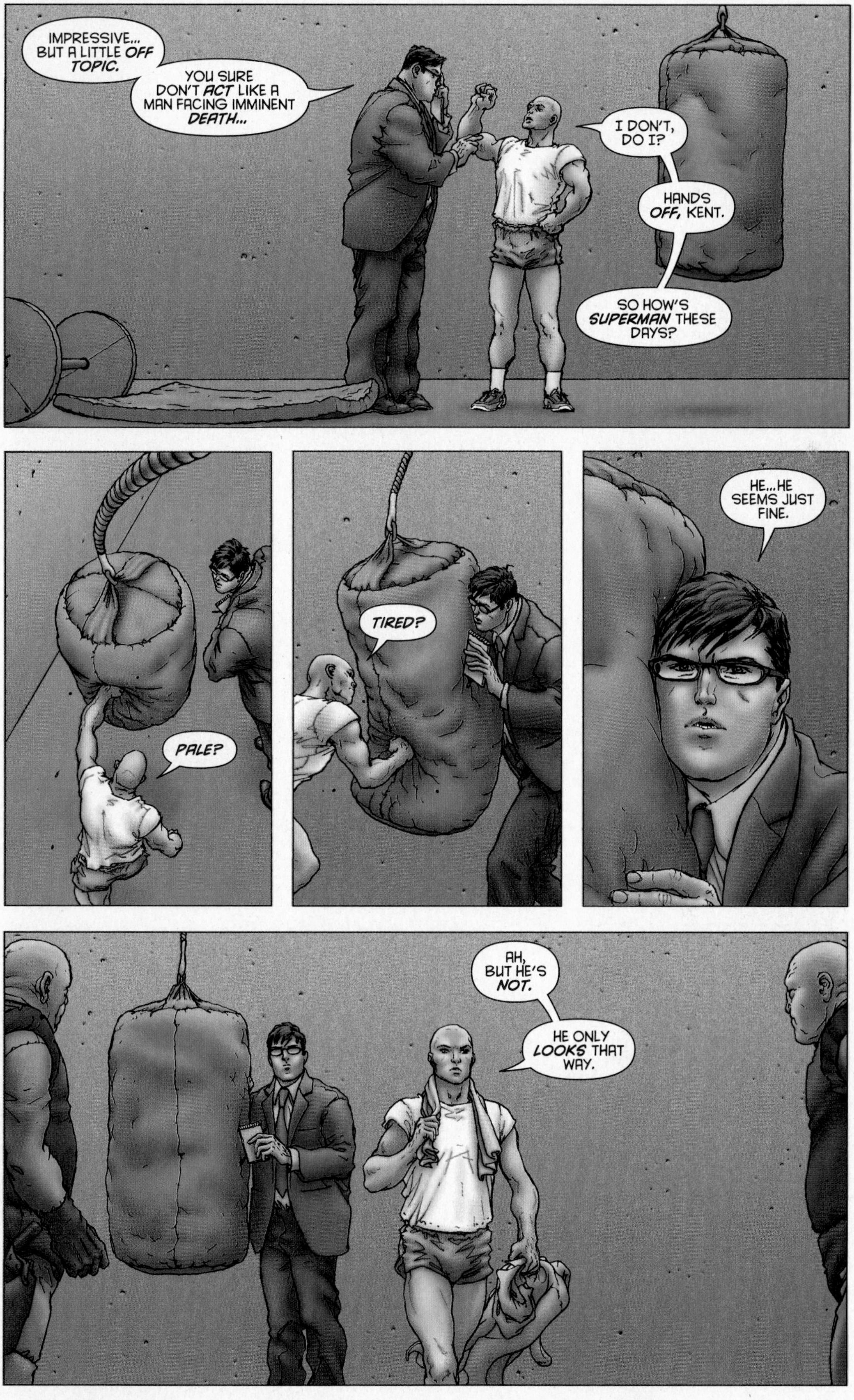
IMPRESSIVE... BUT A LITTLE OFF TOPIC.
YOU SURE DON'T ACT LIKE A MAN FACING IMMINENT DEATH...
I DON'T, DO I?
HANDS OFF, KENT.
SO HOW'S SUPERMAN THESE DAYS?
PALE?
TIRED?
HE...HE SEEMS JUST FINE.
AH, BUT HE'S NOT.
HE ONLY LOOKS THAT WAY.

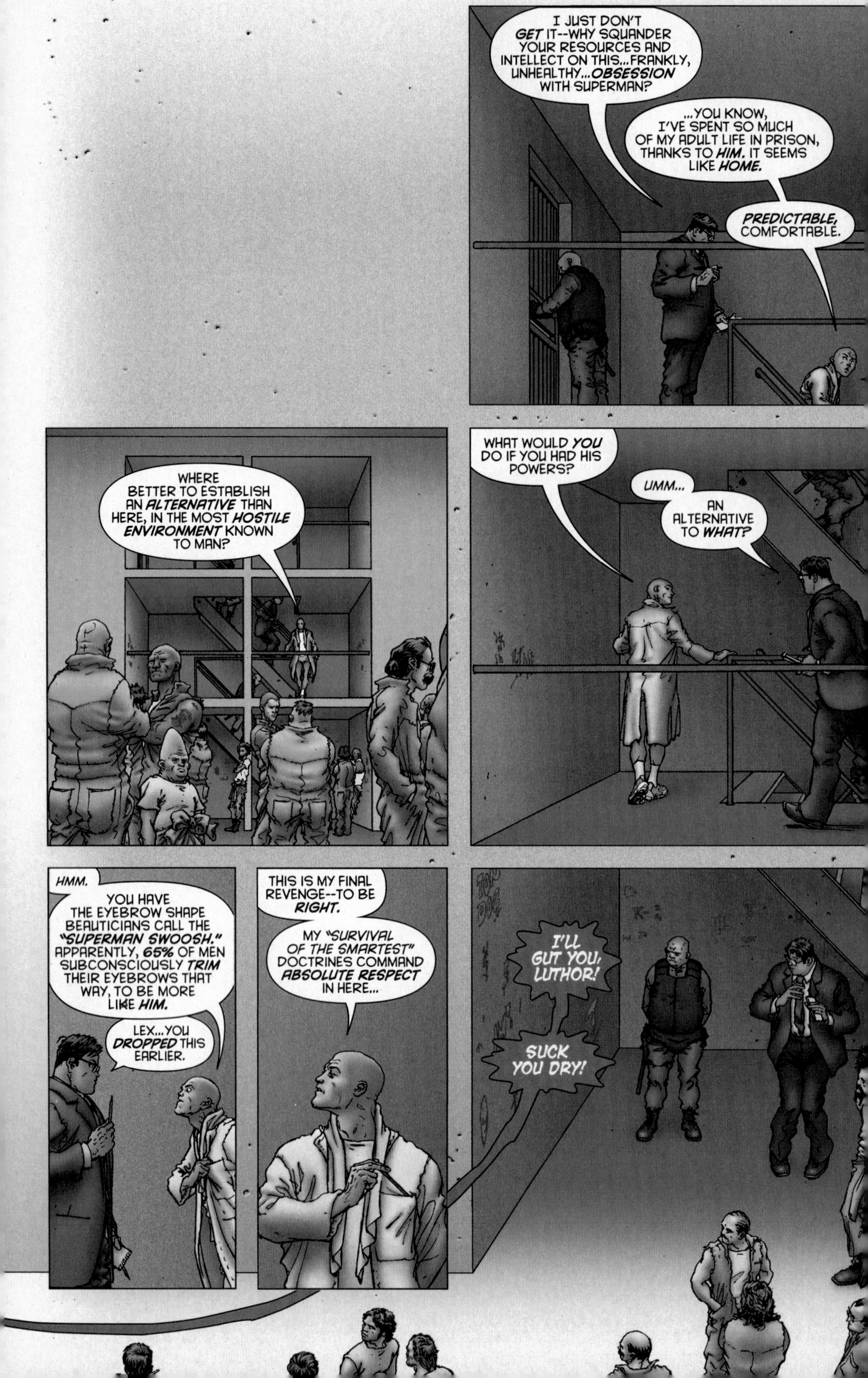
I JUST DON'T GET IT--WHY SQUANDER YOUR RESOURCES AND INTELLECT ON THIS...FRANKLY, UNHEALTHY...OBSESSION WITH SUPERMAN?
...YOU KNOW, I'VE SPENT SO MUCH OF MY ADULT LIFE IN PRISON, THANKS TO HIM. IT SEEMS LIKE HOME.
PREDICTABLE, COMFORTABLE.
WHERE BETTER TO ESTABLISH AN ALTERNATIVE THAN HERE, IN THE MOST HOSTILE ENVIRONMENT KNOWN TO MAN?
WHAT WOULD YOU DO IF YOU HAD HIS POWERS?
UMM...
AN ALTERNATIVE TO WHAT?
HMM.
YOU HAVE THE EYEBROW SHAPE BEAUTICIANS CALL THE "SUPERMAN SWOOSH." APPARENTLY, 65% OF MEN SUBCONSCIOUSLY TRIM THEIR EYEBROWS THAT WAY, TO BE MORE LIKE HIM.
LEX...YOU DROPPED THIS EARLIER.
THIS IS MY FINAL REVENGE--TO BE RIGHT.
MY "SURVIVAL OF THE SMARTEST" DOCTRINES COMMAND ABSOLUTE RESPECT IN HERE...
I'LL GUT YOU, LUTHOR!
SUCK YOU DRY!

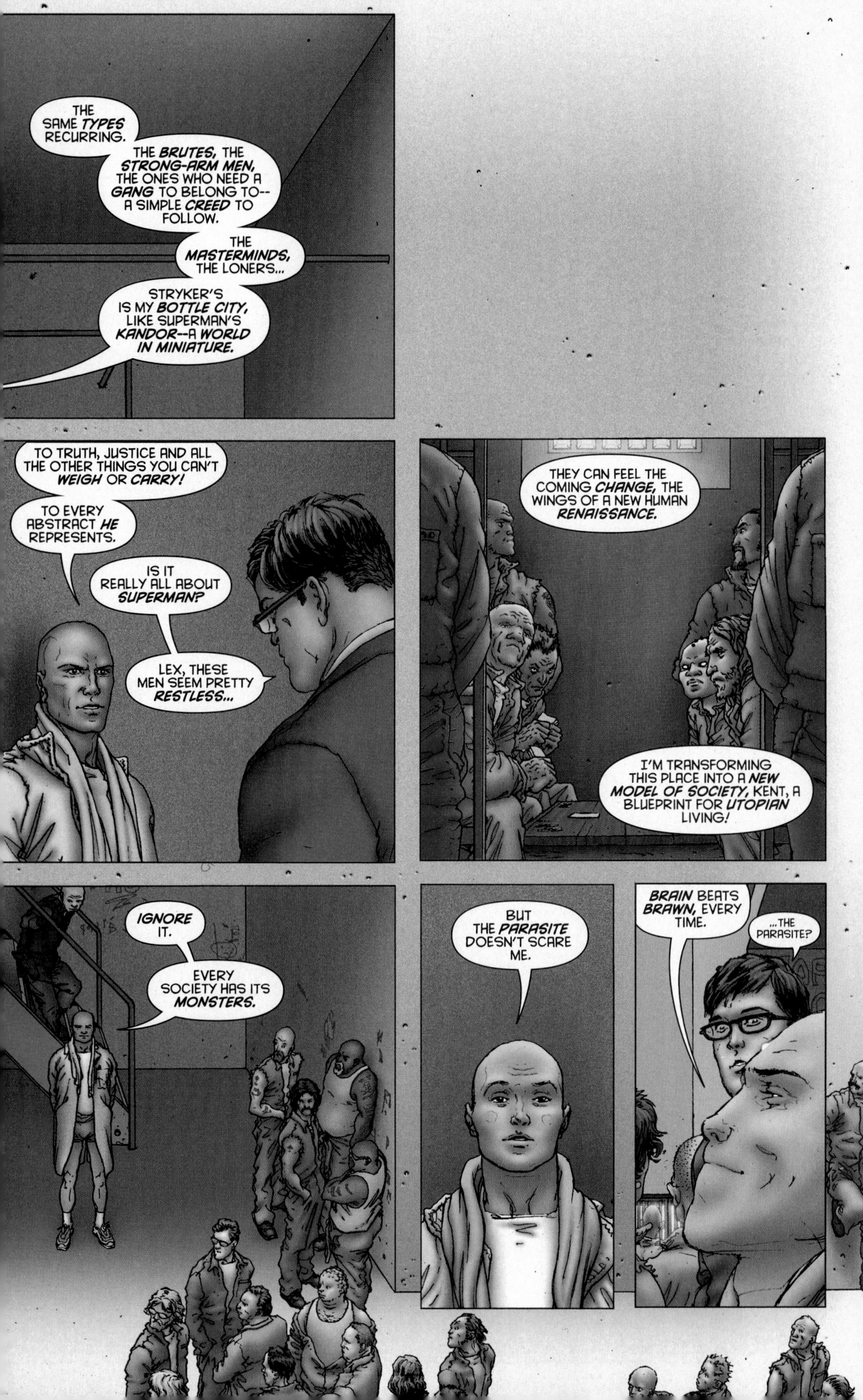
THE SAME TYPES RECURRING.
THE BRUTES, THE STRONG-ARM MEN, THE ONES WHO NEED A GANG TO BELONG TO--A SIMPLE CREED TO FOLLOW.
THE MASTERMINDS, THE LONERS...
STRYKER'S IS MY BOTTLE CITY, LIKE SUPERMAN'S KANDOR--A WORLD IN MINIATURE.
TO TRUTH, JUSTICE AND ALL THE OTHER THINGS YOU CAN'T WEIGH OR CARRY!
TO EVERY ABSTRACT HE REPRESENTS.
IS IT REALLY ALL ABOUT SUPERMAN?
LEX, THESE MEN SEEM PRETTY RESTLESS...
THEY CAN FEEL THE COMING CHANGE, THE WINGS OF A NEW HUMAN RENAISSANCE.
I'M TRANSFORMING THIS PLACE INTO A NEW MODEL OF SOCIETY, KENT, A BLUEPRINT FOR UTOPIAN LIVING!
IGNORE IT.
EVERY SOCIETY HAS ITS MONSTERS.
BUT THE PARASITE DOESN'T SCARE ME.
BRAIN BEATS BRAWN, EVERY TIME.
...THE PARASITE?

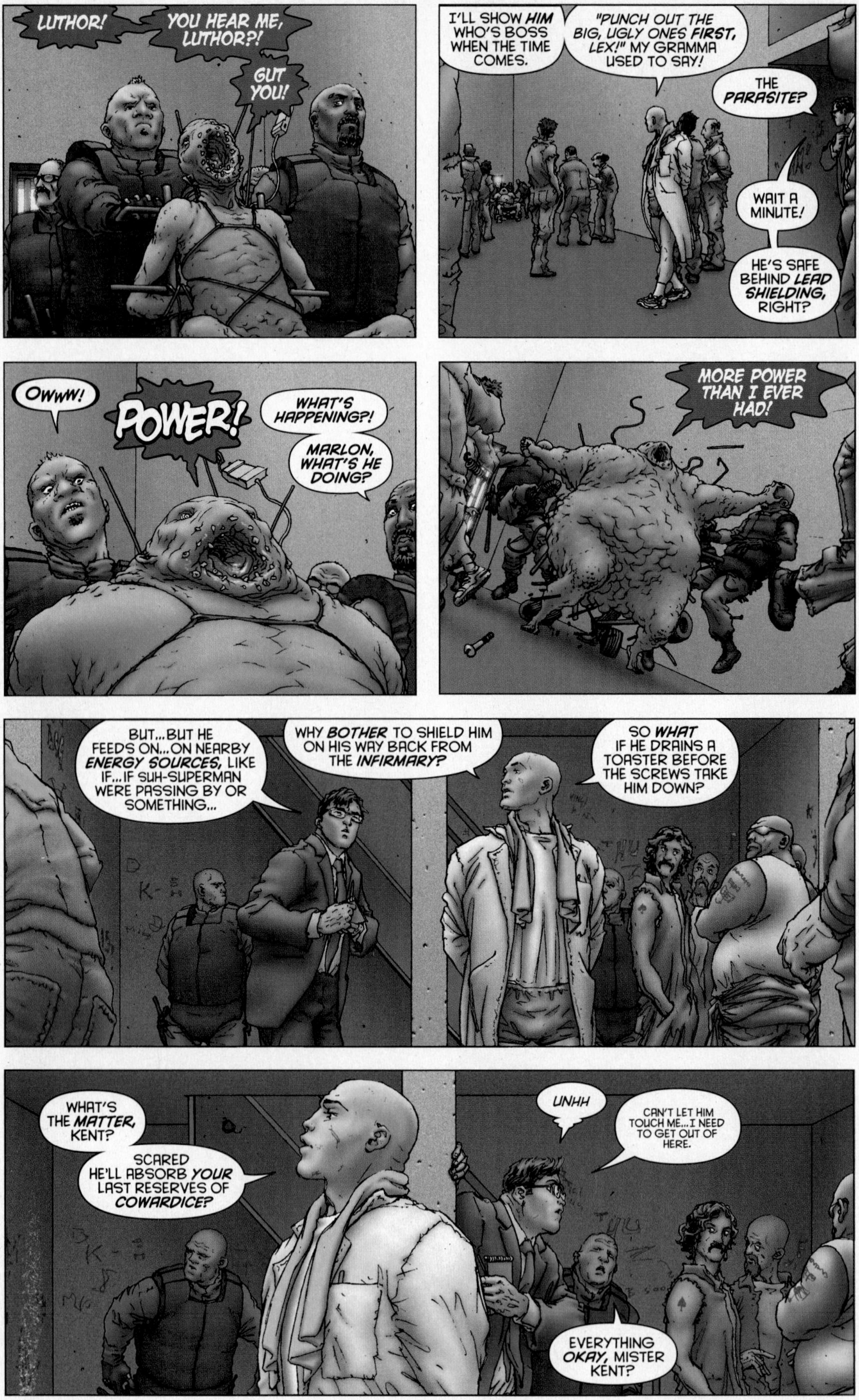
LUTHOR!
YOU HEAR ME, LUTHOR?!
GUT YOU!
I'LL SHOW HIM WHO'S BOSS WHEN THE TIME COMES.
"PUNCH OUT THE BIG, UGLY ONES FIRST, LEX!" MY GRAMMA USED TO SAY!
THE PARASITE?
WAIT A MINUTE!
HE'S SAFE BEHIND LEAD SHIELDING, RIGHT?
OWWW!
POWER!
WHAT'S HAPPENING?!
MARLON, WHAT'S HE DOING?
MORE POWER THAN I EVER HAD!
BUT...BUT HE FEEDS ON...ON NEARBY ENERGY SOURCES, LIKE IF...IF SUH-SUPERMAN WERE PASSING BY OR SOMETHING...
WHY BOTHER TO SHIELD HIM ON HIS WAY BACK FROM THE INFIRMARY?
SO WHAT IF HE DRAINS A TOASTER BEFORE THE SCREWS TAKE HIM DOWN?
WHAT'S THE MATTER, KENT?
SCARED HE'LL ABSORB YOUR LAST RESERVES OF COWARDICE?
UNHH
CAN'T LET HIM TOUCH ME...I NEED TO GET OUT OF HERE.
EVERYTHING OKAY, MISTER KENT?

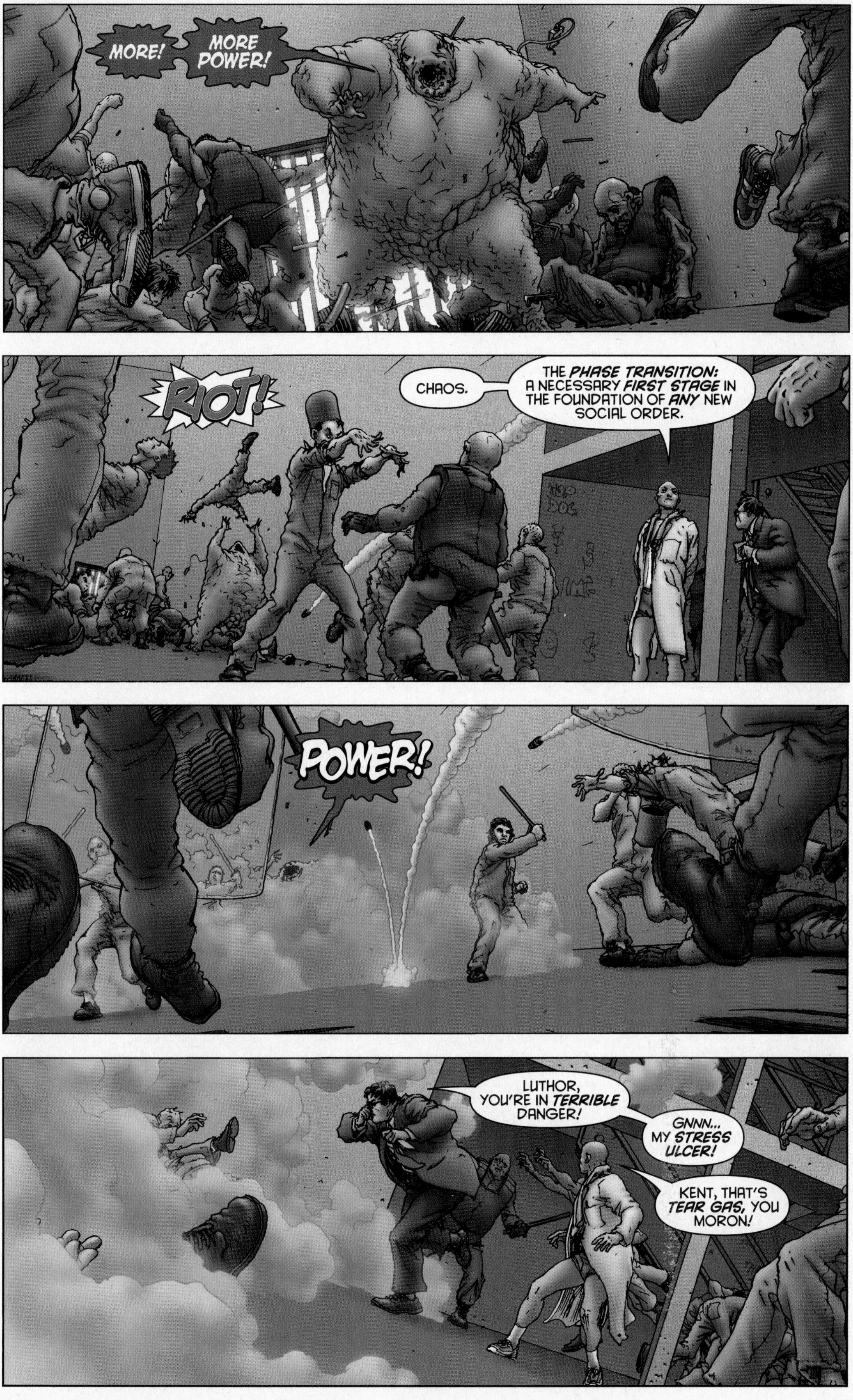
MORE!
MORE POWER!
RIOT!
CHAOS.
THE PHASE TRANSITION: A NECESSARY FIRST STAGE IN THE FOUNDATION OF ANY NEW SOCIAL ORDER.
POWER!
LUTHOR, YOU'RE IN TERRIBLE DANGER!
GNNN... MY STRESS ULCER!
KENT, THAT'S TEAR GAS, YOU MORON!

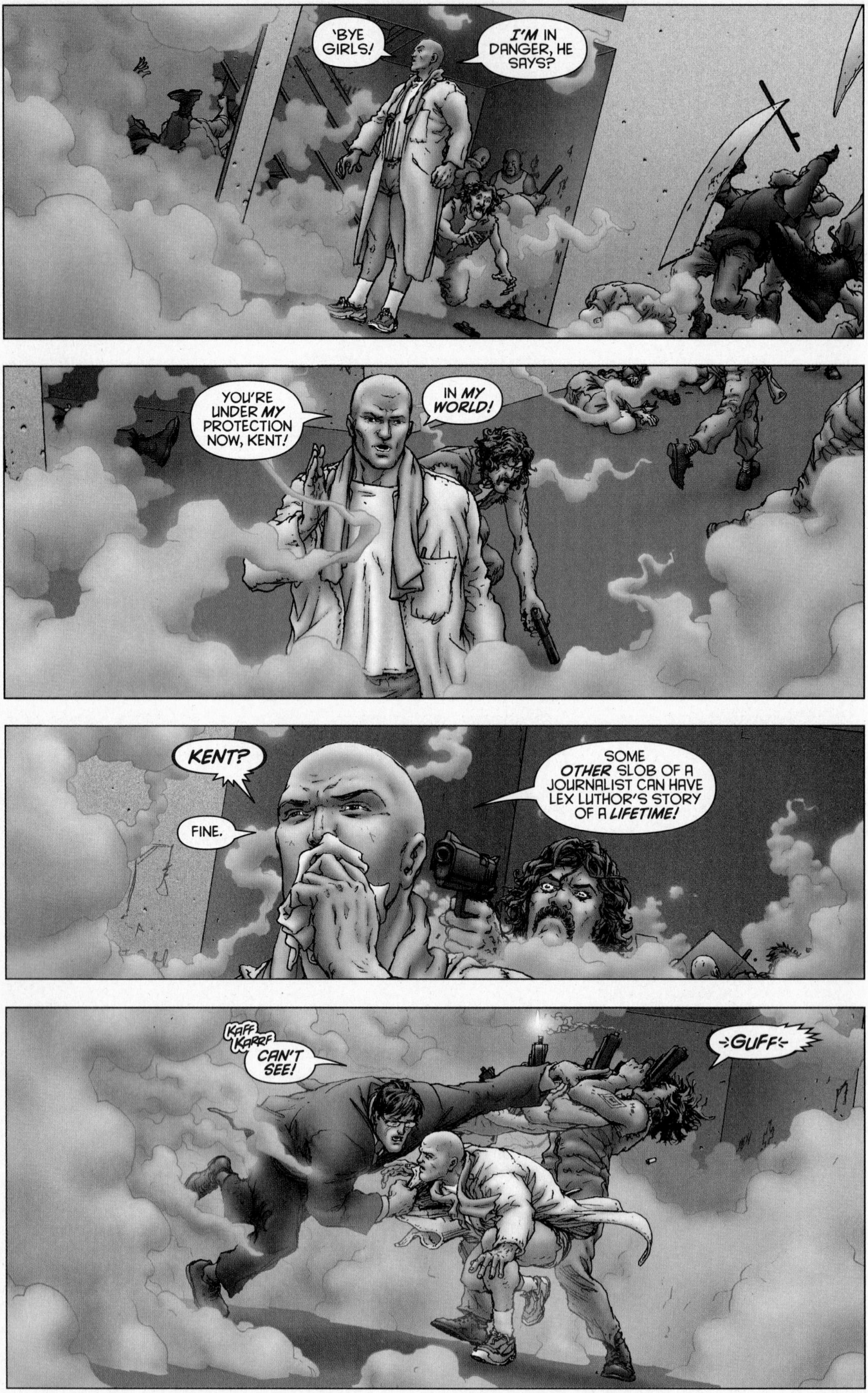
'BYE GIRLS!
I'M IN DANGER, HE SAYS?
YOU'RE UNDER MY PROTECTION NOW, KENT!
IN MY WORLD!
KENT?
FINE.
SOME OTHER SLOB OF A JOURNALIST CAN HAVE LEX LUTHOR'S STORY OF A LIFETIME!
KAFF KARRF
CAN'T SEE!
GUFF

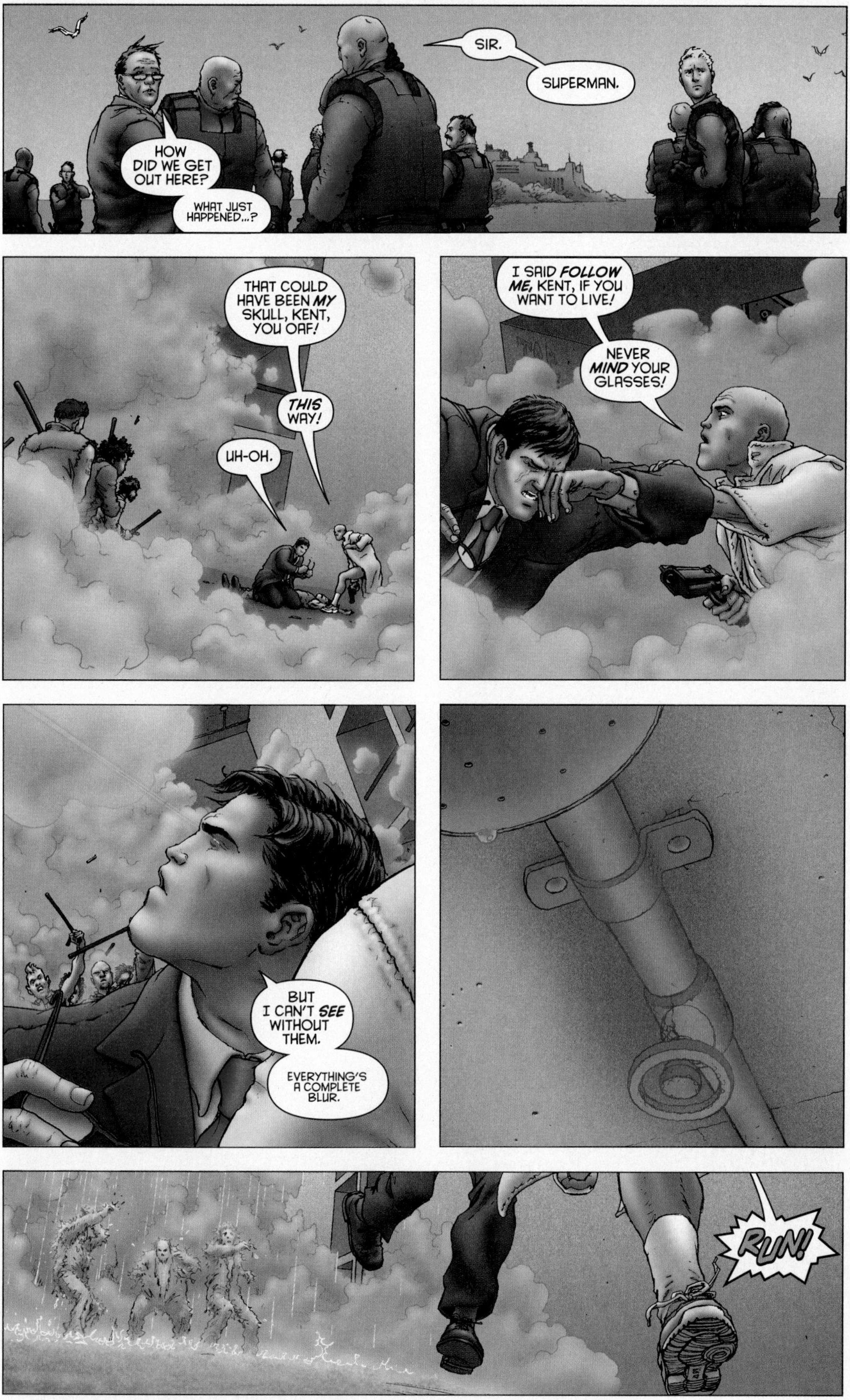
SIR.
SUPERMAN.
HOW DID WE GET OUT HERE?
WHAT JUST HAPPENED...?
THAT COULD HAVE BEEN *MY* SKULL, KENT, YOU OAF!
THIS WAY!
UH-OH.
I SAID *FOLLOW ME,* KENT, IF YOU WANT TO LIVE!
NEVER *MIND* YOUR GLASSES!
BUT I CAN'T *SEE* WITHOUT THEM.
EVERYTHING'S A COMPLETE BLUR.
RUN!

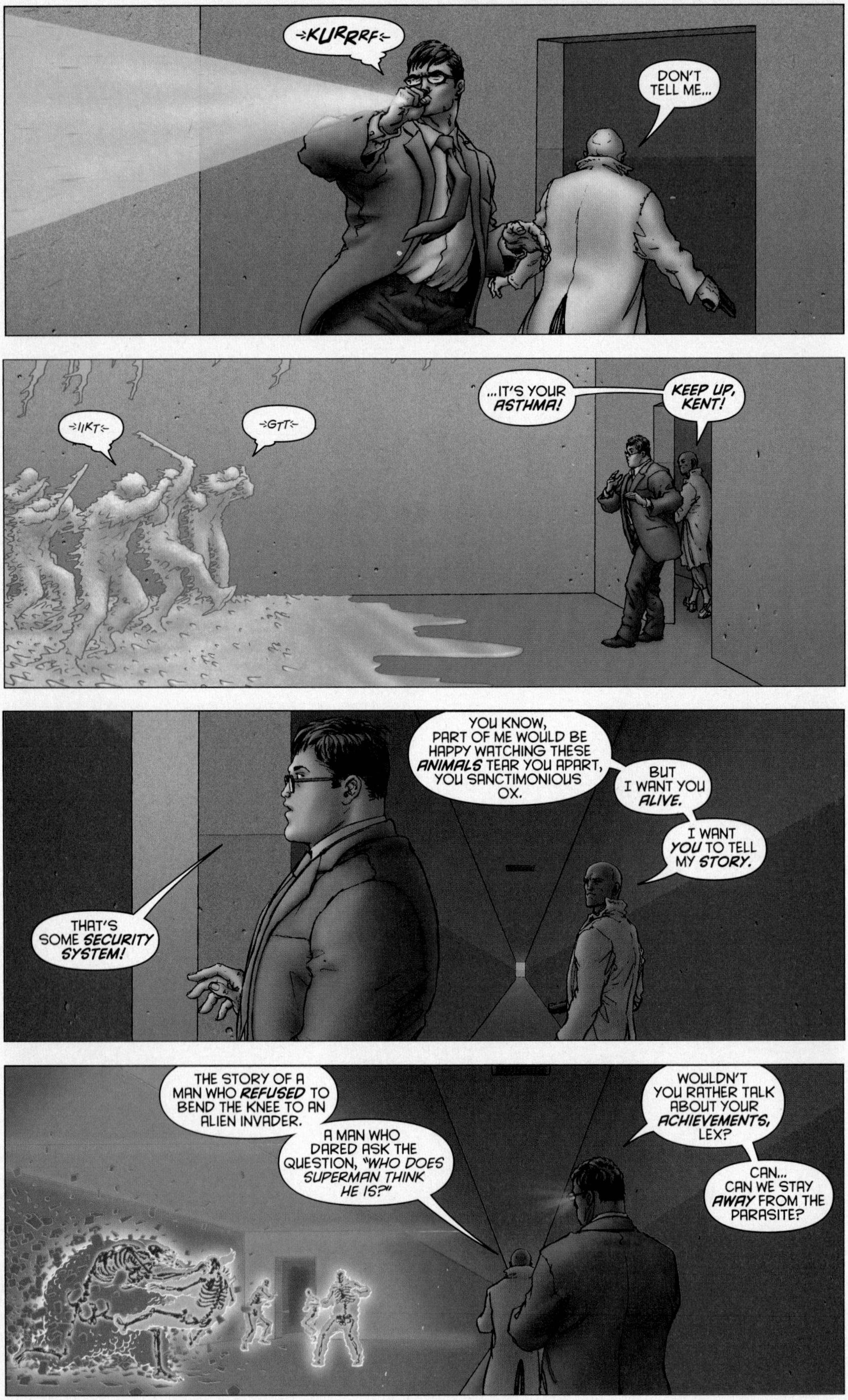

KURRRF
DON'T TELL ME...
IIKT
GTT
...IT'S YOUR ASTHMA!
KEEP UP, KENT!
THAT'S SOME SECURITY SYSTEM!
YOU KNOW, PART OF ME WOULD BE HAPPY WATCHING THESE ANIMALS TEAR YOU APART, YOU SANCTIMONIOUS OX.
BUT I WANT YOU ALIVE.
I WANT YOU TO TELL MY STORY.
THE STORY OF A MAN WHO REFUSED TO BEND THE KNEE TO AN ALIEN INVADER.
A MAN WHO DARED ASK THE QUESTION, "WHO DOES SUPERMAN THINK HE IS?"
WOULDN'T YOU RATHER TALK ABOUT YOUR ACHIEVEMENTS, LEX?
CAN... CAN WE STAY AWAY FROM THE PARASITE?

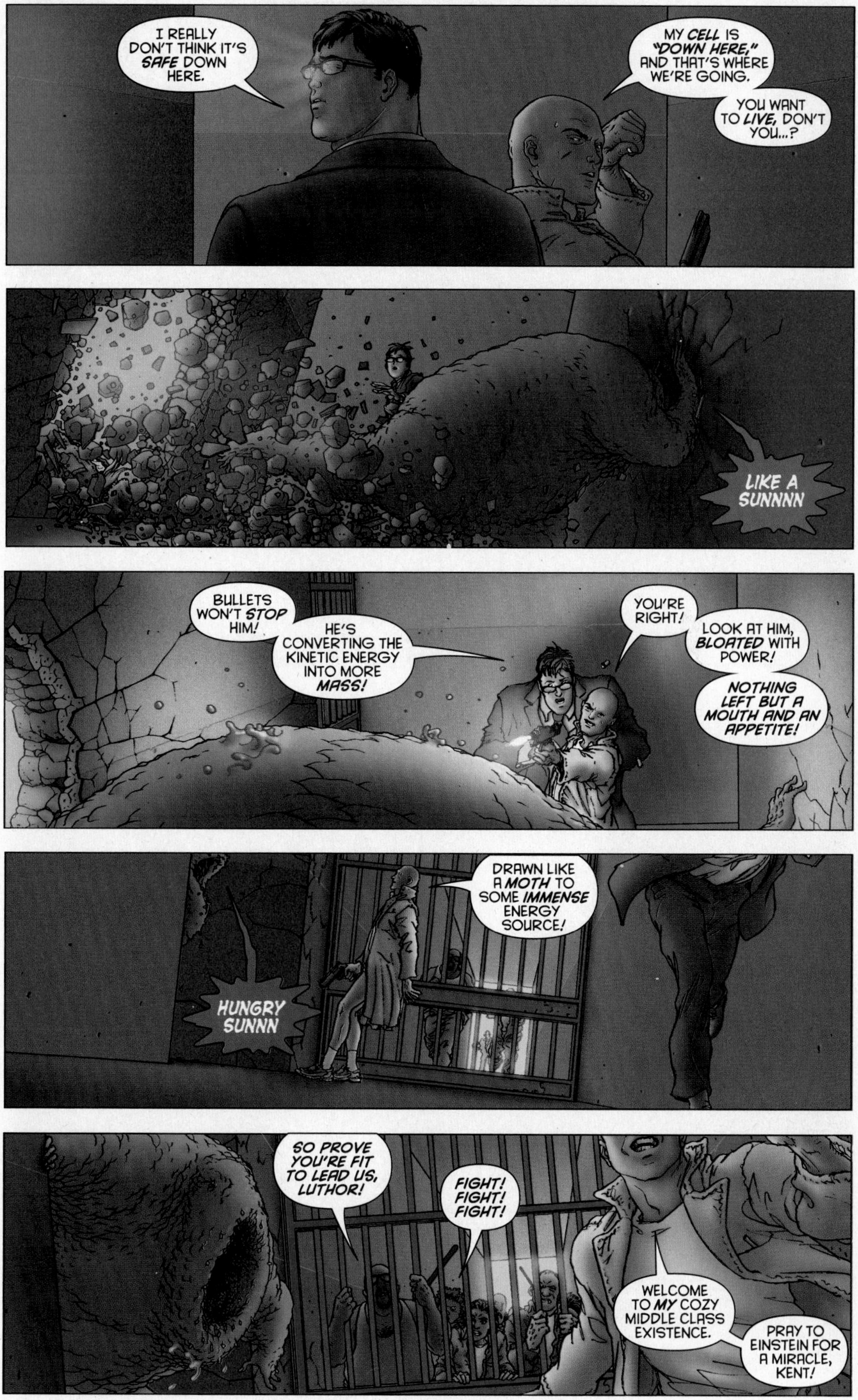
I REALLY DON'T THINK IT'S SAFE DOWN HERE.
MY CELL IS "DOWN HERE," AND THAT'S WHERE WE'RE GOING.
YOU WANT TO LIVE, DON'T YOU...?
LIKE A SUNNNN
BULLETS WON'T STOP HIM!
HE'S CONVERTING THE KINETIC ENERGY INTO MORE MASS!
YOU'RE RIGHT!
LOOK AT HIM, BLOATED WITH POWER!
NOTHING LEFT BUT A MOUTH AND AN APPETITE!
DRAWN LIKE A MOTH TO SOME IMMENSE ENERGY SOURCE!
HUNGRY SUNNN
SO PROVE YOU'RE FIT TO LEAD US, LUTHOR!
FIGHT! FIGHT! FIGHT!
WELCOME TO MY COZY MIDDLE CLASS EXISTENCE.
PRAY TO EINSTEIN FOR A MIRACLE, KENT!

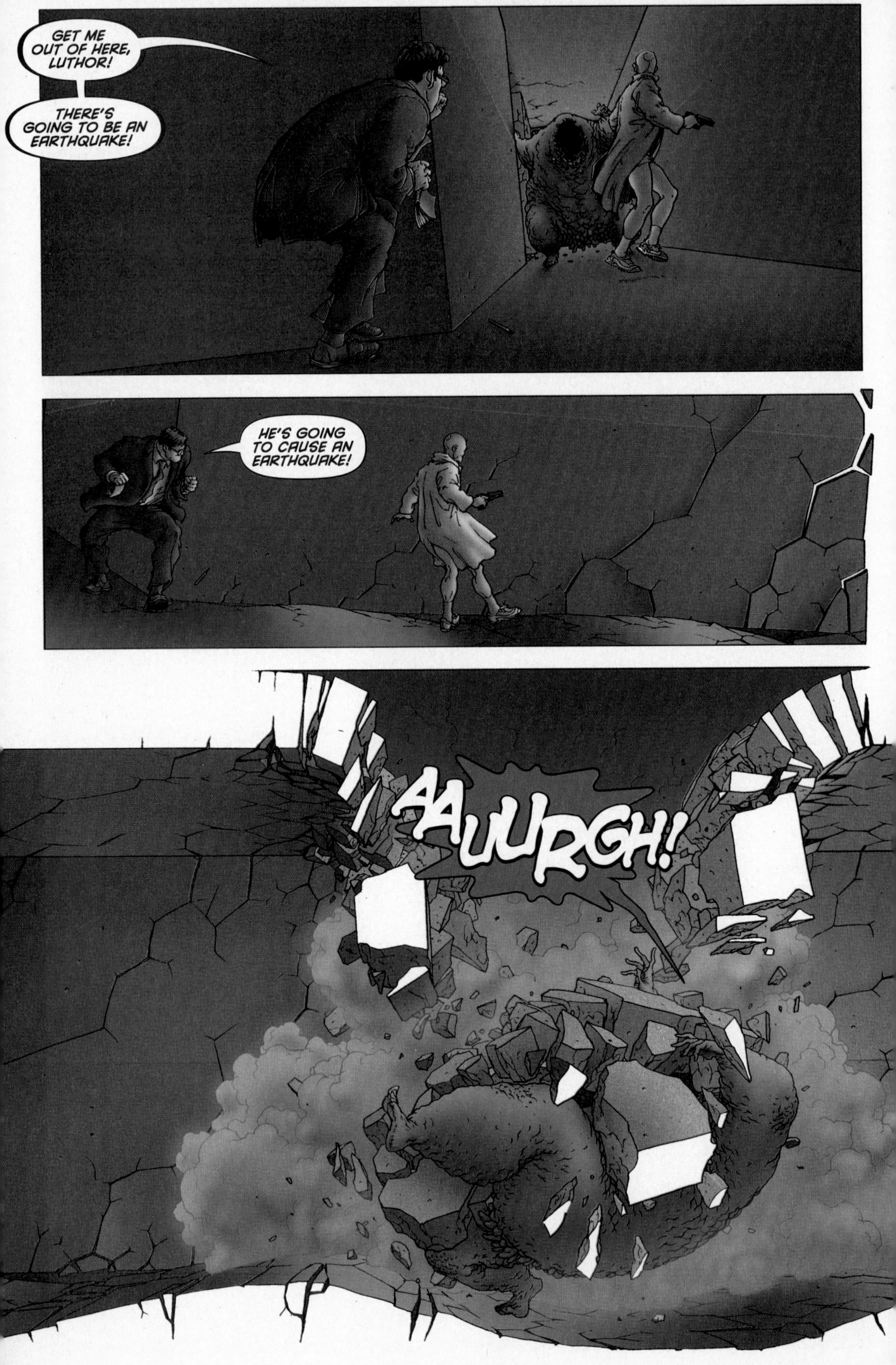
GET ME OUT OF HERE, LUTHOR!
THERE'S GOING TO BE AN EARTHQUAKE!
HE'S GOING TO CAUSE AN EARTHQUAKE!
AAUURGH!

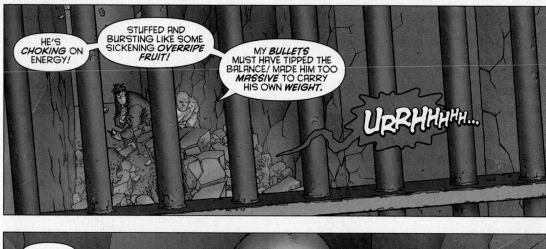

HE'S *CHOKING* ON ENERGY!

STUFFED AND BURSTING LIKE SOME SICKENING *OVERRIPE FRUIT!*

MY *BULLETS* MUST HAVE TIPPED THE BALANCE! MADE HIM TOO *MASSIVE* TO CARRY HIS OWN *WEIGHT.*

URRHHHHH...

I GUESS SO.

POOR MAN.

HIS OWN *GREED* ENGULFED HIM.

SEE WHAT HAPPENS TO *ANYONE* WHO *CROSSES* ME, KENT?

ANYONE WHO UNDERESTIMATES *LEX LUTHOR?*

LIQUEFYING!

AND THAT'S *EXACTLY HOW* HE'LL LOOK!

THAT'S HOW SUPERMAN WILL LOOK AT THE END!

NOBODY THREATENS ME!

NOBODY GETS IN LUTHOR'S WAY!

LEX.

MY SHORTHAND CAN'T HANDLE THE VOLUME.

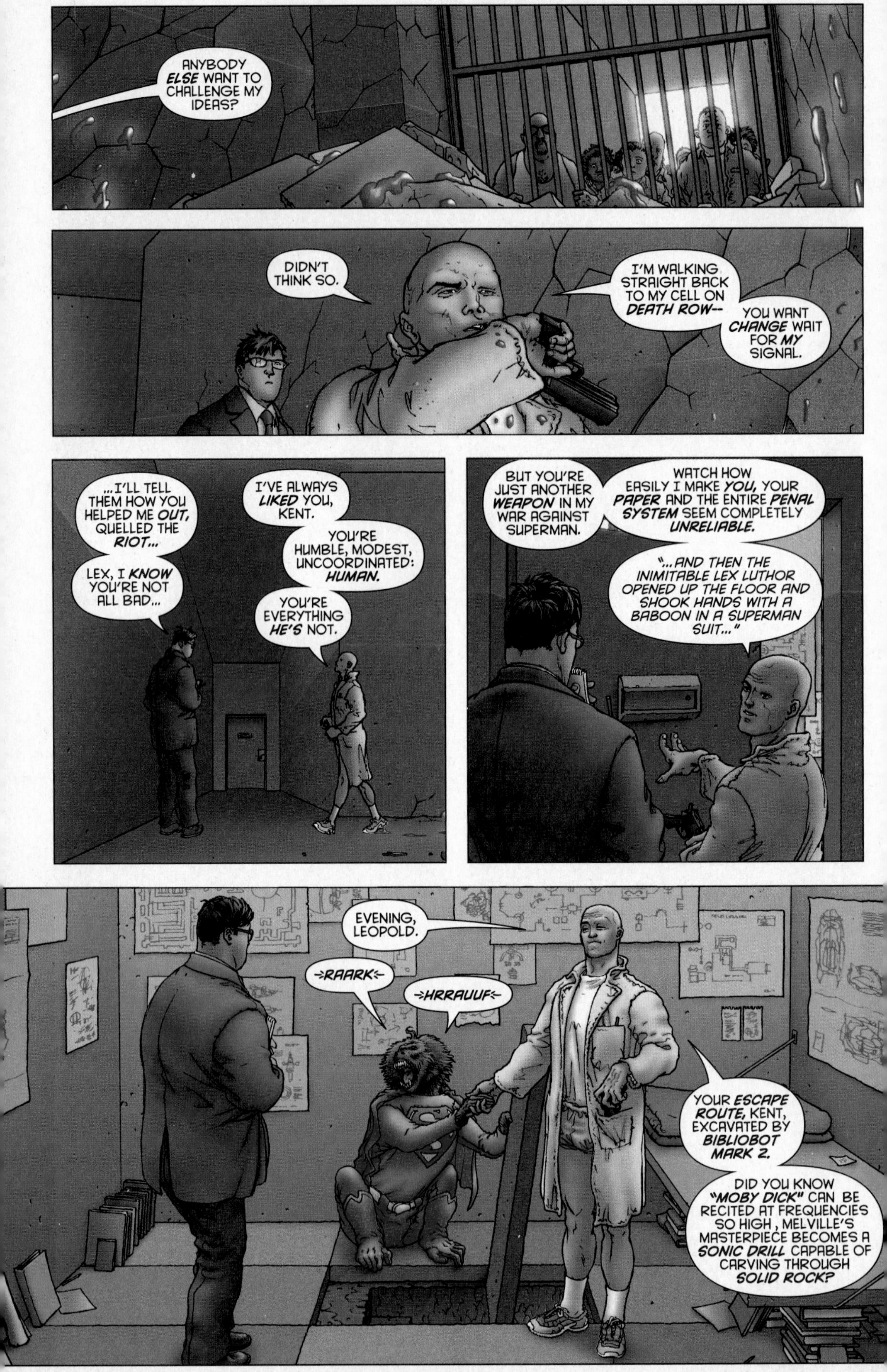
ANYBODY ELSE WANT TO CHALLENGE MY IDEAS?
DIDN'T THINK SO.
I'M WALKING STRAIGHT BACK TO MY CELL ON DEATH ROW--
YOU WANT CHANGE WAIT FOR MY SIGNAL.
...I'LL TELL THEM HOW YOU HELPED ME OUT, QUELLED THE RIOT...
LEX, I KNOW YOU'RE NOT ALL BAD...
I'VE ALWAYS LIKED YOU, KENT.
YOU'RE HUMBLE, MODEST, UNCOORDINATED: HUMAN.
YOU'RE EVERYTHING HE'S NOT.
BUT YOU'RE JUST ANOTHER WEAPON IN MY WAR AGAINST SUPERMAN.
WATCH HOW EASILY I MAKE YOU, YOUR PAPER AND THE ENTIRE PENAL SYSTEM SEEM COMPLETELY UNRELIABLE.
"...AND THEN THE INIMITABLE LEX LUTHOR OPENED UP THE FLOOR AND SHOOK HANDS WITH A BABOON IN A SUPERMAN SUIT..."
EVENING, LEOPOLD.
RAARK
HRRAUUF
YOUR ESCAPE ROUTE, KENT, EXCAVATED BY BIBLIOBOT MARK 2.
DID YOU KNOW "MOBY DICK" CAN BE RECITED AT FREQUENCIES SO HIGH, MELVILLE'S MASTERPIECE BECOMES A SONIC DRILL CAPABLE OF CARVING THROUGH SOLID ROCK?

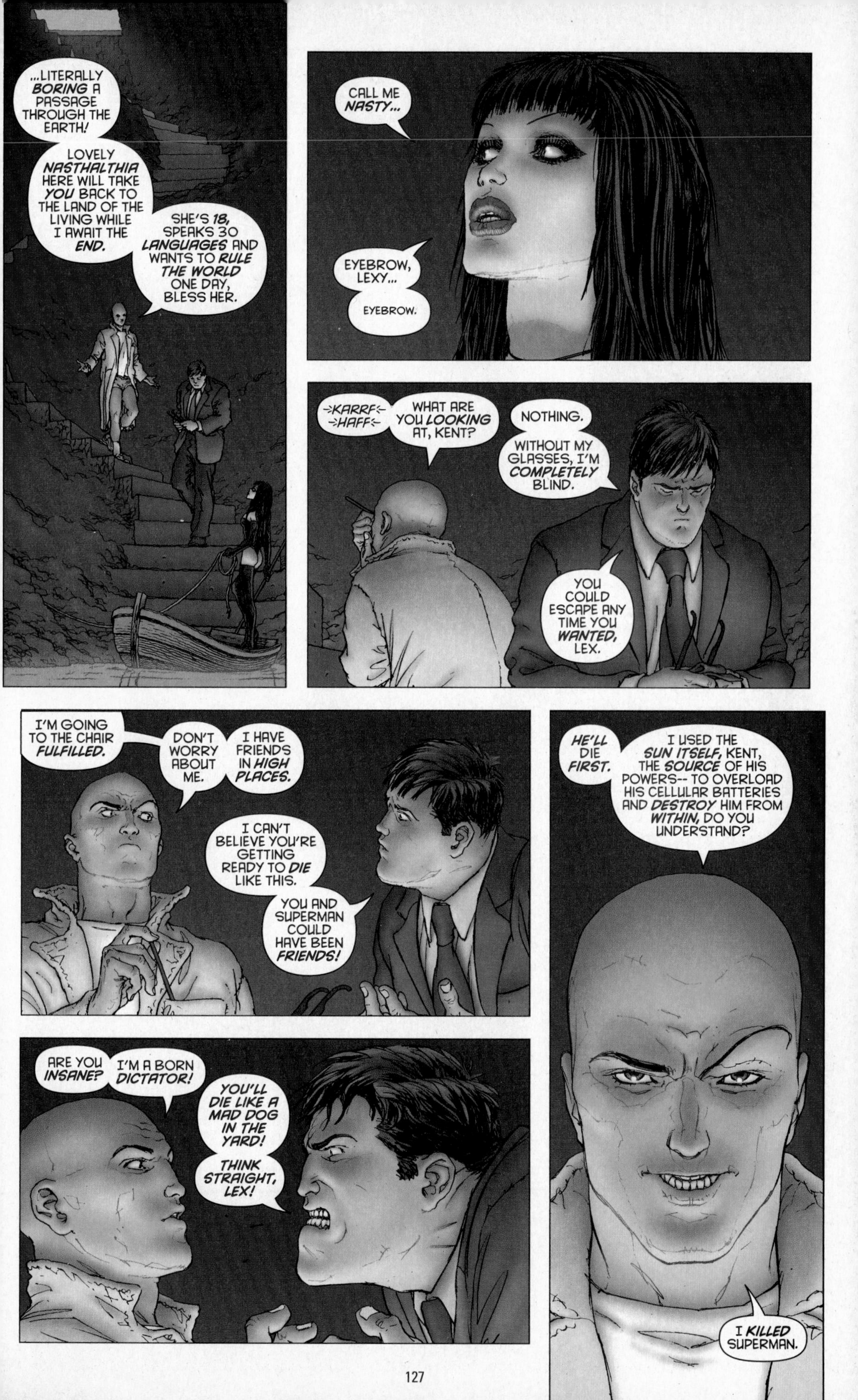
...LITERALLY BORING A PASSAGE THROUGH THE EARTH!
LOVELY NASTHALTHIA HERE WILL TAKE YOU BACK TO THE LAND OF THE LIVING WHILE I AWAIT THE END.
SHE'S 18, SPEAKS 30 LANGUAGES AND WANTS TO RULE THE WORLD ONE DAY, BLESS HER.
CALL ME NASTY...
EYEBROW, LEXY...
EYEBROW.
-KARRF- -HAFF-
WHAT ARE YOU LOOKING AT, KENT?
NOTHING.
WITHOUT MY GLASSES, I'M COMPLETELY BLIND.
YOU COULD ESCAPE ANY TIME YOU WANTED, LEX.
I'M GOING TO THE CHAIR FULFILLED.
DON'T WORRY ABOUT ME.
I HAVE FRIENDS IN HIGH PLACES.
I CAN'T BELIEVE YOU'RE GETTING READY TO DIE LIKE THIS.
YOU AND SUPERMAN COULD HAVE BEEN FRIENDS!
ARE YOU INSANE?
I'M A BORN DICTATOR!
YOU'LL DIE LIKE A MAD DOG IN THE YARD!
THINK STRAIGHT, LEX!
HE'LL DIE FIRST.
I USED THE SUN ITSELF, KENT, THE SOURCE OF HIS POWERS-- TO OVERLOAD HIS CELLULAR BATTERIES AND DESTROY HIM FROM WITHIN, DO YOU UNDERSTAND?
I KILLED SUPERMAN.

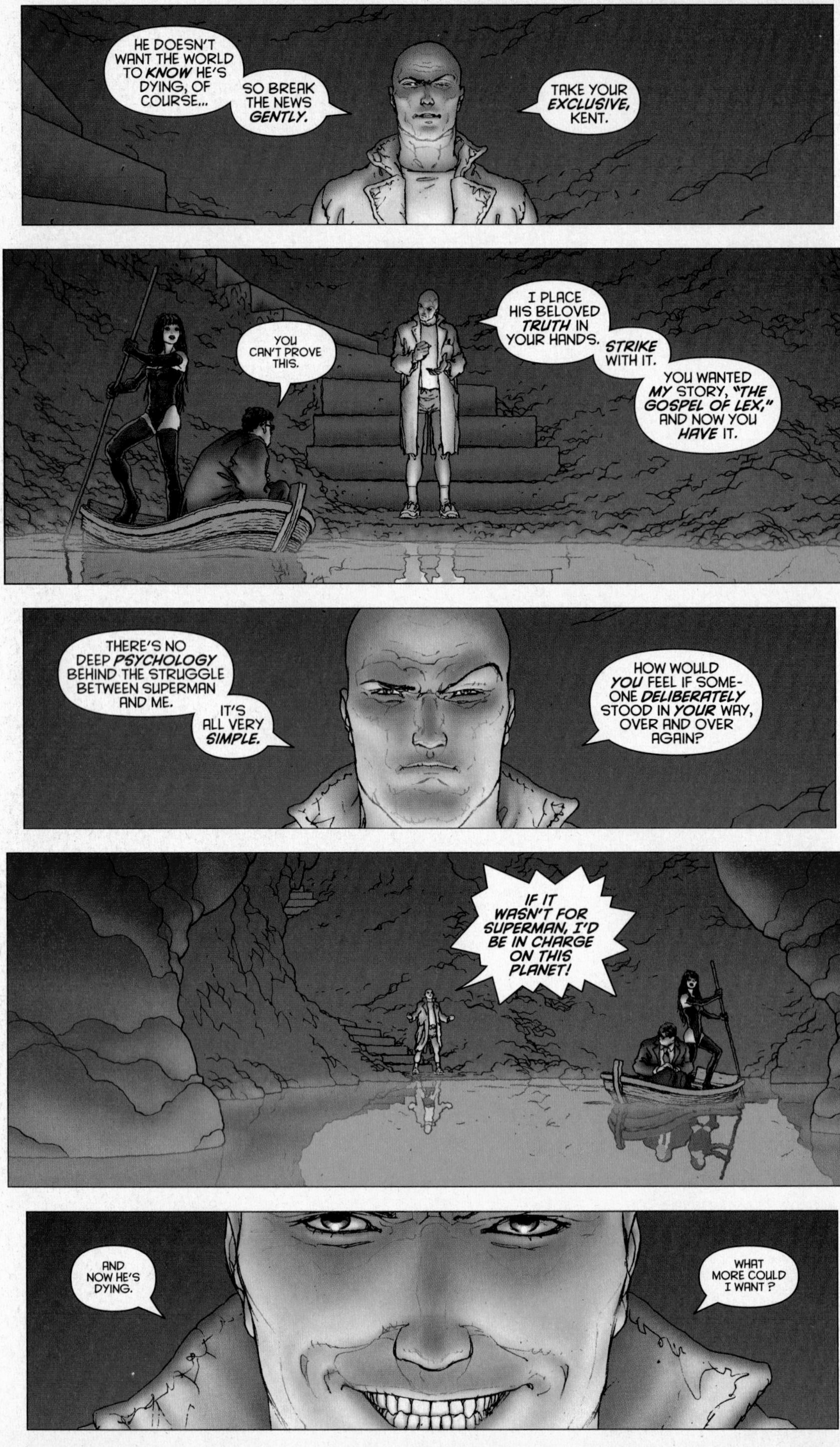
HE DOESN'T WANT THE WORLD TO KNOW HE'S DYING, OF COURSE...
SO BREAK THE NEWS GENTLY.
TAKE YOUR EXCLUSIVE, KENT.
YOU CAN'T PROVE THIS.
I PLACE HIS BELOVED TRUTH IN YOUR HANDS.
STRIKE WITH IT.
YOU WANTED MY STORY, "THE GOSPEL OF LEX," AND NOW YOU HAVE IT.
THERE'S NO DEEP PSYCHOLOGY BEHIND THE STRUGGLE BETWEEN SUPERMAN AND ME.
IT'S ALL VERY SIMPLE.
HOW WOULD YOU FEEL IF SOME-ONE DELIBERATELY STOOD IN YOUR WAY, OVER AND OVER AGAIN?
IF IT WASN'T FOR SUPERMAN, I'D BE IN CHARGE ON THIS PLANET!
AND NOW HE'S DYING.
WHAT MORE COULD I WANT ?

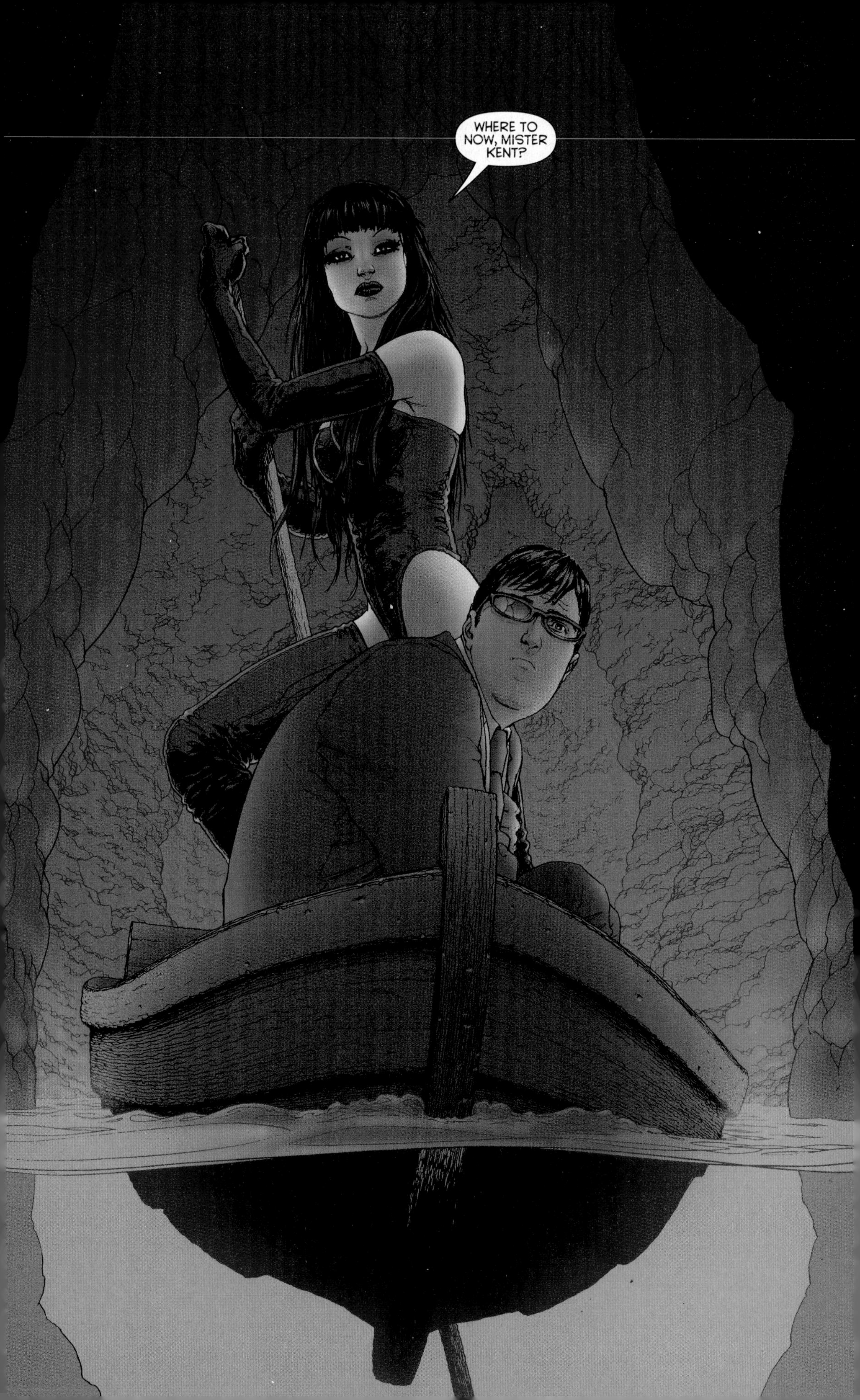
WHERE TO NOW, MISTER KENT?

Episode 6

FUNERAL IN SMALLVILLE

Cover FRANK QUITELY

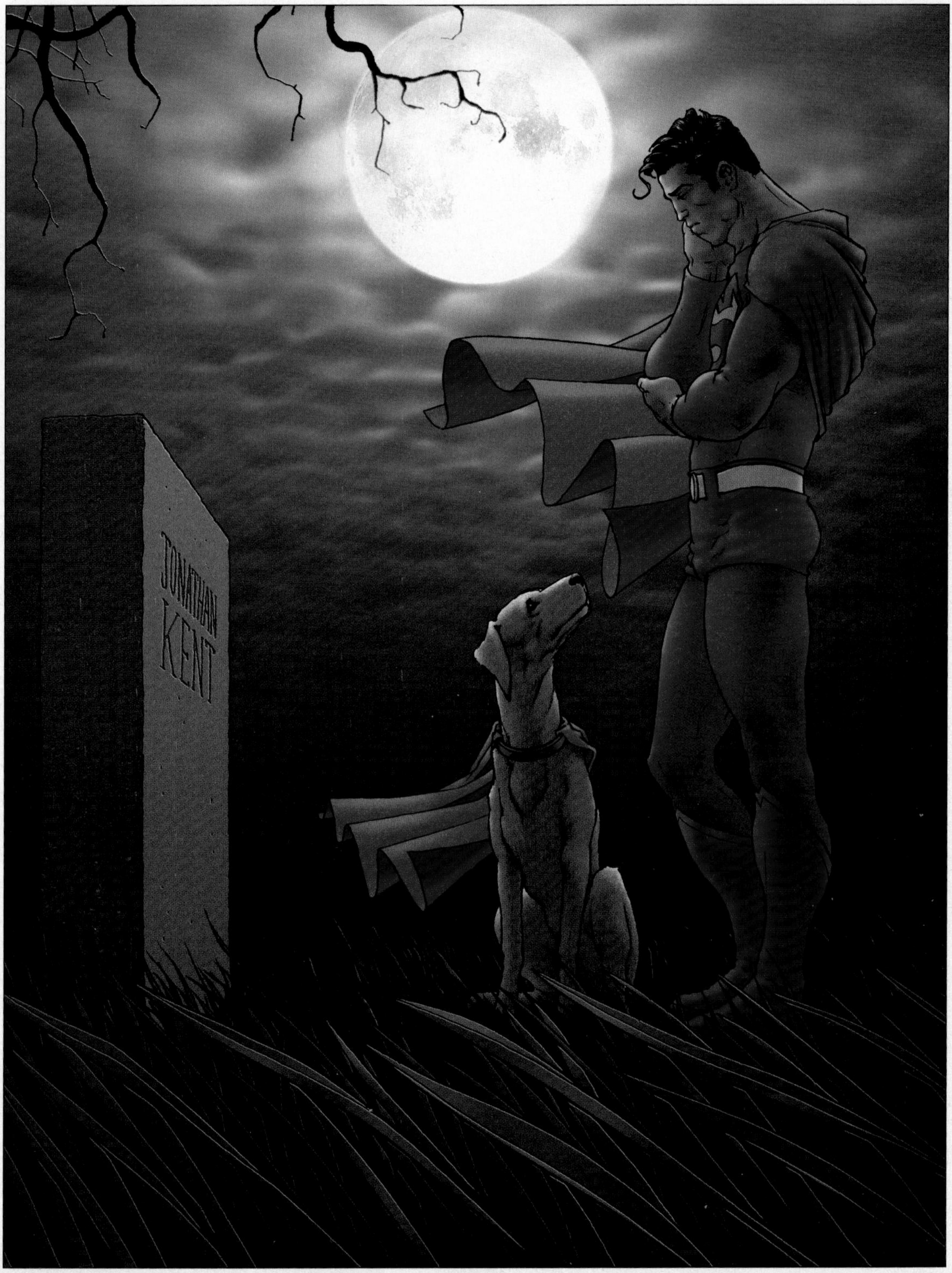
JONATHAN
KENT

6

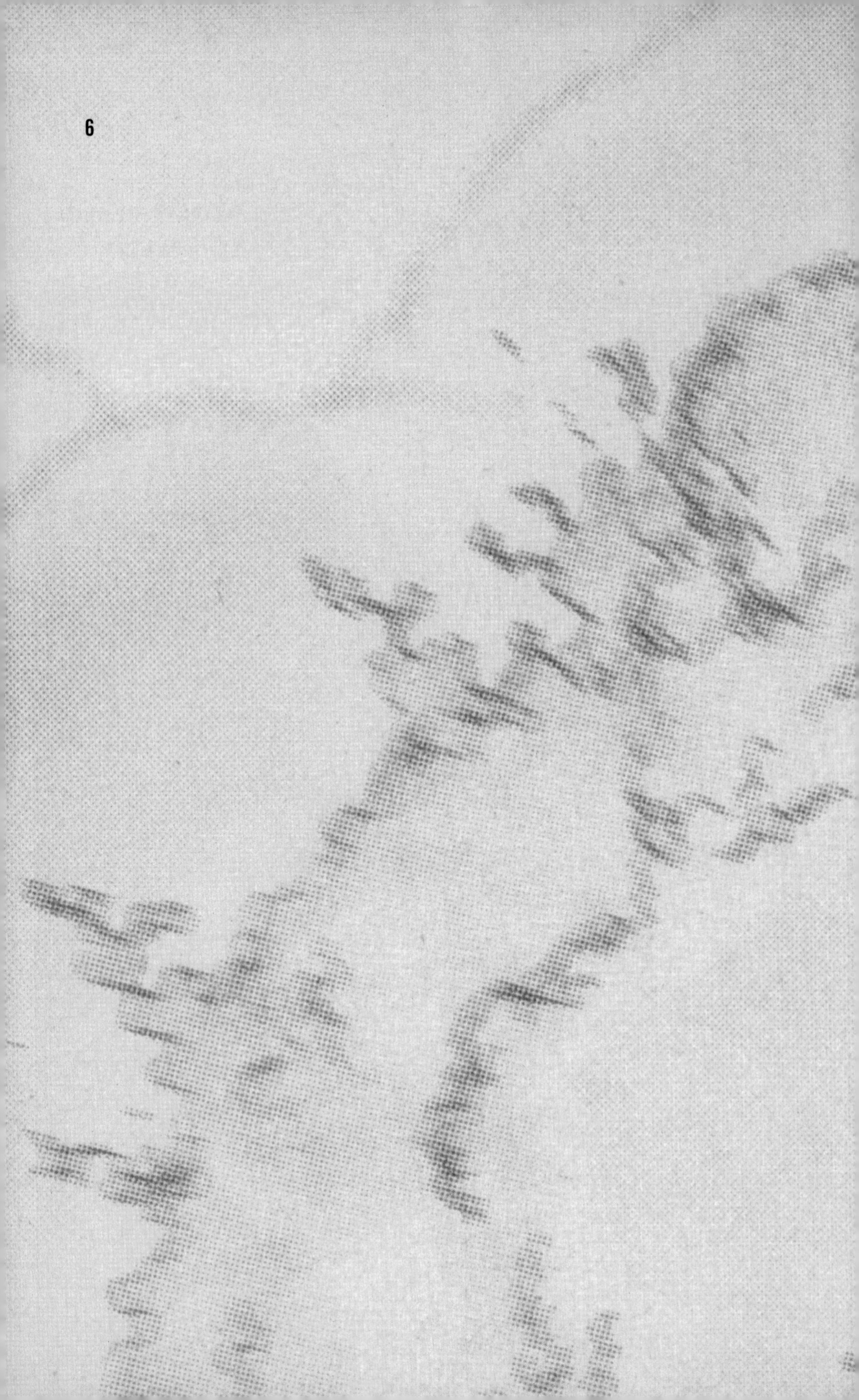

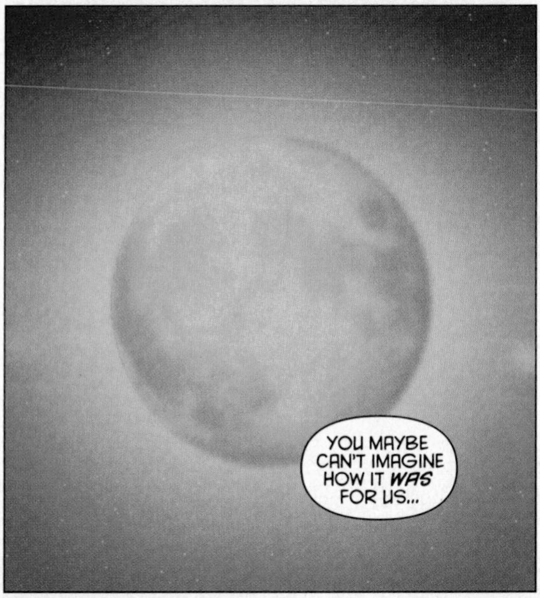
YOU MAYBE CAN'T IMAGINE HOW IT *WAS* FOR US...

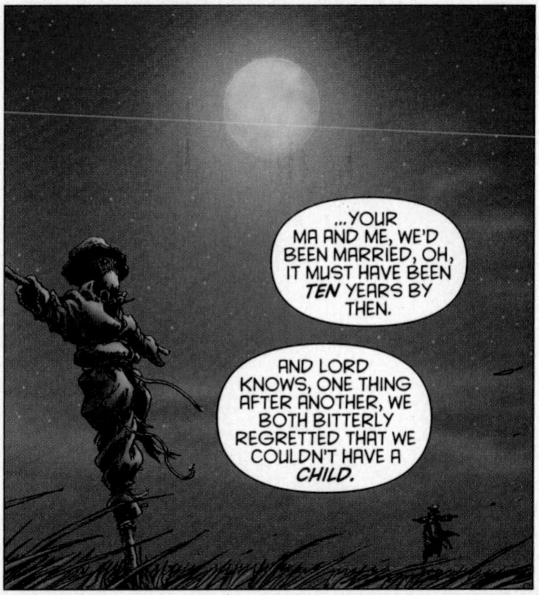
...YOUR MA AND ME, WE'D BEEN MARRIED, OH, IT MUST HAVE BEEN *TEN* YEARS BY THEN.
AND LORD KNOWS, ONE THING AFTER ANOTHER, WE BOTH BITTERLY REGRETTED THAT WE COULDN'T HAVE A *CHILD.*

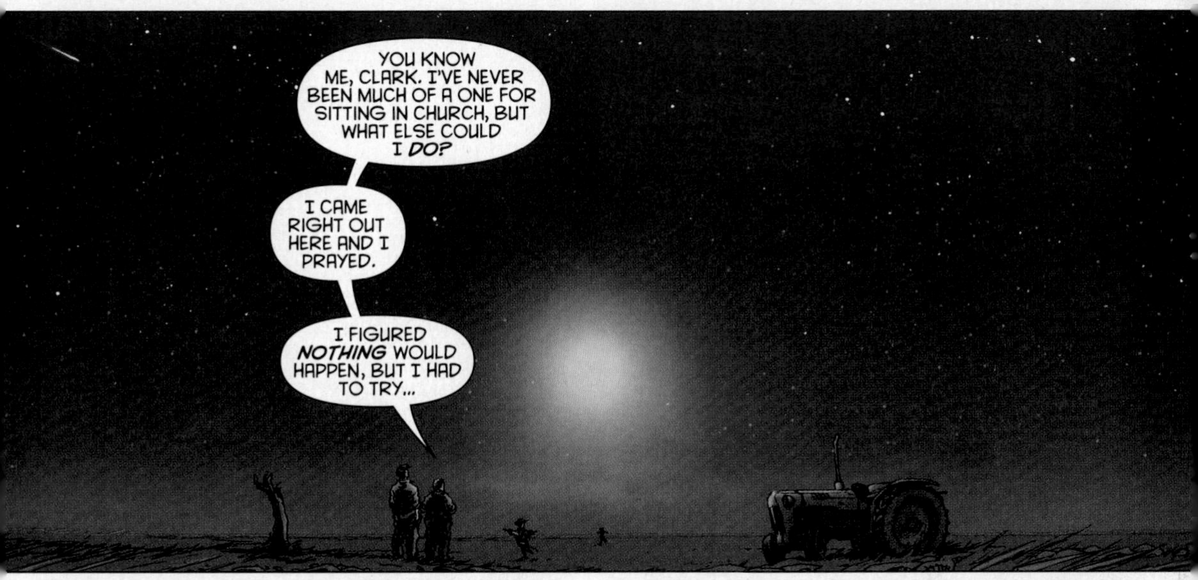
YOU KNOW ME, CLARK. I'VE NEVER BEEN MUCH OF A ONE FOR SITTING IN CHURCH, BUT WHAT ELSE COULD I *DO?*
I CAME RIGHT OUT HERE AND I PRAYED.
I FIGURED *NOTHING* WOULD HAPPEN, BUT I HAD TO TRY...

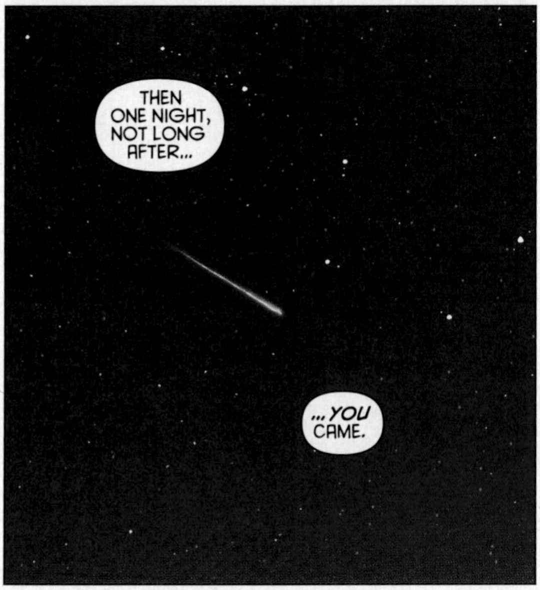
THEN ONE NIGHT, NOT LONG AFTER...
...YOU CAME.

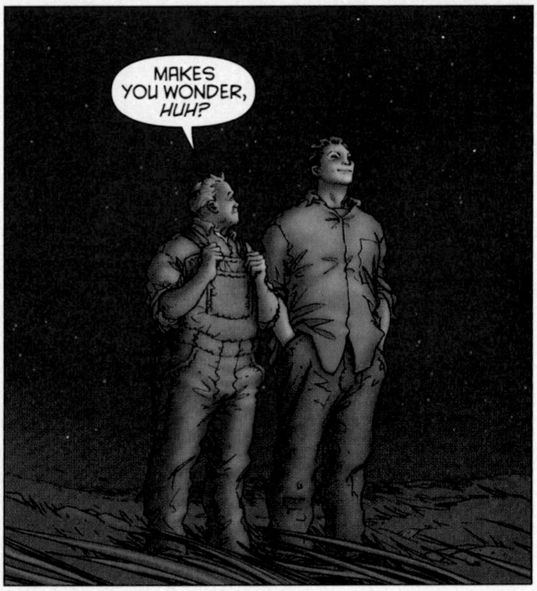
MAKES YOU WONDER, *HUH?*

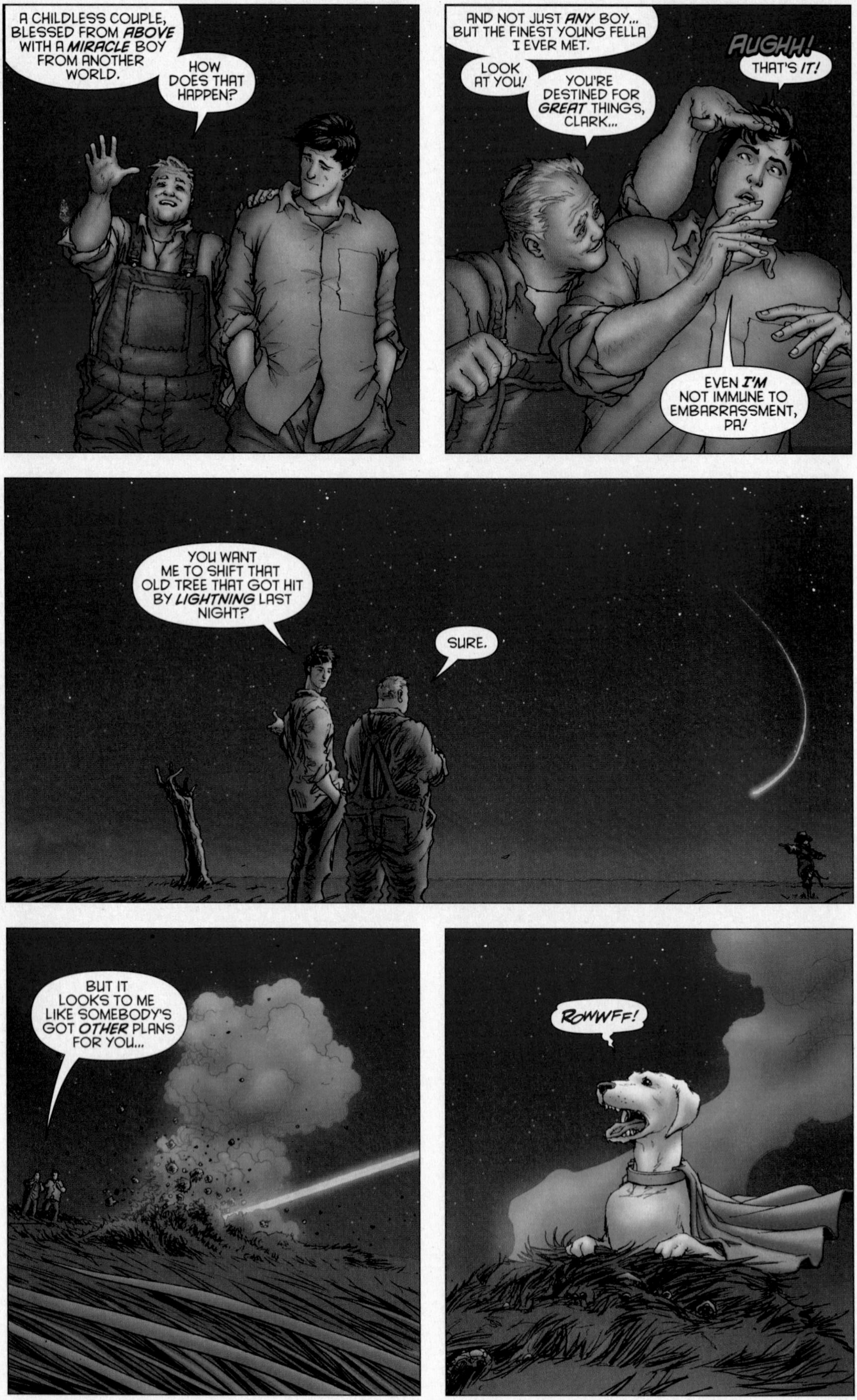

A CHILDLESS COUPLE, BLESSED FROM ABOVE WITH A MIRACLE BOY FROM ANOTHER WORLD.
HOW DOES THAT HAPPEN?
AND NOT JUST ANY BOY... BUT THE FINEST YOUNG FELLA I EVER MET.
LOOK AT YOU!
YOU'RE DESTINED FOR GREAT THINGS, CLARK...
AUGHH!
THAT'S IT!
EVEN I'M NOT IMMUNE TO EMBARRASSMENT, PA!
YOU WANT ME TO SHIFT THAT OLD TREE THAT GOT HIT BY LIGHTNING LAST NIGHT?
SURE.
BUT IT LOOKS TO ME LIKE SOMEBODY'S GOT OTHER PLANS FOR YOU...
ROWWFF!

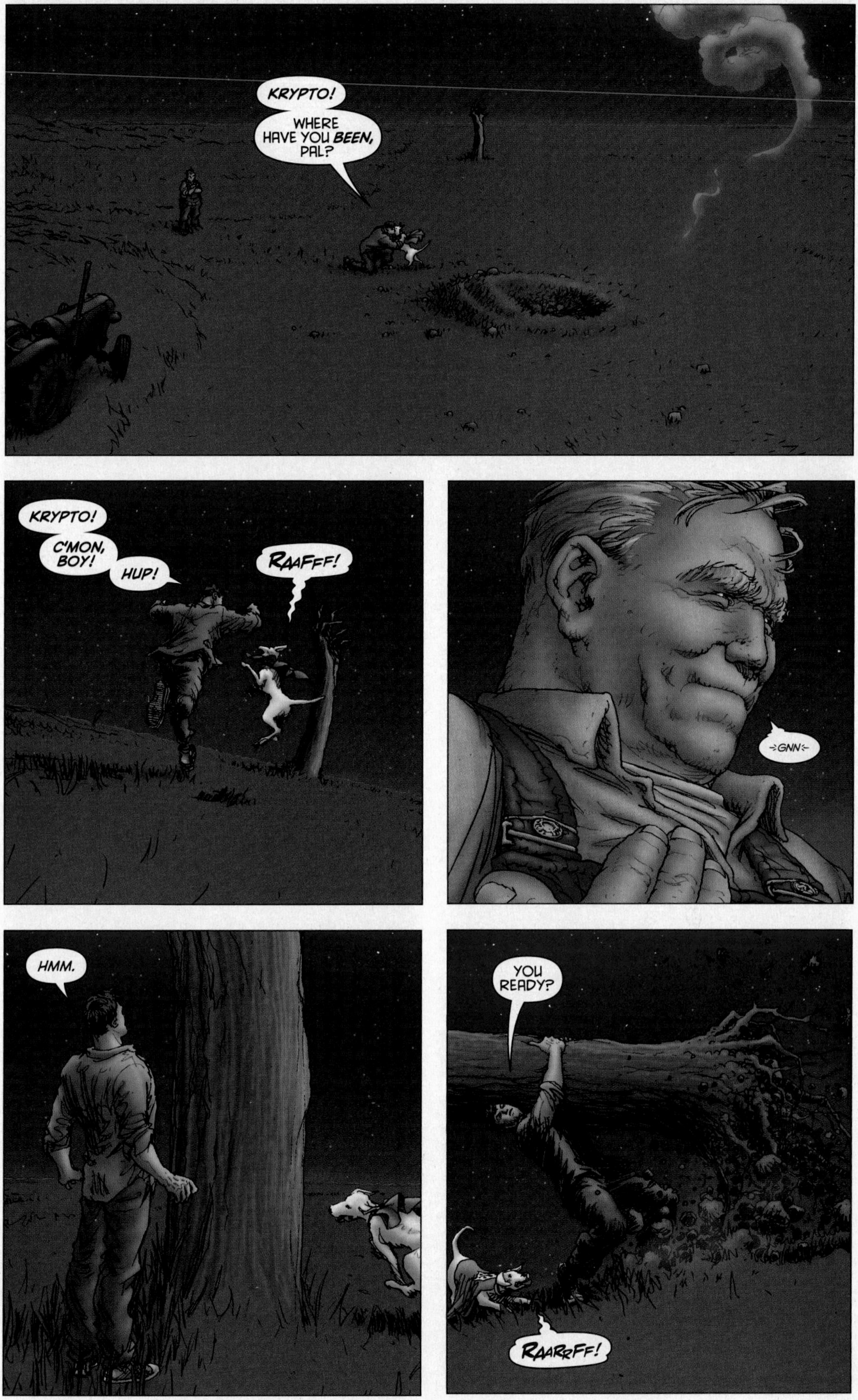
KRYPTO!
WHERE HAVE YOU BEEN, PAL?
KRYPTO!
C'MON, BOY!
HUP!
RAAFFF!
GNN
HMM.
YOU READY?
RAARRFF!

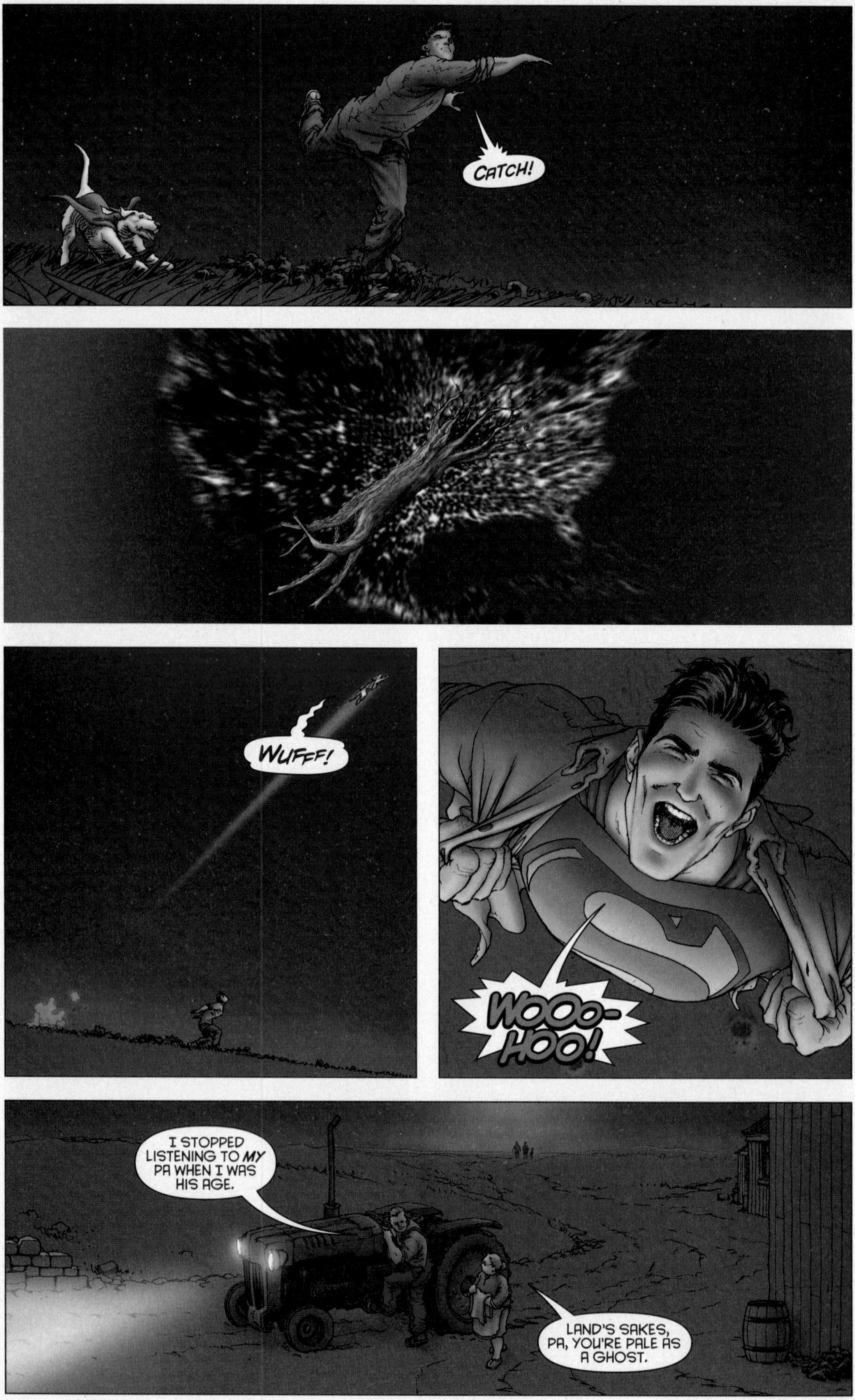
CATCH!
WUFFF!
WOOO-HOO!
I STOPPED LISTENING TO MY PA WHEN I WAS HIS AGE.
LAND'S SAKES, PA, YOU'RE PALE AS A GHOST.

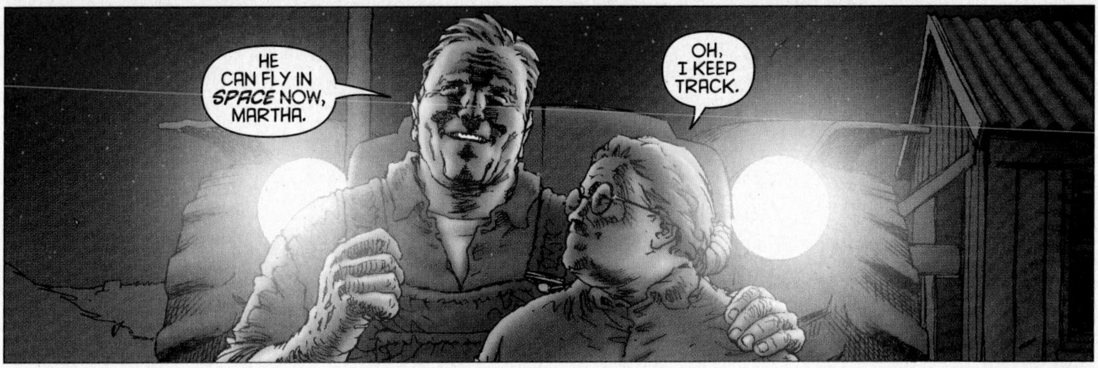
HE CAN FLY IN SPACE NOW, MARTHA.
OH, I KEEP TRACK.

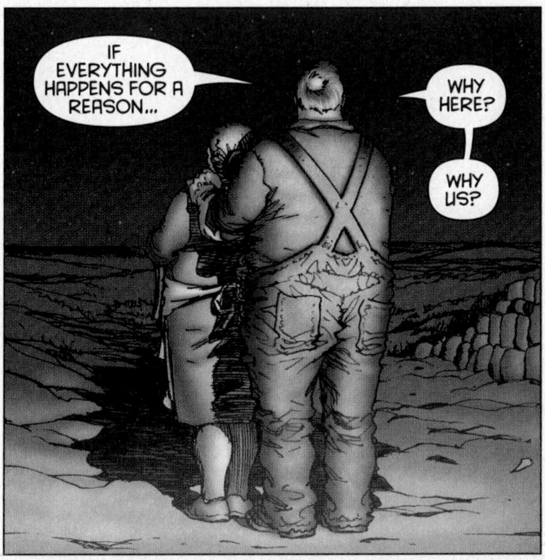
IF EVERYTHING HAPPENS FOR A REASON...
WHY HERE?
WHY US?

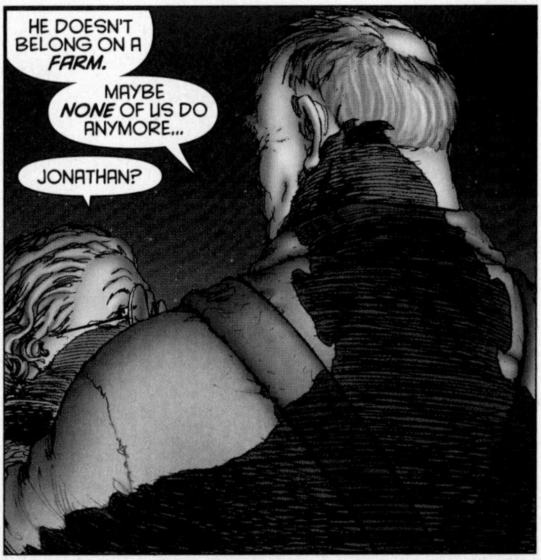
HE DOESN'T BELONG ON A FARM.
MAYBE NONE OF US DO ANYMORE...
JONATHAN?

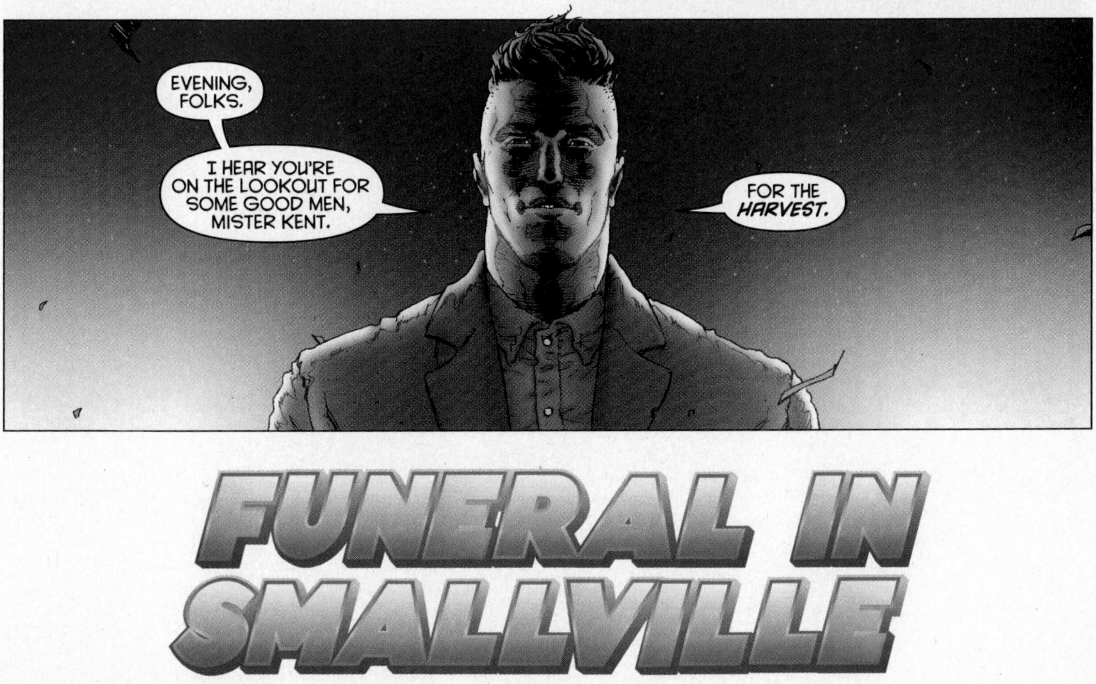
EVENING, FOLKS.
I HEAR YOU'RE ON THE LOOKOUT FOR SOME GOOD MEN, MISTER KENT.
FOR THE HARVEST.

FUNERAL IN SMALLVILLE

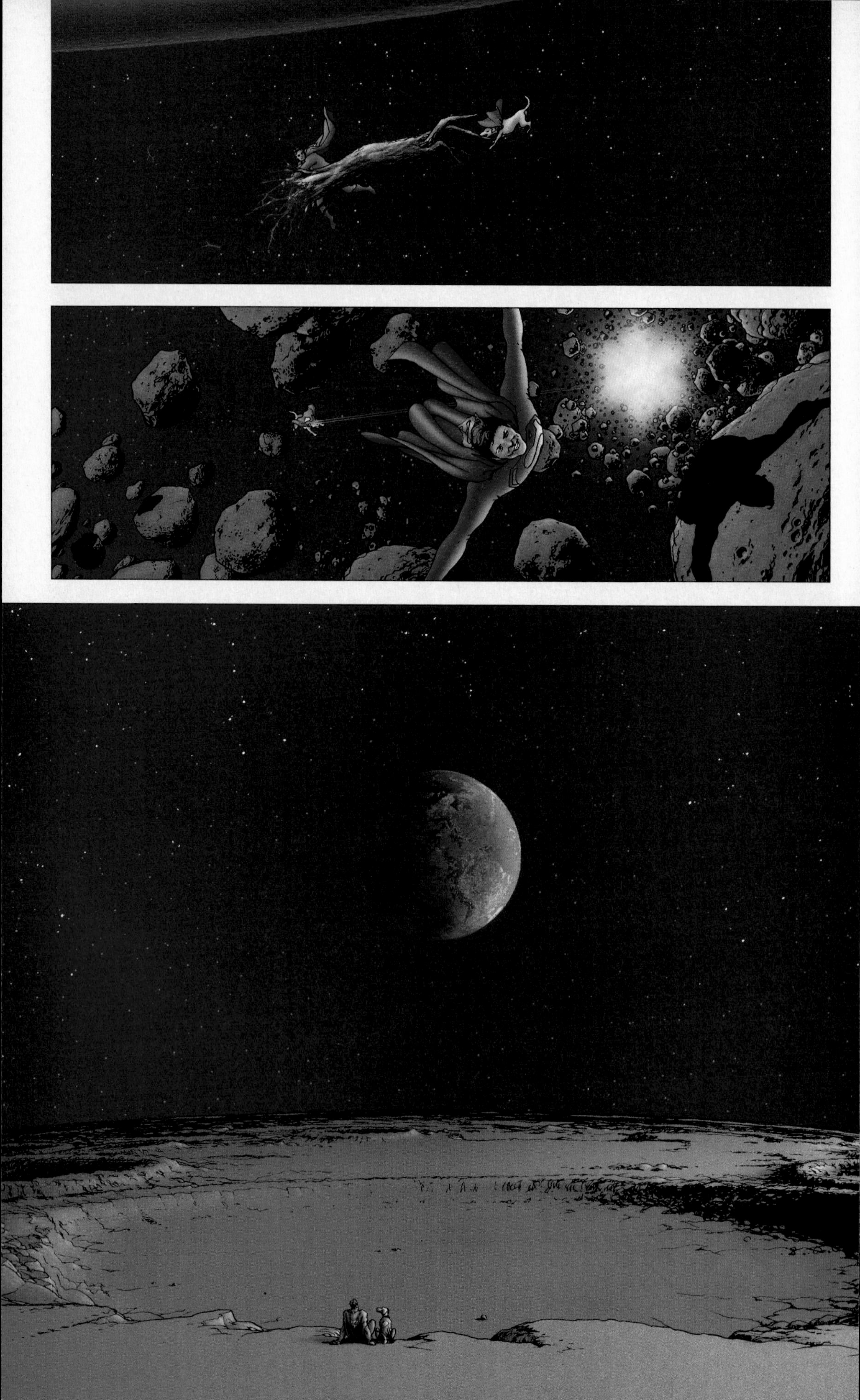

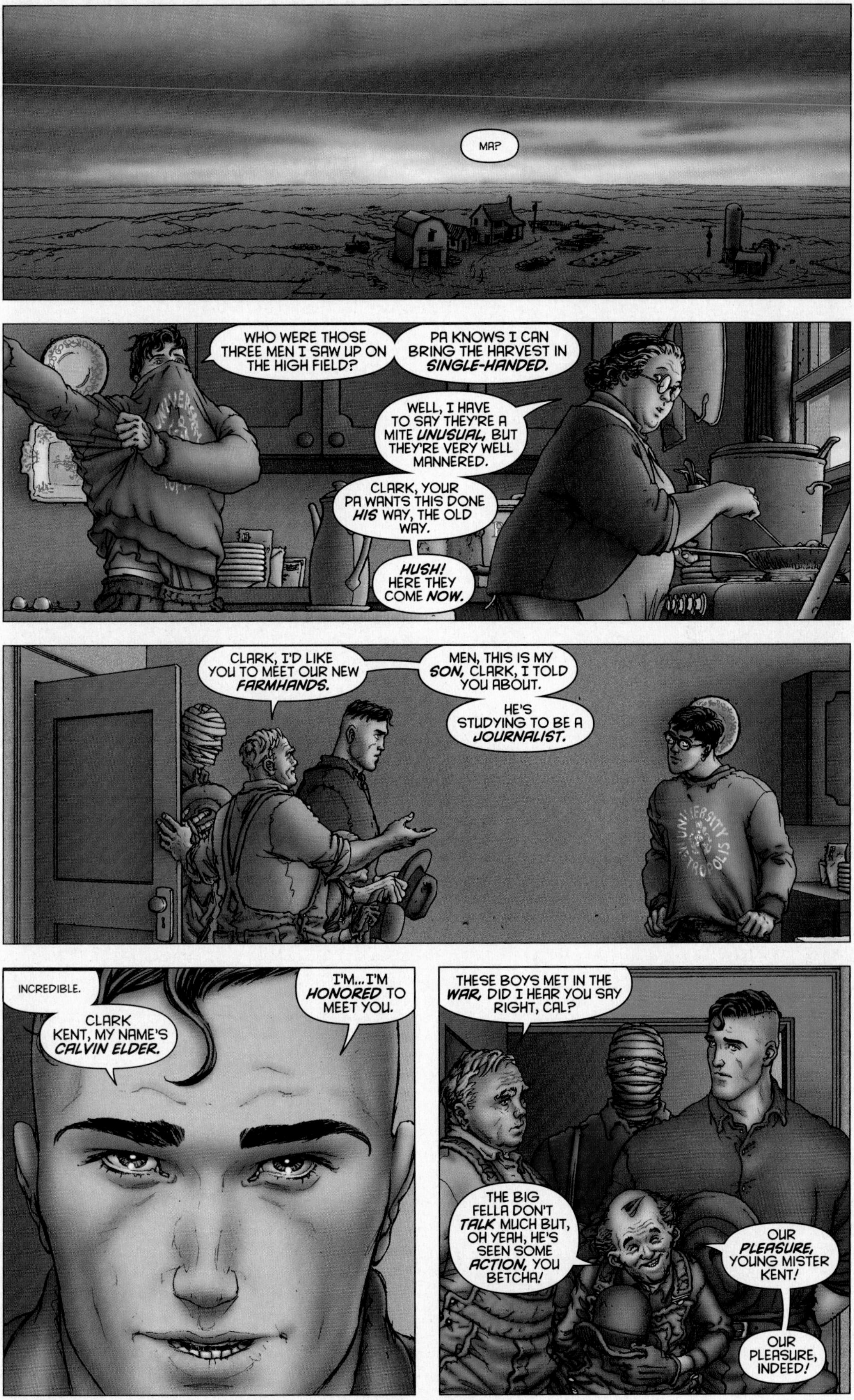
MA?
WHO WERE THOSE THREE MEN I SAW UP ON THE HIGH FIELD?
PA KNOWS I CAN BRING THE HARVEST IN SINGLE-HANDED.
WELL, I HAVE TO SAY THEY'RE A MITE UNUSUAL, BUT THEY'RE VERY WELL MANNERED.
CLARK, YOUR PA WANTS THIS DONE HIS WAY, THE OLD WAY.
HUSH! HERE THEY COME NOW.
CLARK, I'D LIKE YOU TO MEET OUR NEW FARMHANDS.
MEN, THIS IS MY SON, CLARK, I TOLD YOU ABOUT.
HE'S STUDYING TO BE A JOURNALIST.
INCREDIBLE.
CLARK KENT, MY NAME'S CALVIN ELDER.
I'M... I'M HONORED TO MEET YOU.
THESE BOYS MET IN THE WAR, DID I HEAR YOU SAY RIGHT, CAL?
THE BIG FELLA DON'T TALK MUCH BUT, OH YEAH, HE'S SEEN SOME ACTION, YOU BETCHA!
OUR PLEASURE, YOUNG MISTER KENT!
OUR PLEASURE, INDEED!

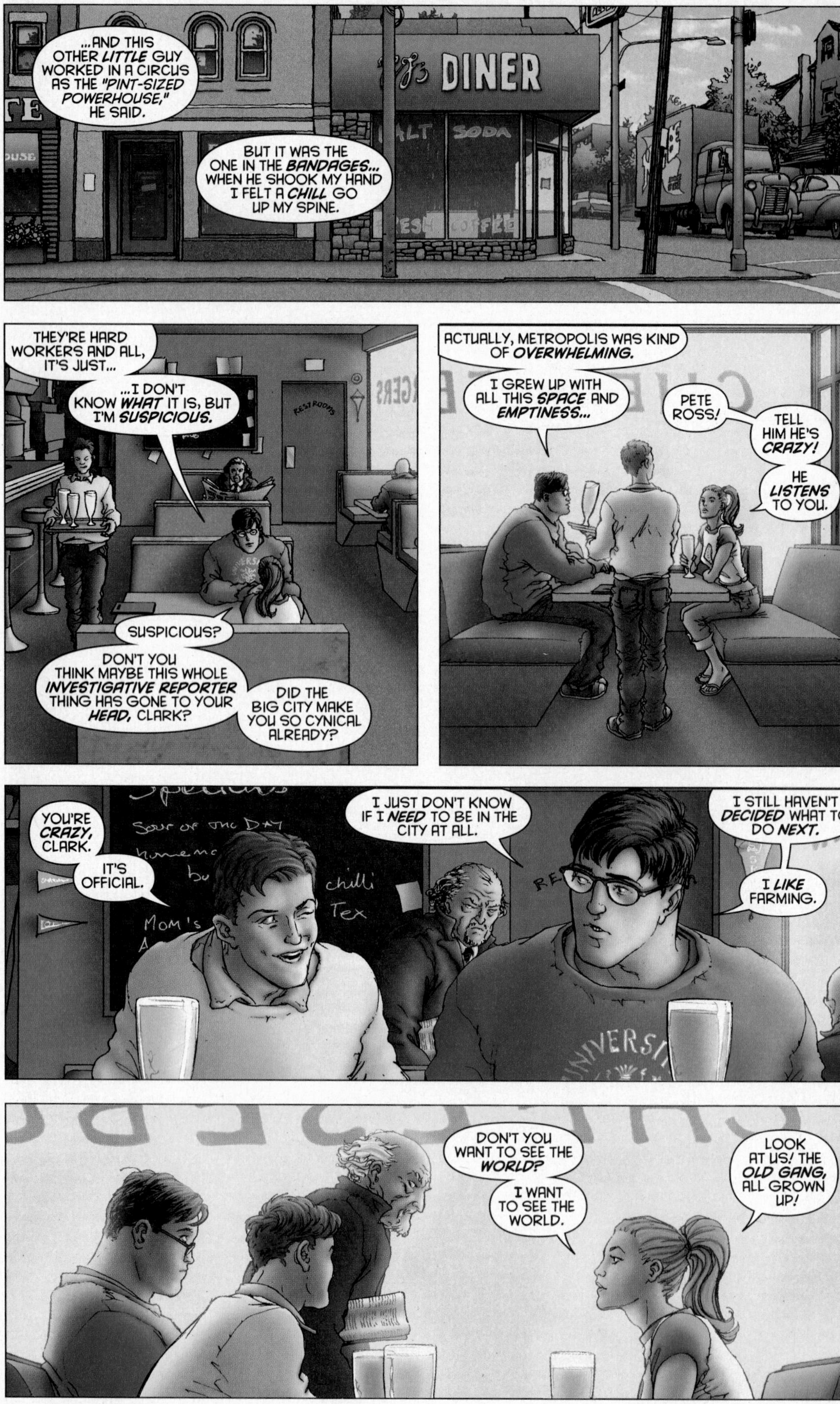
...AND THIS OTHER *LITTLE* GUY WORKED IN A CIRCUS AS THE *"PINT-SIZED POWERHOUSE,"* HE SAID.
BUT IT WAS THE ONE IN THE *BANDAGES...* WHEN HE SHOOK MY HAND I FELT A *CHILL* GO UP MY SPINE.
DINER
THEY'RE HARD WORKERS AND ALL, IT'S JUST...
...I DON'T KNOW *WHAT* IT IS, BUT I'M *SUSPICIOUS.*
SUSPICIOUS?
DON'T YOU THINK MAYBE THIS WHOLE *INVESTIGATIVE REPORTER* THING HAS GONE TO YOUR *HEAD,* CLARK?
DID THE BIG CITY MAKE YOU SO CYNICAL ALREADY?
ACTUALLY, METROPOLIS WAS KIND OF *OVERWHELMING.*
I GREW UP WITH ALL THIS *SPACE* AND *EMPTINESS...*
PETE ROSS!
TELL HIM HE'S *CRAZY!*
HE *LISTENS* TO YOU.
YOU'RE *CRAZY,* CLARK.
IT'S OFFICIAL.
I JUST DON'T KNOW IF I *NEED* TO BE IN THE CITY AT ALL.
I STILL HAVEN'T *DECIDED* WHAT TO DO *NEXT.*
I *LIKE* FARMING.
DON'T YOU WANT TO SEE THE *WORLD?*
I WANT TO SEE THE WORLD.
LOOK AT US! THE *OLD GANG,* ALL GROWN UP!

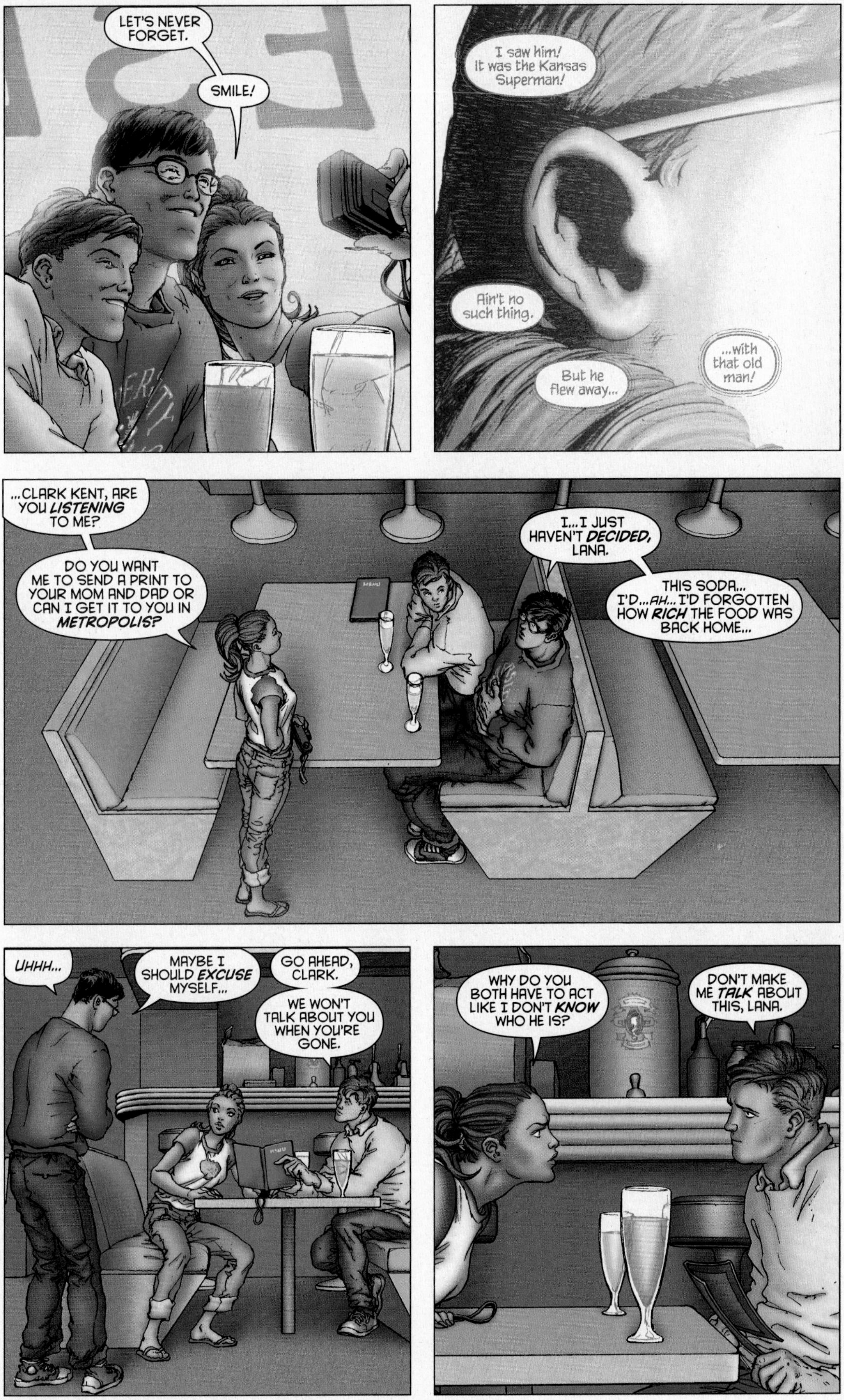
LET'S NEVER FORGET.
SMILE!
I saw him! It was the Kansas Superman!
Ain't no such thing.
But he flew away...
...with that old man!
...CLARK KENT, ARE YOU LISTENING TO ME?
DO YOU WANT ME TO SEND A PRINT TO YOUR MOM AND DAD OR CAN I GET IT TO YOU IN METROPOLIS?
I...I JUST HAVEN'T DECIDED, LANA.
THIS SODA... I'D...AH...I'D FORGOTTEN HOW RICH THE FOOD WAS BACK HOME...
UHHH...
MAYBE I SHOULD EXCUSE MYSELF...
GO AHEAD, CLARK.
WE WON'T TALK ABOUT YOU WHEN YOU'RE GONE.
WHY DO YOU BOTH HAVE TO ACT LIKE I DON'T KNOW WHO HE IS?
DON'T MAKE ME TALK ABOUT THIS, LANA.

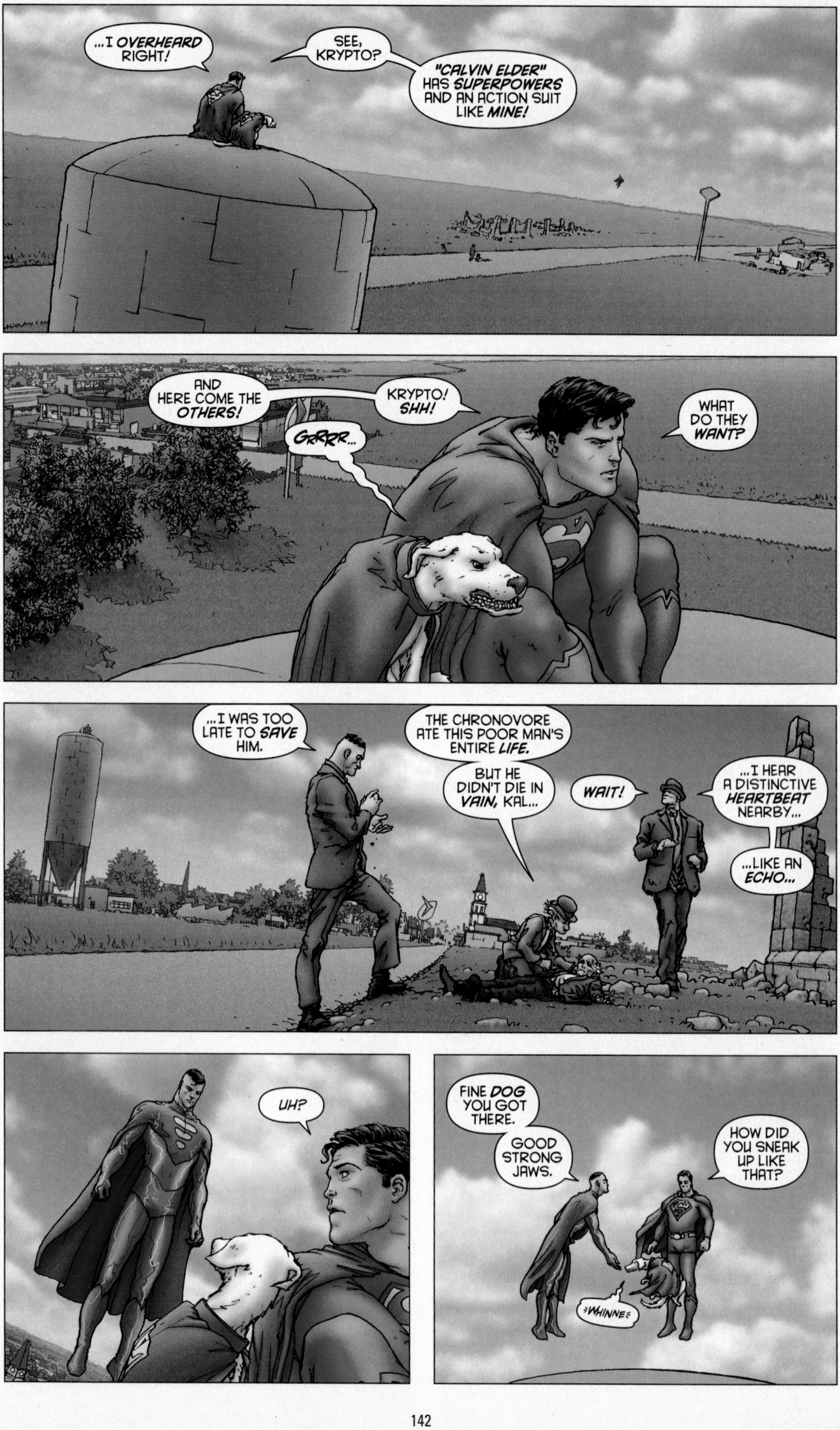
...I OVERHEARD RIGHT!
SEE, KRYPTO?
"CALVIN ELDER" HAS SUPERPOWERS AND AN ACTION SUIT LIKE MINE!
AND HERE COME THE OTHERS!
KRYPTO! SHH!
GRRRR...
WHAT DO THEY WANT?
...I WAS TOO LATE TO SAVE HIM.
THE CHRONOVORE ATE THIS POOR MAN'S ENTIRE LIFE.
BUT HE DIDN'T DIE IN VAIN, KAL...
WAIT!
...I HEAR A DISTINCTIVE HEARTBEAT NEARBY...
...LIKE AN ECHO...
UH?
FINE DOG YOU GOT THERE.
GOOD STRONG JAWS.
HOW DID YOU SNEAK UP LIKE THAT?
WHINNE

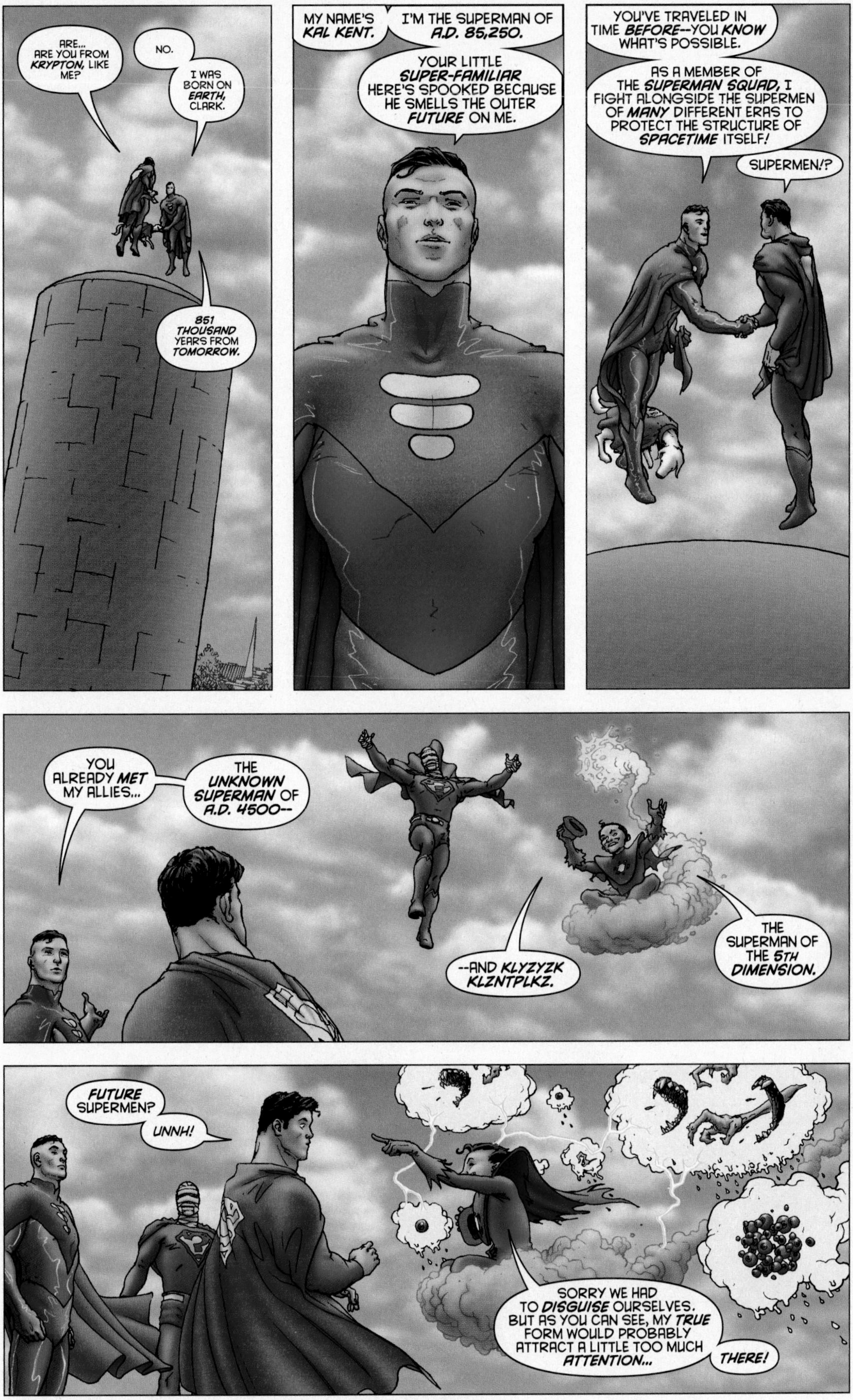
ARE... ARE YOU FROM KRYPTON, LIKE ME?
NO.
I WAS BORN ON EARTH, CLARK.
851 THOUSAND YEARS FROM TOMORROW.
MY NAME'S KAL KENT.
I'M THE SUPERMAN OF A.D. 85,250.
YOUR LITTLE SUPER-FAMILIAR HERE'S SPOOKED BECAUSE HE SMELLS THE OUTER FUTURE ON ME.
YOU'VE TRAVELED IN TIME BEFORE--YOU KNOW WHAT'S POSSIBLE.
AS A MEMBER OF THE SUPERMAN SQUAD, I FIGHT ALONGSIDE THE SUPERMEN OF MANY DIFFERENT ERAS TO PROTECT THE STRUCTURE OF SPACETIME ITSELF!
SUPERMEN!?
YOU ALREADY MET MY ALLIES...
THE UNKNOWN SUPERMAN OF A.D. 4500--
--AND KLYZYZK KLZNTPLKZ.
THE SUPERMAN OF THE 5TH DIMENSION.
FUTURE SUPERMEN?
UNNH!
SORRY WE HAD TO DISGUISE OURSELVES. BUT AS YOU CAN SEE, MY TRUE FORM WOULD PROBABLY ATTRACT A LITTLE TOO MUCH ATTENTION...
THERE!

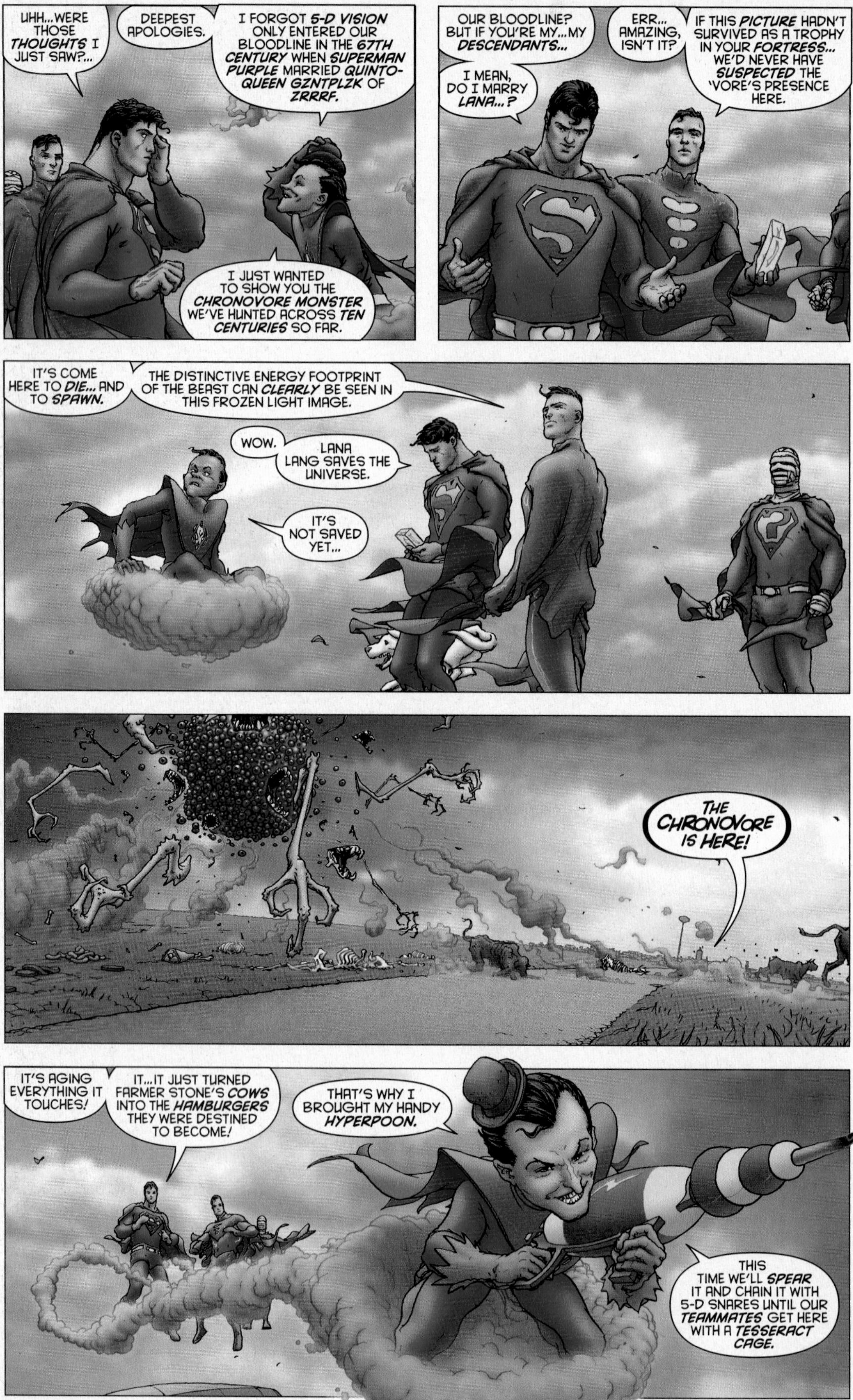
UHH...WERE THOSE THOUGHTS I JUST SAW?...
DEEPEST APOLOGIES.
I FORGOT 5-D VISION ONLY ENTERED OUR BLOODLINE IN THE 67TH CENTURY WHEN SUPERMAN PURPLE MARRIED QUINTO-QUEEN GZNTPLZK OF ZRRRF.
I JUST WANTED TO SHOW YOU THE CHRONOVORE MONSTER WE'VE HUNTED ACROSS TEN CENTURIES SO FAR.
OUR BLOODLINE? BUT IF YOU'RE MY...MY DESCENDANTS...
I MEAN, DO I MARRY LANA...?
ERR... AMAZING, ISN'T IT?
IF THIS PICTURE HADN'T SURVIVED AS A TROPHY IN YOUR FORTRESS... WE'D NEVER HAVE SUSPECTED THE 'VORE'S PRESENCE HERE.
IT'S COME HERE TO DIE... AND TO SPAWN.
THE DISTINCTIVE ENERGY FOOTPRINT OF THE BEAST CAN CLEARLY BE SEEN IN THIS FROZEN LIGHT IMAGE.
WOW.
LANA LANG SAVES THE UNIVERSE.
IT'S NOT SAVED YET...
THE CHRONOVORE IS HERE!
IT'S AGING EVERYTHING IT TOUCHES!
IT...IT JUST TURNED FARMER STONE'S COWS INTO THE HAMBURGERS THEY WERE DESTINED TO BECOME!
THAT'S WHY I BROUGHT MY HANDY HYPERPOON.
THIS TIME WE'LL SPEAR IT AND CHAIN IT WITH 5-D SNARES UNTIL OUR TEAMMATES GET HERE WITH A TESSERACT CAGE.

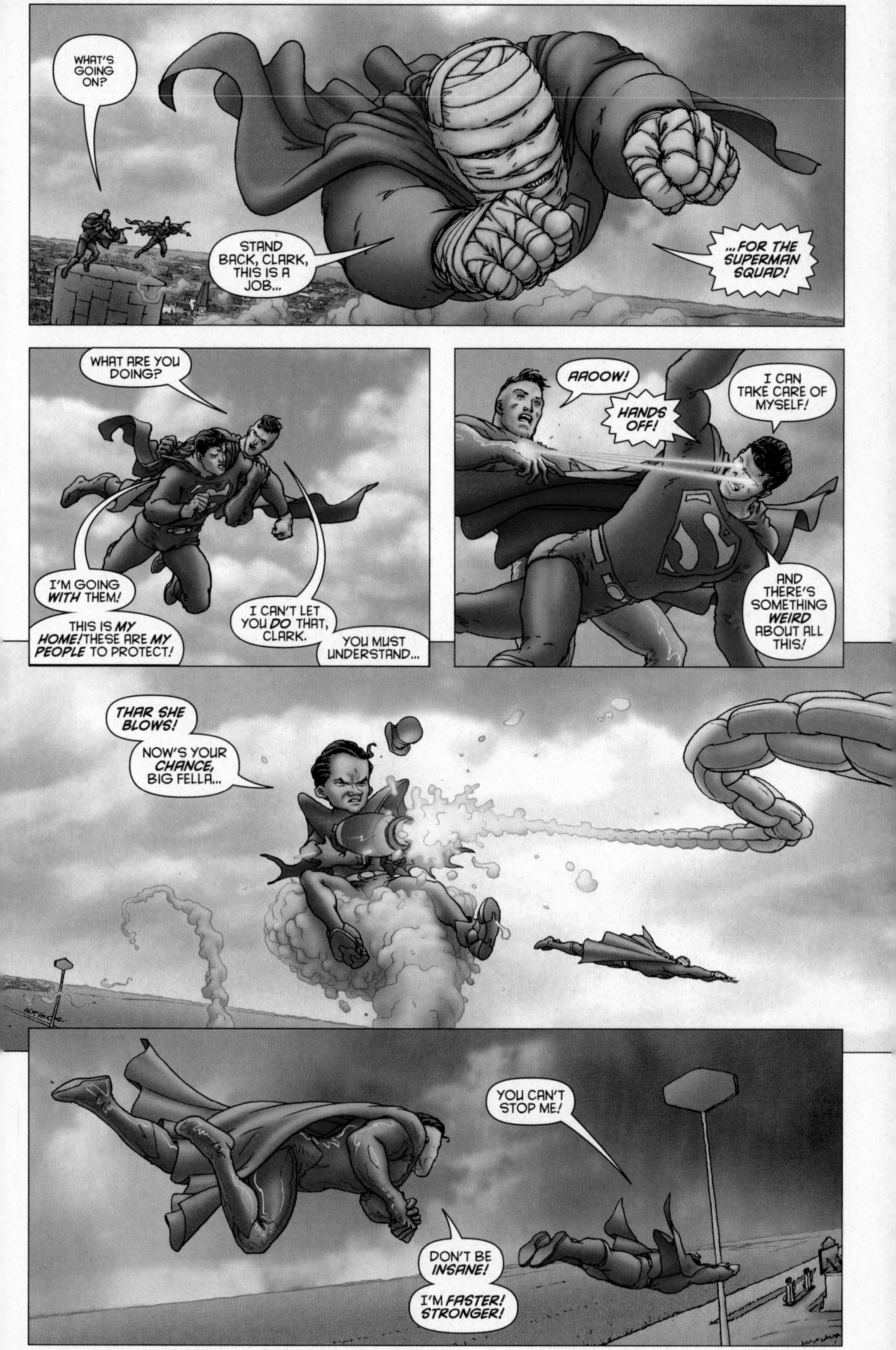
WHAT'S GOING ON?
STAND BACK, CLARK, THIS IS A JOB...
...FOR THE SUPERMAN SQUAD!
WHAT ARE YOU DOING?
I'M GOING WITH THEM!
THIS IS MY HOME! THESE ARE MY PEOPLE TO PROTECT!
I CAN'T LET YOU DO THAT, CLARK.
YOU MUST UNDERSTAND...
AAOOW!
HANDS OFF!
I CAN TAKE CARE OF MYSELF!
AND THERE'S SOMETHING WEIRD ABOUT ALL THIS!
THAR SHE BLOWS!
NOW'S YOUR CHANCE, BIG FELLA...
YOU CAN'T STOP ME!
DON'T BE INSANE!
I'M FASTER! STRONGER!

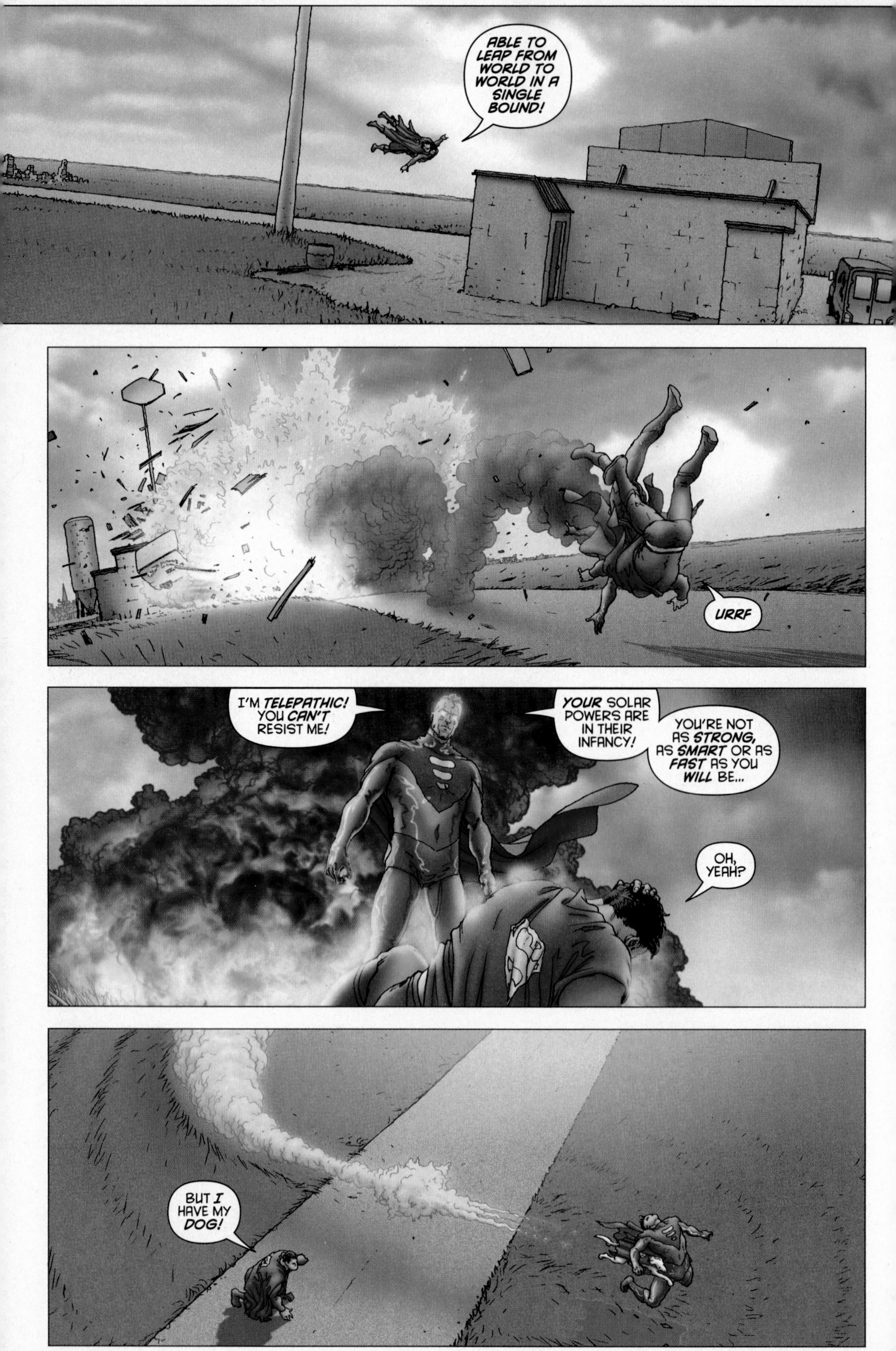
ABLE TO LEAP FROM WORLD TO WORLD IN A SINGLE BOUND!
URRF
I'M TELEPATHIC! YOU CAN'T RESIST ME!
YOUR SOLAR POWERS ARE IN THEIR INFANCY!
YOU'RE NOT AS STRONG, AS SMART OR AS FAST AS YOU WILL BE...
OH, YEAH?
BUT I HAVE MY DOG!

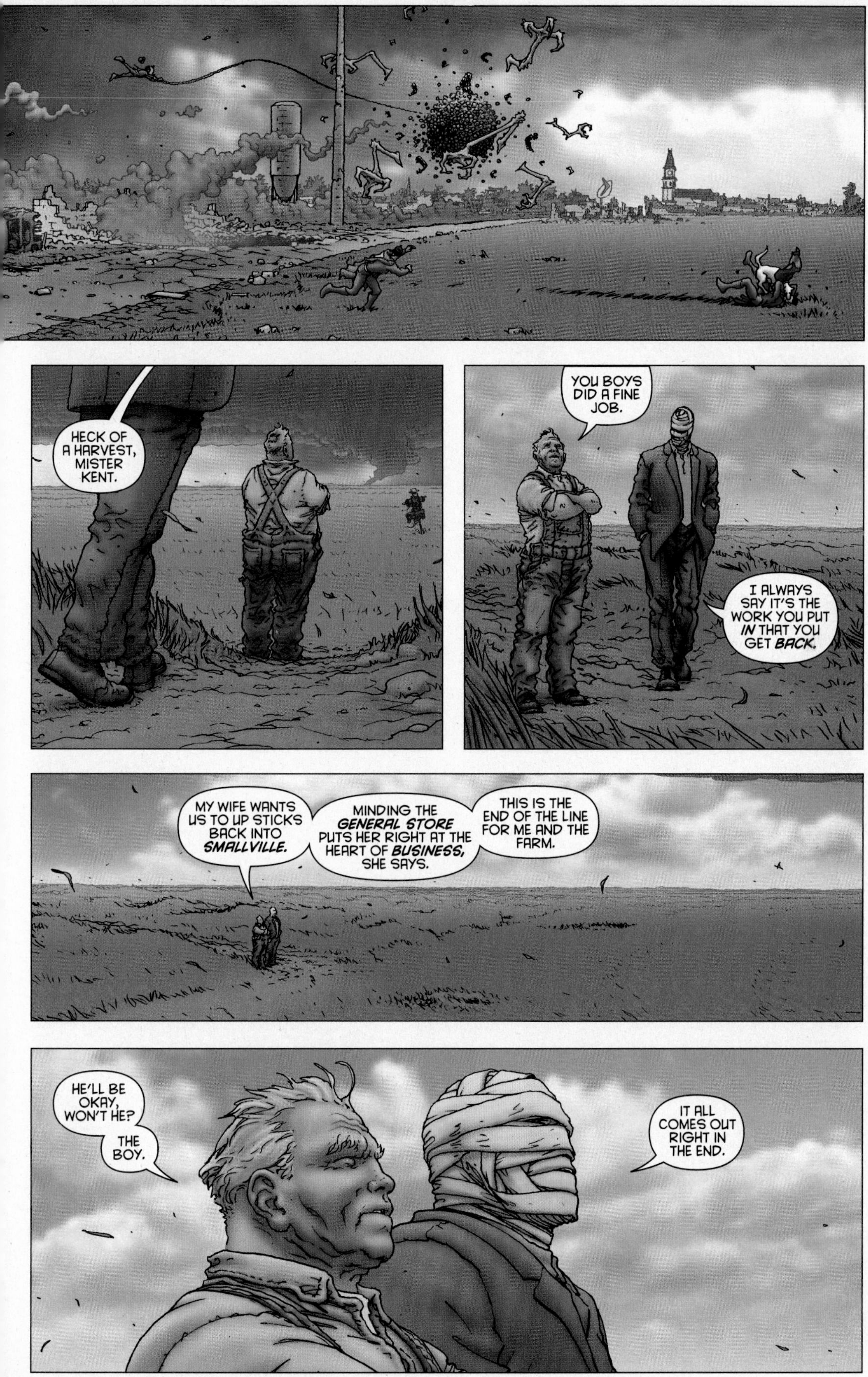
HECK OF A HARVEST, MISTER KENT.
YOU BOYS DID A FINE JOB.
I ALWAYS SAY IT'S THE WORK YOU PUT IN THAT YOU GET BACK.
MY WIFE WANTS US TO UP STICKS BACK INTO SMALLVILLE.
MINDING THE GENERAL STORE PUTS HER RIGHT AT THE HEART OF BUSINESS, SHE SAYS.
THIS IS THE END OF THE LINE FOR ME AND THE FARM.
HE'LL BE OKAY, WON'T HE?
THE BOY.
IT ALL COMES OUT RIGHT IN THE END.

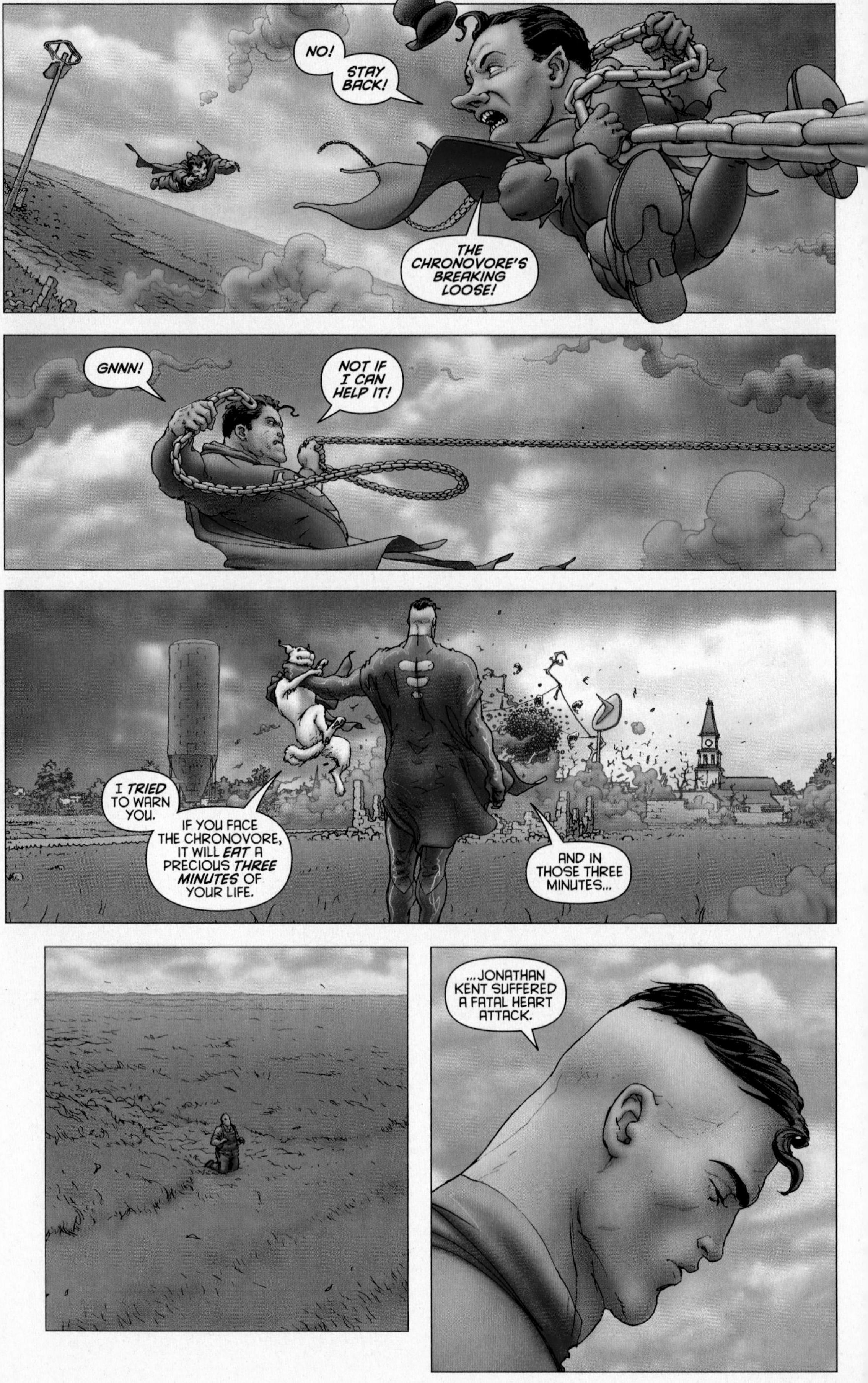
NO!
STAY BACK!
THE CHRONOVORE'S BREAKING LOOSE!
GNNN!
NOT IF I CAN HELP IT!
I TRIED TO WARN YOU.
IF YOU FACE THE CHRONOVORE, IT WILL EAT A PRECIOUS THREE MINUTES OF YOUR LIFE.
AND IN THOSE THREE MINUTES...
...JONATHAN KENT SUFFERED A FATAL HEART ATTACK.

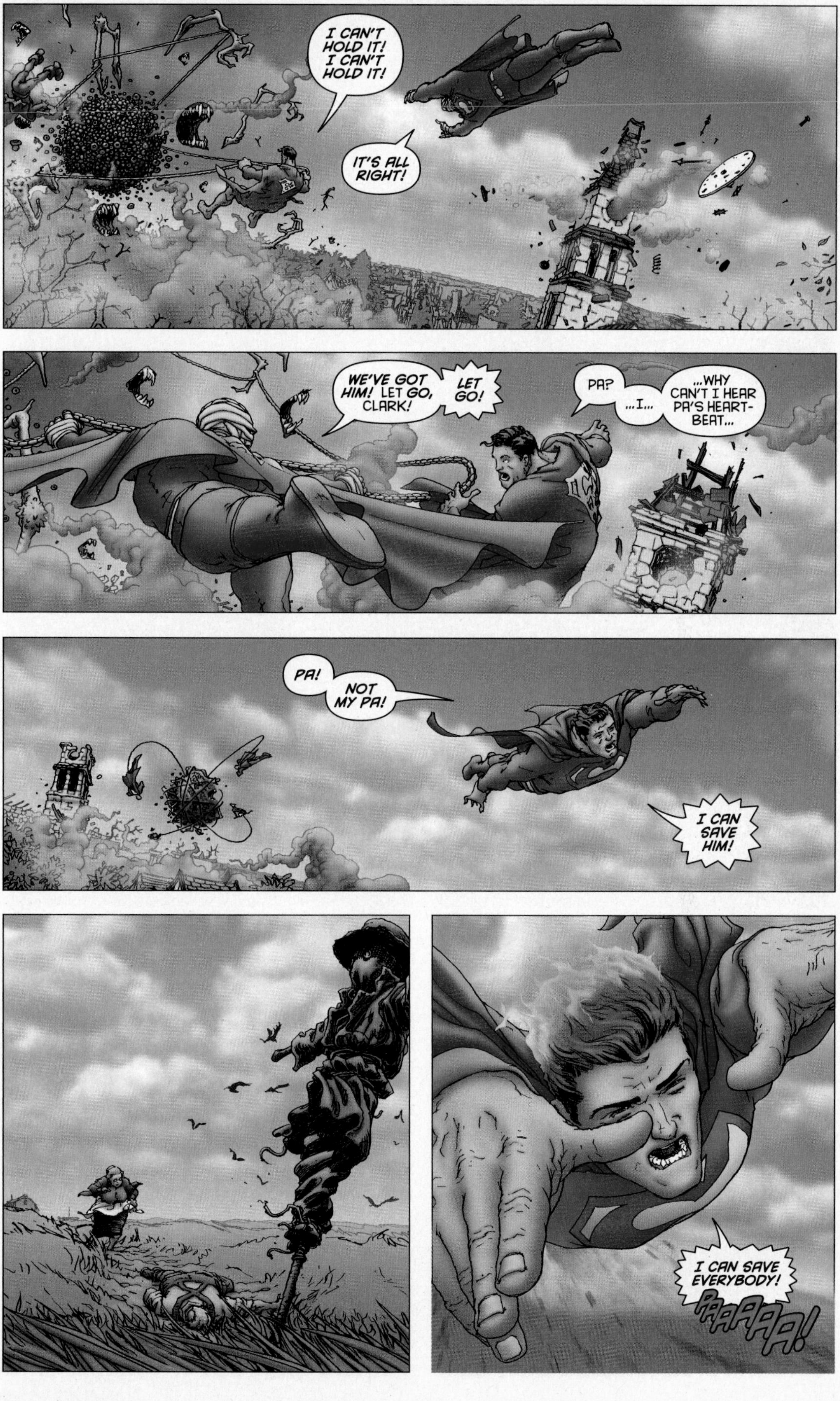
I CAN'T HOLD IT! I CAN'T HOLD IT!
IT'S ALL RIGHT!
WE'VE GOT HIM! LET GO, CLARK!
LET GO!
PA?
...I...
...WHY CAN'T I HEAR PA'S HEART-BEAT...
PA!
NOT MY PA!
I CAN SAVE HIM!
I CAN SAVE EVERYBODY!
PAAAAA!

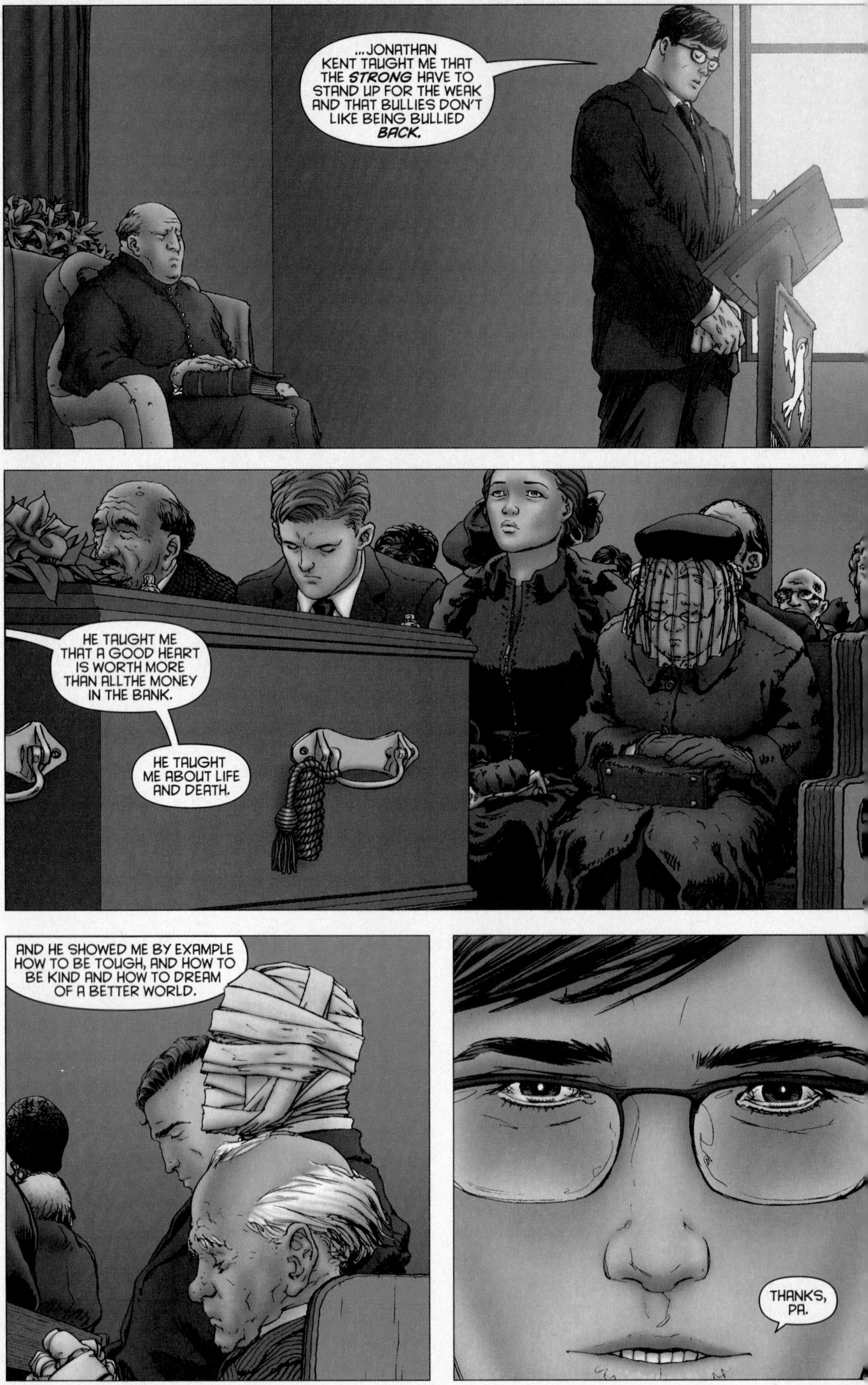
...JONATHAN KENT TAUGHT ME THAT THE STRONG HAVE TO STAND UP FOR THE WEAK AND THAT BULLIES DON'T LIKE BEING BULLIED BACK.
HE TAUGHT ME THAT A GOOD HEART IS WORTH MORE THAN ALL THE MONEY IN THE BANK.
HE TAUGHT ME ABOUT LIFE AND DEATH.
AND HE SHOWED ME BY EXAMPLE HOW TO BE TOUGH, AND HOW TO BE KIND AND HOW TO DREAM OF A BETTER WORLD.
THANKS, PA.

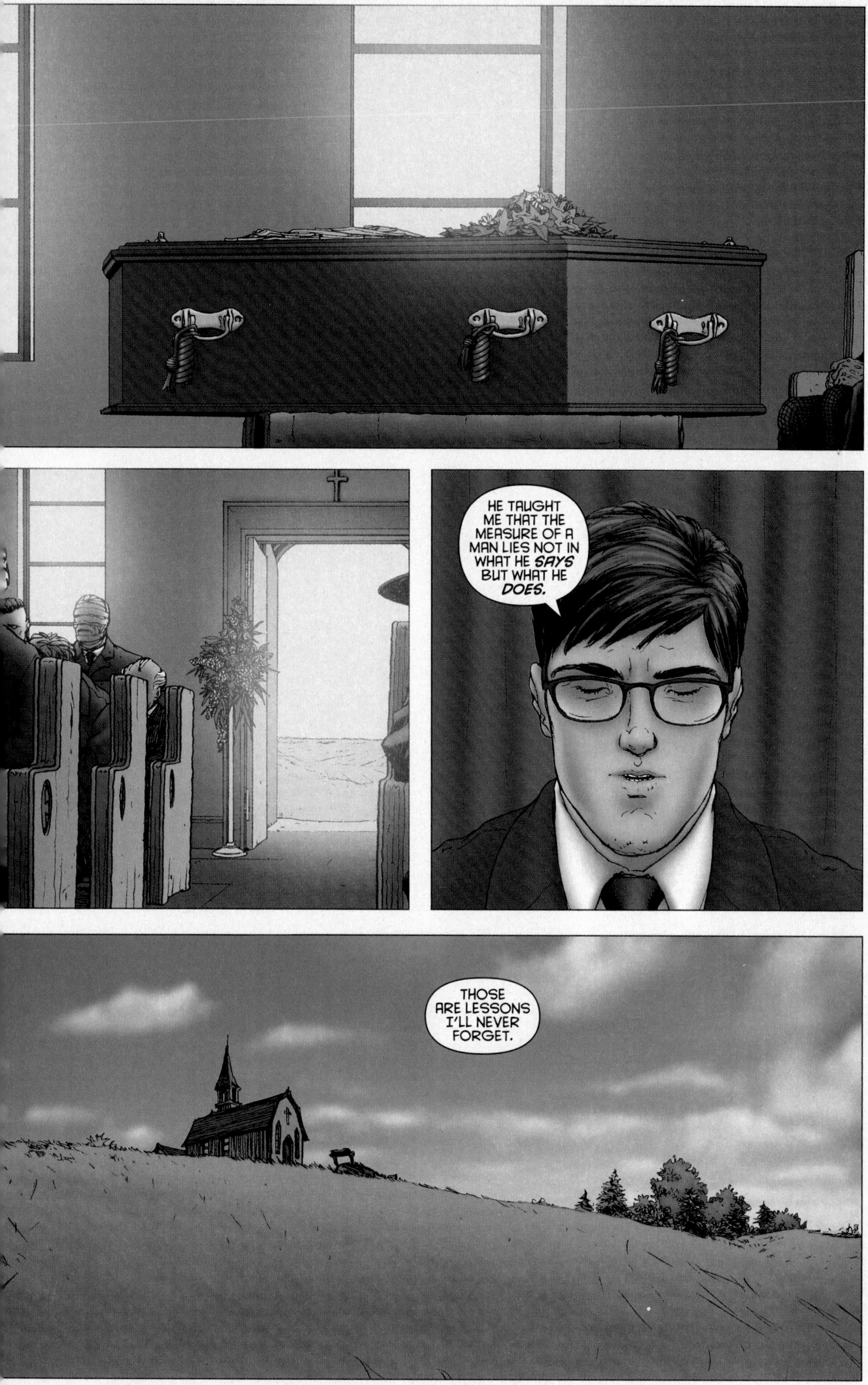
HE TAUGHT ME THAT THE MEASURE OF A MAN LIES NOT IN WHAT HE *SAYS* BUT WHAT HE *DOES.*
THOSE ARE LESSONS I'LL NEVER FORGET.

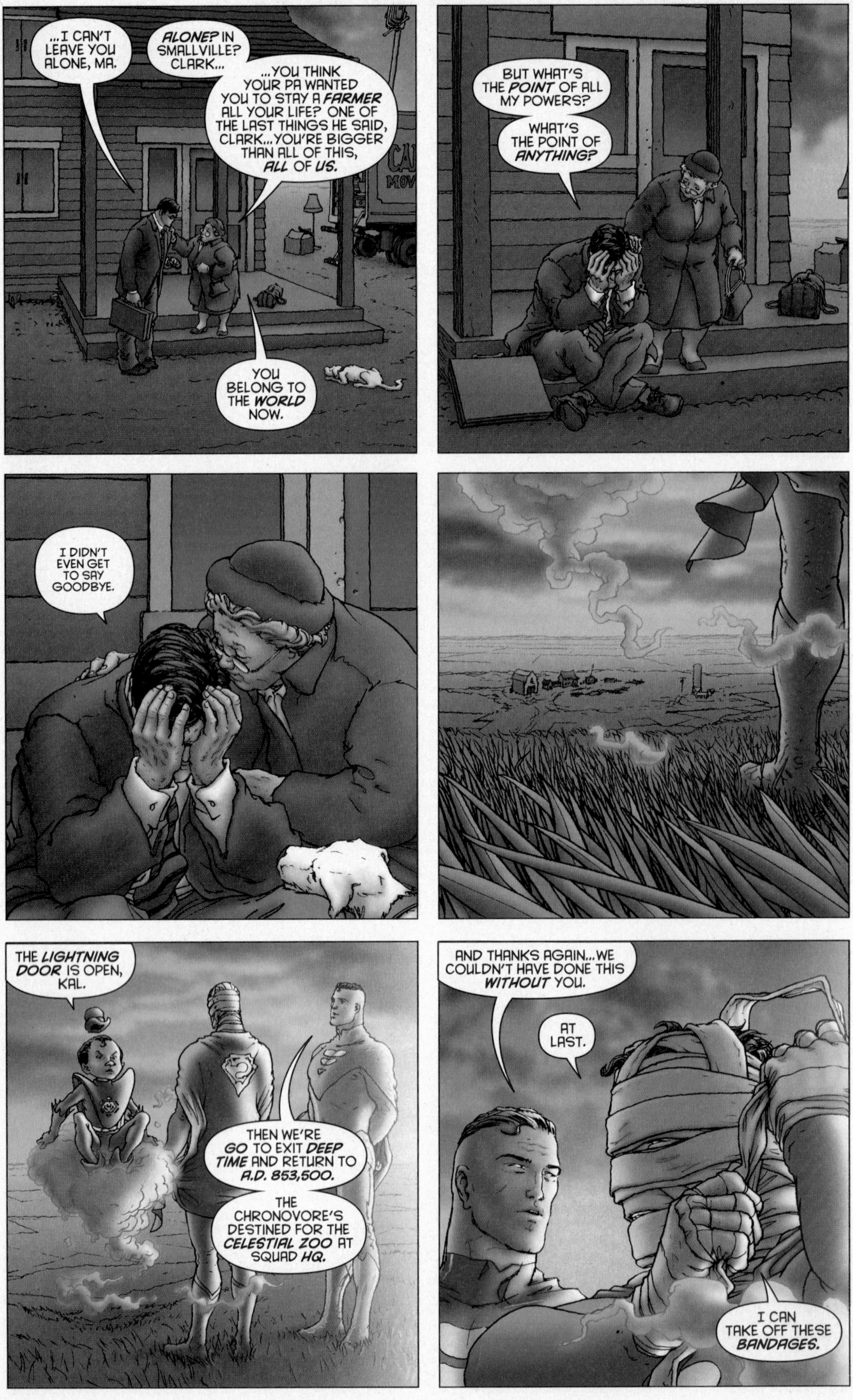
...I CAN'T LEAVE YOU ALONE, MA.
ALONE? IN SMALLVILLE? CLARK...
...YOU THINK YOUR PA WANTED YOU TO STAY A FARMER ALL YOUR LIFE? ONE OF THE LAST THINGS HE SAID, CLARK...YOU'RE BIGGER THAN ALL OF THIS, ALL OF US.
YOU BELONG TO THE WORLD NOW.
BUT WHAT'S THE POINT OF ALL MY POWERS?
WHAT'S THE POINT OF ANYTHING?
I DIDN'T EVEN GET TO SAY GOODBYE.
THE LIGHTNING DOOR IS OPEN, KAL.
THEN WE'RE GO TO EXIT DEEP TIME AND RETURN TO A.D. 853,500.
THE CHRONOVORE'S DESTINED FOR THE CELESTIAL ZOO AT SQUAD HQ.
AND THANKS AGAIN...WE COULDN'T HAVE DONE THIS WITHOUT YOU.
AT LAST.
I CAN TAKE OFF THESE BANDAGES.

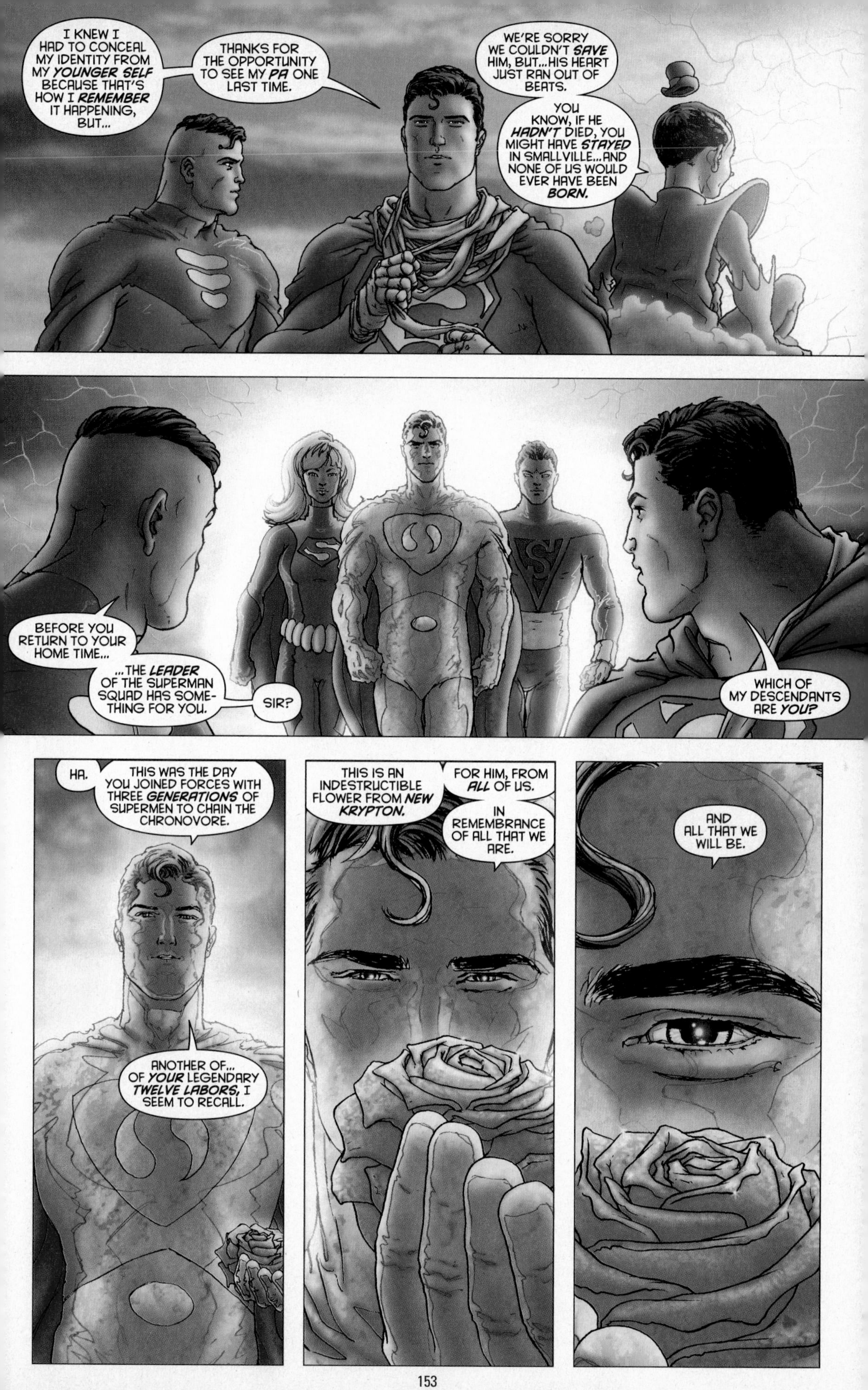

I KNEW I HAD TO CONCEAL MY IDENTITY FROM MY YOUNGER SELF BECAUSE THAT'S HOW I REMEMBER IT HAPPENING, BUT...
THANKS FOR THE OPPORTUNITY TO SEE MY PA ONE LAST TIME.
WE'RE SORRY WE COULDN'T SAVE HIM, BUT...HIS HEART JUST RAN OUT OF BEATS.
YOU KNOW, IF HE HADN'T DIED, YOU MIGHT HAVE STAYED IN SMALLVILLE...AND NONE OF US WOULD EVER HAVE BEEN BORN.
BEFORE YOU RETURN TO YOUR HOME TIME...
...THE LEADER OF THE SUPERMAN SQUAD HAS SOME-THING FOR YOU.
SIR?
WHICH OF MY DESCENDANTS ARE YOU?
HA.
THIS WAS THE DAY YOU JOINED FORCES WITH THREE GENERATIONS OF SUPERMEN TO CHAIN THE CHRONOVORE.
ANOTHER OF... OF YOUR LEGENDARY TWELVE LABORS, I SEEM TO RECALL.
THIS IS AN INDESTRUCTIBLE FLOWER FROM NEW KRYPTON.
FOR HIM, FROM ALL OF US.
IN REMEMBRANCE OF ALL THAT WE ARE.
AND ALL THAT WE WILL BE.

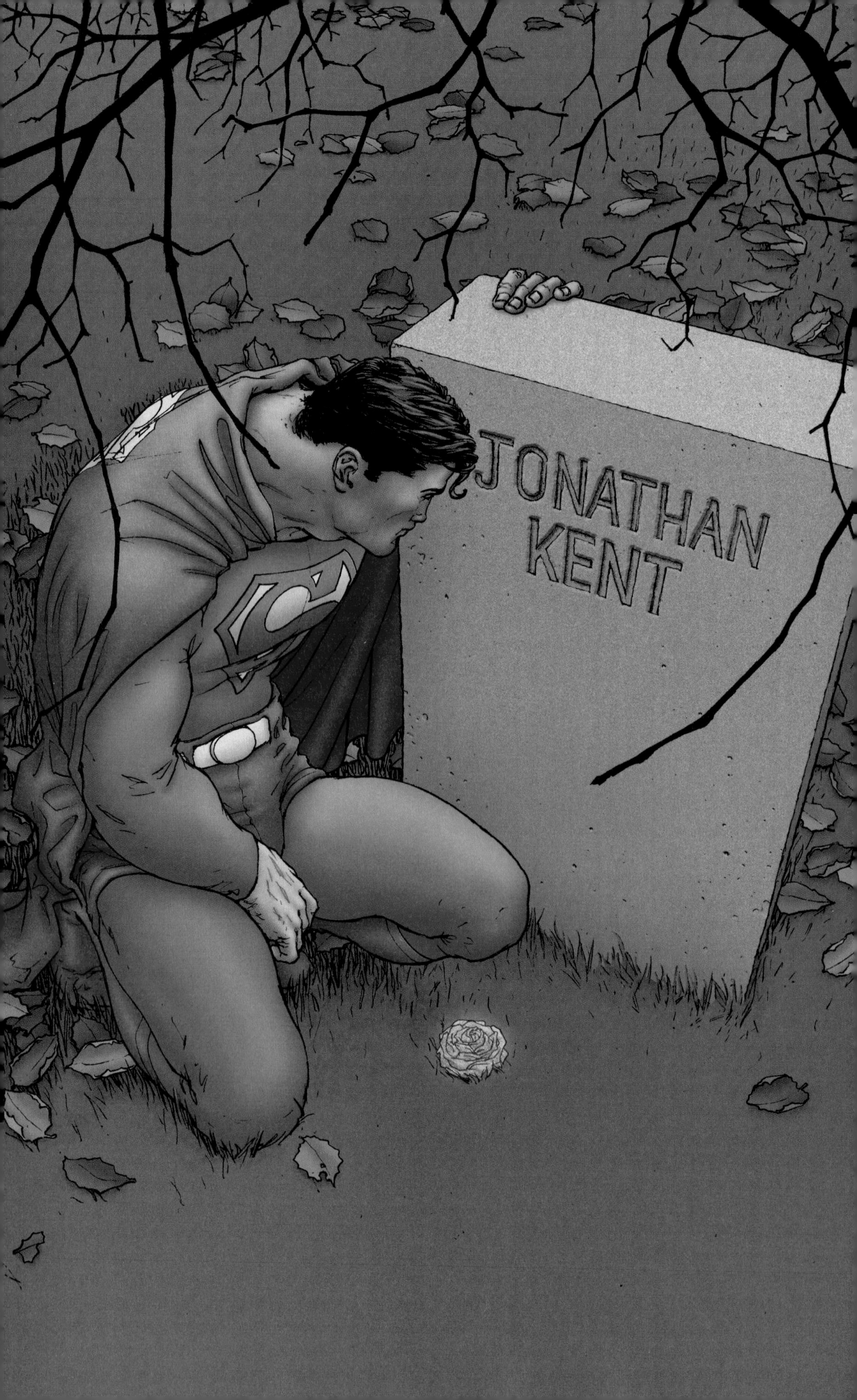
JONATHAN
KENT

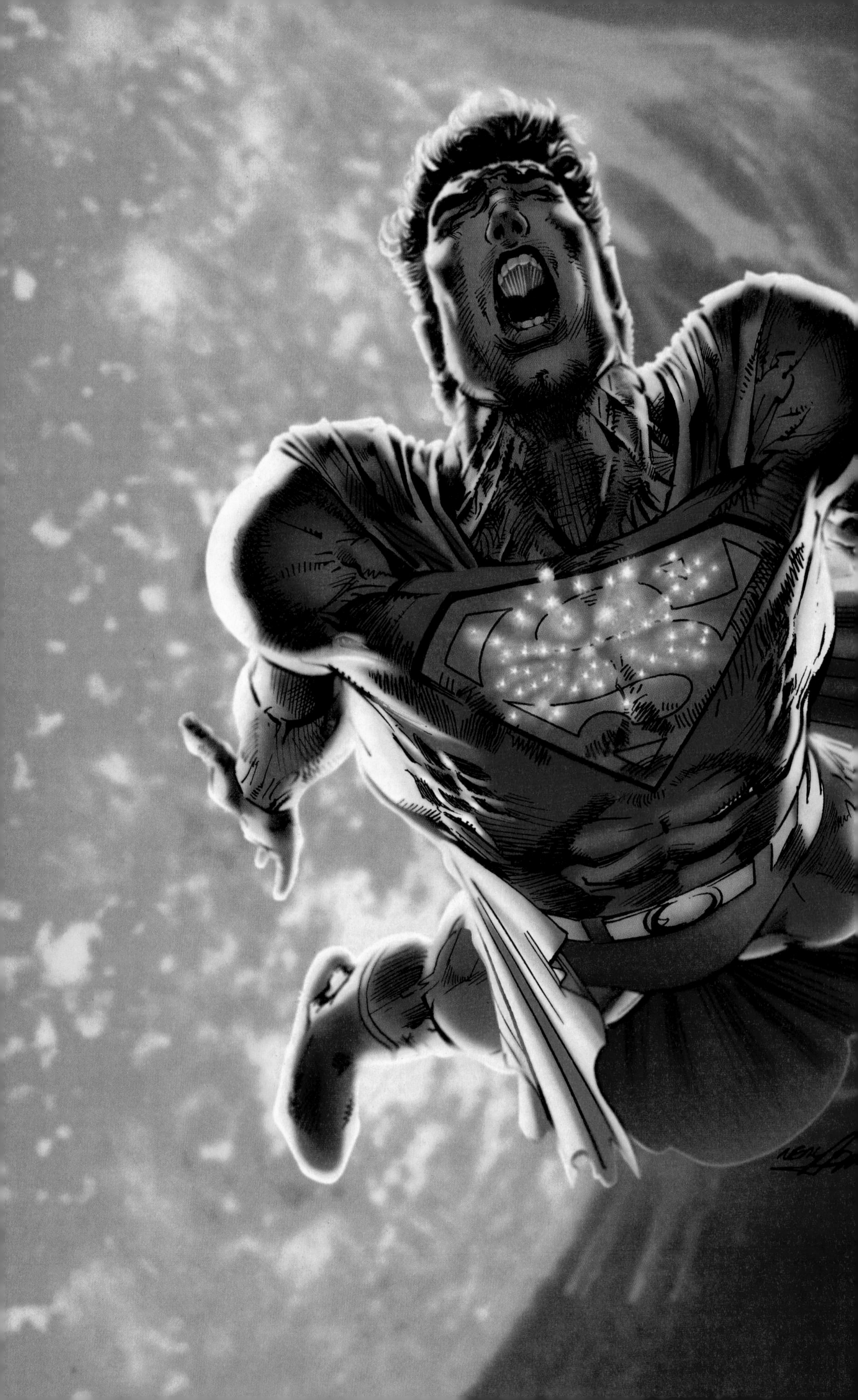

Episode 1

ALTERNATE COVER

Art by NEAL ADAMS and JAMIE GRANT

BIOGRAPHIES

GRANT MORRISON

Grant Morrison has been working at DC Comics for 20 years, starting his U.S. career with acclaimed runs on ANIMAL MAN and DOOM PATROL. Since then he has written best-selling titles, JLA, BATMAN and *New X-Men*, as well as his subversive creator-owned titles such as THE INVISIBLES, SEAGUY, THE FILTH and WE3. He has been hard at work helping to reinvent the DC Universe in titles from Eisner Award-winning SEVEN SOLDIERS and ALL-STAR SUPERMAN to the hit of 2006, the weekly comic 52.

In his secret identity, he is a "counterculture" spokesperson, a musician, an award-winning playwright and a chaos magician. He lives and works between L.A. and his homes in Scotland.

FRANK QUITELY

Frank Quitely was born in Glasgow in 1968. Since 1988 he has drawn *The Greens* (self-published), *Blackheart, Missionary Man, Shimura, Inaba,* ten Paradox Press shorts, six VERTIGO shorts, FLEX MENTALLO, 20/20 VISIONS, BATMAN: THE SCOTTISH CONNECTION, THE KINGDOM: OFFSPRING, JLA: EARTH 2 hardcover, THE INVISIBLES, TRANSMETROPOLITAN, THE AUTHORITY, *Captain America, New X-Men,* SANDMAN: ENDLESS NIGHTS, WE3 and now ALL-STAR SUPERMAN. He has also created covers for *Negative Burn, Judge Dredd Megazine, Classic 2000AD,* JONAH HEX, BOOKS OF MAGICK: LIFE DURING WARTIME, BITE CLUB and AMERICAN VIRGIN.

He lives in Glasgow with his wife and three children. He used to design his own hats and clothing. Currently his favorite hobby is cooking.

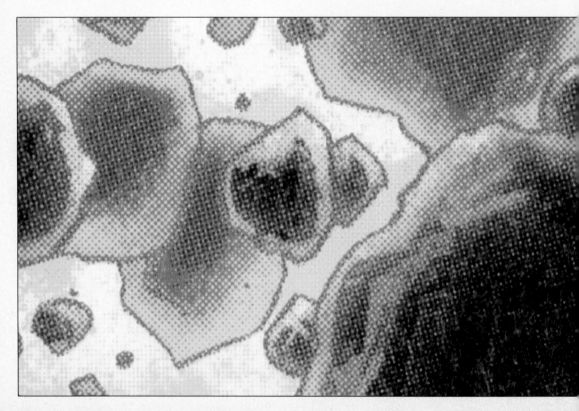

JAMIE GRANT

Jamie Grant first appeared in 1968, Dunfermline, Scotland. As he grew to reading size he began to read A LOT of comics. Later (when bigger) he penned *Blank Expression* (self-published) and painted *Missionary Man* for the *Judge Dredd Megazine*, while performing many other demeaning commercial art services in exchange for money (which he spent on comics).

Since 1999 he's lived and got thoroughly wasted in Glasgow, publishing many issues of *Northern Lightz* — an underground anthology comic. He also founded Hope Street Studios (a true comic den) where he crafted the digital inking and coloring techniques applied to Vertigo's WE3 before tackling ALL-STAR SUPERMAN. His favorite music to color comic book super-spandex to is *Devo, the Mothers of Invention* and *Frank Black*.

Jamie's personal coat of arms: "It doesn't take me long, to work half an hour. No job too dangerous!"

READ MORE OF THE MAN OF STEEL'S ADVENTURES IN THESE COLLECTIONS FROM DC COMICS:

SUPERMAN

BRIAN AZZARELLO JIM LEE SCOTT WILLIAMS
SUPERMAN
FOR TOMORROW
VOLUME ONE

SUPERMAN: FOR TOMORROW

VOLUME 1

Brian Azzarello, Jim Lee and Scott Williams tell the epic tale of a cataclysmic event that strikes the Earth, affecting millions – including those closest to the Man of Steel.

"A BIG HERO NEEDS A BIG STORY, AND THIS TEAM DOESN'T DISAPPOINT."

— THE WASHINGTON POST

SUPERMAN
THE MAN OF STEEL VOLUME 1

JOHN BYRNE DICK GIORDANO
SUPERMAN
THE MAN OF STEEL

JOHN BYRNE
DICK GIORDANO

SUPERMAN
FOR ALL SEASONS

Superman
For All Seasons
Jeph Loeb
Tim Sale
with Bjarne Hansen

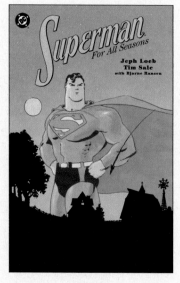

JEPH LOEB
TIM SALE

THE DEATH OF
SUPERMAN

THE BEST-SELLING GRAPHIC NOVEL OF ALL TIME!
THE DEATH OF
SUPERMAN

DAN JURGENS
JERRY ORDWAY
JACKSON GUICE

SEARCH THE GRAPHIC NOVELS SECTION OF

www.DCCOMICS.com

FOR ART AND INFORMATION ON ALL OF OUR BOOKS!